Macmillan/McGraw-Hill

Treasures

Online Interactive Student Book

www.macmillanmh.com

LOG ON StudentWorks Plus™ Interactive Student Book

VIEW IT

- Preview weekly concepts and selections

READ IT

- Word-by-Word Reading

LEARN IT

- Comprehension Questions
- Research and Media Activities

FIND OUT

- Summaries and Glossary in other Languages

LOG ON **Online Activities**
www.macmillanmh.com

- **Interactive activities** and **animated lessons** for guided instruction and practice

IWB Interactive White Board Ready!

Treasures

A Reading/Language Arts Program

Macmillan/McGraw-Hill

Contributors

Time Magazine, The Writers' Express, Accelerated Reader

Students with print disabilities may be eligible to obtain an accessible, audio version of the pupil edition of this textbook. Please call Recording for the Blind & Dyslexic at 1-800-221-4792 for complete information.

B

The McGraw·Hill Companies

Macmillan/McGraw-Hill

Published by Macmillan/McGraw-Hill, of McGraw-Hill Educati Two Penn Plaza, New York, New York 10121.

Printed in the United States of America

ISBN: 978-0-02-201735-4

MHID: 0-02-201735-6

4 5 6 7 8 9 QVR/LEH 13 12 11

Treasures

A Reading/Language Arts Program

Program Authors

Diane August
Donald R. Bear
Janice A. Dole
Jana Echevarria
Douglas Fisher
David Francis
Vicki Gibson
Jan E. Hasbrouck
Scott G. Paris
Timothy Shanahan
Josefina V. Tinajero

Macmillan/McGraw-Hill

Unit 1

Personal Experiences

Growing Up

The Big Question

THEME: Making a Move

THEME: Changing

THEME: Kids at Work

THEME: Mentors

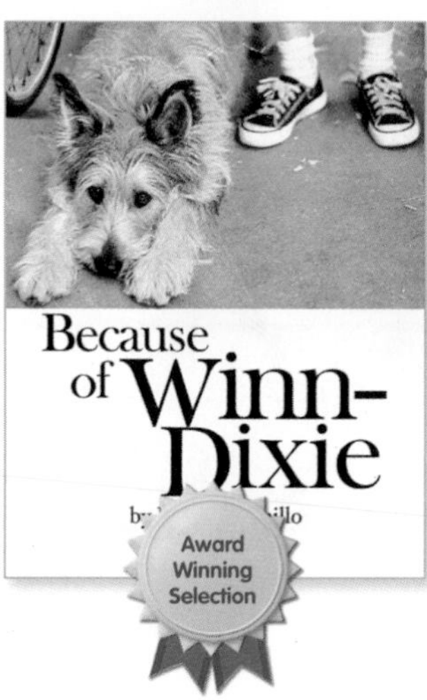

THEME: Friends of All Ages

Show What You Know • REVIEW

Unit 2

Social Studies

Making a Difference

The Big Question

THEME: Civil Rights

THEME: Inspiring Women

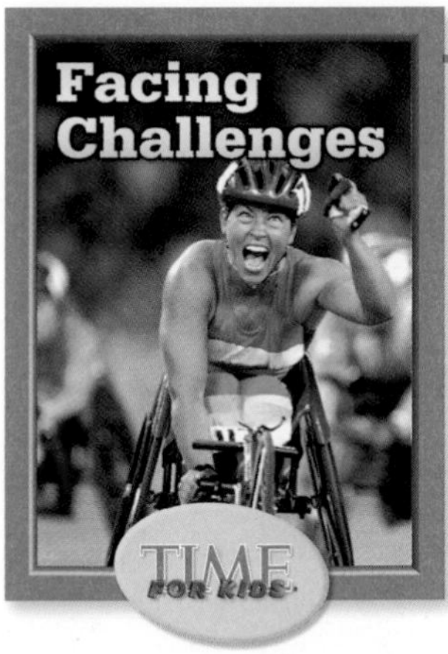

THEME: Facing Challenges

THEME: Saving Animals

THEME: Courage

Show What You Know • REVIEW

Unit 3

Creative Expression

The Power of Words

The Big Question

THEME: Letters

THEME: The Art of Persuasion

THEME: From Words to Action

THEME: Keeping Promises

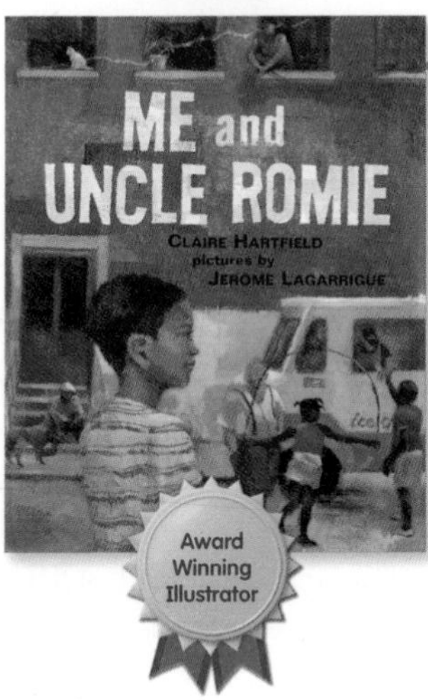

THEME: Expression Through Art

Show What You Know • REVIEW

Unit 4

Teamwork

Working Together

The Big Question

THEME: Value of Friendship

THEME: Animal Teams

THEME: Energy

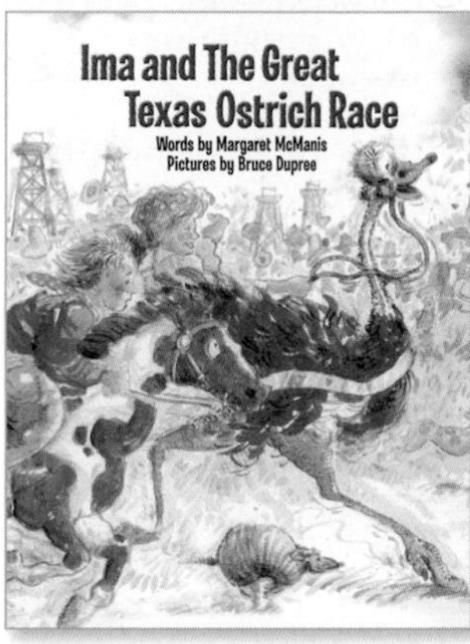

THEME: Teaming Up

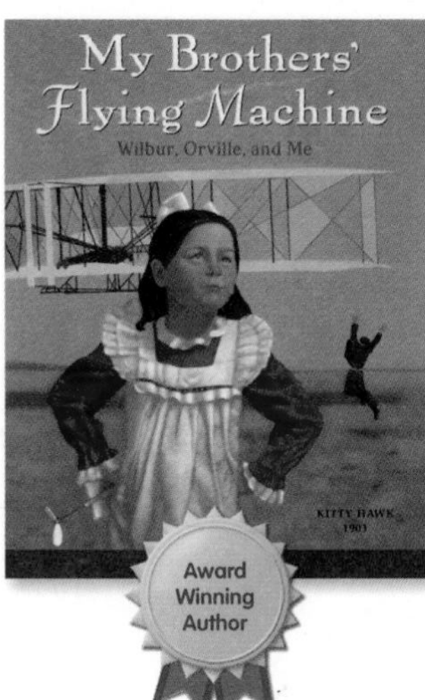

THEME: Family Teams

Show What You Know • REVIEW

Unit 5

Science

Habitats

The Big Question

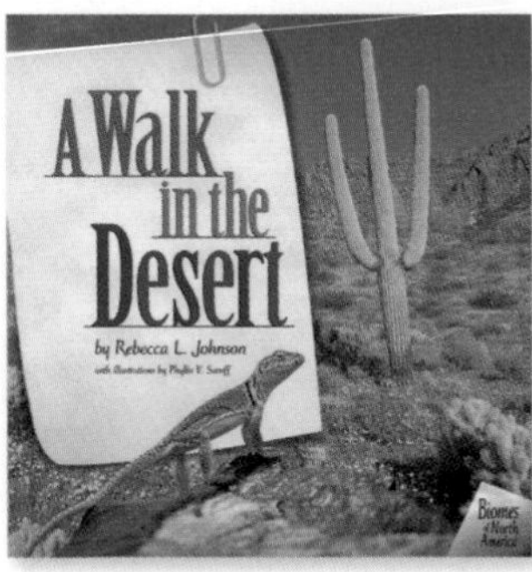

THEME: Adapting to Survive

THEME: Desert Animals

THEME: National Parks

THEME: Oceans

THEME: Ocean Animals

Show What You Know • REVIEW

Unit 6

We're in Grade 4 Now

Problem Solving

SAVE OUR HOSPITAL
Improving Lives
TIME FOR KIDS

SNOWFLAKE BENTLEY
Award Winning Selection

How Ben Franklin Stole the Lightning
Rosalyn Schanzer
Award Winning Author and Illustrator

Unit 1
Growing Up

The Big Question

What experiences can cause a person to change?

LOG ON VIEW IT **Theme Video** Growing Up
www.macmillanmh.com

What experiences can cause a person to change?

People change as they get older and experience new things. When you are young, little things can affect you, such as becoming a big brother or sister, starting a new grade, joining a club, adopting a pet, learning something new, or making a new friend. As you get older, experiences like helping out in your home or community, working, traveling, meeting new people, or learning a new language can change you. These changes can affect what you think, how you feel, and how you look. Learning how people change can help you as you make decisions in your own life.

Research Activities

Throughout the unit, you will be gathering information on people who have gone through life-changing experiences. Choose one person to focus your research on, and then create a short biography. This person can be famous, historical, or someone close to you. Use time lines and other graphic aids to illustrate your biography.

Keep Track of Ideas

As you read, keep track of all you are learning about people and their life-changing experiences. Use the **Layered Book Foldable**. On the top section, write the Unit Theme: *Growing Up*. On each layer of the book, write facts you learn each week that will help you in your research and in your understanding of the Unit Theme.

FOLDABLES® Study Organizer

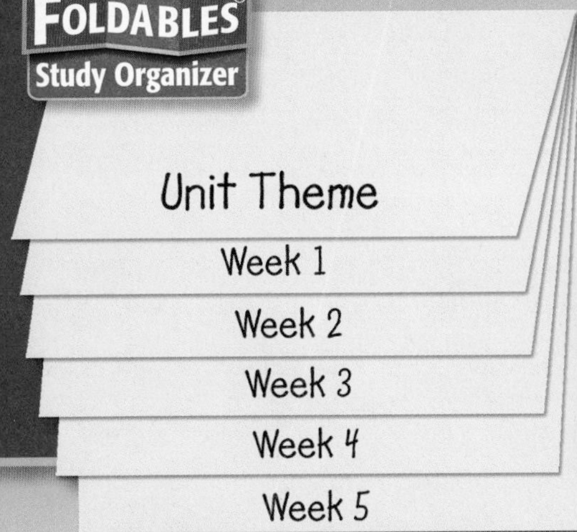

Digital Learning

LOG ON FIND OUT www.macmillanmh.com

StudentWorks™ Plus

Interactive Student Book

- **Research Roadmap**
  Follow a step-by-step guide to complete your research project.

Online Resources

- Topic Finder and Other Research Tools
- Videos and Virtual Field Trips
- Photos and Drawings for Presentations
- Related Articles and Web Resources
- Web Site Links

People and Places

Norman Rockwell, Artist

A famous 20th-century painter and illustrator, Rockwell is best known for the covers he did for *The Saturday Evening Post*. His paintings and illustrations are a record of American life and are still popular today.

MAKING A MOVE

Talk About It

How do you feel about new people, places, and things?

LOG ON VIEW IT

Oral Language Activities
Making a Move
www.macmillanmh.com

Vocabulary

opportunities **strikes**
border **citizen**
unions **boycotts**

Dictionary

Word Origins Where a word comes from and how it came to be in use is its origin. You can determine a word's origin in a dictionary. Use a dictionary to find the origin of *boycotts*.

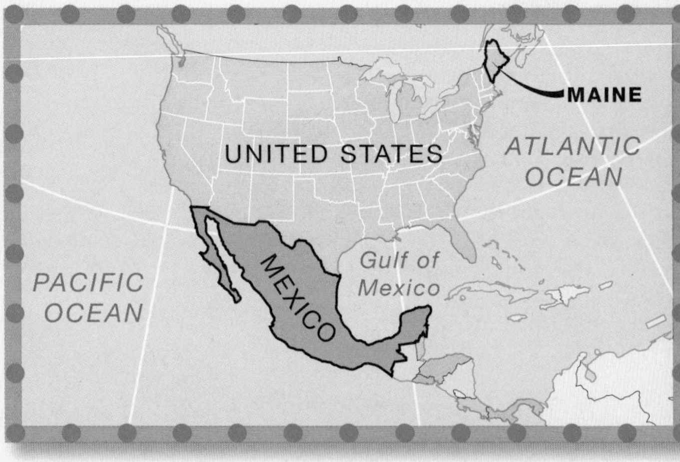

Mexico: My New Home

by Harold Johnson

Dear Grandpa,

Remember when Mom and Dad thought I was asleep and I overheard them talking about moving to Mexico? You said that it would be an adventure. You were right!

I was a little scared when we left Maine. All my friends were there. Living in Mexico is very different.

Guess what? I ate my first *tamale*. Do you know what that is? It's cornmeal wrapped in corn husks and steamed. I have had many chances and **opportunities** to try new foods.

But sometimes I go to my favorite fast food place. So it's not a totally different world. We actually live less than 100 miles from the U.S.–Mexico boundary line or **border**.

The farmers here work very hard but don't make much money to support their families. Some farmers join **unions**, organizations just for them, to protect their rights. Sometimes there are **strikes**, and people stop working, hoping that will make a difference.

Farmers are asking every visitor and **citizen** not to buy produce that comes from outside Mexico. They hope these **boycotts** will improve their working conditions.

I'm learning a lot about Mexican culture. Local harvests are really important here. There are fairs, called *ferias*, to celebrate. There's lots of music, dancing, and eating. I hope we can go to a *feria* when you visit!

Adios!

Paul (or should I say Pablo?)

Reread for Comprehension

Analyze Story Structure

Make Inferences As you read, pay attention to the details the author gives about the characters and events in the story. These story clues will help you make inferences about the characters. Reread the selection and make an inference about Paul. How does he feel about his new home in Mexico? Use an Inferences Web to help record evidence from the text.

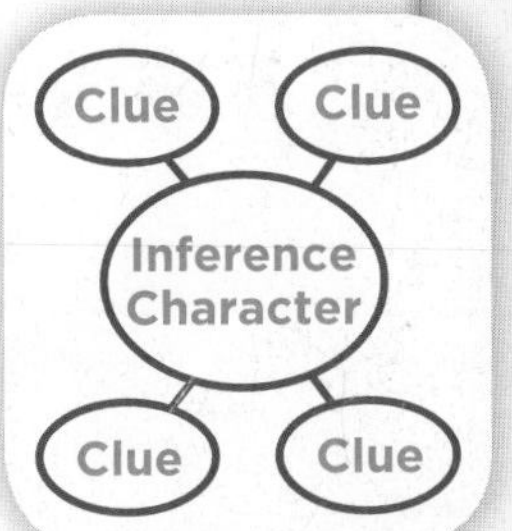

LOG ON LEARN IT Comprehension www.macmillanmh.com

Comprehension

Genre

Fiction is a made-up story that could have happened in real life.

Analyze Story Structure

Make Inferences

As you read, fill in your Inferences Web.

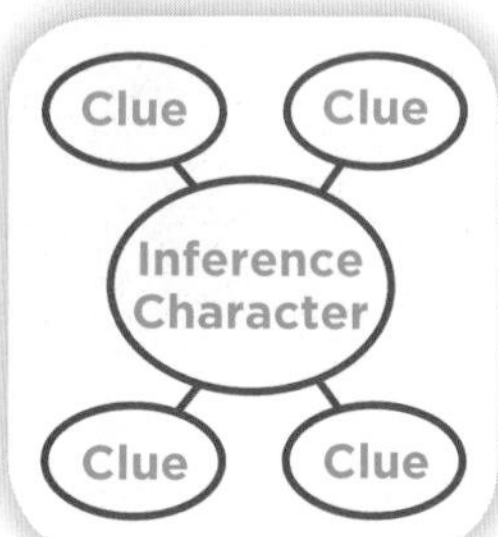

Read to Find Out

What benefits does Amada get from keeping a diary?

My Diary from Here to There

by Amada Irma Pérez
illustrated by Maya Christina Gonzalez

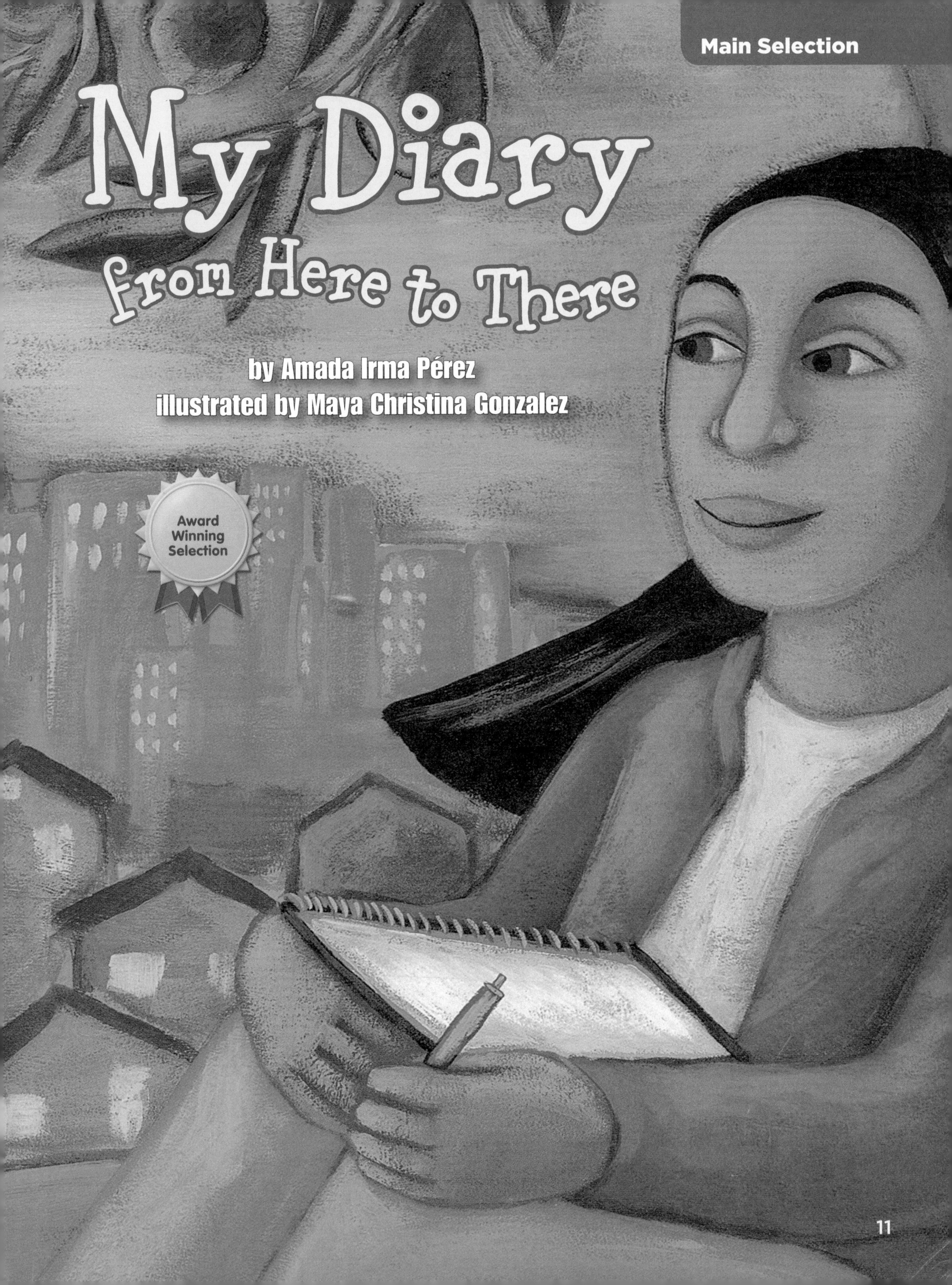

Sé que ya debería
estar dormida pero
no me importa.
Siento que sí

Dear Diary, I know I should be asleep already, but I just can't sleep. If I don't write this all down, I'll burst! Tonight after my brothers—Mario, Víctor, Héctor, Raúl, and Sergio—and I all climbed into bed, I overheard Mamá and Papá whispering. They were talking about leaving our little house in Juárez, Mexico, where we've lived our whole lives, and moving to Los Angeles in the United States. But why? How can I sleep knowing we might leave Mexico forever? I'll have to get to the bottom of this tomorrow.

Today at breakfast, Mamá explained everything. She said, "Papá lost his job. There's no work here, no jobs at all. We know moving will be hard, but we want the best for all of you. Try to understand." I thought the boys would be upset, but instead they got really excited about moving to the States.

"The big stores in El Paso sell all kinds of toys!"

"And they have escalators to ride!"

"And the air smells like popcorn, yum!"

Am I the only one who is scared of leaving our home, our beautiful country, and all the people we might never see again?

My best friend Michi and I walked to the park today. We passed Don Nacho's corner store and the women at the tortilla shop, their hands blurring like hummingbird wings as they worked the dough over the griddle.

At the park we braided each other's hair and promised never to forget each other. We each picked out a smooth, heart-shaped stone to remind us always of our friendship, of the little park, of Don Nacho and the tortilla shop. I've known Michi since we were little, and I don't think I'll ever find a friend like her in California.

"You're lucky your family will be together over there," Michi said. Her sisters and father work in the U.S. I can't imagine leaving anyone in our family behind.

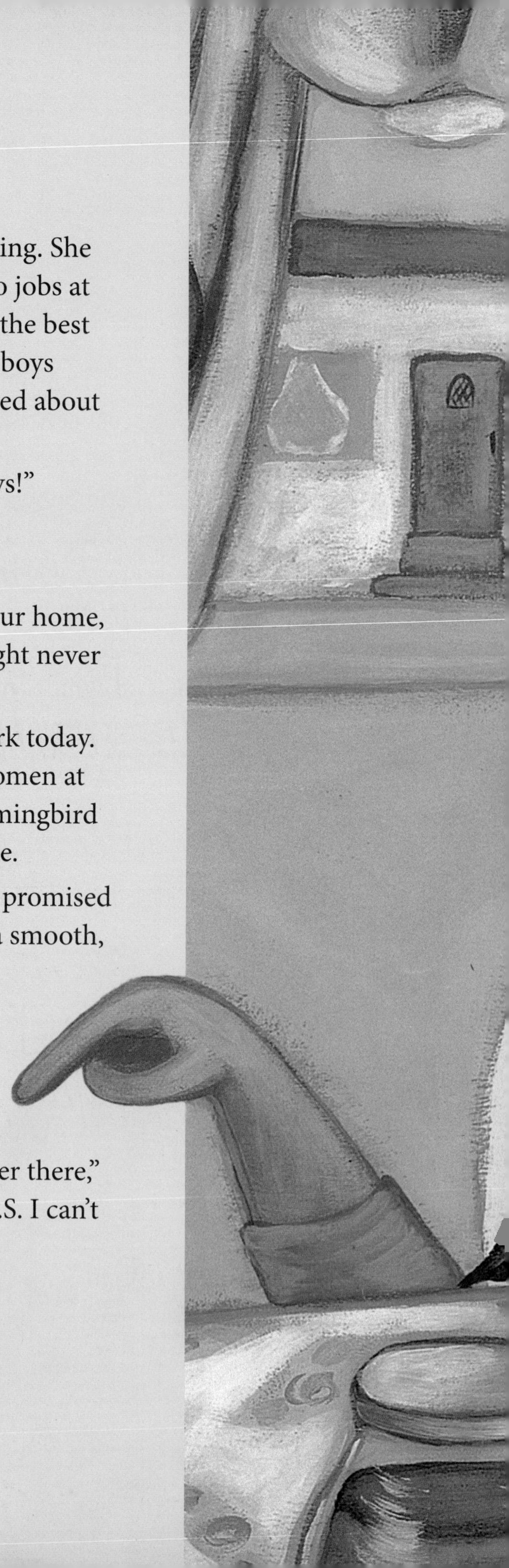

OK, Diary, here's the plan—in two weeks we leave for my grandparents' house in Mexicali, right across the **border** from Calexico, California. We'll stay with them while Papá goes to Los Angeles to look for work. We can only take what will fit in the old car Papá borrowed—we're selling everything else. Meanwhile, the boys build cardboard box cities and act like nothing bothers them. Mamá and Papá keep talking about all the **opportunities** we'll have in California. But what if we're not allowed to speak Spanish? What if I can't learn English? Will I ever see Michi again? What if we never come back?

COCINA
COCINA
GATO

Today while we were packing, Papá pulled me aside. He said, "Amada, *m'ija*, I can see how worried you've been. Don't be scared. Everything will be all right."

"But how do you know? What will happen to us?" I said.

He smiled. "*M'ija*, I was born in Arizona, in the States. When I was six—not a big kid like you—my Papá and Mamá moved our family back to Mexico. It was a big change, but we got through it. I know you can, too. You are stronger than you think." I hope he's right. I still need to pack my special rock (and you, Diary!). We leave tomorrow!

Make Inferences

Based on Amada's journal entries, how do you think she is feeling about the move? How do you know?

Our trip was long and hard. At night the desert was so cold we had to huddle together to keep warm. We drove right along the border, across from New Mexico and Arizona. Mexico and the U.S. are two different countries, but they look exactly the same on both sides of the border, with giant saguaros pointing up at the pink-orange sky and enormous clouds. I made a wish on the first star I saw. Soon there were too many stars in the sky to count. Our little house in Juárez already seems so far away.

We arrived in Mexicali late at night and my grandparents Nana and Tata, and all our aunts, uncles and cousins (there must be fifty of them!) welcomed us with a feast of *tamales*, beans, *pan dulce*, and hot chocolate with cinnamon sticks. It's so good to see them all! Everyone gathered around us and told stories late into the night. We played so much that the boys fell asleep before the last blanket was rolled out onto the floor. But, Diary, I can't sleep. I keep thinking about Papá leaving tomorrow.

Papá left for Los Angeles this morning. Nana comforted Mamá, saying that Papá is a U.S. **citizen**, so he won't have a problem getting our "green cards" from the U.S. government. Papá told us that we each need a green card to live in the States, because we weren't born there.

I can't believe Papá's gone. Tío Tito keeps trying to make us laugh instead of cry. Tío Raúl let me wear his special *medalla*. And Tío Chato even pulled a silver coin out of my ear. The boys try to copy his tricks but coins just end up flying everywhere. They drive me nuts sometimes, but today it feels good to laugh.

We got a letter from Papá today! I'm pasting it into your pages, Diary.

My dear family,

I have been picking grapes and strawberries in the fields of Delano, 140 miles north of Los Angeles, saving money and always thinking of you. It is hard, tiring work. There is a man here in the fields named César Chávez, who speaks of ***unions***, ***strikes***, *and* ***boycotts***. *These new words hold the hope of better conditions for us farmworkers.*

So far, getting your green cards has been difficult, for we are not the only family trying to start a new life here. Please be patient. It won't be long before we are all together again.

Hugs and kisses, Papá

Make Inferences

What can you tell about Amada's father from the letter he writes to his family?

I miss Papá so much—it feels like he left ages ago. It's been tough to stay hopeful. So far we've had to live in three different houses with some of Mamá's sisters. First, the boys broke Tía Tuca's jewelry box and were so noisy she kicked us out. Then, at Nana's house, they kept trying on Tía Nena's high heels and purses. Even Nana herself got mad when they used her pots and pans to make "music." And they keep trying to read what I've written here, and to hide my special rock. Tía Lupe finally took us in, but where will we go if she decides she's had enough of us?

FINALLY! Papá sent our green cards—we're going to cross the border at last! He can't come for us but will meet us in Los Angeles.

The whole family is making a big farewell dinner for us tonight. Even after all the trouble the boys have caused, I think everyone is sad to see us go. Nana even gave me a new journal to write in for when I finish this one. She said, "Never forget who you are and where you are from. Keep your language and culture alive in your diary and in your heart."

We leave this weekend. I'm so excited I can hardly write!

My first time writing in the U.S.A.! We're in San Ysidro, California, waiting for the bus to Los Angeles. Crossing the border in Tijuana was crazy. Everyone was pushing and shoving. There were babies crying, and people fighting to be first in line. We held hands the whole way. When we finally got across, Mario had only one shoe on and his hat had fallen off. I counted everyone and I still had five brothers. Whew!

Papá is meeting us at the bus station in Los Angeles. It's been so long—I hope he recognizes us!

What a long ride! One woman and her children got kicked off the bus when the immigration patrol boarded to check everyone's papers. Mamá held Mario and our green cards close to her heart.

Papá was waiting at the station, just like he promised. We all jumped into his arms and laughed, and Mamá even cried a little. Papá's hugs felt so much better than when he left us in Mexicali!

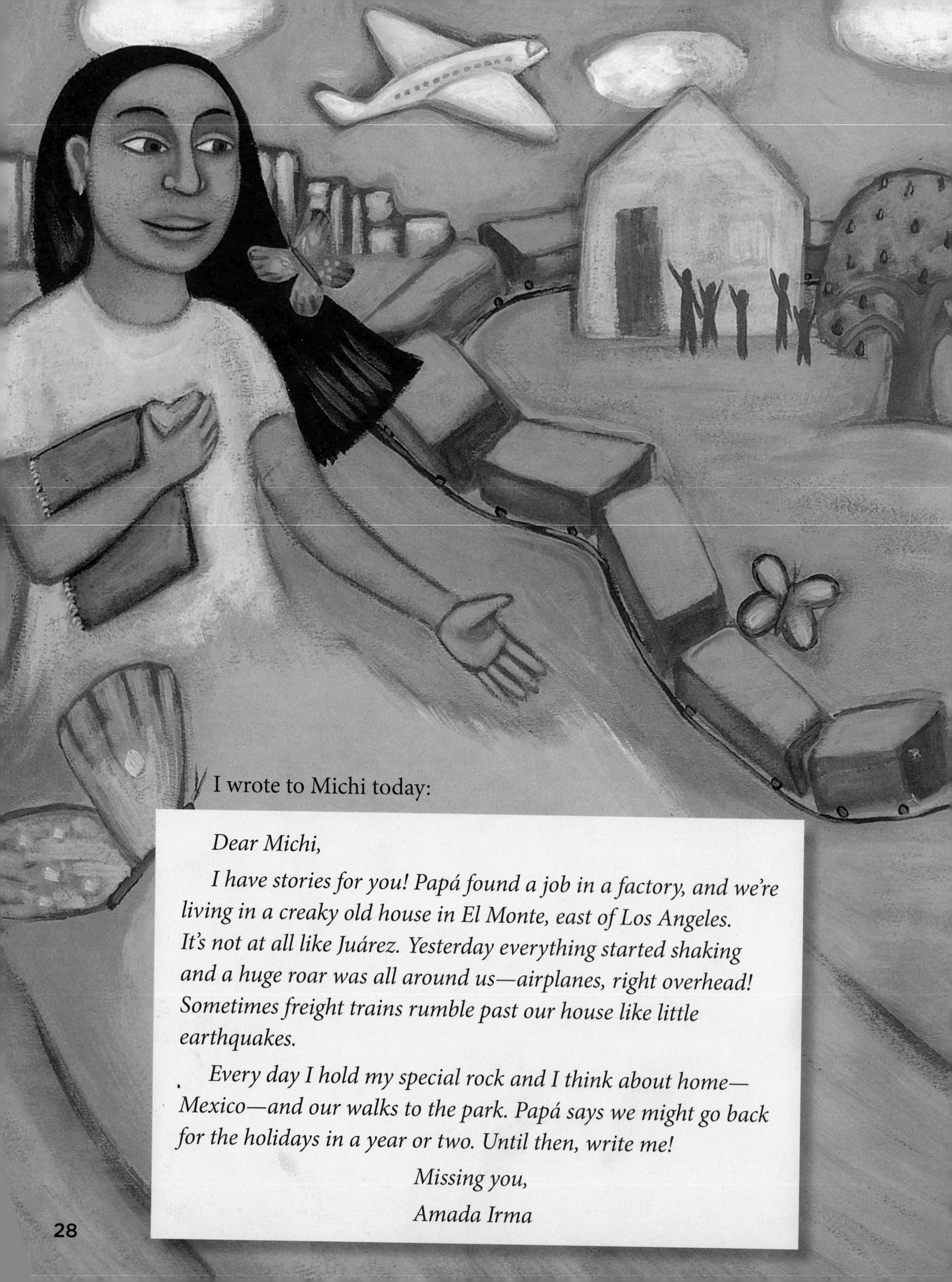

I wrote to Michi today:

Dear Michi,

I have stories for you! Papá found a job in a factory, and we're living in a creaky old house in El Monte, east of Los Angeles. It's not at all like Juárez. Yesterday everything started shaking and a huge roar was all around us—airplanes, right overhead! Sometimes freight trains rumble past our house like little earthquakes.

Every day I hold my special rock and I think about home—Mexico—and our walks to the park. Papá says we might go back for the holidays in a year or two. Until then, write me!

Missing you,
Amada Irma

Well, Diary, I finally found a place where I can sit and think and write. It may not be the little park in Juárez, but it's pretty. You know, just because I'm far away from Juárez and Michi and my family in Mexicali, it doesn't mean they're not here with me. They're inside my little rock; they're here in your pages and in the language that I speak; and they're in my memories and my heart. Papá was right. I AM stronger than I think—in Mexico, in the States, anywhere.

P.S. I've almost filled this whole journal and can't wait to start my new one. Maybe someday I'll even write a book about our journey!

From the Diaries of . . .

Amada Irma Pérez says, "When I was only five years old, my family left Mexico for the United States. That time—when we left Juárez behind, stayed with my Nana in Mexicali, waited breathlessly for my father's letters—was exciting, but also painful." She used those memories of her own journey from Mexico to the United States to write this story. Just like the main character, she was both excited and scared about moving.

Today Amada still writes in a journal. About her first diary, she remembers, "My mother gave me my first diary as a birthday present when I turned 11. It was a beautiful white little book with gold lettering and a tiny lock and key. Each page was divided up into five sections as it was a 5-year diary. Wow! A whole book for me to fill up."

Maya Christina Gonzalez has always loved to draw. When she was a child, she could not find any pictures of Mexican American children like herself in books. Today Maya's books show lots of people of color so readers can feel proud of who they are.

LOG ON FIND OUT

Author Amada Irma Pérez
Illustrator Maya Christina Gonzalez
www.macmillanmh.com

Author's Purpose

Identify some similarities between *My Diary from Here to There* and events in Amada Irma Pérez's life. Why did the author write this story?

LOG ON LEARN IT Comprehension
www.macmillanmh.com

Comprehension Check

Summarize

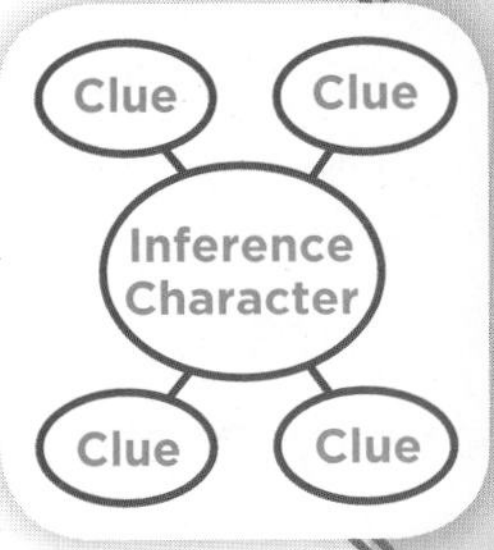

To summarize *My Diary from Here to There* use the most important details from the selection. Information from your Inferences Web may help you.

Think and Compare

1. Who is Amada's best friend in Mexico? Details
2. Why does Amada's family have to sell most of their belongings before they go to her grandparents' house in Mexicali? Cause and Effect
3. What does Amada think about her new home and the **opportunities** it offers? Use evidence from the story in your answer. Analyze Story Structure: Make Inferences
4. Why did the author choose to write the story as a series of diary entries? Author's Purpose
5. Read "Mexico: My New Home" on pages 8–9. How is Paul's situation similar to Amada's? How is it different? Reading/Writing Across Texts

Social Studies

Genre

Expository articles explain topics by presenting facts, information, photos, and graphic aids.

Text Feature

Time lines show historical events in the order in which they occurred.

Content Vocabulary

migrant workers **labor**
conditions **bargained**

César Chávez

by Sam Hiller

César Chávez was born in Arizona on March 31, 1927, into a large and loving Mexican American family. César's mother taught her six children never to solve problems by fighting. Instead, she encouraged them to work out disagreements by using their minds and talking things over. César never forgot this lesson.

A New Home in California

In 1937, César's family was forced to give up their land and leave Arizona. Homeless and almost penniless, the family joined the thousands of other people going west to look for work on California's huge farms.

César Chávez was one of America's most important civil rights leaders.

For the next ten years, César and his family were **migrant workers**. The entire family worked in the fields—planting, weeding, and picking crops. Working **conditions** were harsh, and the pay was very low. When work ended in one place, the family packed up and moved to a different part of California where they might find work.

Farm workers in California harvest crops.

THE LIFE OF CÉSAR CHÁVEZ

Reading a Time Line

Read the time line starting on the left with the earliest event. Continue reading the events in the correct time order.

1930 | 1960 | 1990

- **1927** Born
- **1937** Family moves to California to become migrant workers
- **1942** Quits school to work full time in the fields
- **1944** Serves in the U.S. Navy
- **1948** Marries Helen Fabela
- **1952** Joins the Community Service Organization
- **1962** Forms the National Farm Workers Association
- **1965** Leads a strike against grape growers
- **1993** Dies
- **1994** Receives the Medal of Freedom

César Chávez Grows Up

César Chávez attended school until eighth grade when he had to begin to work full time to support his family. In 1944, he joined the U.S. Navy and fought in World War II. When Chávez returned to California, he went back to work in the fields. In 1948, he married Helen Fabela, who was also from a family of migrant workers. Conditions for farm workers had not changed, and Chávez wanted a better life for his growing family.

César Chávez with grape pickers in 1968.

Working for Change

In 1952, Chávez went to work for the Community Service Organization (CSO). He helped Mexican American migrant workers become U.S. citizens. As citizens, the workers would be able to vote on **labor** issues. Under Chávez's leadership, the organization became the strongest Mexican American civil rights group in the United States.

Building a Union

Chávez believed that farm workers would be stronger if they **bargained** as a group for better working conditions and higher wages. In 1962, Chávez and Dolores Huerta started the National Farm Workers Association, a labor union.

Chávez used nonviolent methods to achieve his goals. He was inspired by Dr. Martin Luther King, Jr., and Mahatma Gandhi.

A Victory for Farm Workers

In 1965, Chávez led farm workers in a strike against grape growers. The strike angered many business owners. Other people across the United States showed their support by refusing to buy grapes. After five years of struggle, the farm owners agreed to give the workers better conditions and higher wages. Chávez continued working for the rights of farm laborers until the end of his life.

Helen Chávez accepting the Medal of Freedom on behalf of her husband.

Connect and Compare

1. Using the time line, explain when and how César Chávez began working to improve the civil rights of farm workers. **Reading a Time Line**
2. Why was César Chávez's work important? Explain using details from the selection. **Apply**
3. Think about this article and *My Diary from Here to There*. Compare how the two selections present information about César Chávez. **Reading/Writing Across Texts**

Social Studies Activity

César Chávez changed farm workers' lives all over the country. Research the founding of farm workers' unions in Texas or the Midwest. Use reference texts, time lines, and online resources. Write a summary of your findings.

LOG ON FIND OUT César Chávez www.macmillanmh.com

Reading and Writing Connection

Writing

Trait: Ideas

Writers provide details, such as precise action and sensory words, to describe a specific **moment** in time.

Read the passage below. Notice how the author Amada Irma Pérez focuses on a moment of time in her story.

An excerpt from
My Diary from Here to There

Papá was waiting at the station, just like he promised. We all jumped into his arms and laughed, and Mamá even cried a little. Papá's hugs felt so much better than when he left us in Mexicali!

The author focuses on the moment when the family is reunited. In the focused moment, her details help us imagine what happened, even if there weren't any pictures.

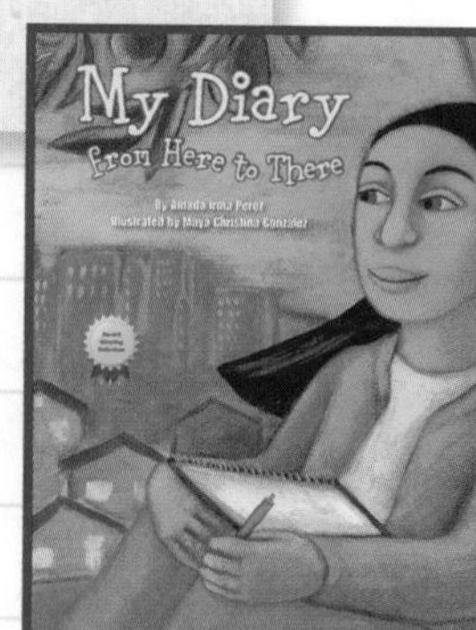

Read and Find

Read Pablo's writing below. What did he do to focus on a moment? Use the checklist below to help you.

Birthday Gift

by Pablo M.

After dinner, Nana pulled out a big box. It was wrapped in red paper, decorated with footballs and had a yellow ribbon around it. As soon as she placed it in my hands, I yanked at the ribbon. I had to strain to get it off the box. Then I ripped into the paper. Strips were flying everywhere! And there it was: a new helmet.

Read about Pablo's birthday gift.

Writer's Checklist

- ☑ Does the writer write about a short amount of time?
- ☑ Does the writer use specific details?
- ☐ Can you picture the **moment** the way Pablo experienced it?

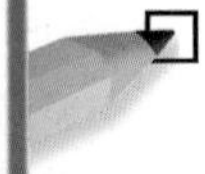

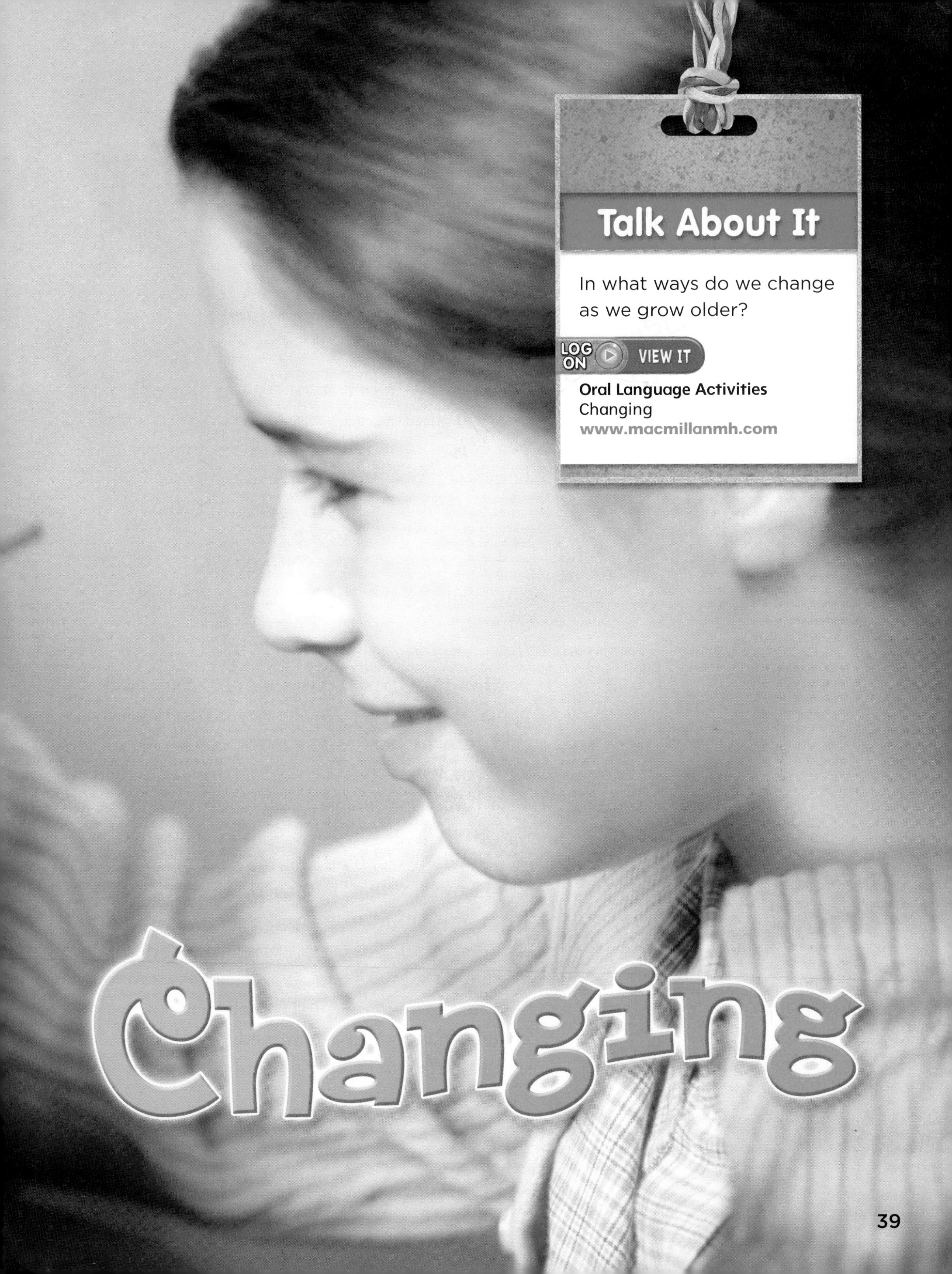

Talk About It

In what ways do we change as we grow older?

LOG ON VIEW IT

Oral Language Activities
Changing
www.macmillanmh.com

Changing

The Surprise

Vocabulary

several | **policy**
ranged | **temporary**
curious | **frequently**

Thesaurus

Synonyms are words that have the same, or nearly the same, meaning. Use a thesaurus to find a synonym for the word *curious*.

by Eleanor McClain

Emily lay in bed staring up at the ceiling. **Several** fluorescent stars glowed faintly above her. She counted four small stars and three bigger stars.

"Are you still awake?" her sister Anna asked from the bottom bunk.

"Yeah, I can't sleep," Emily said, sighing. She wished she could just make a decision. The way she saw it, their choices **ranged** from bad to horrible.

"Emily, what's the worst thing that could happen?" Anna asked. She was **curious** to find out why her sister was so nervous.

"The worst thing? What if Mom gets mad at us for planning a surprise birthday party and grounds us for life?"

"Maybe we should cancel it," Anna said.

"I can't do that. Twenty of Mom's friends are coming tomorrow. And the bakery has a strict **policy** about canceling cake orders. I'll lose my money if I cancel now."

The next evening, Emily felt nervous. Twenty people were crammed into their small apartment. Emily had turned on the fan.

She and Anna had set up a **temporary** party area in the living room. Balloons **frequently** twisted back and forth in the fan's breeze.

Emily and Anna heard a key turning in the lock. Suddenly, the room became silent. Their mother came in carrying her briefcase and a bag of groceries.

"Hi, girls," their mother said. Then she looked up and saw all the people. "What's going on here?"

"HAPPY BIRTHDAY!" everyone shouted.

"Oh," said their mother and dropped the bag of groceries. Then she hugged Emily, and laughing, wiped some tears from her eyes.

Reread for Comprehension

Analyze Story Structure

Character, Setting, Plot The setting is where the story takes place. Knowing the setting of a story can help a reader analyze how the setting affects the characters, their actions, and the plot. Use the Story Flowchart to help you keep track of the setting, characters, and events of a story.

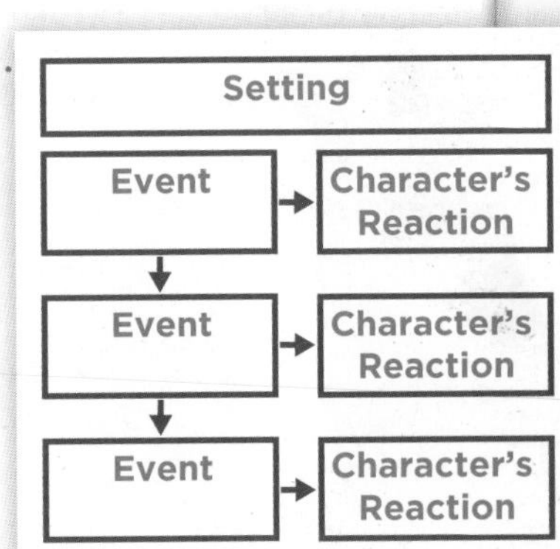

LOG ON LEARN IT Comprehension www.macmillanmh.com

Comprehension

Genre

Fiction is a made-up story that could happen in real life.

Analyze Story Structure

Character, Setting, Plot
As you read, fill in your Story Flowchart.

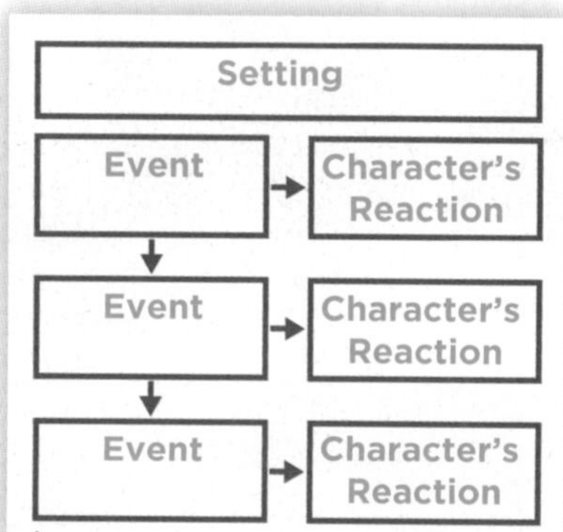

Read to Find Out

What adventures does Ali Baba Bernstein have?

David Bernstein

David Bernstein

David Bernstein

David Bernstein

David Bernstein

David Bernstein

from

The Adventures of Ali Baba Bernstein

Award Winning Author

by Johanna Hurwitz

illustrated by Brian Biggs

David (Ali Baba) Bernstein

How Ali Baba Got His Name

David Bernstein was eight years, five months, and seventeen days old when he chose his new name.

There were already four Davids in David Bernstein's third-grade class. Every time his teacher, Mrs. Booxbaum, called, "David," all four boys answered. David didn't like that one bit. He wished he had an exciting name like one of the explorers he learned about in social studies—Vasco Da Gama. Once he found two unusual names on a program his parents brought home from a concert—Zubin Mehta and Wolfgang Amadeus Mozart. Now those were names with pizzazz!

David Bernstein might have gone along forever being just another David if it had not been for the book report that his teacher assigned.

"I will give extra credit for fat books," Mrs. Booxbaum told the class.

She didn't realize that all of her students would try to outdo one another. That afternoon when the third grade went to the school library, everyone tried to find the fattest book.

Melanie found a book with eighty pages.

Sam found a book with ninety-seven pages.

Jeffrey found a book with one hundred nineteen pages.

David K. and David S. each took a copy of the same book. It had one hundred forty-five pages.

None of the books were long enough for David Bernstein. He looked at a few that had over one hundred pages. He found one that had two hundred fourteen pages. But he wanted a book that had more pages than the total of all the pages in all the books his classmates were reading. He wanted to be the best student in the class—even in the entire school.

That afternoon he asked his mother what the fattest book was. Mrs. Bernstein thought for a minute. "I guess that would have to be the Manhattan telephone book," she said.

David Bernstein rushed to get the phone book. He lifted it up and opened to the last page. When he saw that it had over 1,578 pages, he was delighted.

He knew that no student in the history of P.S. 35 had ever read such a fat book. Just think how much extra credit he would get! David took the book and began to read name after name after name. After turning through the A pages, he skipped to the name Bernstein. He found the listing for his father, Robert Bernstein. There were fifteen of them. Then he counted the number of David Bernsteins in the telephone book. There were seventeen. There was also a woman named Davida and a man named Davis, but he didn't count them. Right at that moment, David decided two things: he would change his name and he would find another book to read.

The next day David went back to the school library. He asked the librarian to help him pick out a very fat book. "But it must be very exciting, too," he told her.

"I know just the thing for you," said the librarian.

She handed David a thick book with a bright red cover. It was *The Arabian Nights*. It had only three hundred thirty-seven pages, but it looked a lot more interesting than the phone book. David checked the book out of the library and spent the entire evening reading it. When he showed the book to his teacher the next day, she was very pleased.

"That is a good book," she said. "David, you have made a fine choice."

It was at that moment that David Bernstein announced his new name. He had found it in the library book.

"From now on," David said, "I want to be called Ali Baba Bernstein."

Mrs. Booxbaum was surprised. David's parents were even more surprised. "David is a beautiful name," said his mother. "It was my grandfather's name."

"You can't just go around changing your name when you feel like it," his father said. "How will I ever know who I'm talking to?"

"You'll know it's still me," Ali Baba told his parents.

Mr. and Mrs. Bernstein finally agreed, although both of them **frequently** forgot and called their son David.

So now in Mrs. Booxbaum's class, there were three Davids and one Ali Baba. Ali Baba Bernstein was very happy. He was sure that a boy with an exciting name would have truly exciting adventures.

Only time would tell.

Character, Setting, Plot
What does David's choice of the name Ali Baba tell you about his character?

The Gathering of David Bernsteins

When Ali Baba Bernstein was eight years, eleven months, and four days old, his mother asked him how he wanted to celebrate his ninth birthday. He could take his friends to the bowling alley or to a movie. Or he could have a roller-skating party. None of these choices seemed very exciting to Ali Baba. Two boys in his class had already given bowling parties, another had invited all the boys in the class to a movie, and a third classmate was giving a roller-skating party next week. Ali Baba wanted to do something different.

"Do you remember when I counted all the David Bernsteins in the telephone book?"

Mrs. Bernstein nodded.

"I'd like to meet them all," said David. "I want to invite them here for my birthday."

"But you don't know them," his mother said. "And they are not your age."

"I want to see what they are all like," said Ali Baba. "If I can't invite them, then I don't want to have any party at all."

A week later, when Ali Baba was eight years, eleven months and twelve days old, his mother asked about his birthday again.

"I told you what I decided," said Ali Baba.

That night Ali Baba's parents talked about the David Bernstein party. Mr. Bernstein liked his son's idea. He thought the other David Bernsteins might be **curious** to meet one another. So it was agreed that Ali Baba would have the party he wanted.

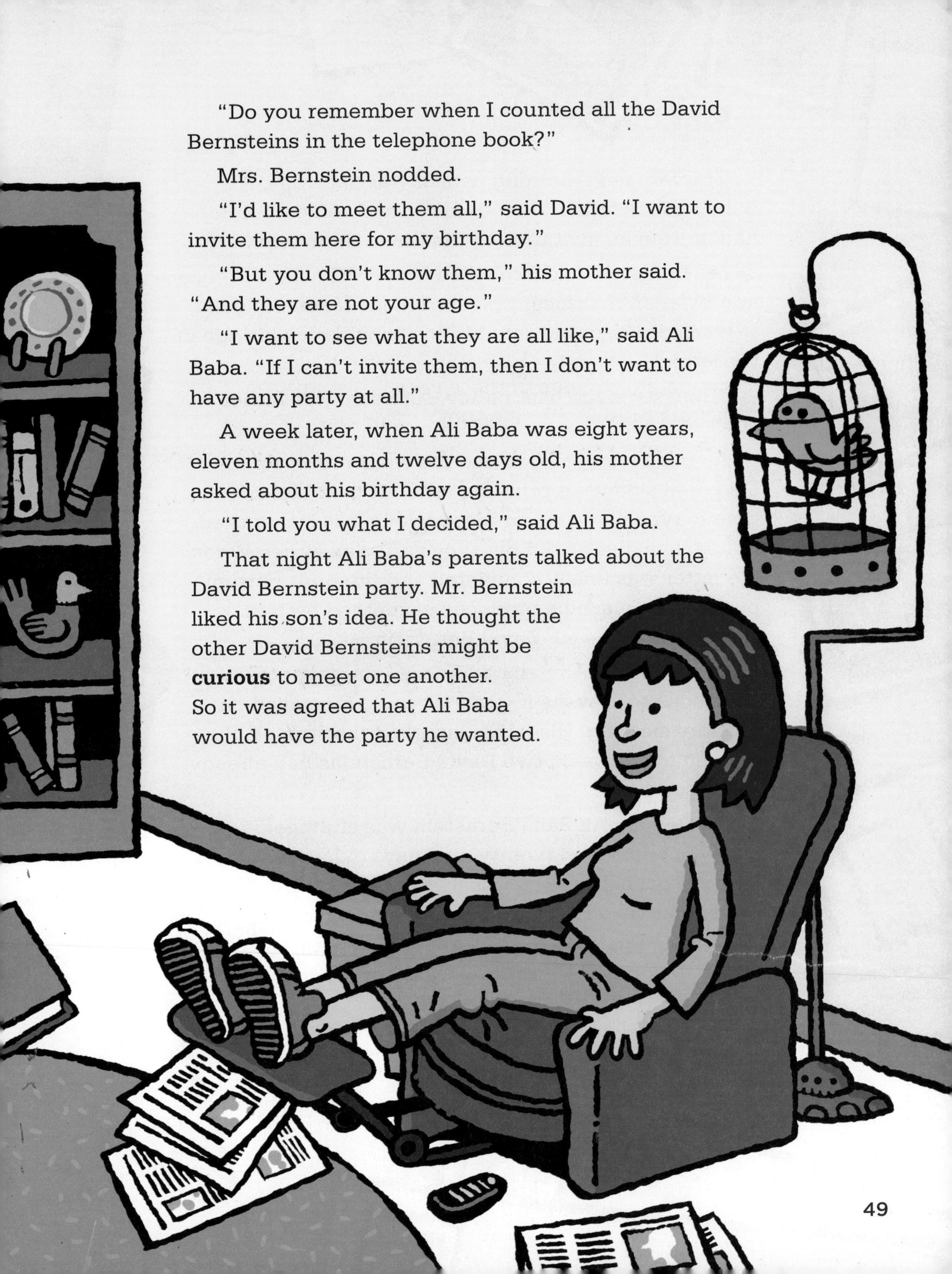

The very next morning, which was Saturday, Ali Baba and his father went to his father's office. Ali Baba had written an invitation to the David Bernstein party.

Mr. Bernstein had explained that RSVP was a French abbreviation that meant please tell me if you are going to come. He also said that his son should give his age in the letter.

"Honesty is the best **policy**, Ali Baba," his father advised.

Ali Baba was going to use the word processor in his father's office to print the letter. It took him a long time to type his letter on the machine. His father tried to help him, but he did not type very well either. When the letter was finally completed and the print button pushed, the machine produced seventeen perfect copies—one for each David Bernstein.

That evening Ali Baba addressed the seventeen envelopes so that the invitations could be mailed on Monday morning. His father supplied the stamps. By the end of the week, two David Bernsteins had already called to accept.

By the time Ali Baba Bernstein was eight years, eleven months, and twenty nine days old, seven David Bernsteins had accepted his invitation. Four David Bernsteins called to say they couldn't come.

Six David Bernsteins did not answer at all.

Dear David Bernstein:

I found your name in the Manhattan telephone book. My name is David Bernstein, too. I want to meet all the David Bernsteins in New York. I am having a party on Friday, May 12th at 7:00 P.M., and I hope you can come. My mother is cooking supper. She is a good cook.

Yours truly,
David Bernstein
(also known as Ali Baba Bernstein)

P.S. May 12th is my ninth birthday, but you don't have to bring a present.
RSVP: 211-3579

Ali Baba and his mother chose the menu for his birthday dinner. There would be a pot roast, corn (Ali Baba's favorite vegetable), rolls, applesauce, and salad. They were also having kasha varnishkas (a combination of buckwheat groats and noodles), which one of the guests had requested.

The evening of the party finally arrived. Ali Baba had decided to wear a pair of slacks, a sport jacket, and real dress shoes. It was not at all the way he would have dressed for a bowling party.

Ali Baba was surprised when the first guest arrived in a jogging suit and running shoes.

"How do you do," he said when Ali Baba answered the door. "I'm David Bernstein."

"Of course," said the birthday boy. "Call me Ali Baba."

Soon the living room was filled with David Bernsteins. They **ranged** in age from exactly nine years and three hours old to seventy-six years old (he was the David Bernstein who had asked for kasha varnishkas). There was a television director, a delicatessen owner, a mailman, an animal groomer, a dentist, a high-school teacher, and a writer. They all lived in Manhattan now, but they had been born in Brooklyn, the Bronx, Michigan, Poland, Germany, and South Africa. None of them had ever met any of the others before.

All of the guests enjoyed the dinner.

"David, will you please pass those delicious rolls," asked the mailman.

"Certainly, David," said the animal groomer on his left.

"David, would you please pass the pitcher of apple cider this way," asked the dentist.

"Here it is, David," said the television director.

"I have trouble remembering names," the seventy-six-year-old David Bernstein told Ali Baba. "At this party I can't possibly forget." He smiled at Ali Baba. "What did you say your nickname was?"

"Ali Baba is not a nickname. I have chosen it to be my real name. There are too many David Bernsteins. There were even more in the telephone book who didn't come tonight."

"I was the only David Bernstein to finish the New York City Marathon," said David Bernstein the dentist. He was the one wearing running shoes.

"The poodles I clip don't care what my name is," said David Bernstein the animal groomer.

"It's not what you're called but what you do that matters," said the seventy-six-year-old David Bernstein.

All of them agreed to that.

"I once read that in some places children are given **temporary** names. They're called 'milk names.' They can then choose whatever names they want when they get older," said David Bernstein the high-school teacher.

Character, Setting, Plot
What does Ali Baba Bernstein learn from meeting the other David Bernsteins at his party?

"I'd still choose David Bernstein," said David Bernstein the delicatessen owner. "Just because we all have the same name doesn't make us the same."

"You're right," agreed David Bernstein the mailman.

"Here, here," called out David Bernstein the television director. He raised his glass of apple cider. "A toast to the youngest David Bernstein in the room."

Everyone turned to Ali Baba. He was about to say that he didn't want to be called David. But somehow he didn't mind his name so much now that he had met all these other David Bernsteins. They *were* all different. There would never be another David Bernstein like himself. One of these days he might go back to calling himself David again. But not just now.

"Open your presents," called out David Bernstein the writer.

Even though he had said that they didn't have to, **several** guests had brought gifts. So after singing "Happy Birthday" and cutting into the ice-cream cake that was shaped like the Manhattan phone book, Ali Baba began to open the packages. There was a pocket calculator the size of a business card, just like the one his father had. There was a jigsaw puzzle that looked like a subway map of Manhattan, a model airplane kit, and a few books. One was a collection of Sherlock Holmes stories. "I used to call myself Sherlock Bernstein," the high-school teacher recalled. There was an atlas, and, best of all, there was *The Arabian Nights*.

"Now I have my own copy!" said Ali Baba. This was the best birthday he had ever had.

Finally, it was time for the guests to leave. "I never thought I would meet all the David Bernsteins," said David Bernstein the writer.

"You haven't," said Ali Baba. "Besides the seventeen David Bernsteins in the telephone book, there are six hundred eighty-three other Bernsteins listed between Aaron Bernstein and Zachary Bernstein. There must be members of their families who are named David. I bet there are thousands of David Bernsteins that I haven't met yet."

"You're right," said the seventy-six-year-old David Bernstein, patting Ali Baba on the back.

"Maybe I could invite them all next year," said Ali Baba. He was already nine years and six hours old.

"You could put an advertisement in the newspaper," suggested the mailman.

Ali Baba liked that idea.

David Bernstein the writer said, "I just might go home and write all about this. When did you get so interested in all the David Bernsteins?"

"It goes back a long time," said Ali Baba. "It all started on the day that I was eight years, five months, and seventeen days old."

The Gathering of Johanna Hurwitz and Brian Biggs

Johanna Hurwitz likes to write about everyday boys and girls, like Ali Baba Bernstein, and their funny adventures. Johanna gets her story ideas from many places. She thinks about children she knew as a librarian and about people and places she has seen on trips. She also gets ideas from her family. You can read more about Ali Baba and his adventures in *Hurray for Ali Baba Bernstein* and *Ali Baba Bernstein, Lost and Found*.

Other books
by Johanna Hurwitz

LOG ON FIND OUT

Author Johanna Hurwitz
Illustrator Brian Briggs
www.macmillanmh.com

Brian Biggs was born in Arkansas and has lived many other places, including Texas, New York City, Paris, and San Francisco. He likes to draw and write, and he also works with animation and other exciting forms of multimedia. After all of his traveling, Brian now lives in Philadelphia with his two children.

Author's Purpose

What clues from the story can you use to figure out Johanna Hurwitz's purpose for writing? Did she want to inform or entertain? How do you know?

LOG ON LEARN IT Comprehension
www.macmillanmh.com

Comprehension Check

Summarize

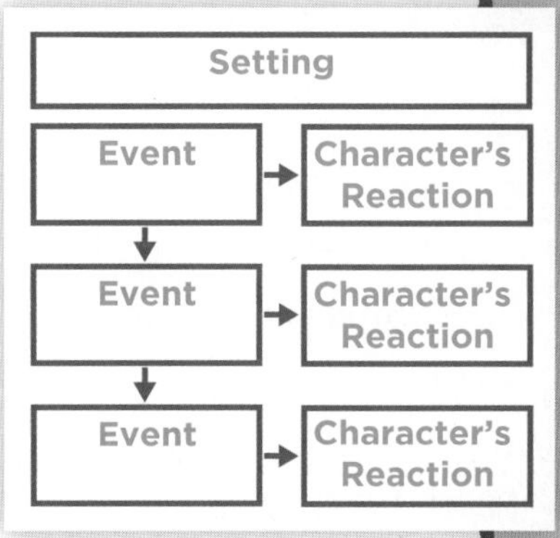

To summarize *The Adventures of Ali Baba Bernstein* use the most important details from the selection. Information from your Story Flowchart may help you.

Think and Compare

1. How many students named "David" are in Ali Baba's third-grade class? Details

2. David tries to read the phone book for his book report. What book does he read next? Sequence

3. Ali Baba is **curious** to meet the other David Bernsteins in the phone book. How does Ali Baba's curiosity influence the events of the plot? Analyze Story Structure: Character, Setting, Plot

4. What message or lesson is the author communicating through the story of Ali Baba's birthday party? Author's Purpose

5. Read "The Surprise" on pages 40–41. How are Emily and Ali Baba similar? How are they different? What do the characters discover? Use details from both selections in your answer. Reading/Writing Across Texts

Social Studies

Genre

Expository text, such as magazine articles, give facts and information about a topic.

Text Feature

Maps are drawings of geographic locations, such as continents or countries.

Content Vocabulary

Silk Road
sultan
civilizations
translation

One Thousand Nights and a Night

The Story of the Arabian Nights
by Neena Akram

The Arabian Nights, also known as *The Thousand and One Nights*, is one of the most famous collections of stories in the world. Most of the stories are believed to be Arabic, Persian, Asian, and Indian and changed over many, many years of storytelling before they were written down. The stories started as tales told by travelers along the trade route known as the **Silk Road** from China to Persia, and through what is today the Middle East. The first known written version of the stories was found in Syria and may date back to the fourteenth or fifteenth century. *The Arabian Nights* has inspired writers around the world with the power of its storytelling.

Stories Within a Story

The very first tale in *The Arabian Nights* is a story about a clever woman named Shahrazad, who told her husband, the **sultan**, or ruler, stories for 1,001 nights! This is why *The Arabian Nights*

is sometimes known as *The Thousand and One Nights*. The stories include fairy tales, fables, parables, romances, and adventures. There are tales of truth and justice. There are also stories that use fantastic imagination to express the spirit of the great **civilizations** in which the stories take place.

The Journey of *The Arabian Nights*

A French writer named Antoine Galland wrote the first European **translation**, or version, of the tales in the early 1700s. There were twelve books in all. He added some of the most well-known tales, including "Aladdin" and "Ali Baba and the Forty Thieves."

In 1885 an Englishman named Sir Richard Francis Burton penned *The Book of The Thousand Nights and a Night*, what we know today as the stories of *The Arabian Nights*.

The Arabian Nights includes these famous tales:

- ***Aladdin and the Wonderful Lamp*** The famous story of Aladdin, the boy who agrees to find a magical lamp for a wizard. When he sees the wizard has tricked him, Aladdin keeps the lamp and becomes the master of the djini, or genie, who lives inside of it.
- ***Ali Baba and the Forty Thieves*** Ali Baba, a poor woodcutter, one day overhears the leader of the Forty Thieves describe the secret location of their loot—a cave that is sealed by magic. He listens further and discovers the cave's magic password: "Open sesame!"
- ***The Ebony Horse*** The tale of King Sabur, ruler of the Persians, his three daughters, and the magical wooden horse that comes to life and flies when someone climbs upon it.
- ***The Seven Voyages of Sinbad the Sailor*** A cycle of seven stories, each describing a different journey of Sinbad and his crew. Sinbad and his men set sail for adventure and treasure, but usually find themselves shipwrecked and having to fight villains and monsters to find their way home.

Reading a Map

This map shows the locations of countries important to the history of the tales of *The Arabian Nights*.

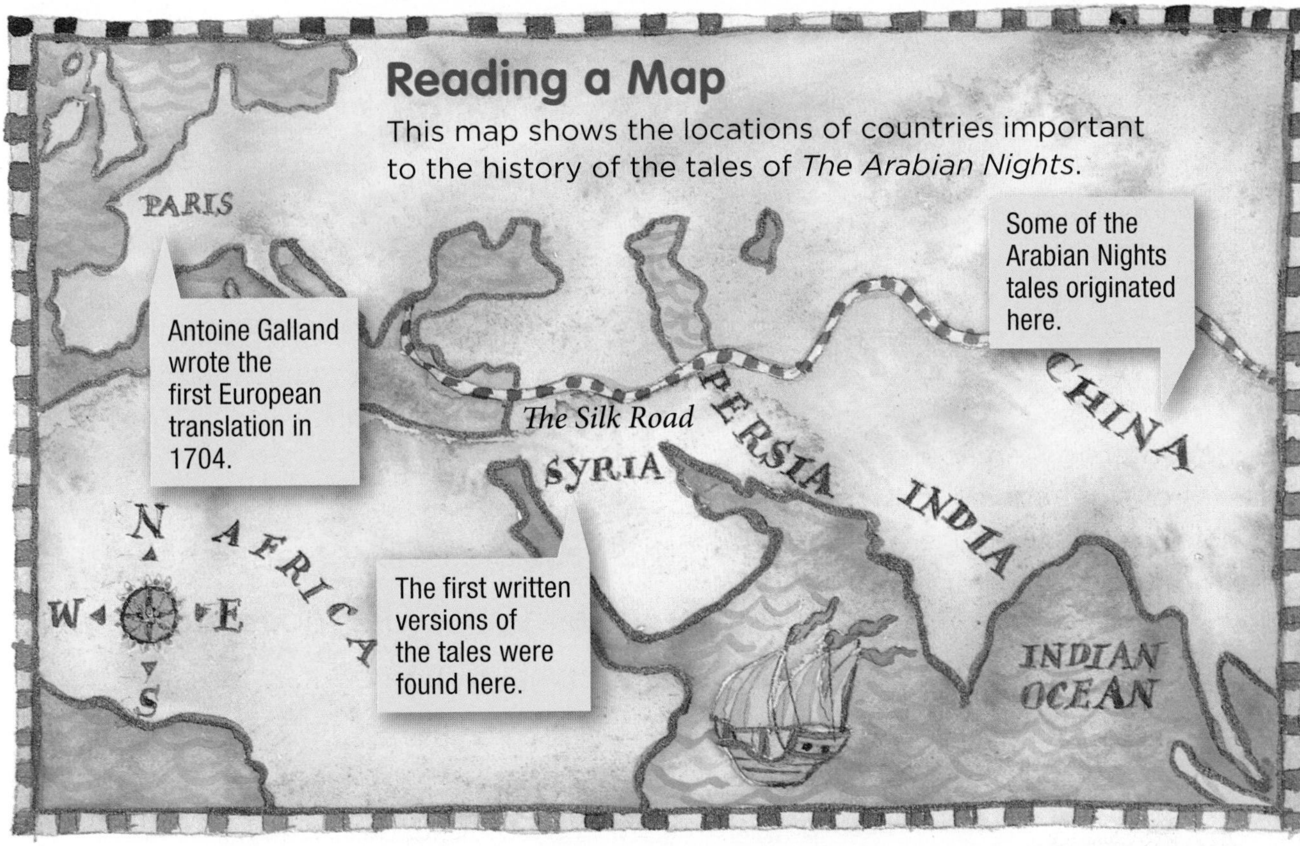

Connect and Compare

1. According to the map, where was the first written version of *The Arabian Nights* found? **Reading a Map**

2. Read the map. Name two countries the Silk Road passed through. **Apply**

3. Think about *The Adventures of Ali Baba Bernstein* and what you know about the character Ali Baba. Why does Ali Baba enjoy reading *The Arabian Nights*? **Reading/Writing Across Texts**

RESEARCH INQUIRY

Social Studies Activity

Choose a classic folktale such as *Stone Soup*. On your own, read two versions of the story you have chosen from two different countries. Locate these countries on a map. Then make a Venn diagram comparing the characters and events in the two different stories.

LOG ON FIND OUT *The Arabian Nights*
www.macmillanmh.com

Reading and Writing Connection

Writing

Trait: Ideas

Good writers give readers details of sight and sound to help them experience the **moment** the writer is describing.

Read the passage below. Notice how the author Johanna Hurwitz focuses on one moment in time in her story.

The author focuses on the moment Ali Baba was writing his invitation. By including details about where he was and what he did, we can imagine what it was like for him to write it.

An excerpt from
The Adventures of Ali Baba Bernstein

Ali Baba was going to use the word processor in his father's office to print the letter. It took him a long time to type his letter on the machine. His father tried to help him, but he did not type very well either. When the letter was finally completed and the print button pushed, the machine produced seventeen perfect copies—one for each David Bernstein.

Read and Find

Read Mary's writing below. What did she do to focus on a moment? Use the checklist below to help you.

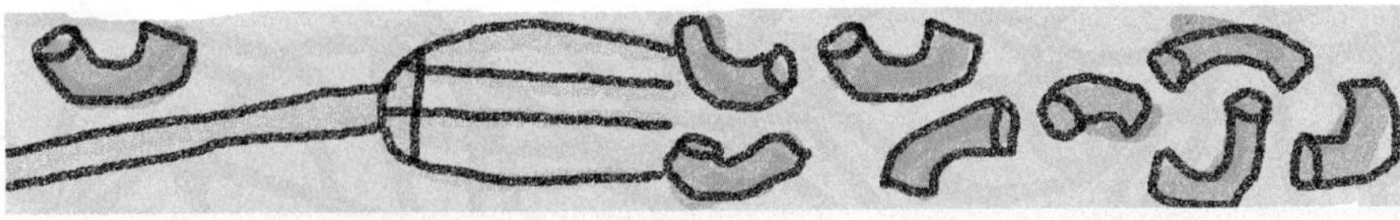

The Delicious Dish

by Mary M.

I rushed to the dinner table because I knew my mom had made my favorite–macaroni and cheese. I could hear the creaminess as I mixed it around with my fork. The soft yellowish noodles kind of made a crackling noise. I dug out a large forkful and opened wide. Happiness spread across my face as I chewed my tasty treat.

Read about Mary's favorite dish.

Writer's Checklist

- [x] Did the writer write about a short amount of time?
- [x] Did the writer use specific details of sight and sound?
- [ ] Can you picture the **moment** as Mary experienced it?

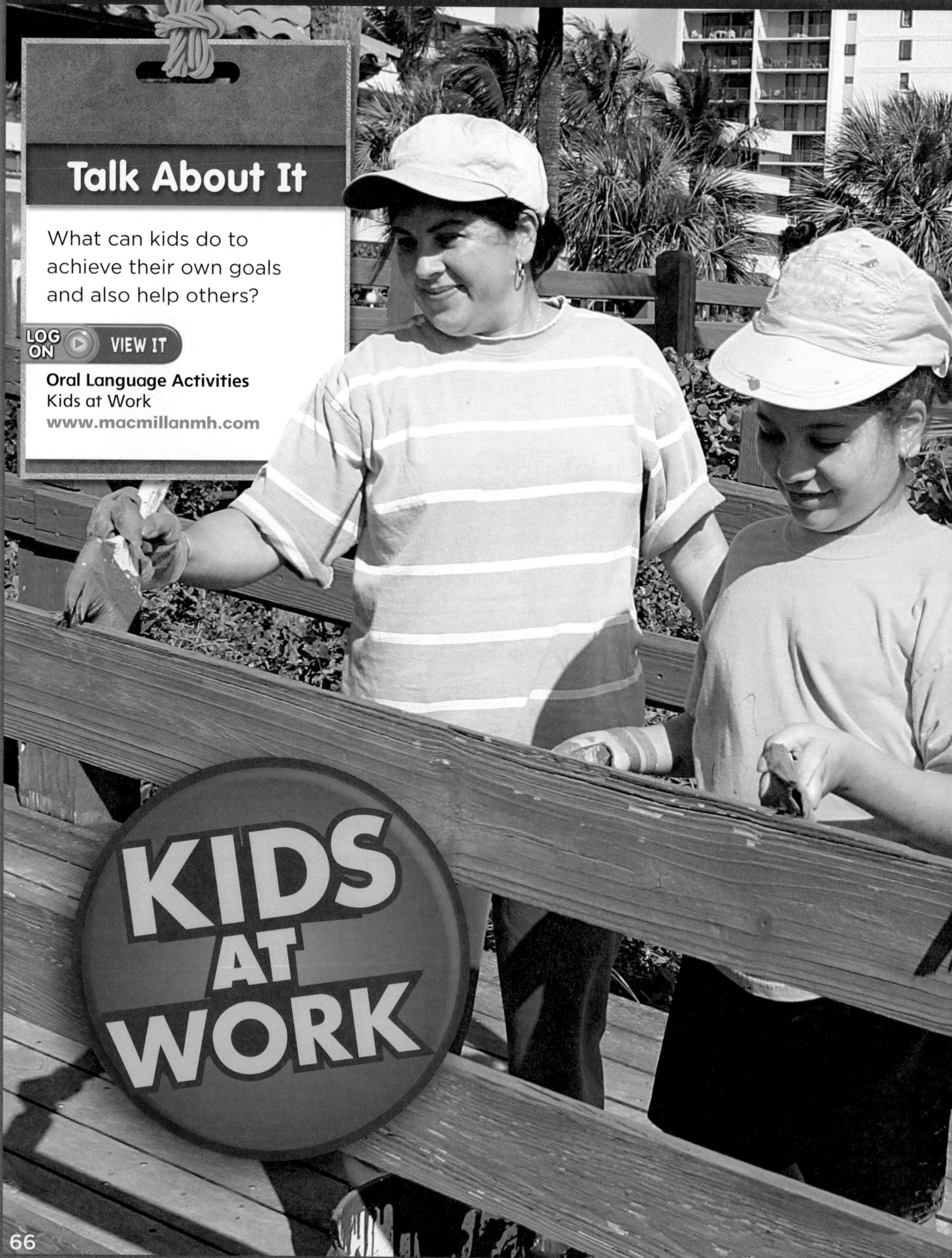

Talk About It

What can kids do to achieve their own goals and also help others?

LOG ON VIEW IT

Oral Language Activities
Kids at Work
www.macmillanmh.com

KIDS AT WORK

TIME FOR KIDS®

Vocabulary

identified
enterprising
persistence
venture

Their Way All the Way!

Gidget Schultz couldn't bear to see kids living on the streets near her Encinitas, California, home. So Gidget, now 14, started her own charity.

Gidget's Way gives backpacks, jackets, and school supplies to homeless kids. Gidget also gives teddy bears to local police to keep in their cars. Officers give the bears to kids who are scared, sad, or hurt. "Running Gidget's Way is a full-time job," says Gidget.

Jhordan Logan of New Castle, Indiana, **identified** a different need. She discovered there were hardly any good books for kids to read at Riley Hospital for Children in Indianapolis. Jhordan organized a Read It Again drive that collected over 5,000 books. Another program she started matches elementary school students with nursing home residents.

Gidget and Jhordan share an **enterprising**, creative, high-energy attitude. "No matter what age you are, you can always volunteer," says Jhordan.

Tips for Planning a Service Project

Kids around the world use their skills and time to help make our world a better place. A service project can be as big as building a home for a family or as simple as collecting coins for charity. Choose something that will inspire you—something that you really care about and makes you want to work hard. Here are some helpful tips.

1. Identify a problem that exists in your community.
2. Learn more about the problem; think about ways to solve it.
3. Set a goal for the project.
4. Decide what supplies and help you'll need.
5. Get others involved.
6. Stick with it! Your **persistence** and hard work will keep the project on track.
7. Have fun! Knowing that you are helping your community should make you feel proud.

Kids' Jobs

Do you think about getting a job when you're older? The chart below shows the types of businesses that employ the most teenagers. Use the chart to identify the most popular job for teenage girls. Don't forget, you can also start your own venture—business or project—and be your own boss!

Male	Percent of All Youths Who Work
Restaurants	31.3%
Grocery Stores	13.6
Entertainment and Recreation Services	4.5
Agriculture	3.6
Construction	3.6
Department Stores	3.1

Female	Percent of All Youths Who Work
Restaurants	32.6%
Grocery Stores	9.9
Private Households (baby-sitting, etc.)	5.7
Department Stores	4.4
Entertainment and Recreation Services	4.0

Source: U.S. Department of Labor

☆ KID ☆ REPORTERS AT WORK

Comprehension

Genre

An **Expository** article in a newspaper or magazine tells a true story.

Analyze Text Structure

Compare and Contrast
When you look for similarities, you compare two or more things or ideas. When you look for differences, you contrast two or more things or ideas.

How do kid reporters tell the story when the news is about improving the lives of children?

Each year the news magazine *Time For Kids* selects several young people to serve as TFK kid reporters. These **enterprising** kids are not professional journalists, but like adult reporters they still have to show they are qualified for the job. Three skills they must have are **persistence** in tracking down a story, good interviewing skills, and the ability to write clearly about complicated topics.

Here's a behind-the-scenes look at two TFK reporters and two of the stories they covered for the magazine. The reporters don't have much in common, except that they are both determined to do a good job as reporters covering an interesting story. The stories seem quite different at first, too. However, they have some strong similarities.

REPORTER: TERRENCE CHEROMCKA

STORY:

A World Conference Just for Kids

Terrence, from Pennsylvania, plays softball, basketball, and field hockey. She loves to read and write. She's also very interested in travel, and has visited France and Thailand. In 2002, however, she had the chance to meet people from all over the world without traveling very far at all. That year Terrence got an assignment from TFK to go to New York City to cover the opening ceremonies of the United Nations Special Session on Children.

The event was a follow-up to a conference held at the U.N. in 1990 to promote the rights of children. World leaders and 375 young people met to discuss what had been accomplished since 1990 and how much more needed to be done. Issues with the highest priority were health care, education, and basic rights for the children of the world. U.N. Secretary General Kofi Annan addressed the opening session. Speaking directly to the young people in attendance, he said, "Your voices will be heard, I promise you."

For her story Terrence interviewed kids from several different countries about what they hoped the conference would accomplish. "We hope to get kids closer to the government and making decisions," said Bala Subrayanya of India.

Terrence also reported on her tour of the United Nations building. Her tour ended with an exhibit showing the devastating effects of war. She saw pictures of child soldiers fighting in war-torn countries. She wrote: "It really reminded me of why the U.N. is working so hard to help improve children's lives and why its mission is so important."

In the large room where the United Nations General Assembly meets, young people from many countries perform at the opening ceremonies of the special session. Others sit in the U.N. delegates' seats.

REPORTER: MARTIN JACOBS

STORY:

Kid Scientist Starts Kids' Charity

Martin, who lives in New York, is a computer buff, plays the piano, and wants to be an airline pilot when he grows up. When he got the assignment to interview Andrew Hsu, he expected to be talking about science. After all, Andrew had just become the youngest winner of the Washington State Science and Engineering Fair. The 11-year-old scientist won the grand prize for identifying a particular gene that plays an important role in keeping the human body healthy.

Martin soon discovered that being a science whiz is just one of Andrew's accomplishments. He's also an athlete who competes in swimming. But the main thing Andrew wanted to tell Martin about was the World Children Organization (WCO). Andrew founded this organization along with his brother Patrick. The brothers started this **venture** in order to help improve the lives of children. In that way its mission is similar to that of the U.N. Special Session on Children. The U.N. special session **identified** three high-priority issues. In contrast, WCO focuses on a single issue for now.

Andrew and Patrick believe that improving education is the best way they can make a positive difference for children. They know that, unlike the United States, there are places where a free education isn't available to all kids.

Andrew Hsu, 11, receives the grand prize award at the 2003 Washington State Science and Engineering Fair. He became the youngest person to ever win that prize.

To help meet that need, Andrew and Patrick had the idea of producing videos about science, math, and languages for children in countries where there aren't enough qualified teachers. "Without education," Andrew said, "the problems of poverty, hunger, child labor, and other abuses of children's rights will never end."

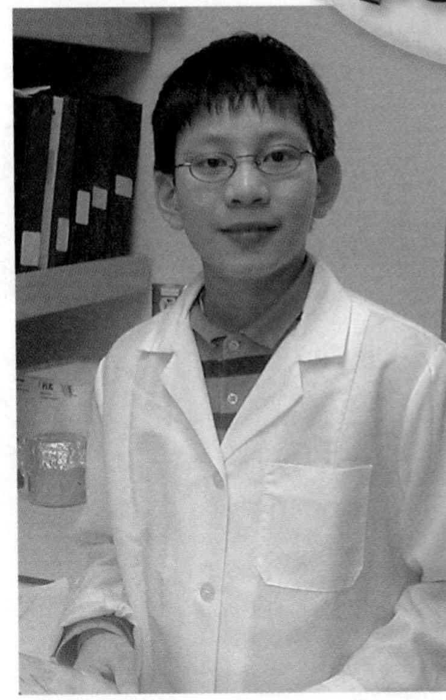

Andrew finished high school at age 9. By age 11 he was already a "working" scientist.

STORY: Different Reporters, Different Stories, a Common Theme

Terrence and Martin both wrote about kids and organizations involved in helping children. In Terrence's story, the organization—the United Nations—is a large one that was founded by the nations of the world. The kids involved came from many different countries. The size and political power of the U.N. enables it to work on several high-priority issues at once. In Martin's story, the organization is a small one—the World Children Organization—founded by two kids. For now, the WCO focuses on education as its single issue.

Clearly, all of these kids—at the U.N. special session, Andrew and Patrick at WCO, and reporters Terrence and Martin—share a commitment to making the world a better place for everyone, especially children.

Think and Compare

1. Who founded the World Children Organization?
2. How were the stories that Terrence and Martin wrote similar?
3. Summarize the main idea of this article.
4. How are Gidget Schultz in "Their Way All the Way!" and Andrew Hsu alike? Use details from both articles in your answer.

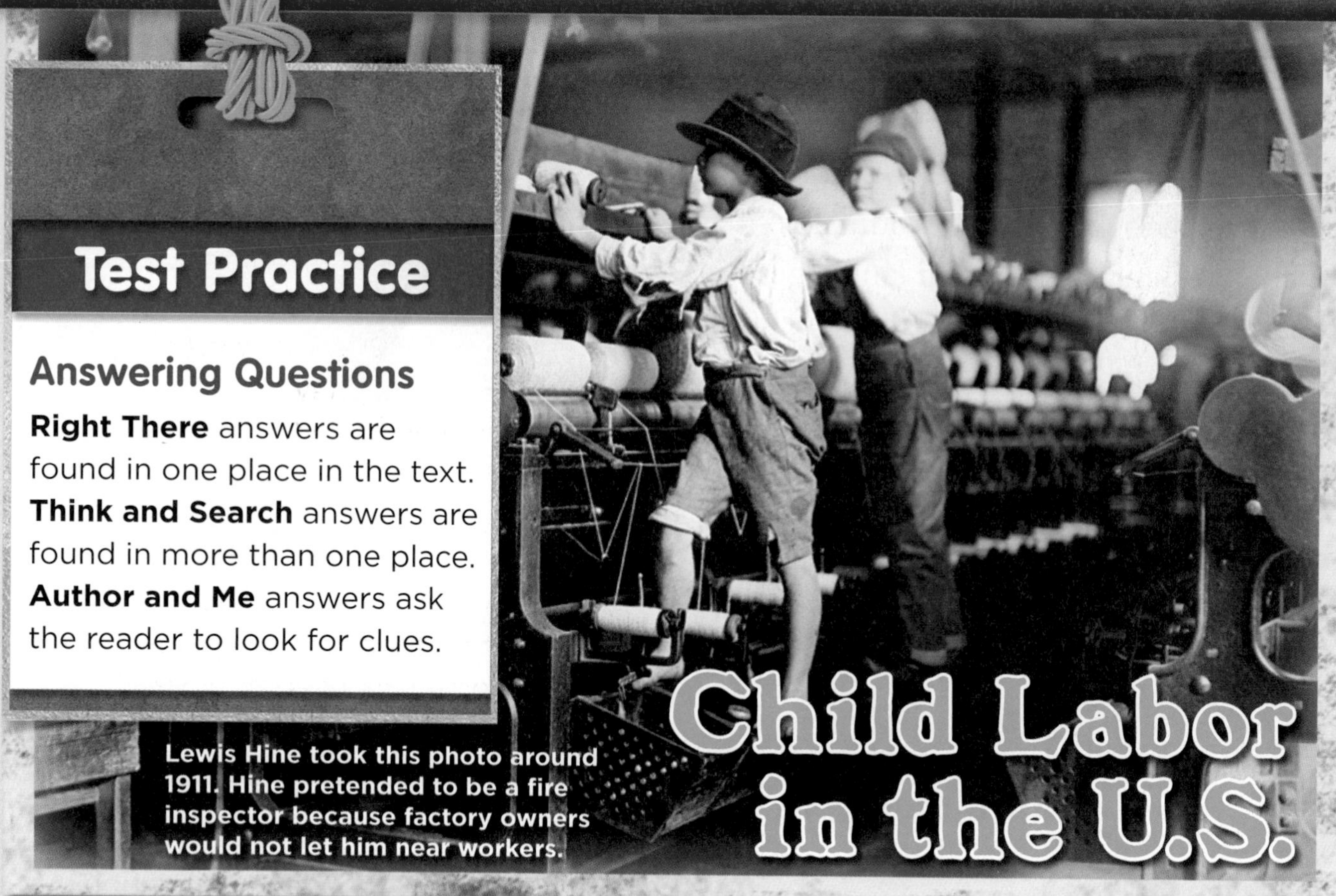

Test Practice

Answering Questions

Right There answers are found in one place in the text.
Think and Search answers are found in more than one place.
Author and Me answers ask the reader to look for clues.

Lewis Hine took this photo around 1911. Hine pretended to be a fire inspector because factory owners would not let him near workers.

Child Labor in the U.S.

1 Throughout its early history, the United States counted on kids to work on farms and in mines and factories. There was a time when employers hired kids because they were cheap labor and easy to manage. In the 1800s kids as young as seven worked in textile mills for 12 hours a day. By the end of the nineteenth century, almost 2 million kids performed hazardous jobs.

2 Besides working long hours, conditions and wages for the laborers were very bad. Anyone who misbehaved was punished and sent to a "whipping room." Workers were rarely given breaks and most had to eat their lunches while working. Many concerned citizens tried to change these conditions, including photographer Lewis Hine. He was hired by the National Child Labour Committee to investigate and photograph working kids. His photographs showed just how badly kids were treated in the workforce.

In 1938 a U.S. law called the 3
Fair Labor Standards Act was passed. This law limited work hours and set the minimum age for children to work. The Fair Labor Standards Act still exists, but some employers do not follow it. It is estimated that 800,000 children work illegally in the United States today. Close to 1 million children work long hours on farms with heavy machinery or poisonous chemicals, or under other harmful conditions.

Use "Child Labor in the U.S." to answer questions 1–4.

1 What happened before the 1938 Fair Labor Standards Act was passed?

- **A** Kids worked long hours at unsafe jobs.
- **B** Kids were only allowed to work a few hours a day.
- **C** Kids were not allowed to work in factories.
- **D** Kids were prevented from working on farms.

2 The National Child Labour Commitee hired Lewis Hine to —

- **F** pass a law
- **G** work in a factory
- **H** visit farms and textile mills
- **J** photograph working kids

3 What has not changed since the 1800s?

- **A** Kids still work in textile mills.
- **B** Kids still work under conditions that could harm them.
- **C** Kids still work in mines and factories.
- **D** Lewis Hine is still photographing kids.

4 Which is the best summary of the selection?

- **F** In the 1800s kids worked in factories. They had to eat their lunches while they worked. Lewis Hine took photographs. He gave them to the National Child Labour Committee.
- **G** In 1938 the Fair Labor Standards Act was passed. Some kids used to work 12 hours a day. Kids worked in factories and mills.
- **H** Children used to work long hours in very dangerous conditions. In 1938, a U.S. law called the Fair Labor Standards Act was passed. This law limited the number of hours children could work.
- **J** The National Child Labour Committee investigated how hard kids were working. They hired Lewis Hine to take photographs. He had to pretend to be a fire inspector so he could take photographs.

Write to a Prompt

Write a composition about living in a new and unfamiliar place.

Think about the purpose of your composition.

Think about how to express your ideas clearly and develop them in a logical order.

Below, see how one student begins a response to the prompt above.

The writer included an opinion to express a point of view.

I grew up in a small town. I knew everyone there, and I was very happy. Then one day my mother said we were moving. She had a great new job, in a city a thousand miles away.

The city was very different. I felt uncomfortable because I didn't know anybody. I was scared to go out because there was lots of traffic outside. People spoke many different languages. And I didn't like the food very much.

I was unhappy for about three days. Then I met my new neighbor, a kid my age. He introduced me to his friends. When school started, I met even more new friends. That's when many good things started happening to me.

Writing Prompt

Respond to the prompt below. Review the hints below before and after you write.

Write a composition about a time that you faced a new situation or experience.

Writing Hints

- ☑ Remember to write about a new situation or experience. Think about the genre.
- ☑ Plan your writing by organizing your ideas.
- ☑ Include important details to support your ideas.
- ☑ Check that each sentence you write helps the reader to understand your story.
- ☑ Use correct spelling, capitalization, punctuation, grammar, and sentences.
- ☑ Review and edit your writing.

MENTORS

Talk About It

How can people in your community help you learn new things?

LOG ON VIEW IT

Oral Language Activities
Mentors
www.macmillanmh.com

Vocabulary

display	**sensible**
paralyzed	**protested**
endless	**realistic**

Dictionary

Using a Dictionary will help you to learn the pronunciation, syllabication, and meaning of a word you may not know.

Look up the meaning, syllabication, and pronunciation of *sensible*.

Astronaut Adventure

by Benjamin Telicki

Ana Gomez saw Larry Waters looking at a **display** of fresh fruit in the cafeteria. "Hi, Larry!" she called out.

"Hi, Ana, I heard you had an adventure yesterday," he remarked as he sat down. "What happened?"

Ana laughed, "Meteors almost hit my ship."

"I can't believe you can laugh about it!" Larry exclaimed.

"Well, I can laugh now. But when it was happening, I was so **paralyzed** with fear that I couldn't move. It took all my skill to escape!" said Ana. "It started out as a typical day. I waited in what seemed an **endless** line on the runway.

Finally, I made it to the head of the line and was cleared for takeoff. I was taking a load of grain to Space Station G17, usually a boring trip. I made good time and got to G17 in time for lunch. Before I left, a mechanic checked out my ship. He warned me that there might be a meteor shower in the area."

"Why did you take off when you knew there might be meteors?" Larry asked, shaking his head. "It would have been much more **sensible** to wait on G17 until it was safe to leave."

"Larry, I hate waiting," Ana **protested**. "Why would I wait around for meteors that might not appear? Anyway, I took off." Ana grinned as she continued the story. "Sure enough, I ran right into a thick meteor shower. It was like being inside a video game full of falling rocks. Luckily, my ship is really fast and I made it through."

"Let's be **realistic**, Ana. The truth is it wasn't the speed of your ship. You dodged those meteors because you're the best pilot on this station. But next time, try to be more sensible and less daring," said Larry.

Reread for **Comprehension**

Summarize

Character Looking at a character's thoughts, words, feelings, and actions will help you to identify character traits. Character traits are special qualities of a character's personality. You can identify a character's traits based on what he or she does, says, feels, or thinks in the story. A Character Web can help you summarize a character's traits. Reread the selection to find Ana's character traits.

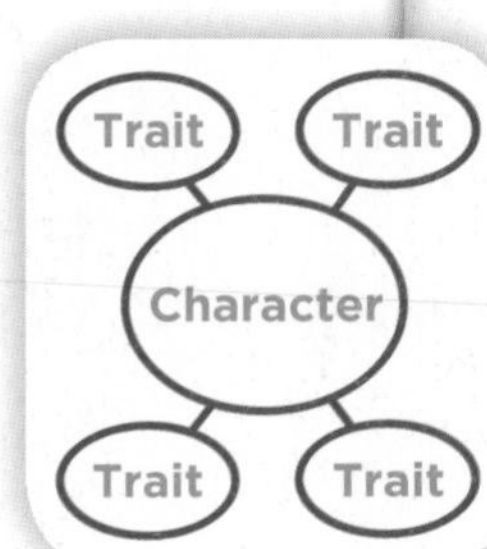

LOG ON LEARN IT **Comprehension** www.macmillanmh.com

Comprehension

Genre

Fiction is a made-up story that could have happened in real life.

Summarize

Character

As you read, fill in your Character Web.

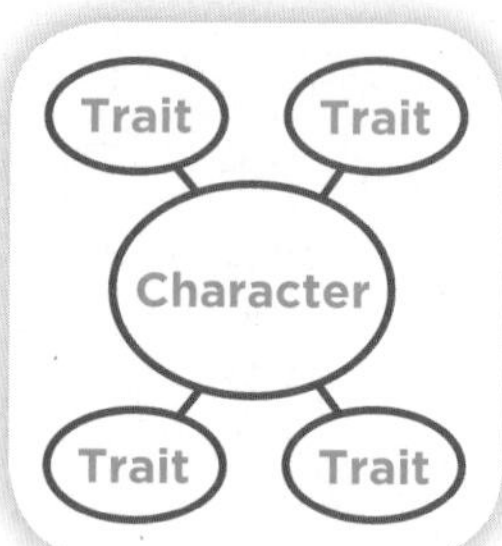

Read to Find Out

How does a trip to the supermarket change Gloria?

The Astronaut and the Onion

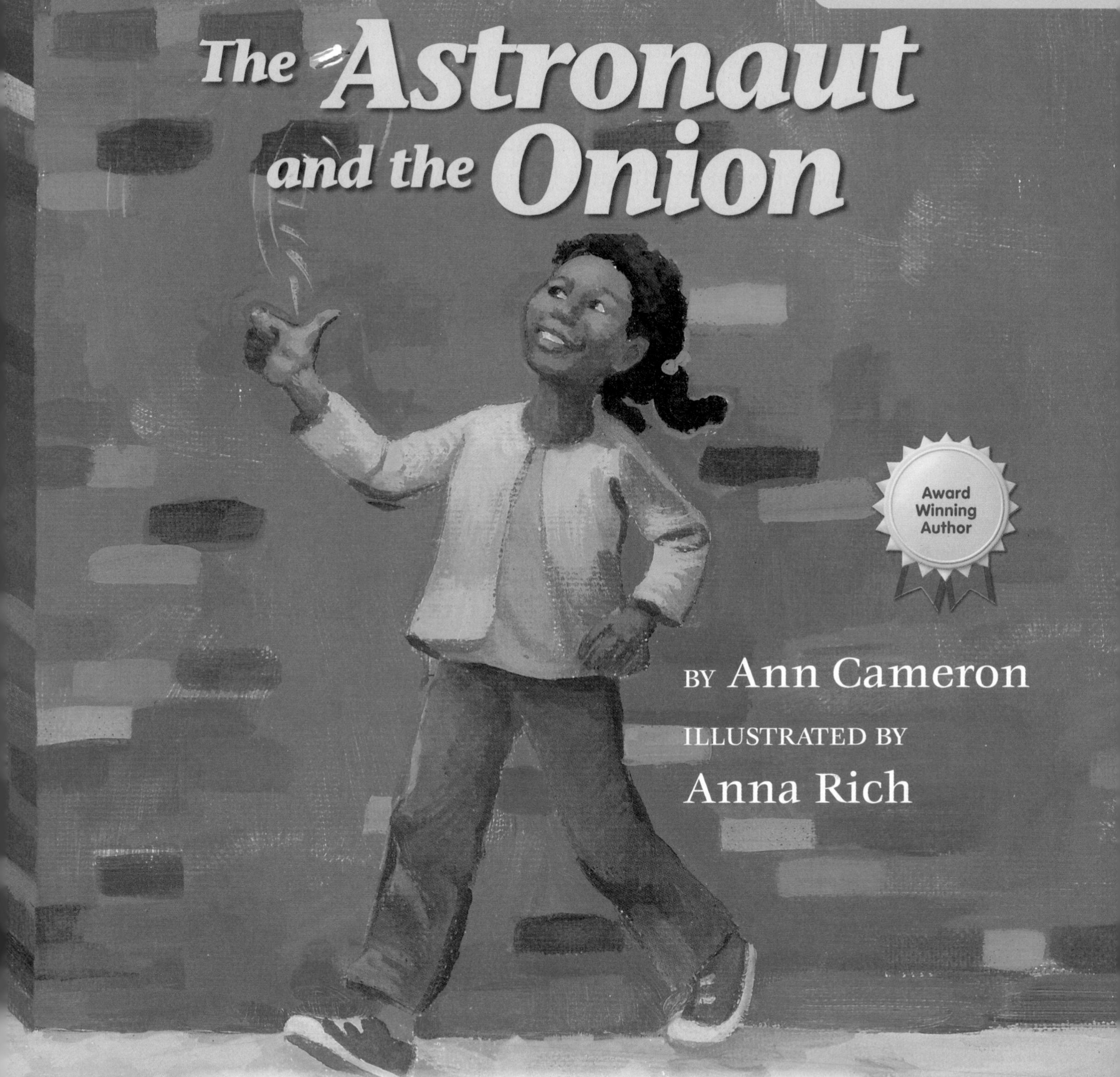

BY Ann Cameron

ILLUSTRATED BY Anna Rich

MY MOTHER was making spaghetti sauce. She said, "Gloria, honey, would you go buy me an onion?"

"Sure," I said. She gave me some money, and I went.

The store was crowded with old people holding tightly to their shopping carts, little kids hollering to their parents for candy, and lots of people staring at shopping lists and blocking the aisles.

I ducked around all the carts and went to the back where the vegetables are. From all the onions in the bin, I took the prettiest—a big round one, light tan and shiny, with a silvery glow to its skin.

I carried it to the express checkout and stood at the end of a very long line.

Next to me there was a giant Berkbee's Baby Food **display**. It was like a wall of glass, and taller than I am. All the little jars were stacked up to look like a castle, with pennants that said "Baby Power" sticking out above the castle doorways and windows. At the top there was a high tower with a red-and-white flag that said "Berkbee's Builds Better Babies!" I started counting the jars, but when I got to 346, I gave up. There must have been at least a thousand.

The checkout line didn't move. To pass the time, I started tossing my onion from hand to hand. I tried to improve and make my throws harder to catch.

A woman wearing a sky-blue jogging suit got in line behind me. She was holding a cereal box. She smiled at me, and I smiled back.

I decided to show her what a really good catcher I am. I made a wild and daring onion throw.

Character
What was wild and daring about Gloria's actions?

I missed the catch. The onion kept going, straight for the middle of the baby food castle. The castle was going to fall!

My folks would have to pay for every broken jar! The store manager would kill me. After that, my folks would bring me back to life to tell me things that would be much worse than death.

I was **paralyzed**. I shut my eyes.

I didn't hear a crash. Maybe I had gone deaf from fright. Or maybe I was in a time warp because of my fear. In fifty years the onion would land, and that would be the end of me.

I felt a tap on my shoulder. If I opened my eyes, I would see the store manager and all the broken jars.

I didn't want to see him. I didn't want to know how bad it was.

There came a tap again, right on the top of my head.

I heard a woman's voice. "I have your onion."

I opened my eyes. The woman in the jogging suit handed the onion to me.

"Lucky I used to play baseball," she said.

"O-o-o-h," I said. I clutched the onion.

"O-o-o-h," I moaned again.

"You're welcome," was all she said.

She had brown eyes with a sparkle in them, and her hair was in shiny black ringlets. She wore blue-green earrings that hung on tiny gold chains. When she tilted her head, her earrings spun around, and I saw they were the Earth—I mean, made to look like the Earth, jeweled with green continents and blue oceans.

"Your earrings are beautiful," I said.

She smiled. "Some friends got them for me," she said, "to remind me of a trip we made."

When she said "trip," her face started to look familiar, but I didn't know why. Then I remembered.

"I've seen you!" I said. "I saw you on TV!"

She smiled. "Could be."

"And you come from right here in town, but you don't live here anymore," I said.

"That's right," she said.

"And you are—aren't you?—Dr. Grace Street, the astronaut!"

She tilted her head, and the little Earths on both her ears spun round. "That's me," she said.

I was amazed, because I never thought I would meet a famous person in my life, and yet one was right beside me in the supermarket, and I myself, Gloria Jones, was talking to her, all because of my onion throw.

"We learned about the space station in school last year," I said. "You were up there, orbiting the Earth."

"My team and I were there," Dr. Street said.

"What is space like?"

"You know," she said.

"How could I know?" I said.

"We're always in space," Dr. Street said. "We're in space right now."

"Yes," I said, "but what was it like out there, where you went? Out there it must seem different."

"Do you really want to know?" she asked, and I said yes.

Q's!

“The most awesome part was when we had to fix things on the outside of the station. We got our jobs done and floated in our space suits, staring out into the universe. There were zillions of stars—and space, deep and black, but it didn’t seem exactly empty. It seemed to be calling to us, calling us to go on an **endless** journey. And that was very scary.

“So we turned and looked at Earth. We were two hundred miles above it. We saw enormous swirls of clouds and the glow of snowfields at the poles. We saw water like a giant blue cradle for the land. One big ocean, not ‘oceans.’ The Earth isn’t really chopped up into countries, either. Up there you see it is one great big powerful living being that knows a lot, lot more than we do.”

“What does it know?” I said.

“It knows how to be Earth,” Dr. Street said. “And that’s a lot.”

I tried to imagine everything she had seen. It gave me a shiver.

“I wish I could see what you saw,” I said. “I’d like to be an astronaut. Of course, probably I couldn’t.”

Dr. Street frowned. “Why do you say ‘Probably I couldn’t?’ ”

“Practically nobody gets to do that,” I said.

“You might be one of the people who do,” she said. “But you’ll never do anything you want to do if you keep saying ‘Probably I couldn’t’.”

“But maybe I can’t!” I **protested**. I looked down at my onion. I didn’t think a very poor onion thrower had a chance to be an astronaut.

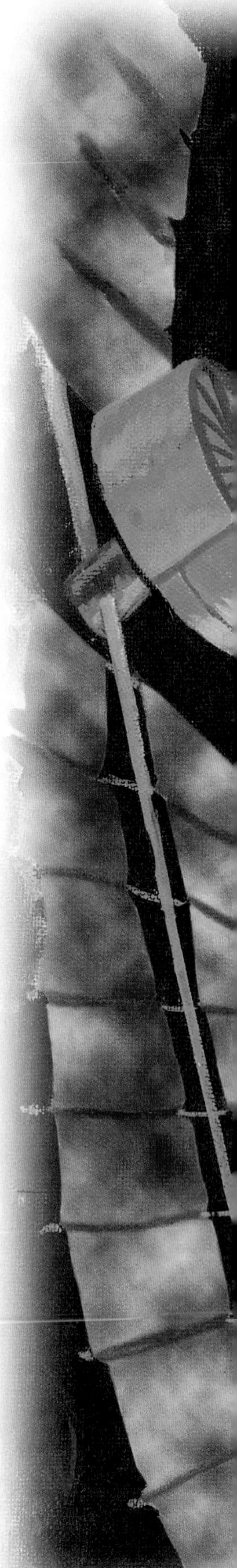

5555

Dr. Street looked at my onion, too. "It was a good throw—just a bad catch," she said. "Anyhow—saying 'Maybe I can't' is different. It's okay. It's **realistic**.

"Even 'I can't' can be a good, **sensible** thing to say. It makes life simpler. When you really know you can't do one thing, that leaves you time to try some of the rest. But when you don't even know what you can do, telling yourself 'Probably I couldn't' will stop you before you even start. It's paralyzing. You don't want to be paralyzed, do you?"

"I just was paralyzed," I said. "A minute ago, when I threw my onion. I didn't enjoy it one bit."

"If you don't want to be paralyzed," Dr. Street said, "be careful what you tell yourself—because whatever you tell yourself you're very likely to believe."

I thought about what she said. "If maybe I could be an astronaut," I asked, "how would I get to be one?"

"You need to do well in school," she said. "And you need to tame your fears. Not get rid of them—just tame them."

The line moved forward suddenly, and we moved up. Maybe the people in line behind us thought Dr. Street and I were mother and daughter having a serious conversation, because they left some space around us.

"So how does a person tame fears?"

"By doing things that are difficult, and succeeding," Dr. Street said. "That's how you learn you can count on yourself. That's how you get confidence. But even then, you keep a little bit of fear inside—a fear that keeps you careful."

Character
What character traits does Dr. Street have that tell you how she reacts in space?

The checkout line moved again, and we moved with it.

"Big things are really little," Dr. Street said. "That's a great secret of life."

"How—" I began. But I never got to ask how big things are really little, because I was the first person in line.

The checkout man looked at my onion.

"Young lady, didn't you weigh that?" he asked.

"No, sir," I said.

"Go back to Produce and have it weighed."

So I had to go.

"Goodbye," Dr. Street said.

"Goodbye," I said. On the way to Produce, I looked back at her. She was walking toward the exit with her cereal box. I waved, but she didn't notice.

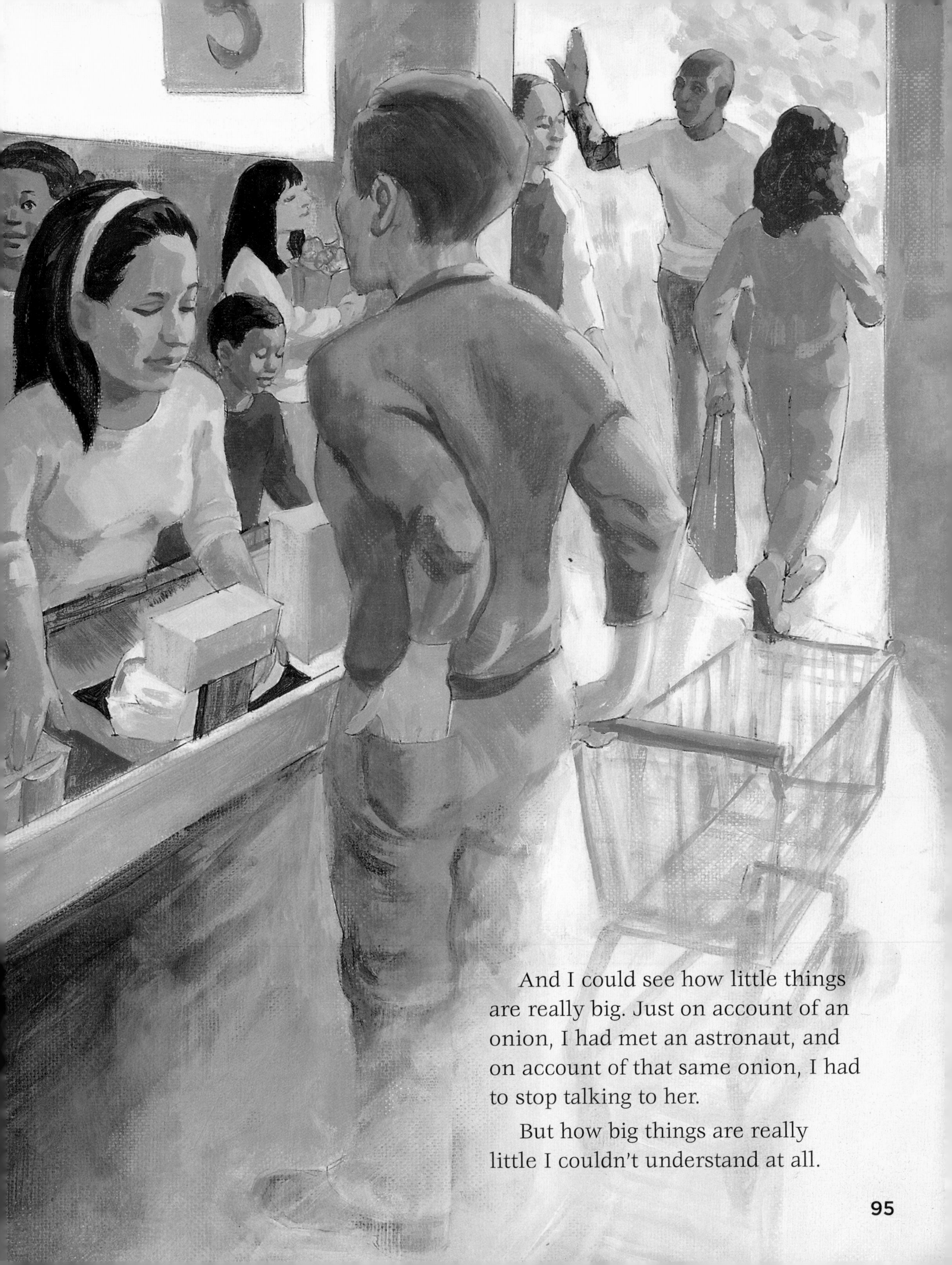

And I could see how little things are really big. Just on account of an onion, I had met an astronaut, and on account of that same onion, I had to stop talking to her.

But how big things are really little I couldn't understand at all.

Blast Off with Ann and Anna

Ann Cameron is a well-known writer. When she was a young girl, like Gloria, she was always outside exploring and wondering about the world around her. Ann did not have a TV until she was nine years old. She spent time listening to stories on the radio and reading books. Today Ann still loves nature and books. She lives in Guatemala, near a waterfall and volcanoes.

Other books by Ann Cameron

Anna Rich has always loved to draw. From an early age, her mother saw her talent and encouraged Anna to follow her dream. Her passion for illustration eventually became a full-time job. Good thing, too, because Anna has never considered doing anything else as a career. Anna, a native New Yorker, still lives there with her family.

LOG ON ▶ FIND OUT

Author Ann Cameron
Illustrator Anna Rich
www.macmillanmh.com

Author's Purpose

Why did Ann Cameron write *The Astronaut and the Onion*? Did she write to entertain the reader or to inform the reader? How do you know?

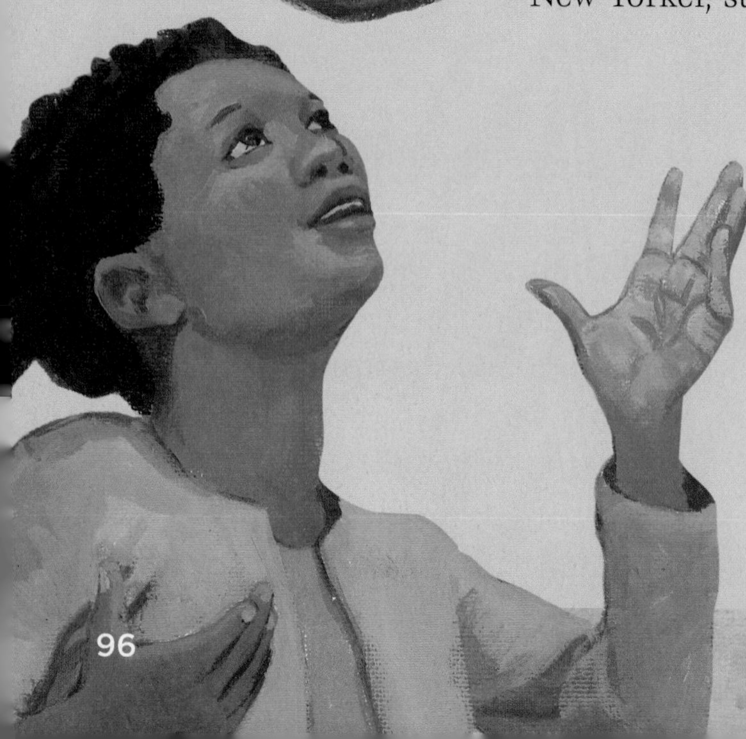

Comprehension Check

Summarize

To summarize *The Astronaut and the Onion* use the most important details from the selection. Information from your Character Web may help you.

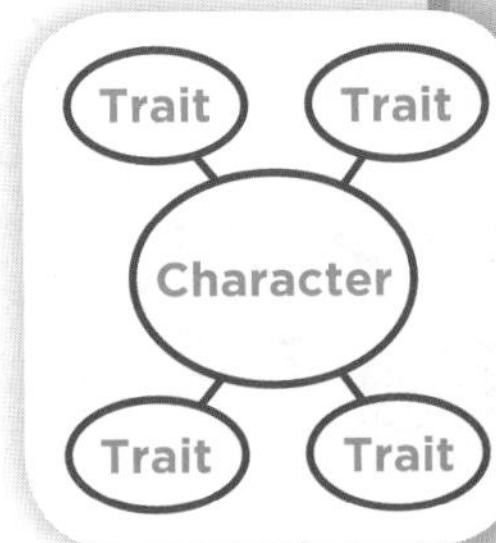

Think and Compare

1. Where does this story take place? Setting
2. What happened to make Gloria feel **paralyzed** after she tossed the onion in the air? Plot
3. What can you tell about Gloria's personality? Use the Character Web and story details to support your answer. Summarize: Character
4. Why did the author choose to tell the story from Gloria's point of view? Author's Purpose
5. Read "Astronaut Adventure" on pages 80–81. Compare Ana's character to Dr. Street's character. In what ways are they alike? How are they different? Reading/Writing Across Texts

Science

Genre

Expository articles present facts about a topic. They may also provide photos, captions, and procedural text, such as recipes.

Text Feature

Recipes give directions on how to prepare food.

Content Vocabulary

condensed **freeze-dried** **spinoff**

Sky-High Dining

Eating Like the Astronauts

by Mel Dorsett

Our nation's space program, NASA, faced many challenges. One of these was how to feed astronauts well in space. Healthful foods had to be easy to transport, simple to cook, and safe to eat. Oh, and they had to taste good, too!

At first, scientists dried and **condensed** foods into powder and cube form. They also created pastes that could be squeezed out of tubes. These worked well, but they were not very popular with the astronauts. Over time, scientists invented new ways to process and package food. You can see the results of their hard work in any grocery store.

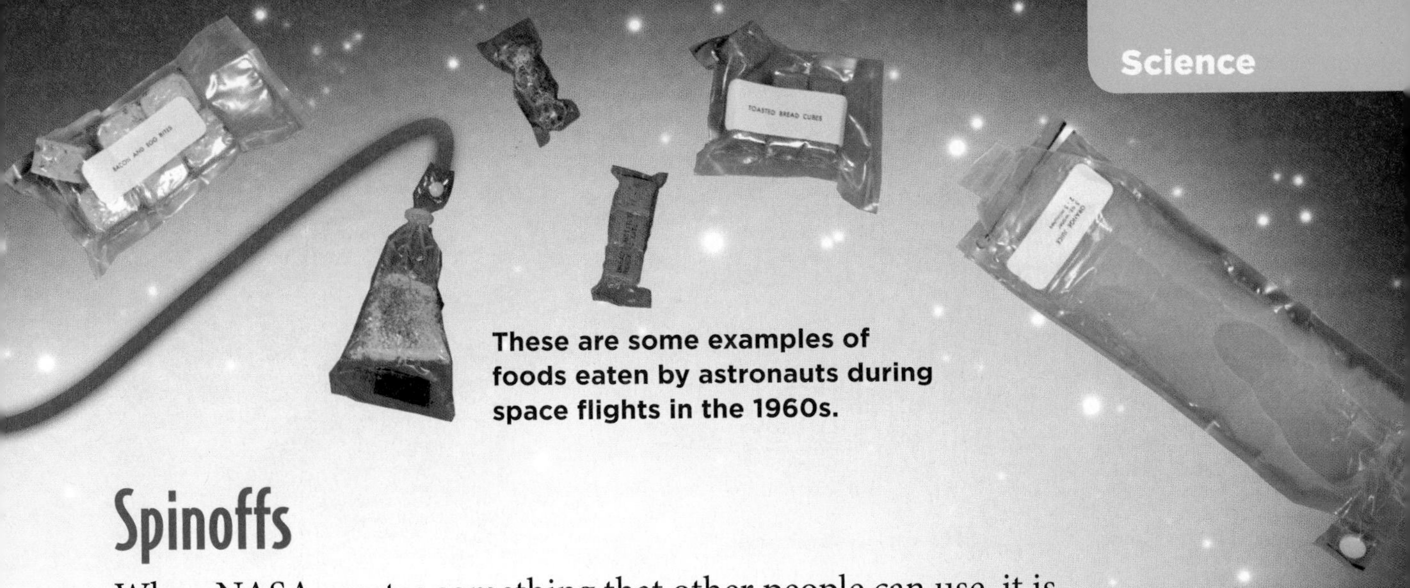

These are some examples of foods eaten by astronauts during space flights in the 1960s.

Spinoffs

When NASA creates something that other people can use, it is called a **spinoff**. For example, the Texas government asked NASA to use their food technology to help design and make meals for the elderly. Together they created healthful meals that were easy to cook, serve, and eat. Other people also liked these convenient foods. You can find some examples of these spinoffs in the frozen foods section at the store.

Hikers and campers also rely on NASA technology. They can buy **freeze-dried** stews and casseroles packaged in sturdy pouches and bags. Many nutritious meals are made simply by adding hot water and stirring. Emergency workers in disaster areas can use these meals to feed people in trouble. Soldiers in distant lands can enjoy meals that taste like their home-cooked favorites.

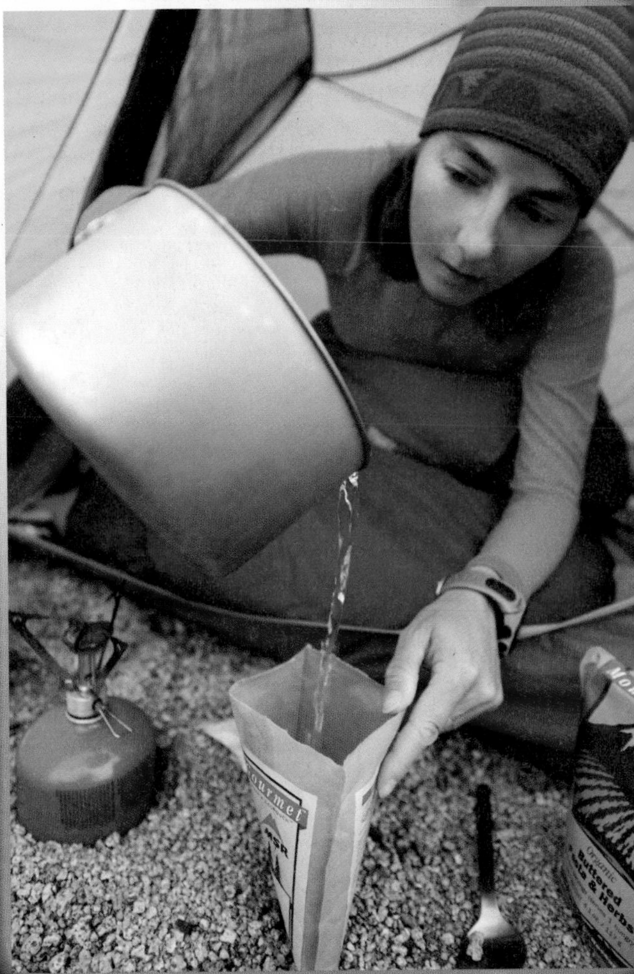

This camper is adding boiling water to her freeze-dried meal.

Astronaut Granola Bars

Recipe

Granola bars are one of the astronauts' favorite foods to eat in space. Ask an adult to help you make some to find out why!

- 2 cups dried rolled oats
- ¾ cup brown sugar
- ½ cup wheat germ
- ¾ teaspoon cinnamon
- 1 cup all-purpose flour
- ½ cup raisins
- ¾ teaspoon salt
- ½ cup honey
- 1 egg (beaten)
- ½ cup vegetable oil
- 2 teaspoons vanilla extract

1. Preheat the oven to 350 degrees F (175 degrees C).
2. Grease a 9" x 13" baking pan.
3. Mix the dry ingredients (oats, brown sugar, wheat germ, cinnamon, flour, raisins, and salt) in a large bowl.
4. Mix the wet ingredients (honey, egg, oil, and vanilla) in a large cup.
5. Make a hole in the center of the dry ingredients and pour the wet ingredients into it. Mix well.
6. Pour the mixture into the pan and spread out evenly.
7. Bake for 30 to 35 minutes or until the edges turn golden brown.
8. Let cool for 5 minutes, then cut into bars while still warm.

What Goes Up

Today's astronauts no longer rely on powders and pastes for their meals. In fact, they eat many of the same foods you can buy in the grocery store. Spinoff technology helps to keep these foods fresh and safe for long periods of time. They provide excellent nutrition and are easy to prepare. As the saying goes, "What goes up must come down." NASA used its new ideas to feed people in space. Now those same ideas are making life better here on Earth.

Astronauts Jan Davis and Mae Jemison eat aboard the shuttle *Endeavor*, September 12, 1992.

Connect and Compare

1. Look at the recipe. What is the next step after mixing the wet ingredients together? **Reading a Recipe**
2. What is this article mainly about? Use details from the selection to support your answer. **Apply**
3. What might Dr. Street from "The Astronaut and the Onion" say to Gloria about how spinoff technology from NASA helps make life better? **Reading/Writing Across Texts**

Science Activity

Use online resources to find out the process for freeze-drying food. Then create a diagram that shows how food is freeze-dried.

LOG ON FIND OUT **Science** Space Food
www.macmillanmh.com

Writing

Trait: Ideas

When writers **describe an object**, they should use words that help their readers see the object.

Reading and Writing Connection

Read the passage below. Notice how the author Ann Cameron focuses on an object in her story.

An excerpt from
The Astronaut and the Onion

Next to me there was a giant Berkbee's Baby Food display. It was like a wall of glass, and taller than I am. All the little jars were stacked up to look like a castle, with pennants that said "Baby Power" sticking out above the castle doorways and windows. At the top there was a high tower with a red-and-white flag that said "Berkbee's Builds Better Babies!" I started counting the jars, but when I got to 346, I gave up. There must have been at least a thousand.

The author describes an object by focusing on what Gloria saw next to her. By describing the object, the writer helps us see what's around Gloria.

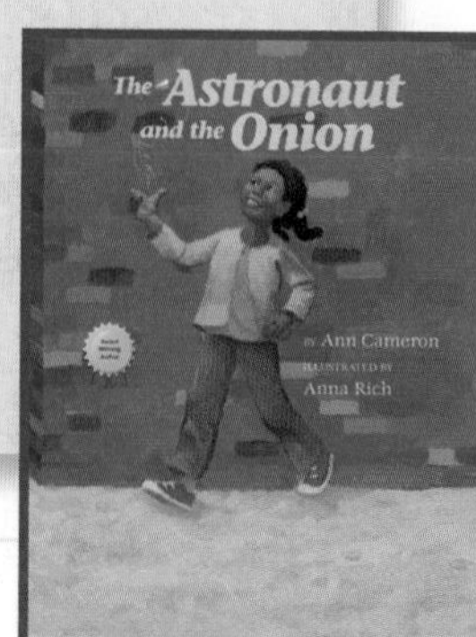

Read and Find

Read Wyatt's writing below. What did he do to describe an object? Use the checklist below to help you.

Read about a giant tomato plant.

Tomato Plant

by Wyatt R.

In the sunny patch on our patio a huge tomato plant grows in an orange pot. Its green leafy stems wind around a bamboo stake stuck in the middle of the pot. Three large, red tomatoes hang from the plant, their weight pulling the branches toward the ground. They feel warm from the sun. Two small green tomatoes hang among the leaves.

Writer's Checklist

- [x] Does the writer pick an object to write about?
- [x] Does the writer include specific details about the object he is describing?
- [ ] Do you feel like you can picture the plant from the words Wyatt uses to **describe** it?

FRIENDS OF ALL AGES

Talk About It

What are these friends doing? How do you think they learn from each other?

LOG ON VIEW IT

Oral Language Activities
Friends of All Ages
www.macmillanmh.com

Vocabulary

aware	**selecting**
peculiar	**consisted**
positive	**advanced**

Dictionary

Connotation/Denotation
Connotation is the feeling associated with a word. Denotation is the dictionary meaning. What are the connotations and denotation of *peculiar*?

A Library Card for Emilio

by Susan Pinter

"Hurry or we'll miss the bus to the library, Emilio!" called Mrs. Mendoza. The Mendoza family had moved to Boston, from San Juan, Puerto Rico, last month, and Emilio was going to get his library card today.

On the bus, Emilio's grandmother became **aware** of something **peculiar**. She saw Emilio was very quiet and looked rather sad. "Is something wrong, honey?" she asked.

Emilio snuffled. He then took out a tissue to blow his nose. "My speaking of English is not good. What if the library lady is not able to understand what I am saying?" he said.

"Your English gets better and better every day. I'm one hundred percent **positive** that the librarian will understand you," Mrs. Mendoza said confidently. "I am sure that you will be able to take some books home today."

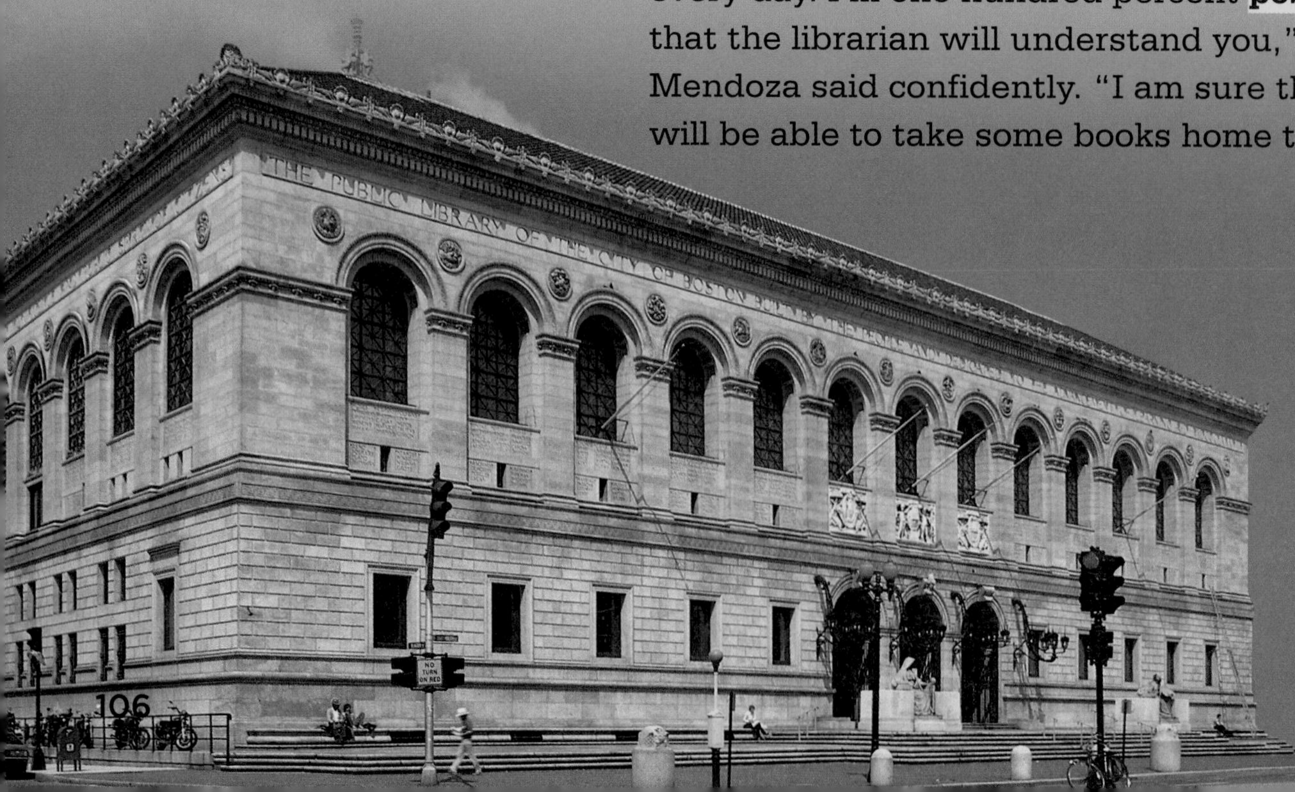

When they finally got to the library, there were lots of people. Some were reading newspapers. Others were **selecting** books that they wanted to borrow from the shelves. As Emilio looked around in wonder, a smiling librarian asked, "May I help you with anything?"

Emilio stuttered a little as he began to explain. "I ... I am here for my card for library books."

"That's just terrific!" said the librarian. She asked him to complete a form that **consisted** of questions about Emilio and where he and his family lived.

Mrs. Mendoza smiled. She noticed that her grandson had no trouble understanding the form. He filled it in quickly and then returned it to the librarian.

"It will take a few minutes to process your card, Emilio," said the librarian. "Why don't you select a few books to borrow today? If you're an **advanced** reader, the novels are over there."

"Thank you," said Emilio.

"*Abuela*," Emilio whispered to Mrs. Mendoza, "my English must be better than I thought!"

Reread for Comprehension

Summarize

Sequence is the order in which the events of a story take place. Certain words and phrases can help readers identify the sequence of events in a **plot**. Fill in your Sequence Chart to help you identify the order of events. This will help you summarize the plot's main events and explain their influence on future events.

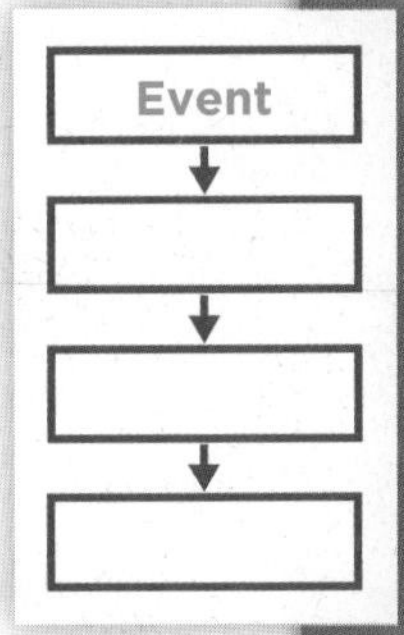

LOG ON ▶ LEARN IT **Comprehension**
www.macmillanmh.com

Comprehension

Genre

Fiction is an invented story that could have happened in real life.

Summarize

Sequence

As you read, fill in your Sequence Chart.

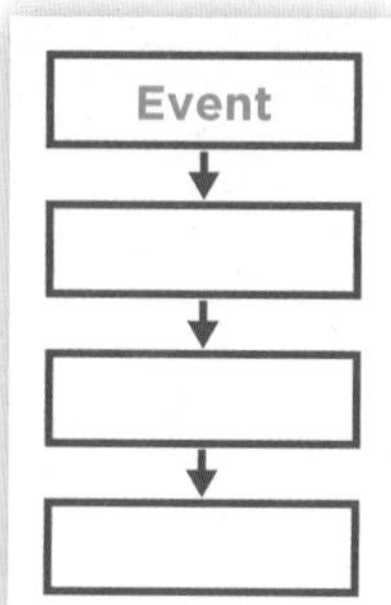

Read to Find Out

What happened that day at the library?

Because of Winn-Dixie

by Kate DiCamillo

I spent a lot of time that summer at the Herman W. Block Memorial Library. The Herman W. Block Memorial Library sounds like it would be a big fancy place, but it's not. It's just a little old house full of books, and Miss Franny Block is in charge of them all. She is a very small, very old woman with short gray hair, and she was the first friend I made in Naomi.

It all started with Winn-Dixie not liking it when I went into the library, because he couldn't go inside, too. But I showed him how he could stand up on his hind legs and look in the window and see me in there, **selecting** my books; and he was okay, as long as he could see me. But the thing was, the first time Miss Franny Block saw Winn-Dixie standing up on his hind legs like that, looking in the window, she didn't think he was a dog. She thought he was a bear.

This is what happened: I was picking out my books and kind of humming to myself, and all of a sudden, there was this loud and scary scream. I went running up to the front of the library, and there was Miss Franny Block, sitting on the floor behind her desk.

"Miss Franny?" I said. "Are you all right?"

"A bear," she said.

"A bear?" I asked.

"He has come back," she said.

"He has?" I asked. "Where is he?"

"Out there," she said and raised a finger and pointed at Winn-Dixie standing up on his hind legs, looking in the window for me.

"Miss Franny Block," I said, "that's not a bear. That's a dog. That's my dog. Winn-Dixie."

"Are you **positive**?" she asked.

"Yes ma'am," I told her. "I'm positive. He's my dog. I would know him anywhere."

Miss Franny sat there trembling and shaking.

"Come on," I said. "Let me help you up. It's okay." I stuck out my hand and Miss Franny took hold of it, and I pulled her up off the floor. She didn't weigh hardly anything at all. Once she was standing on her feet, she started acting all embarrassed, saying how I must think she was a silly old lady, mistaking a dog for a bear, but that she had a bad experience with a bear coming into the Herman W. Block Memorial Library a long time ago and she never had quite gotten over it.

"When did that happen?" I asked her.

"Well," said Miss Franny, "it is a very long story."

Sequence

Sequence the events leading up to the narrator finding Miss Franny on the floor.

"That's okay," I told her. "I am like my mama in that I like to be told stories. But before you start telling it, can Winn-Dixie come in and listen, too? He gets lonely without me."

"Well, I don't know," said Miss Franny. "Dogs are not allowed in the Herman W. Block Memorial Library."

"He'll be good," I told her. "He's a dog who goes to church." And before she could say yes or no, I went outside and got Winn-Dixie, and he came in and lay down with a "huummmppff" and a sigh, right at Miss Franny's feet.

She looked down at him and said, "He most certainly is a large dog."

"Yes ma'am," I told her. "He has a large heart, too."

"Well," Miss Franny said. She bent over and gave Winn-Dixie a pat on the head, and Winn-Dixie wagged his tail back and forth and snuffled his nose on her little old-lady feet. "Let me get a chair and sit down so I can tell this story properly."

"Back when Florida was wild, when it **consisted** of nothing but palmetto trees and mosquitoes so big they could fly away with you," Miss Franny Block started in, "and I was just a little girl no bigger than you, my father, Herman W. Block, told me that I could have anything I wanted for my birthday. Anything at all."

Miss Franny looked around the library. She leaned in close to me. "I don't want to appear prideful," she said, "but my daddy was a very rich man. A very rich man." She nodded and then leaned back and said, "And I was a little girl who loved to read. So I told him, I said, 'Daddy, I would most certainly love to have a library for my birthday, a small little library would be wonderful.' "

"You asked for a whole library?"

"A small one," Miss Franny nodded. "I wanted a little house full of nothing but books and I wanted to share them, too. And I got my wish. My father built me this house, the very one we are sitting in now. And at a very young age, I became a librarian. Yes ma'am."

"What about the bear?" I said.

"Did I mention that Florida was wild in those days?" Miss Franny Block said.

"Uh-huh, you did."

"It was wild. There were wild men and wild women and wild animals."

"Like bears!"

"Yes ma'am. That's right. Now, I have to tell you, I was a little-miss-know-it-all. I was a miss-smarty-pants with my library full of books. Oh, yes ma'am, I thought I knew the answers to everything. Well, one hot Thursday, I was sitting in my library with all the doors and windows open and my nose stuck in a book, when a shadow crossed the desk. And without looking up, yes ma'am, without even looking up, I said, 'Is there a book I can help you find?'

"Well, there was no answer. And I thought it might have been a wild man or a wild woman, scared of all these books and afraid to speak up. But then I became **aware** of a very **peculiar** smell, a very strong smell. I raised my eyes slowly. And standing right in front of me was a bear. Yes ma'am. A very large bear."

"How big?" I asked.

"Oh, well," said Miss Franny, "perhaps three times the size of your dog."

"Then what happened?" I asked her.

"Well," said Miss Franny, "I looked at him and he looked at me. He put his big nose up in the air and sniffed and sniffed as if he was trying to decide if a little-miss-know-it-all librarian was what he was in the mood to eat. And I sat there. And then I thought, 'Well, if this bear intends to eat me, I am not going to let it happen without a fight. No ma'am.' So very slowly and very carefully, I raised up the book I was reading."

"What book was that?" I asked.

"Why, it was *War and Peace*, a very large book. I raised it up slowly and then I aimed it carefully and I threw it right at that bear and screamed, 'Be gone!' And do you know what?"

"No ma'am," I said.

"He went. But this is what I will never forget. He took the book with him."

"Nuh-uh," I said.

"Yes ma'am," said Miss Franny. "He snatched it up and ran."

"Did he come back?" I asked.

"No, I never saw him again. Well, the men in town used to tease me about it. They used to say, 'Miss Franny, we saw that bear of yours out in the woods today. He was reading that book and he said it sure was good and would it be all right if he kept it for just another week.' Yes ma'am. They did tease me about it." She sighed. "I imagine I'm the only one left from those days. I imagine I'm the only one that even recalls that bear. All my friends, everyone I knew when I was young, they are all dead and gone."

She sighed again. She looked sad and old and wrinkled. It was the same way I felt sometimes, being friendless in a new town and not having a mama to comfort me. I sighed, too.

Winn-Dixie raised his head off his paws and looked back and forth between me and Miss Franny. He sat up then and showed Miss Franny his teeth.

"Well now, look at that," she said. "That dog is smiling at me."

"It's a talent of his," I told her.

"It is a fine talent," Miss Franny said. "A very fine talent." And she smiled back at Winn-Dixie.

"We could be friends," I said to Miss Franny. "I mean you and me and Winn-Dixie, we could all be friends."

Miss Franny smiled even bigger. "Why, that would be grand," she said, "just grand."

Sequence
How did Miss Franny and the narrator become friends? List the events in the correct order.

And right at that minute, right when the three of us had decided to be friends, who should come marching into the Herman W. Block Memorial Library but old pinch-faced Amanda Wilkinson. She walked right up to Miss Franny's desk and said, "I finished *Johnny Tremain* and I enjoyed it very much. I would like something even more difficult to read now, because I am an **advanced** reader."

"Yes dear, I know," said Miss Franny. She got up out of her chair.

Amanda pretended like I wasn't there. She stared right past me. "Are dogs allowed in the library?" she asked Miss Franny as they walked away.

"Certain ones," said Miss Franny, "a select few." And then she turned around and winked at me. I smiled back. I had just made my first friend in Naomi, and nobody was going to mess that up for me, not even old pinch-faced Amanda Wilkinson.

Because of Kate

Kate DiCamillo wrote this story while she was shivering in Minnesota one winter. Kate had moved there from Florida and was very homesick. She also felt sad because she was not allowed to have a dog in her apartment. When Kate went to sleep, she dreamed she heard a girl say she had a dog named Winn-Dixie. Kate started writing the story as soon as she woke up.

Because of Winn-Dixie became the first book that Kate published. It won a Newbery Honor, which is one of the most respected awards a children's book can receive. She is also the author of *The Tiger Rising* and of *The Tale of Despereaux: Being the Story of a Mouse, a Princess, Some Soup, and a Spool of Thread*, which received the Newbery Medal in 2004.

When Kate wrote *Because of Winn-Dixie*, she would get up early every day to write two pages before leaving for her job at a bookstore. She no longer works at the bookstore, but she still writes two pages every morning.

Other books
by Kate DiCamillo

LOG ON ▶ FIND OUT

Author Kate DiCamillo
www.macmillanmh.com

Author's Purpose

The story is set in Florida and one of the characters in it is a dog. Why did the author write this story? Use information from page 120 to support your answer.

LOG ON LEARN IT **Comprehension** www.macmillanmh.com

Comprehension Check

Summarize

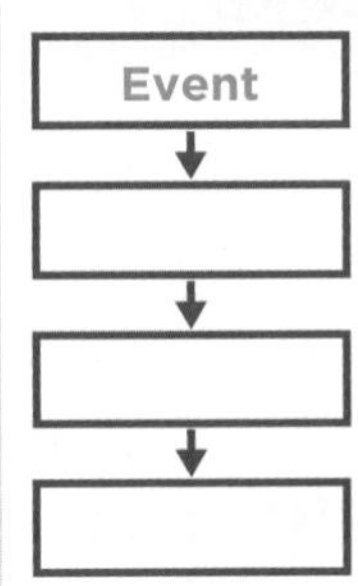

To summarize *Because of Winn-Dixie* use the most important details from the story. Information from your Sequence Chart may help you.

Think and Compare

1. What did Miss Franny think she saw outside the window? **Details**
2. After Miss Franny realized a bear was standing in front of her desk, what did she do? **Sequence**
3. Summarize the **peculiar** story Miss Franny tells the narrator from her childhood. Describe the events of her story in correct sequence. **Summarize: Sequence**
4. At the end of the story, how does the author show how Miss Franny feels about the narrator? **Author's Craft**
5. Read "A Library Card for Emilio" on pages 106–107. How is Emilio like the narrator in *Because of Winn-Dixie*? How are they different? Use details from both selections to explain. **Reading/Writing Across Texts**

Poetry

Free Verse Poems often contain rhythmic patterns and other poetic elements.

Literary Elements

Stanzas are groups of lines that give the poem its form. A **Line Break** is the place where the line ends.

A **Simile** compares two different things, usually by using the words *like* or *as*.

I Love the Look of Words

Popcorn leaps, popping from the floor
of a hot black skillet
and into my mouth.
Black words leap,
snapping from the white
page. Rushing into my eyes. Sliding
into my brain which gobbles them
the way my tongue and teeth
chomp the buttered popcorn.

This **line break** at the word *leap* helps to highlight the word's meaning.

When I have stopped reading,
ideas from the words stay stuck
in my mind, like the sweet
smell of butter perfuming my
fingers long after the popcorn
is finished.

> This **simile** compares ideas sticking in the poet's mind to the smell of butter sticking to her fingers.

I love the book and the look of words
the weight of ideas that popped into my mind
I love the tracks
of new thinking in my mind.

— *Maya Angelou*

Connect and Compare

1. Why do you think the poet chose to **break** the **line** on the word *stuck* in the second **stanza**? **Stanza/Line Breaks**

2. Look at each stanza. Explain how the poet used each stanza to organize her thoughts about reading. **Apply**

3. Compare the narrator in this poem with the narrator in *Because of Winn-Dixie*. How are they alike? How are they different? **Reading/Writing Across Texts**

4. Write a free verse poem about why you like to read. Include at least one simile in your poem. **Apply**

LOG ON FIND OUT Free verse poems
www.macmillanmh.com

Writing

Trait: Ideas

When writers **focus on setting**, their readers should be able to picture the place in their minds.

Reading and Writing Connection

Read the passage below. Notice how the author Kate DiCamillo focuses on a setting in her story.

An excerpt from
Because of Winn-Dixie

The author focuses on the setting by describing what the library looks like. By focusing on the setting, we can imagine the characters' surroundings as we read further.

I spent a lot of time that summer at the Herman W. Block Memorial Library. The Herman W. Block Memorial Library sounds like it would be a big fancy place, but it's not. It's just a little old house full of books, and Miss Franny Block is in charge of them all.

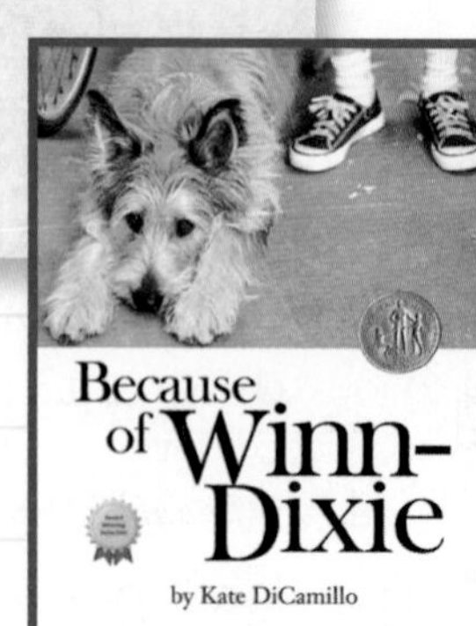

Read and Find

Read Elena's writing below. What did she do to focus on the setting? Use the checklist below to help you.

Read about Elena's trip.

A Trip to Cape Cod

by Elena J.

We drove up to the beach. The smell of salty air hit my nose before I could even see the sand. The reeds and grass were blowing in the hot breeze, and a seagull was munching on a piece of cracker that another kid had left behind.

Writer's Checklist

- [x] Does the writer pick one **setting** and write a lot about it?
- [x] Is the writer able to include specific details about the place she's describing?
- [ ] Do you feel like you can picture the beach Elena describes?

Review

Make Inferences
Character, Setting, Plot
Compare and Contrast
Synonyms
Map

A Walk on the Beach

Jenny stared at her cousin disapprovingly. "Tony, is it true you've really never seen the ocean?"

Tony felt exhausted. Why had he told his parents he would come on this trip? It seemed like a great idea last month. Now that he was actually here, he wasn't so sure. Jenny sounded mean. Tony felt like she wasn't happy to see him.

"No, I've never seen it," he answered quietly.

"Tony lives in New Mexico, Jen. Look it up on the map. It's nowhere near the ocean. That's one of the reasons your cousin came to visit us. Right, Tony?" said Jenny's dad.

"Right," said Tony. Then he thought of something. "Jenny, when was the last time you saw a desert?"

"I've never seen a desert but that doesn't matter. I mean, who would want to go to a desert anyway?" she said coldly.

"You've never seen a desert? Are you kidding?" said Tony, sounding as surprised as Jenny.

Jenny's dad smiled at them. "Okay, you two. Put your sneakers on. Mom's taking you to the beach."

Twenty minutes later, Tony stood on the beach staring at the Atlantic Ocean. He'd had no idea that it was so big.

"Beautiful, isn't it?" asked his aunt as she stood next to him. Tony nodded and watched in amazement as a line of pelicans swooped low over the waves.

"Check out the dunes, Tony. They're beautiful, too," said Jenny. She waved her hand at the huge hills of sand.

Tony turned to look behind him. "How can all those plants grow in the sand?" he asked.

"Some have leaves with a waxy coating or little hairs to keep the water inside," his aunt explained.

"Hey, desert plants do that too!" Tony exclaimed. He turned and looked at the ocean again. All of a sudden he saw three black fins in a row, swimming in a line.

"Sharks!" he yelled, pointing at the fins.

Jenny looked at where Tony was pointing. She laughed.

"Those aren't sharks, Tony. Those are dolphins. I don't see how you could mistake them."

Tony turned and started walking down the beach. *Jenny doesn't seem thrilled about my visit*, he thought. Maybe coming to visit his aunt and uncle was not such a great idea after all, but he had really wanted to see the ocean.

Jenny watched Tony walk away. "Tony, wait up," Jenny called. "I'm sorry. A lot of people think of sharks when they see dolphin fins. I bet if I went to New Mexico, I'd think everything in the desert was poisonous. I'd probably be too scared to get out of the car."

Tony laughed. "You probably would. One time this guy started yelling because he thought some tiny harmless spider was really a tarantula."

"Are you two ready for a swim?" Jenny's mother yelled from down the beach.

"Race you back," Tony grinned, and took off running down the beach.

"No fair, you got a head start!" shouted Jenny as she ran after him laughing.

DIAMONDS FOR THE TAKING

HAVE YOU EVER WONDERED how it would feel to be a prospector? Imagine what it would be like to tap rocks with a hammer, hour after hour, in the hopes of discovering a glittering diamond.

Each year hundreds of people do just that in upper New York State. Herkimer County, New York, is the only place in the world where Herkimer diamonds can be found. The map below shows exactly where Herkimer County is in New York State.

Actually the diamonds found here are not really diamonds. They are natural quartz crystals, and what is unusual about them is that they have points at both ends.

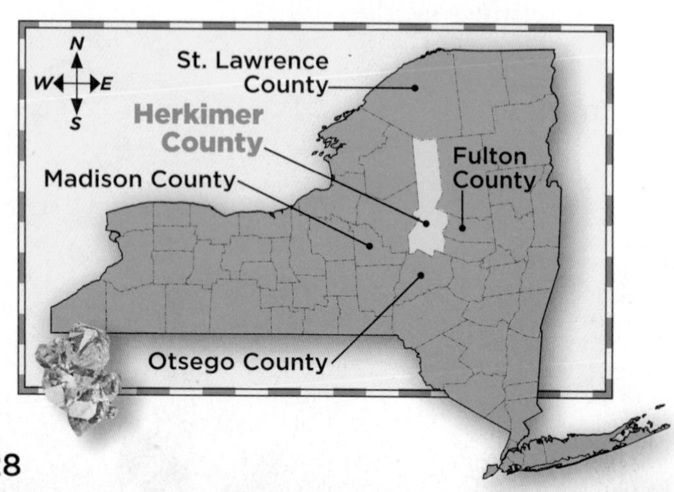

When true diamonds are taken from the earth, they need to be cut and polished to make them sparkle and shine. Herkimer diamonds come out of their rocky homes already shaped and polished by nature!

How Herkimer Diamonds Began

Some 500 million years ago, a shallow sea covered parts of what is now New York State. Particles of rock and earth settled to the bottom. Over millions of years, this sediment built up. The weight of the sediment on top pressed down on the bottom layers. Gradually the layers of sediment turned into rock. Water seeped through pores in the rock and eventually became trapped in pockets inside the rock. Over time crystals formed in those pockets.

Long ago the sea dried up. Glaciers and storms wore away the top layers of rock. This weathering exposed the hidden crystals and the first Herkimer diamonds came to light!

Prospecting for Diamonds

Herkimer "mines" are actually rocky, open pits. The ground is rough and uneven. Prospectors are told to wear hiking boots, and goggles are also recommended.

Some collectors just wander around, hoping to spot a diamond. Some sift through the dirt. Serious prospectors use crowbars, rock hammers, and heavy chisels. Most miners use hammers that weigh two or three pounds. They pound the rock until it breaks apart. If they are lucky, a crystal will be there.

The luckiest prospectors find pockets of crystals. These pockets can be as much as six feet wide and can contain thousands of crystals. Most pockets contain crystals in a wide range of sizes, up to eight or more inches long. Sometimes people find crystals with water bubbles inside. Twin crystals, double crystals, and smoky crystals are all exciting discoveries as well.

Shouts of "I found one!" encourage other prospectors to keep working. If they keep at it, they may get lucky, too. If not, they can always buy a Herkimer diamond in the gift shop.

Show What You Know

Comprehension

Reading Directions

- Directions explain how to do something. Many directions include a list of materials that you will need. Sometimes numbered steps are given to tell the reader the order in which things should be done.
- Look at the granola bar recipe in the article "Sky-High Dining" on page 100. Answer the questions below on a separate sheet of paper.
- How many ingredients does the recipe require?
- Explain what might happen if you were to skip step #5.
- What temperature should the oven be?

Genre

Author Tales

- Authors sometimes write stories based on events that have happened in their own lives.
- Think about an author whose stories you enjoy, such as two authors in this unit: Amada Irma Pérez and Johanna Hurwitz.
- Read an autobiography or biography about the author's life. Use online and print resources.
- Write a paragraph comparing events in the author's life to events in a story the author has written.

Word Study

Words, Words, Words

- Dictionaries and glossaries can tell a reader the meaning of a word, its syllabication, pronunciation, and part of speech. A thesaurus can be used to look up alternate word choices.
- Use a dictionary or glossary to look up the following words: *active, cranky, glorious*.
- Write down the definition, syllabication, pronunciation, and part of speech for every word. Then use a thesaurus to locate alternate word choices and write a sentence using the synonyms.

Words from Around the World

- Languages often borrow words from each other. The English language has many words that have their roots in other languages. You can use a dictionary to look up a word's origin—where a word came from, its root, and how it is used in our language.
- Use a dictionary to look up the origins of the following words: *yacht, typhoon, bureau, bronco*.
- Write down the word, its definition, its syllabication, and its origin.
- Then write down two of your favorite words and look up their origins.

MADE EASY

Unit 2
Making a Difference

The Big Question

How do people make a difference in their communities?

LOG ON VIEW IT

Theme Video
Making a Difference
www.macmillanmh.com

How do people make a difference in their communities?

Communities, or large neighborhoods, are shaped by the people living in them. If the community needs something, members can make sure the community gets what it needs. For example, if a community wanted to build a playground, community members could do different things like raise money, send letters to their government for help, or build it themselves. They then make a difference in their community by creating a safe, happy place for children of all ages to play. Learning about how people make a difference in their communities can help you do the same in your community.

Research Activities

In this unit, you will collect information about community projects. Choose a project that would be important for your community. Research resources that would help complete this project, such as visiting completed projects and interviewing the people who worked on them.

Keep Track of Ideas

As you read, keep track of all you are learning about how people make a difference in their communities. Use the **Accordion Book Foldable**. In the first panel, write the Unit Theme: *Making a Difference*. On each of the following panels, write the facts you learn each week that will help you in your research and in your understanding of the Unit Theme.

Digital Learning

LOG ON ▶ FIND OUT www.macmillanmh.com

StudentWorks™ Plus

Interactive Student Book

- **Research Roadmap**
  Follow a step-by-step guide to complete your research project.

Online Resources

- Topic Finder and Other Research Tools
- Videos and Virtual Field Trips
- Photos and Drawings for Presentations
- Related Articles and Web Resources
- Web Site Links

People and Places

Barbara Jordan

In 1966, Barbara Jordan became the first African American woman to be elected to the Texas Senate. In 1973, she was elected to the United States House of Representatives. In 1994, she was awarded the Presidential Medal of Freedom.

Civil Rights

Talk About It

Why is it important for all people to have the same rights?

LOG ON VIEW IT

Oral Language Activities
Civil Rights
www.macmillanmh.com

Vocabulary

unfair	**segregation**
ancestors	**avoided**
numerous	**injustice**

Word Parts

Prefixes are added to the beginnings of words to change their meanings. The prefix *un-* means "not."
unfair = "not fair"
Suffixes are added to the ends of words. The suffix *-ful* means "full of."
peaceful = "full of peace"

IT TOOK COURAGE

by Lily Tuttle

CIVIL RIGHTS are equal opportunities for all citizens regardless of race, religion, or gender. At one time, **unfair** laws gave some people more opportunities than others. Several brave people took a stand against this and made a difference.

Thurgood Marshall

Thurgood Marshall's family had come a long way from the time when their **ancestors** were slaves. But when he wanted to attend the University of Maryland Law School, the school rejected him because he was black. Marshall had to go to a different law school.

Later, in one of his first court cases, Marshall helped a young African American student sue the University of Maryland. The school had denied him admission, too.

Marshall worked hard to win **numerous** cases. One of his best-known trials was *Brown v. Board of Education* in 1954. In this case the Supreme Court decided to end **segregation** in schools. The Court made it illegal for black students and white students to be sent to separate locations.

Ruby Bridges

In 1960 six-year-old Ruby Bridges was the first black child to go to an all-white school in the South. Ruby was young and unsuspecting. She didn't realize how brave she was to do this. White parents decided to take their children out of school. For a whole year Ruby and her teacher were the only people there. Eventually some white children returned. The following year more black children came. Ruby Bridges made a difference.

Dr. Martin Luther King, Jr.

Dr. Martin Luther King, Jr., was a leader in the 1950s and 1960s. He **avoided** violence and asked others to fight in peaceful ways to end **injustice**.

King organized a march on Washington, D.C. There he and thousands of others demanded equal rights for all people. He gave a famous speech that day. He said, "I have a dream." King's dream was that all people would be treated fairly and equally.

Reread for Comprehension

Monitor Comprehension

Author's Purpose One way to monitor comprehension is to identify the author's purpose. The reason an author writes a story is the author's purpose. An author writes to entertain, give information, or persuade. Thinking about how and why an author presents events and other information can help you identify the author's purpose. Reread the selection and fill in the Author's Purpose Map.

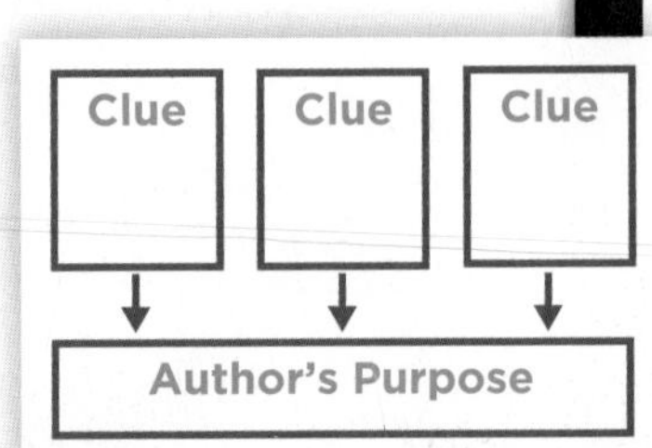

LOG ON LEARN IT **Comprehension** **www.macmillanmh.com**

Comprehension

Genre

A **Biography** is a story about the life of a real person written by someone else.

Monitor Comprehension

Author's Purpose

As you read, fill in your Author's Purpose Map.

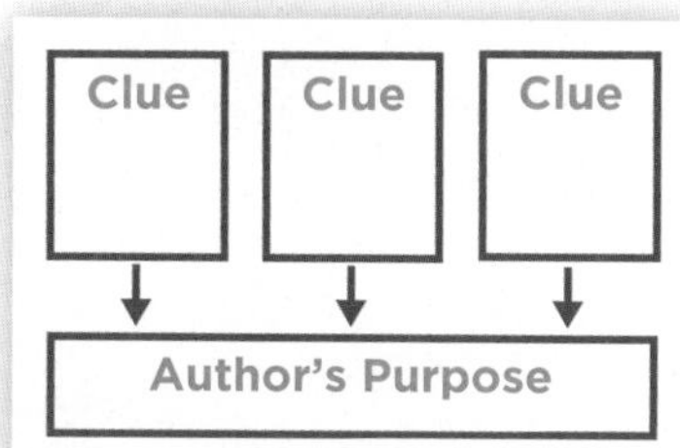

Read to Find Out

What does Rev. Dr. Martin Luther King, Jr.'s sister want you to know about him?

my brother MARTIN

Award Winning Illustrator

A SISTER REMEMBERS
GROWING UP WITH THE REV. DR. MARTIN LUTHER KING JR.

BY CHRISTINE KING FARRIS

ILLUSTRATED BY CHRIS SOENTPIET

We were born in the same room, my brother Martin and I. I was an early baby, born sooner than expected. Mother Dear and Daddy placed me in the chifforobe drawer that stood in the corner of their upstairs bedroom. I got a crib a few days afterward. A year and a half later, Martin spent his first night in that hand-me-down crib in the very same room.

The house where we were born belonged to Mother Dear's parents, our grandparents, the Reverend and

Mrs. A. D. Williams. We lived there with them and our Aunt Ida, our grandmother's sister.

And not long after my brother Martin—who we called M. L. because he and Daddy had the same name—our baby brother was born. His name was Alfred Daniel, but we called him A. D., after our grandfather.

They called me Christine, and like three peas in one pod, we grew together. Our days and rooms were filled with adventure stories and Tinkertoys, with dolls and Monopoly and Chinese checkers.

And although Daddy, who was an important minister, and Mother Dear, who was known far and wide as a musician, often had work that took them away from home, our grandmother was always there to take care of us. I remember days sitting at her feet, as she and Aunt Ida filled us with grand memories of their childhood and read to us about all the wonderful places in the world.

And of course, my brothers and I had each other. We three stuck together like the pages in a brand-new book. And being normal young children, we were almost *always* up to something.

Our best prank involved a fur piece that belonged to our grandmother. It looked almost alive, with its tiny feet and little head and gleaming glass eyes. So, every once in a while, in the waning light of evening, we'd tie that fur piece to a stick, and, hiding behind the hedge in front of our house, we would dangle it in front of unsuspecting passersby. Boy! You could hear the screams of fright all across the neighborhood!

Then there was the time Mother Dear decided that her children should all learn to play piano. I didn't mind too much, but M. L. and A. D. preferred being outside to being stuck inside with our piano teacher, Mr. Mann, who would rap your knuckles with a ruler just for playing the wrong notes. Well, one morning, M. L. and A. D. decided to loosen the legs on the piano bench so we wouldn't have to practice. We didn't tell Mr. Mann, and when he sat . . . *CRASH!* down he went.

But mostly we were good, obedient children, and M. L. did learn to play a few songs on the piano. He even went off to sing with our mother a time or two. Given his love for singing and music, I'm sure he could have become as good a musician as our mother had his life not called him down a different path.

But that's just what his life did.

Author's Purpose
Why does the author tell so much about Martin's childhood?

My brothers and I grew up a long time ago. Back in a time when certain places in our country had **unfair** laws that said it was right to keep black people separate because our skin was darker and our **ancestors** had been captured in far-off Africa and brought to America as slaves.

Atlanta, Georgia, the city in which we were growing up, had those laws. Because of those laws, my family rarely went to the picture shows or visited Grant Park with its famous Cyclorama. In fact, to this very day I don't recall ever seeing my father on a streetcar. Because of those laws, and the indignity that went with them, Daddy preferred keeping M. L., A. D., and me close to home, where we'd be protected.

We lived in a neighborhood in Atlanta that's now called Sweet Auburn. It was named for Auburn Avenue, the street that ran in front of our house. On our side of the street stood two-story frame houses similar to the one we lived in. Across it crouched a line of one-story row houses and a store owned by a white family.

When we were young all the children along Auburn Avenue played together, even the two boys whose parents owned the store.

And since our house was a favorite gathering place, those boys played with us in our backyard and ran with M. L. and A. D. to the firehouse on the corner where they watched the engines and the firemen.

The thought of *not* playing with those kids because they were different, because they were white and we were black, never entered our minds.

Well, one day, M. L. and A. D. went to get their playmates from across the street just as they had done a hundred times before. But they came home alone. The boys had told my brothers that they couldn't play together anymore because A. D. and M. L. were Negroes.

And that was it. Shortly afterward the family sold the store and moved away. We never saw or heard from them again.

Looking back, I realize that it was only a matter of time before the generations of cruelty and **injustice** that Daddy and Mother Dear and Mama and Aunt Ida had been shielding us from finally broke through. But back then it was a crushing blow that seemed to come out of nowhere.

"Why do white people treat colored people so mean?" M. L. asked Mother Dear afterward. And with me and M. L. and A. D. standing in front of her trying our best to understand, Mother Dear gave the reason behind it all.

Her words explained the streetcars our family **avoided** and the WHITES ONLY sign that kept us off the elevator at City Hall. Her words told why there were parks and museums that black people could not visit and why some restaurants refused to serve us and why hotels wouldn't give us rooms and why theaters would only allow us to watch their picture shows from the balcony.

But her words also gave us hope.

She answered simply: "Because they just don't understand that everyone is the same, but someday, it will be better."

And my brother M. L. looked up into our mother's face and said the words I remember to this day.

He said, "Mother Dear, one day I'm going to turn this world upside down."

In the coming years there would be other reminders of the cruel system called **segregation** that sought to keep black people down. But it was Daddy who showed M. L. and A. D. and me how to speak out against hatred and bigotry and stand up for what's right.

Daddy was the minister at Ebenezer Baptist Church. And after losing our playmates, when M. L., A. D., and I heard our father speak from his pulpit, his words held new meaning.

And Daddy practiced what he preached. He always stood up for himself when confronted with hatred and bigotry, and each day he shared his encounters at the dinner table.

When a shoe salesman told Daddy and M. L. that he'd only serve them in the back of the store because they were black, Daddy took M. L. somewhere else to buy new shoes.

Another time, a police officer pulled Daddy over and called him "boy." Daddy pointed to M. L. sitting next to him in the car and said, "This is a boy. I am a man, and until you call me one, I will not listen to you."

These stories were as nourishing as the food that was set before us.

Years would pass, and many new lessons would be learned. There would be **numerous** speeches and marches and prizes. But my brother never forgot the example of our father, or the promise he had made to our mother on the day his friends turned him away.

And when he was much older, my brother M. L. dreamed a dream . . . that turned the world upside down.

Author's Purpose

Why does the author echo Martin's words, "I'm going to turn this world upside down"?

The Stories of Christine and Chris

Christine King Farris wrote this story to show children that her famous brother was once a kid just like them. She saw how young Martin laughed, played, and dreamed of a better world. As Christine says, "Dreams are based on imagination. All leaders dream big dreams that are larger than life."

Chris Soentpiet does a lot of research when he illustrates historical stories like this one. He goes to the library to study what clothes people wore and how they lived. Sometimes he even visits the actual locations where story events took place. That is why it often takes Chris up to a year to illustrate a book.

Other books illustrated by Chris Soentpiet

LOG ON FIND OUT

Author Christine King Farris
Illustrator Chris Soentpiet
www.macmillanmh.com

Author's Purpose

Why did Christine King Farris write *My Brother Martin*? How did the author's relationship with her brother influence this story?

LOG ON LEARN IT Comprehension www.macmillanmh.com

Comprehension Check

Summarize

To summarize *My Brother Martin* use the most important details from the story. Information from your Author's Purpose Map may help you.

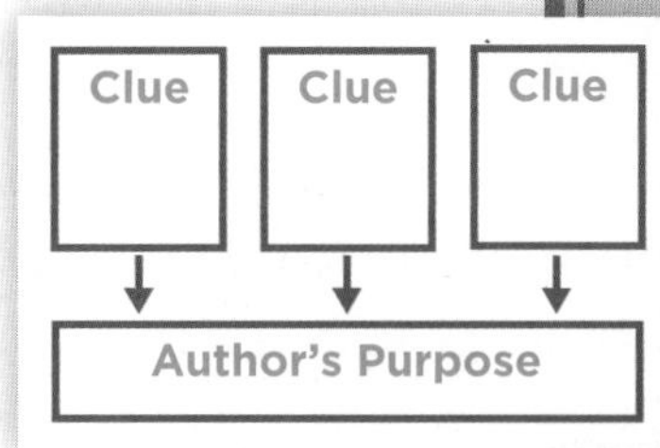

Think and Compare

1. In what city did Christine and her brothers grow up? Details
2. What happened after Mother Dear said, "Because they just don't understand that everyone is the same, but someday, it will be better"? Sequence
3. How did Martin feel about **injustice**? Explain using details from the story to support your answer. Make Inferences
4. Identify the simile used in the first paragraph on page 144. How does the author's use of simile help the reader understand the relationship between Christine and her two brothers? Monitor Comprehension: Author's Purpose
5. Read "It Took Courage" on pages 138–139. Compare the experiences of Thurgood Marshall and Dr. Martin Luther King, Jr. How did segregation affect both men? Use details from both selections to explain. Reading/Writing Across Texts

Social Studies

Genre

Expository selections give information and facts about people, places, or things.

Text Feature

Surveys gather information by asking people for their opinions about specific topics.

Content Vocabulary

orators **opinions**
legacy

Barbara Jordan

A Powerful Speaker

by Jayden Kirksey

Barbara Jordan was one of the greatest **orators** of our time. Her speeches helped many people understand the importance of equal rights.

Barbara Jordan was born in Houston, Texas, in 1936. Her father was a clerk and a former minister. Her grandfather, who lived with the family, was also a former minister. They taught Barbara how powerful and important words could be. As a child, she also learned the value of a school education. She studied how to write and deliver speeches in debates. This experience helped her to become a successful lawyer later in life.

Barbara Jordan at the Watergate hearings in 1974

Jimmy Carter and Barbara Jordan at the 1976 Democratic Convention

Working for Change

At the time, many rules discriminated against African Americans. Barbara wanted people to be treated fairly under the law. She ran for political office in 1966 and became the first African American woman ever elected to the Texas Senate. She was later elected to office in the U.S. House of Representatives in 1972. Presidents, such as Lyndon B. Johnson and Jimmy Carter, depended on Barbara's skills and knowledge. She became a powerful voice for justice and equality in our nation's government.

Barbara left politics due to health reasons. Even when she relied on a wheelchair to get around, she continued to write and speak. She became a teacher to help prepare others to carry on her message. Thirty-one schools and universities awarded her honorary degrees to call attention to her achievements. Many of our nation's greatest orators today continue to honor her **legacy**.

Conducting a Survey

Barbara Jordan cared about people and she wanted to know if people thought they were being treated unfairly. Surveys help people like Barbara Jordan and other politicians to know what the people they represent are thinking about and what might help them most.

Surveys are useful tools for finding out more about something. They can help us to discover **opinions** on important topics. Unlike facts which can be verified, or proven true, opinions are what somebody thinks, feels, or believes. Surveys play an important role in our government. You could even say that voting is a kind of survey.

If you were running for class president, you might conduct a survey in your school to find out how students feel about a particular issue such as raising money to buy books for the library or starting an online school newspaper. In order to get the best results possible, you should interview a large number of students. Ask them simple direct questions that can be answered with "Yes," "No," or "Undecided." These kinds of questions will make it easier for you to record their answers.

Barbara Jordan gave the keynote address at the 1992 Democratic National Convention.

Class President's Survey

Flora Aiken wants to run for president of her class. She created the following survey to help her prepare a speech about why she would make a good class president.

QUESTION	YES	NO	UNDECIDED
1. Do you think we should raise money to buy books for our library?	☐	☐	☐
2. Would you like to see more computers in the library?	☐	☐	☐
3. Do you think we should have more class field trips?	☐	☐	☐
4. Should we serve more fruit in our cafeteria?	☐	☐	☐

Connect and Compare

1. Will Flora find out facts or opinions from the questions on her survey? Explain your answer. **Conducting a Survey**
2. Is it a fact that Barbara Jordan was elected to the Texas Senate? How would you prove it? **Apply**
3. Think about what you learned from *My Brother Martin* about Martin Luther King, Jr. How are he and Barbara Jordan alike? **Reading/Writing Across Texts**

RESEARCH INQUIRY

Social Studies Activity

Create a survey that would help you to write an article about how to improve something in your school. Explain what you hope to learn from each question. Conduct the survey and report what you find to the class.

LOG ON FIND OUT **Barbara Jordan** **www.macmillanmh.com**

Writing

Trait: Ideas

Writers include **details** in their writing that show readers a strong image of what they are writing about.

Reading and Writing Connection

Read the passage below. Notice how the author Christine King Farris shows a moment in her story.

An excerpt from *My Brother Martin*

The author shows us the prank. The details work together to make a clear picture in our minds about the children's funny trick.

Our best prank involved a fur piece that belonged to our grandmother. It looked almost alive, with its tiny feet and little head and gleaming glass eyes. So, every once in a while, in the waning light of evening, we'd tie that fur piece to a stick, and, hiding behind the hedge in front of our house, we would dangle it in front of unsuspecting passersby. Boy! You could hear the screams of fright all across the neighborhood!

Read and Find

Read Damon's writing below. What did he do to show you the moment? Use the checklist below to help you.

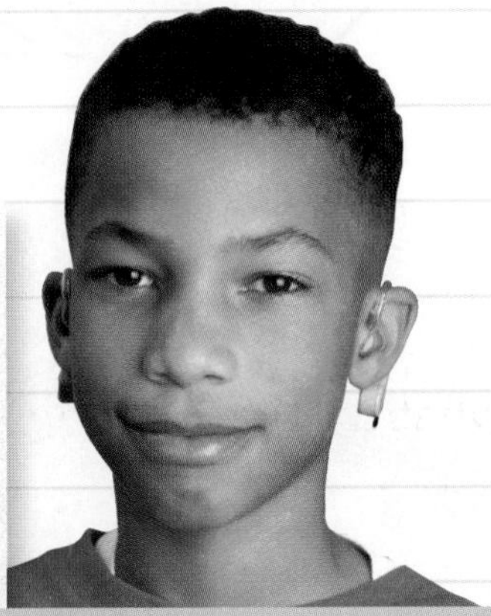

Read about Damon's move.

Muscle Man

by Damon L.

The boxes were only about the size of a loaf of bread, but they each weighed as much as a big dictionary. I stacked up five. I could feel my arm muscles straining, but I stuck with it. When I reached the second flight of stairs, I could feel my knees turn to jelly. My arms felt like too-tight rubber bands. Finally, I staggered into our apartment, dropped the boxes, and collapsed on the couch.

Writer's Checklist

- [x] Does the writer describe exactly what he sees and feels?
- [x] Does the writer include **details** about size, shape, weight, or other features?
- [ ] Can you picture what it was like for Damon in that moment?

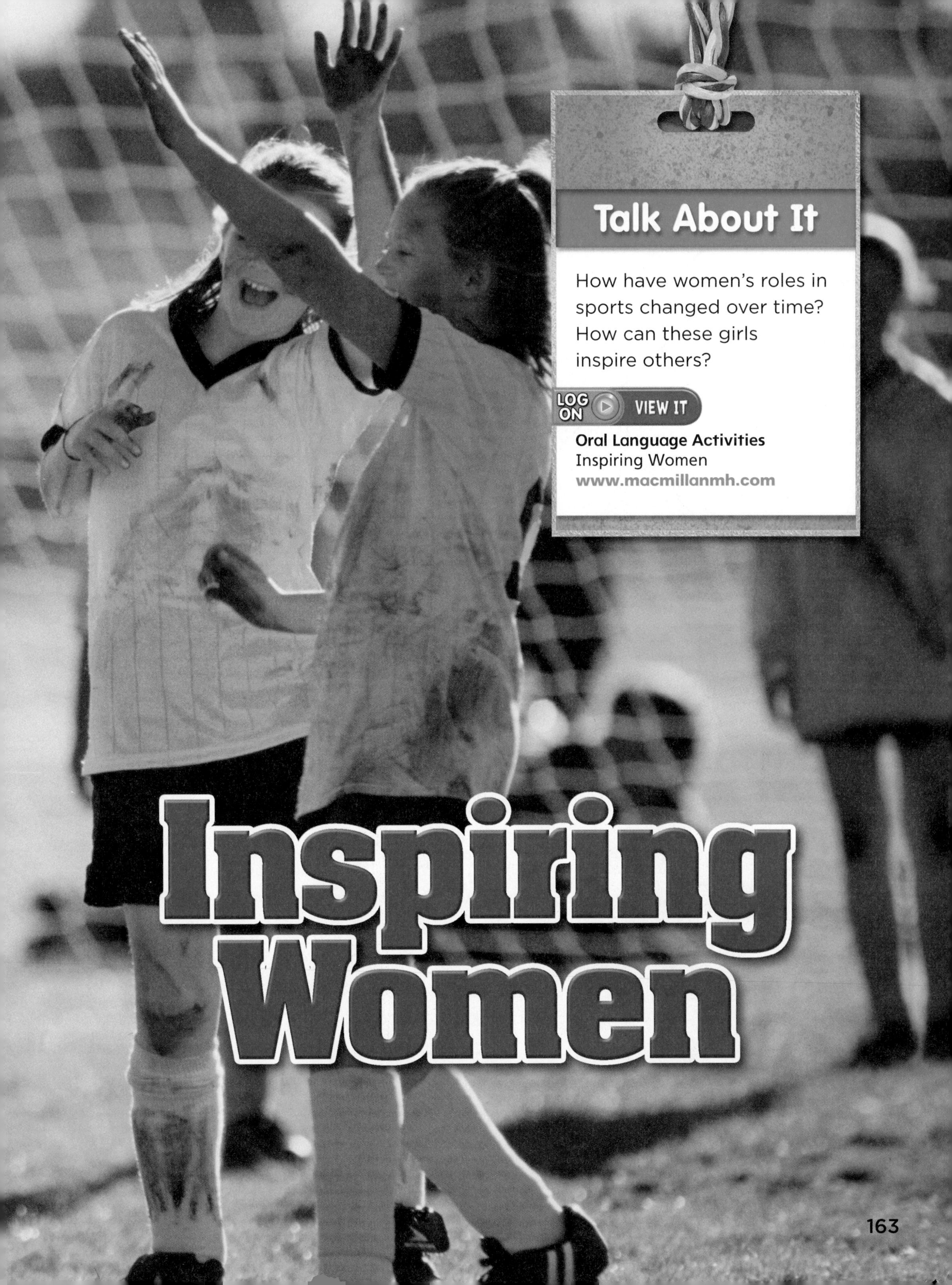

Talk About It

How have women's roles in sports changed over time? How can these girls inspire others?

LOG ON VIEW IT

Oral Language Activities
Inspiring Women
www.macmillanmh.com

Inspiring Women

Vocabulary

legendary
muttered
gaped
snickering
insult
flinched

Context Clues

Descriptions in the text can help you figure out what a word means. Figure out the meaning of *snickering* using descriptions.

WOMEN PICK UP THE BALL

by Jenny Hull

Lucy's class was at Cooperstown—site of the **legendary** Baseball Hall of Fame. Lucy wasn't thrilled to be there. "Who cares about the All-American Girls Professional Baseball League?" Lucy **muttered** quietly to herself.

The League's Beginning

The guide explained that in 1942, most young men were being drafted to fight in World War II. Some feared that major-league baseball parks would close. But Philip Wrigley, the owner of the Chicago Cubs, decided to start a girls' league. Some may have stared and **gaped** at the idea, but it soon caught on.

Lucy wondered what it was like for those girls. If people laughed in a mean way, did the girls notice the baseball fans **snickering**?

A woman baseball player makes a leaping catch.

The League Succeeds

Girls as young as 15 tried out for the league. The $45- to $85-a-week salaries were a big draw. That might seem like an **insult** today, but back then it was a lot of money.

Players had to follow strict rules of behavior and take classes. They were taught how to dress, act, and take care of themselves.

Female players walked with blocks on their heads for balance and posture.

The success of the league was no fluke. During the war many women worked in factories. This changed the image people had of what women could do.

The League Ends

After the war ended, interest lessened and the league fell apart. One reason was that many people got TVs in the early 1950s. They could watch major-league games without buying a ticket or leaving the house!

Time to Leave

Lucy **flinched** and drew back when her teacher called the class together. She wasn't ready to leave. She wanted to learn more. But Lucy would have to wait until her next visit to learn more about this interesting time in baseball history.

Reread for Comprehension

Monitor Comprehension

Author's Purpose One way to monitor comprehension is to identify the author's purpose. An author writes for three purposes, or reasons: to entertain, inform, or persuade. Think about how an author presents events in a person's life. This can help you identify the author's purpose. Reread the selection and fill in the Author's Purpose Map.

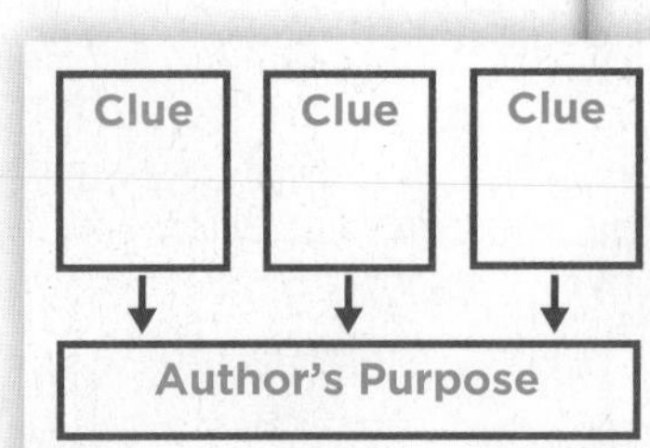

LOG ON LEARN IT **Comprehension** www.macmillanmh.com

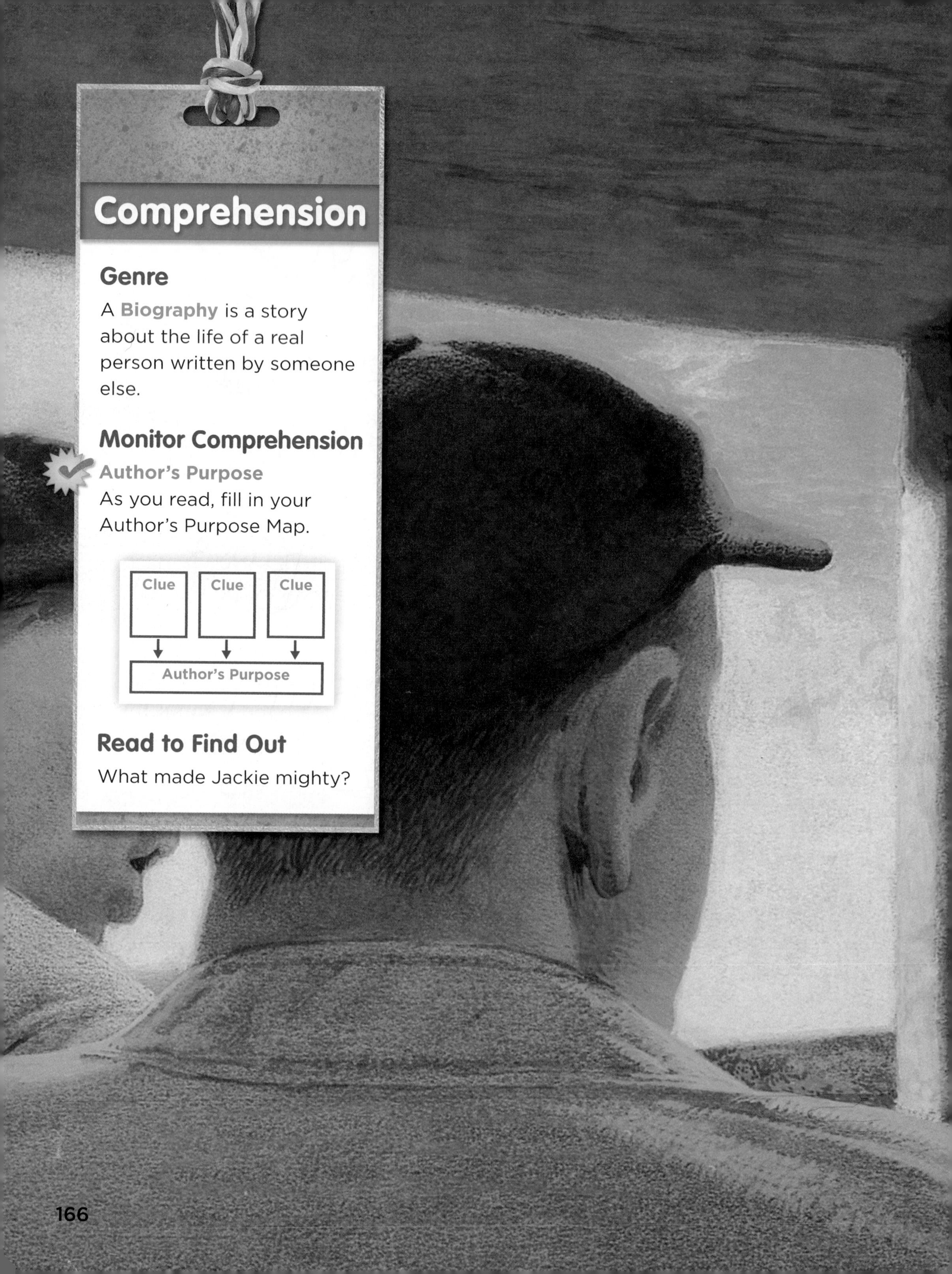

Comprehension

Genre

A **Biography** is a story about the life of a real person written by someone else.

Monitor Comprehension

Author's Purpose

As you read, fill in your Author's Purpose Map.

Clue | Clue | Clue

Author's Purpose

Read to Find Out

What made Jackie mighty?

MIGHTY JACKIE
The Strike-out Queen

by Marissa Moss • illustrated by C.F. Payne

Award Winning Illustrator

It was April 2, 1931, and something amazing was about to happen. In Chattanooga, Tennessee, two teams were about to play an exhibition game of baseball.

One was the New York Yankees, a **legendary** team with famous players—Babe Ruth, Lou Gehrig, and Tony Lazzeri.

The other was the Chattanooga Lookouts, a small team, a nothing team, except for the pitcher, Jackie Mitchell.

Jackie was young, only seventeen years old, but that's not what made people sit up and take notice. Jackie was a girl, and everyone knew that girls didn't play major-league baseball.

The *New York Daily News* sneered that she would swing "a mean lipstick" instead of a bat. A reporter wrote that you might as well have "a trained seal behind the plate" as have a woman standing there. But Jackie was no trained seal. She was a pitcher, a mighty good one. The question was, was she good enough to play against the New York Yankees?

C

As long as she could remember, Jackie had played ball with her father. She knew girls weren't supposed to. All the kids at school, all the boys in her neighborhood told her that. When one boy yelled at another one, "You throw like a girl!" it was an **insult**—everyone knew girls couldn't throw. Or that's what they thought.

Day after day, in the neighborhood sandlot, Jackie's father told her differently. He said she could throw balls, and she did. She ran bases, she swung the bat. By the time she was eight years old, Dazzy Vance, the star pitcher for the Brooklyn Dodgers, had taught her how to pitch. A real pitcher talking to a little girl was all Jackie needed to start dreaming of playing in the World Series. Her father saw her talent and so did Dazzy. He told her she could be good at whatever she wanted, as long as she worked at it. And Jackie worked at baseball. She worked hard.

She practiced pitching till it was too cold and dark to stay outside. She threw balls until her shoulder ached and her fingers were callused. She pitched until her eyes blurred over and she couldn't see where she was throwing. But it didn't matter, her arm knew.

Author's Purpose
Why did the author give so much information about Jackie's childhood?

And now she was finally going to have her chance to play on a *real* baseball team, to pitch to *real* players. The stands were packed. A crowd of four thousand had come to see the strange sight of a woman on the pitcher's mound.

She stood tall on the field and looked back at the crowd in the bleachers. They were waiting for her to make a mistake, and she knew it. They were waiting for her to prove that baseball was a man's game, not *her* game.

"It *is* my game," she **muttered** to herself and bit her lip. The Yankees were up, top of the first, and the batter was walking up to the plate. Jackie was ready for him, the ball tight in her left hand.

Except the batter was Babe Ruth—Babe Ruth, the "Home Run King," a big mountain of a man—and Babe didn't like the idea of a woman pitcher at all. He thought women were "too delicate" for baseball. "They'll never make good," he said. "It would kill them to play ball every day." He walked to the plate and tipped his cap at Jackie. But if she thought he was going to go easy on her, she could forget it! He gripped the bat and got ready to slam the ball out of the ballpark.

Jackie held that ball like it was part of her arm, and when she threw it, she knew exactly where it would go. Right over the plate, right where the Babe wasn't expecting it, right where he watched it speed by and *thwunk* into the catcher's mitt.

"STRRRRRIKE ONE!"

Babe Ruth **gaped**—he couldn't believe it! The crowd roared. Jackie tried to block them out, to see only the ball, to feel only the ball. But Babe Ruth was facing her down now, determined not to let a girl make a fool out of him. She **flinched** right before the next pitch, and the umpire called a ball.

"Hmmmph," the Babe snorted.

"You can do it!" Jackie told herself. "Girls can throw—show them!"

But the next pitch was another ball.

Now the crowd was hooting and jeering. The Babe was **snickering** with them.

Jackie closed her eyes. She felt her fingers tingling around the ball, she felt its heft in her palm, she felt the force of her shoulder muscles as she wound up for the pitch. She remembered what her father had told her: "Go out there and pitch just like you pitch to anybody else."

"STRRRRIKE TWO!"

Now the Babe was mad.

This was serious. The Babe was striking out, and the pitcher was a girl!

Jackie wasn't mad, but she wasn't scared either. She was pitching, really pitching, and it felt like something was happening the way it had always been meant to. She knew the batter would expect the same pitch, close and high, even if the batter was Babe Ruth. So this time she threw the ball straight down the middle with all the speed she could put on it.

"STRRRRIKE THREE!"

Babe Ruth glared at the umpire and threw the bat down in disgust. He told reporters that that would be the last time he'd bat against a woman! The crowd was stunned. A girl had struck out the "Sultan of Swat"! It couldn't be! It was a mistake, a fluke! What would the papers say tomorrow? But wait, here came Lou Gehrig, the "Iron Horse," up to the plate. He'd show her. She couldn't strike him out too.

Lou Gehrig swung with a mighty grunt, but his bat hit nothing but air.

"STRRRRRIKE ONE!"

He looked stunned, then dug in his heels and glared at Jackie.

"STRRRRRIKE TWO!"

Jackie grinned. She was doing what she'd worked so hard and long to do, and nothing could stop her.

She pitched the ball the way she knew best, a lefty pitch with a low dip in it. No one could touch a ball like that when it was thrown right.

"STRRRRRIKE THREE!"

The crowd, so ready to boo her before, rose with a roar, clapping and cheering like crazy. Back to back, Jackie had struck out two of baseball's best batters, Babe Ruth and Lou Gehrig. She'd proven herself and now the fans loved her for it.

But Jackie didn't hear them. She was too proud and too happy. She'd done what she'd always known she could do. She'd shown the world how a girl could throw—as hard and as fast and as far as she wanted.

Author's Purpose
Why did Marissa Moss write this story?

The Winning Team: Marissa and C.F.

Marissa Moss likes to write about real women like Jackie who have done unusual things. She has also written about a female train engineer and the first woman to fly across the English Channel. Marissa hopes that when kids read her books they will discover things about the past that remind them of their own lives.

Other books by Marissa Moss and C.F. Payne

C.F. Payne has stepped up to the plate to illustrate other baseball stories. C.F. often does caricatures, a kind of art that exaggerates the way people look or act, making them seem larger than life.

LOG ON FIND OUT

Author Marissa Moss
Illustrator C.F. Payne
www.macmillanmh.com

Author's Purpose

Identify whether the narrator of the story is first or third person. Why did the author tell the story from this point of view?

LOG ON LEARN IT Comprehension
www.macmillanmh.com

Comprehension Check

Summarize

To summarize *Mighty Jackie* use the most important details from the selection. Information from your Author's Purpose Map may help you.

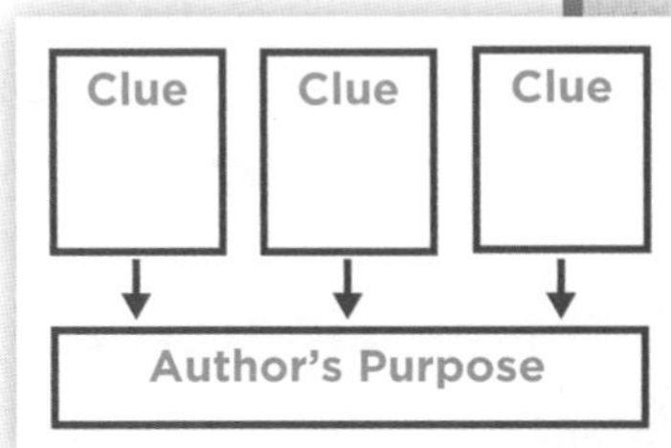

Think and Compare

1. Who taught Jackie how to pitch? Details
2. What happened right after Jackie struck out Babe Ruth and before Lou Gehrig stepped up to the plate? Sequence
3. Why was proving her skill as a pitcher so important to Jackie? Explain using story details. Make Inferences
4. The author states that Ruth and Gehrig were famous baseball players on a **legendary** team. Why does the author say this? Explain using story details. Monitor Comprehension: Author's Purpose
5. Reread "Women Pick Up the Ball" on pages 164–165. Think about *Mighty Jackie*. If Jackie had been in the girls' league, do you think the crowds would have treated her differently? Use details from both selections to explain. Reading/Writing Across Texts

Poetry

Lyric Poems express the thoughts and feelings of the poet. They may sometimes sound like a song.

Literary Elements

Stanzas are groups of lines that give the poem its form. A **Line Break** is the place where the line ends.

Meter is the rhythm of stressed and unstressed syllables in a line of poetry.

Words **Rhyme** when their endings sound the same or nearly the same.

The New Kid

by Mike Makley

illustrated by Steve Cieslawski

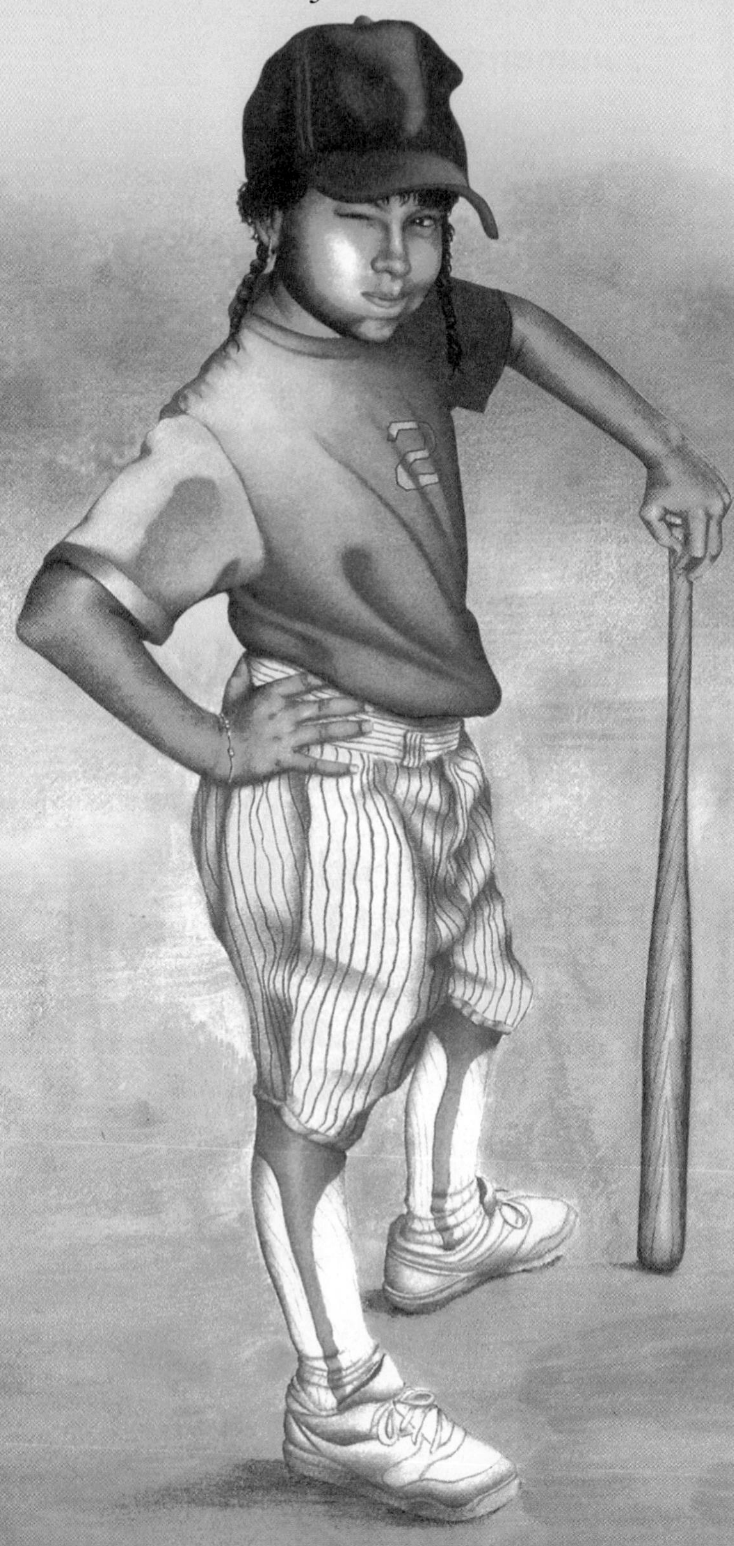

Our baseball team never did very much,
we had me and PeeWee and Earl and Dutch.
And the Oak Street Tigers always got beat
until the new kid moved in on our street.

Each stanza in this poem has four lines and almost all lines have ten syllables.

The kid moved in with a mitt and a bat
and an official New York Yankee hat.
The new kid plays shortstop or second base
and can outrun us all in any place.

The kid never muffs a grounder or fly
no matter how hard it's hit or how high.
And the new kid always acts quite polite,
never yelling or spitting or starting a fight.

We were playing the league champs just last week;
they were trying to break our winning streak.
In the last inning the score was one-one,
when the new kid swung and hit a home run.

The words "league," "week," and "streak" all rhyme.

A few of the kids and their parents say
they don't believe that the new kid should play.
But she's good as me, Dutch, PeeWee, or Earl,
so we don't care that the new kid's a girl.

Connect and Compare

1. Read the third stanza of the poem aloud. Is the rhythm of the stressed and unstressed syllables the same in each line? Explain your answer. **Meter**
2. The last line of the poem ends on the word "girl." How does this emphasize the surprise ending? **Line Breaks**
3. Compare Jackie in *Mighty Jackie* to the girl in this poem. What is similar about their situations? **Reading/Writing Across Texts**
4. Think about a sport or hobby that you like to do. Write a poem about it. Form your lines into stanzas and try to use rhyme in your poem. **Apply**

Writing

Trait: Word Choice

Writers use **descriptive words and phrases** to show actions.

Reading and Writing Connection

Read the passage below. Notice how the author Marissa Moss uses descriptive words to show actions.

An excerpt from *Mighty Jackie*

The author shows us what Jackie thinks and feels right before she pitches the ball. The details help us imagine what it was like for Jackie as she pitched.

Now the crowd was hooting and jeering. The Babe was snickering with them.

Jackie closed her eyes. She felt her fingers tingling around the ball, she felt its heft in her palm, she felt the force of her shoulder muscles as she wound up for the pitch. She remembered what her father had told her: "Go out there and pitch just like you pitch to anybody else."

Read and Find

Read Rasika's writing below. What words did she use to show actions? Use the checklist below to help you.

Elliot J. Hamster

by Rasika W.

I'd like to introduce you to my best friend (and pet), Elliot J. Hamster. He is covered with soft, butterscotch-colored fur. When he crawls up my arm, his tiny claws scratch a little, but his fur tickles me at the same time. Sometimes he sits up in my hand and looks right at me. I laugh when he does that and wiggles his nose!

Read about Elliot J. Hamster.

Writer's Checklist

- [x] Does the writer describe exactly what she sees and feels?
- [x] Does the writer include details about size, shape, color, or other features?
- [ ] Does Rasika use **descriptive words and phrases** to show the actions of her hamster?

Talk About It

What does it take to face challenges in life?

LOG ON VIEW IT

Oral Language Activities
Facing Challenges
www.macmillanmh.com

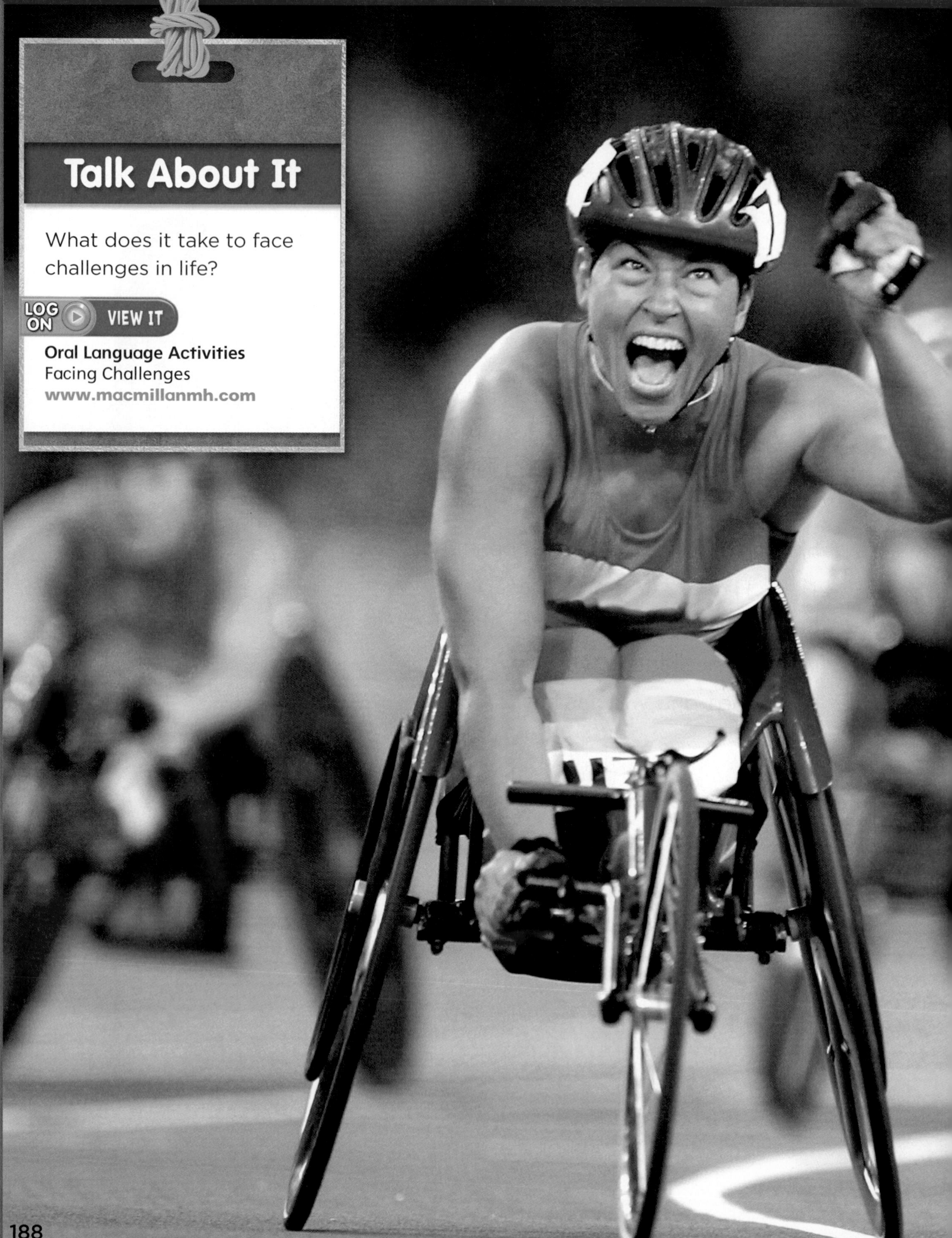

TIME FOR KIDS®

Facing Challenges

Vocabulary

similar **achieved**
challenges **varied**
designed

Mono-skiing lets a paralyzed skier go down a hill while sitting.

The Paralympics

A special group of athletes prepare for the Paralympic Games at the same time athletes prepare for the Olympic Games.

The Paralympics are for athletes with physical disabilities. When the Paralympics began in 1960, 400 athletes from 23 countries took part. Time flies. In the Paralympic Games, 44 years later, 3,806 athletes from 136 countries competed.

In the Paralympics, athletes compete with others who have the same type of disability. They take part in athletic events **similar** to those that Olympic athletes compete in. However, Paralympians use special equipment designed for their disabilities.

One of the goals of the Paralympic Games is to change the way the public views people with disabilities. Paralympians are world-class athletes. They don't shy away from **challenges**, nor do they let themselves be held back.

American mono-skier Muffy Davis competes in the women's slalom. At 16, a skiing accident left her legs paralyzed. At first, Muffy refused to ski again. Then, she did an about-face. "The limits we have are the ones we put on ourselves," she says.

Athletes from Germany took part in the opening ceremonies of the 2004 Winter Paralympics.

The Ride of His Life

California native Alejandro Abor builds handcycles. These bikes are **designed** and made for people who can't use their legs. They are powered by hand pedals.

Alejandro is also a handcycle rider. He lost both of his legs in an accident, but he wanted to continue playing sports. Alejandro learned how to do things without his legs. He taught himself to kayak and to play basketball. He even competed in difficult triathlons.

For years, Alejandro continued training. Today he is a handcycling champion on the U.S. Paralympic Cycling Elite Team. In the 2004 Paralympic Games, he won a silver medal.

Alejandro inspires others to do their best. He talks to people about disabilities and builds handcycles for kids with physical challenges. He also is a great dad to his three children. Through hard work, Alejandro has **achieved** his dreams.

In 2006, Abor won a 267-mile handcycle-wheelchair race.

Good Sports

Football 5-a-side players compete for the ball.

Paralympian sports are **varied**. Many are familiar to most people, such as track and field or skiing. Some sports, like those mentioned below, are just a little different.

Football 5-a-side—In this soccer game, each team has five players who are either blind or vision-impaired. The ball makes a noise when it moves.

Wheelchair Rugby—The goal of this very physical game is for players in wheelchairs to carry a ball over the opponent's goal line.

Ice sledge hockey—Players with lower limb disabilities sit in sleds. They use two short hockey sticks to push themselves around the ice.

Comprehension

Genre

An **Expository** article in a newspaper or magazine presents facts and information.

Monitor Comprehension

Main Idea and Details
To find the main idea of an article, first identify the most important details. Then decide what these details have in common.

Making a Splash

How does a person with physical disabilities become a world-champion athlete?

Rudy Garcia-Tolson is not an ordinary athlete. He holds world records for swimming, running, and biking. He takes part in top competitions around the world, where all eyes are on him. This talented athlete has won many medals and honors. There is one other thing special about Rudy: He has no legs.

Rudy was born in Bloomington, California, with a serious illness. He went through 15 operations as a baby. At five years old, Rudy and his family had to make a big decision. Rudy's legs could no longer function. He could keep his legs and stay in a wheelchair or he could walk with artificial legs. Rudy knew what he wanted; he chose to walk. The brave five-year-old had his legs amputated. From that point on, Rudy's life was never the same.

Flying in the Water

After his operation, Rudy took swimming lessons. He joined a local swim team and soon competed in races. By the time he was eight, Rudy had earned 43 ribbons and 13 medals for swimming. At the age of ten, he completed his first triathlon. Rudy didn't let physical **challenges** get in the way of his dreams. He **achieved** every goal he set. Rudy won many awards for running and biking. "I'm unstoppable," the young Rudy often said.

Now Rudy is a swimmer for the U.S. Paralympic Elite Team. In 2004, Rudy won a gold medal for swimming in the Athens Paralympic Games. In 2006 he finished an Ironman triathlon. Rudy continues to train hard for future Paralympic Games.

Rudy Garcia-Tolson carries the Olympic Flame during the 2002 Salt Lake Olympic Torch Relay in San Francisco, California.

Rudy gets ready for a swimming race at the 2004 Paralympics. The Games were held in Athens, Greece.

Leg Work

When Rudy swims or surfs, he doesn't use artificial legs. He relies on his strong upper body in the water. He chooses his feet and legs depending on his activity. He also uses different feet and legs for running and cycling.

Rudy rides a bike in a special wind tunnel. It helps him test how well his prosthetic legs work.

Going for the Gold

Rudy lives at the Olympic Training Center in Colorado. The center is **designed** to train Olympic athletes for the Games. Rudy and other swimmers use a state-of-the-art swimming pool. Here, swimmers learn to go the extra mile—literally! Underwater cameras film the athletes as they swim. Athletes and coaches study the film to help the swimmers train better.

Olympic swimmers also train in a swimming flume. The flume is like a swimming treadmill that contains 50,000 gallons of water. The water current can be adjusted for each swimmer. The altitude, or height, of the flume can also be changed. Swimmers can train in conditions **similar** to sea level or to more than a mile above sea level.

This **varied** type of technology helps athletes get better and stronger. Rudy knows he'll be ready to go for the gold at future Games. "A brave heart is a powerful weapon," he says.

Working for Others

Rudy's feet are made of carbon fiber, a light material that bends easily. The carbon fiber feet perform like human feet. They bend and help push the body forward. They also absorb shock from walking and running.

People who use artificial legs work with prosthetists. They are doctors who help people choose artificial legs. Rudy and his prosthetist have been working together since he was a child.

The doctor studies new artificial legs and feet. Rudy tests them out during training and racing. Sometimes things go wrong with the legs. They may be uncomfortable. His body may hurt after long races. Rudy and his doctor work together to fix the problems. Over the years, their research has made artificial legs better for all people.

Rudy swam to a world record in the 12th Paralympic Games in Athens.

Think and Compare

1. What did Rudy achieve in 2006?

2. Why are Rudy's artificial feet able to bend?

3. What is this article mainly about? Use details from the text to support your answer.

4. What do the athletes in "The Paralympics" and "Making a Splash" have in common?

Test Practice

Answering Questions

Right There answers are found in one place in the text.
Think and Search answers are found in more than one place.
Author and Me answers ask the reader to look for clues.

STANDING TALL

1 Grayson Rosenberger creates some wild inventions. He once made a go-kart skateboard, but his family didn't think it was safe. However, there was one invention they really liked.

2 Grayson created a covering for a prosthetic, or artificial leg. Some types of artificial legs are made of metal rods. Grayson used bubble-like plastic wrapping material and tape to cover the metal leg. Then he shaped the leg with a heat gun to make it look real.

3 Artificial legs that look real are very expensive. Many amputees, people who no longer have their arms or legs, can't pay $1,000 to buy a real-looking leg, so they use metal legs. Grayson's invention costs $15 to make, so more people can afford it.

4 Grayson's parents run Standing with Hope. This group provides artificial legs to people in Ghana, in Africa. Grayson remembers the story of Daniel, a boy in Ghana who received an artificial metal leg. It didn't have a covering. "He's made fun of in school," says Grayson. Grayson and his family are returning to Ghana, and Grayson's first priority is Daniel.

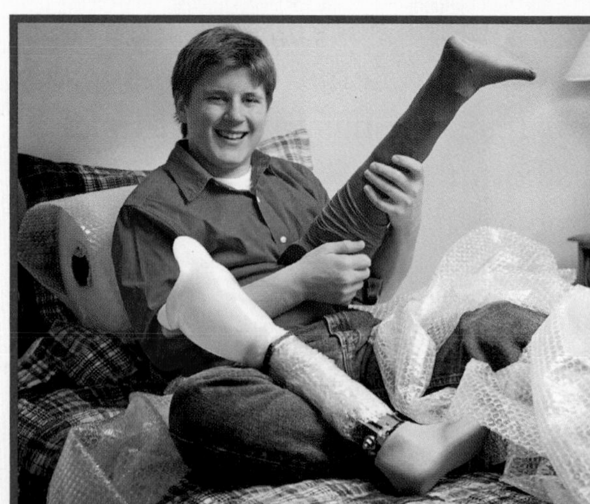

Grayson holds up his invention. One leg is covered only in plastic wrap. The other has a flesh-colored stocking to make it look real. A person who makes prosthetics for a living said, "It surprised me a kid came up with this."

Use "Standing Tall" to answer questions 1–3.

1 Look at the following web of information from the article.

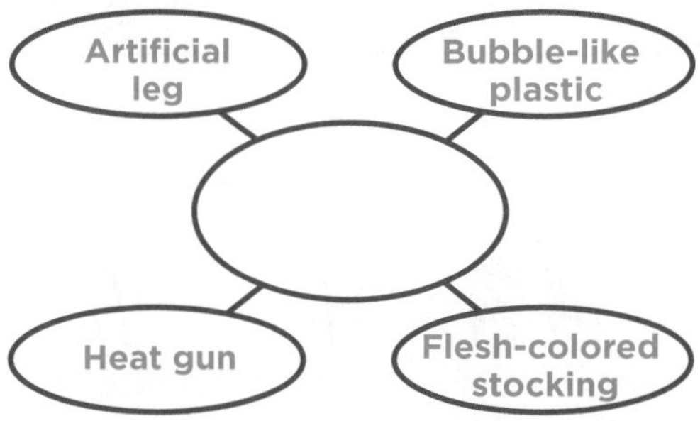

Which would be the best title for this web?

A Go-Kart Skateboard
B Grayson's Invention
C Standing with Hope
D Daniel in Ghana

---

2 Artificial legs that look real are —

F made in Africa
G difficult to use
H made of metal
J very expensive

3 Paragraph 4 is mainly about —

A Daniel, a boy in Ghana
B the go-kart skateboard
C Grayson's parents
D how much artificial legs cost

Write to a Prompt

Write a composition about a job that requires specific skills.

Think about the purpose of the composition.

As you write your composition, think about how to clearly express your ideas.

Below, see how one student begins a response to the prompt above.

The writer listed specific skills.

Explorers need special qualities and skills. They should like danger, traveling, and studying. It's hard to think of a more dangerous job than diving to the bottom of the ocean or digging in a dark chamber. Any problem could result in a serious injury or death. Like the explorer in "Adventures," explorers should probably go to college. They need to study a subject and become experts in their field. This way they can recognize things other people might not notice. A knowledge of their surroundings helps explorers while they are out working. A deep sea explorer should be able to see a fish and figure out if the fish is a threat.

Writing Prompt

Respond in writing to the prompt below. Review the hints below before and after you write.

Write a composition about a job that interests you.

Writing Hints

- ☑ Remember to write about a job that interests you. Think about genre.
- ☑ Plan your writing by organizing your ideas.
- ☑ Include important details to support your ideas.
- ☑ Check that each sentence you write helps the reader to understand your ideas.
- ☑ Use correct spelling and punctuation.
- ☑ Review and edit your writing.

Talk About It

These wild horses live in a big marsh in southern France. Why is it important to save wild animals?

LOG ON VIEW IT

Oral Language Activities
Saving Animals
www.macmillanmh.com

SAVING ANIMALS

Vocabulary

sanctuary
descendants
threatened
emerge
fragile
habitat

Context Clues

Paragraph Clues are words in a sentence or paragraph that help readers figure out the meaning of unfamiliar words. Use paragraph clues, such as examples or definitions, to figure out what *habitat* means.

The Wild Ponies of Chincoteague

by Gregory Searle

Every year since 1924, a pony swim has taken place between two tiny islands in the Atlantic Ocean. Assateague and Chincoteague islands are located off the coasts of Maryland and Virginia.

The calm, quiet privacy of the islands provides a **sanctuary** for the wild ponies. The ponies are **descendants** of wild horses. How the ancestors of these ponies ended up on an island, no one knows for sure.

The Pony Swim

In the 1920s several terrible fires broke out on Chincoteague. In response, the Chincoteague Volunteer Fire Department was founded in 1924. In order to raise money to buy equipment for the fire department, the annual pony swim and auction was started.

Every year, thousands of people come to watch the pony swim and the auction. Many watch from boats out on the water.

The firemen "round up" the wild ponies on Assateague Island. At first the ponies feel **threatened** and head back into the trees. After some coaxing, the ponies swim across the channel to **emerge** from the water onto Chincoteague Island.

These ponies are small, but they are not **fragile**. They are very strong and intelligent animals. Many farmers want to buy a Chincoteague pony. Some of the foals are auctioned off to good homes. The rest of the ponies swim back to Assateague Island a few days later. The fire department uses the money that is raised to update their safety equipment.

Protecting the Ponies

The pony swim is important for another reason, too. The number of horses living on Assateague has to be controlled. If too many horses are born, there won't be enough grass for the rest to eat. Keeping the population of ponies under control protects the **habitat**, the area in which an animal or plant naturally lives, and its natural resources for future generations.

Reread for Comprehension

Analyze Text Structure

Cause and Effect Text structure is the way an author organizes a selection to present information. Cause and effect is a type of text structure. A cause is why something happens. An effect is what happens. Readers can look for explicit and implicit causes and effects in a selection to help them check their understanding. Reread the selection and fill in your Cause and Effect Chart to help you identify what happens in the selection and why.

Cause → Effect
→
→
→
→

LOG ON LEARN IT **Comprehension**
www.macmillanmh.com

Comprehension

Genre

Expository writing can be an account of actual persons, living things, situations, or events.

Analyze Text Structure

Cause and Effect
As you read, fill in your Cause and Effect Chart.

Cause → Effect
→
→
→
→

Read to Find Out

What is it that makes a wild horse wild?

Wild Horses

by Cris Peterson

photographs by Alvis Upitis

In the deepest, darkest part of night, when the crickets and tree frogs are almost silent, shadowy shapes **emerge** from the ponderosa pine ridge and tiptoe down to the glassy Cheyenne River below. Their long tangled manes and tails ruffle in the night breeze. Ever alert and watchful for predators, they swiftly drink their fill. Then they turn on their heels and lunge up the rocky hills to safety.

In the misty glow of dawn, one can see these mysterious visitors aren't backyard pasture mares with swishing tails and docile, trusting eyes. These horses are wild—from another century, another era, another world. They are American mustangs, whose freedom, adaptability, and toughness define the western wilderness.

Some of the mares have names. Medicine Hattie is easy to spot. Her dark ears jut out above her ghostly white face and corn-silk mane. Painted Lady's pure white coat is splashed with brown spots; she always seems to know where the sweetest grasses are.

And there are others. Funny Face has a creamy white blaze that slides down the sides of her face like melting ice cream on a hot day. She loves to stand on the highest rock-strewn spot with her face to the wind. Yuskeya, whose name means freedom in the Sioux language, always stands at the edge of the herd, alert for danger and ready to run.

To find these horses, cross Cascade Creek where the South Dakota Black Hills meet the prairie, and turn right onto a pothole-strewn gravel road. This is the land of silver sagebrush and cowboy legends. Scraggly buzzards perch on fence posts near the entry gate to the Black Hills Wild Horse **Sanctuary**, home for more than three hundred wild horses and one determined cowboy-conservationist named Dayton Hyde.

Dayton was a gangly, growing thirteen-year-old boy when he met his first horse. It was a dirt-colored pony he found drinking from a puddle of old soapy dishwater behind his family's summer cabin in northern Michigan. He recalls that for a time he thought all horses blew bubbles out of their noses.

Soon after that encounter, word came from Dayton's cattle rancher uncle in Oregon that his cowboys had just captured a band of wild horses. Dayton hopped a westbound train and arrived on his uncle's doorstep, where he grew up as a cowboy learning to love the western range and its wild horses.

Mustangs are **descendants** of the horses brought to America by Spanish explorers nearly five hundred years ago. By 1900, more than two million smart, fast, surefooted wild horses roamed the West.

When newly invented barbed wire fences began crisscrossing the rangelands, the horses lost access to sources of food and water and became a pesky problem for local residents. Thousands of them were slaughtered for fertilizer or pet food. By 1950, less than seventeen thousand survived.

After a Congressional act prohibited the capture or slaughter of wild horses in 1971, the wild horse population again grew quickly. Many died of thirst and starvation in the harsh western winters. In an attempt to manage the size of the herds, the United States government gathered up the animals and maintained them in fenced feedlots until they could be adopted.

One day in the early 1980s, Dayton Hyde, who by this time owned his uncle's ranch and had a grown family of his own, drove by one of these feedlots. Shocked and dismayed by the sight of dozens of muddy and dejected horses locked in a corral, he felt he had to do something.

Cause and Effect
Why did the mustang population increase during the 1970s?

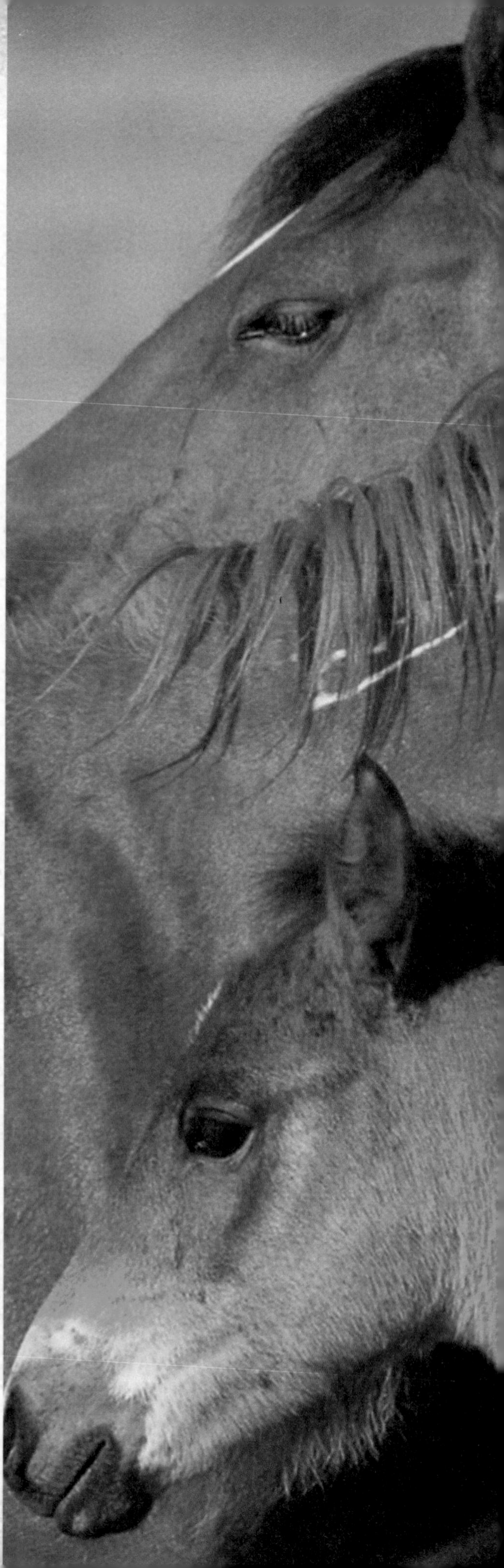

After months of searching and many long days spent convincing government officials to accept his plan of creating a special place for wild horses, he acquired eleven thousand acres of rangeland and rimrock near the Black Hills in South Dakota. Here, among yawning canyons and sun-drenched pastures, he hoped wild horses—some too ugly, old, or knobby kneed to be adopted—could run free forever.

Before he could ship his wild horse rejects to their new home, Dayton had to build eight miles of fences to ensure they wouldn't wander into his neighbors' wheat fields. He also fenced in a fifty-acre training field where the horses would spend their first few days on the ranch adjusting to their new surroundings.

On a miserably cold fall day, huge creaking semi-trailers filled with snorting, stomping steeds finally arrived at the ranch. After hours of coaxing, Dayton succeeded in getting Magnificent Mary to skitter off the trailer. She was a battle-scarred, mean-eyed mare with a nose about twice as long as it should be. The rest of the herd clattered behind her, eyes bulging with fear.

Dayton's worst fear was that the horses would spook and charge through his carefully constructed six-wire fence, scattering across the prairie like dry leaves in a whirlwind. Aware that wild horses often feel **threatened** by being watched, he sat in the cab of his old pickup truck, peeking at them out of a corner of his eye. Finally, after nearly a week of around-the-clock vigilance, he swung open the gate from the training field to his wild horse sanctuary.

Many years have passed since Dayton held his breath and pushed that corral gate open. Every spring, dozens of his wild horses give birth to tottering colts that learn the ways of the back country from their mothers. They share the vast, quiet land with coyotes, mountain lions, and countless deer. Star lilies, bluebells, and prairie roses nod in the wind along with the prairie short grass that feeds the herd.

Thousands of visitors arrive each summer to get a glimpse of wild horses in their natural **habitat**, a habitat that has been preserved through Dayton's careful planning. Throughout the grazing season, he moves the herd from one area of the ranch to another so the horses don't damage the **fragile** rangeland. In the process, he searches for his marker mares: Painted Lady, Medicine Hattie, Funny Face, Yuskeya, Magnificent Mary, and several others. When he spots them all, he knows the whole herd is accounted for.

Sometimes in the fall while he's checking on the horses, Dayton notices a gaunt, aging mare whose ribs stand out through her ragged coat. He knows this old friend won't survive the winter. As the pale December daylight slips over the rimrock, the old mare lies down and goes to sleep for the last time. After years of running free, the wild mustang returns to the earth and completes the circle of life.

The wild mustangs Dayton Hyde once discovered crowded into a feedlot now gallop across the Cheyenne River free as the prairie wind. They splash through the glistening water and bolt up a ravine. Here in this rugged wilderness, one man's vision of a sanctuary for wild horses has become a reality.

Cause and Effect
How did the horses from the feedlot end up in the Black Hills Wild Horse Sanctuary?

Ride Away with Cris and Alvis

Cris Peterson lives on a big dairy farm in Wisconsin. Tending 500 cows keeps Cris pretty busy, but she still finds time to write. Cris writes a lot about farm life and animals. She often uses her own experiences to inspire her books. Cris believes it is very important to give readers a true picture of farms and animals, so she chooses her details carefully.

Alvis Upitis has provided the photographs for many of Cris's books. He is a good partner. When Cris was very busy with farm work and did not think she'd have time to write, Alvis encouraged her to try.

Other books by Cris and Alvis

LOG ON FIND OUT

Author Cris Peterson
Illustrator Alvis Upitis
www.macmillanmh.com

Author's Purpose

Cris Peterson tried to create a true picture of the animals in her story *Wild Horses*. What does this suggest about her purpose for writing? Explain using story details.

LOG ON LEARN IT Comprehension www.macmillanmh.com

Comprehension Check

Summarize

To summarize *Wild Horses* use the most important details from the selection. Information from your Cause and Effect Chart may help you.

Cause → Effect
→
→
→
→

Think and Compare

1. By 1950, how many wild horses were left? Details
2. Why did Dayton Hyde want to help the wild horses? Explain your answer. Analyze Text Structure: Cause and Effect
3. Explain how Dayton manages to care for the **fragile** land while allowing the horses free range. Include details from the selection. Summarize
4. How does the author let the reader know how she feels about Dayton Hyde's wild horse sanctuary? Use details from the selection to explain your answer. Author's Purpose
5. Read "The Wild Ponies of Chincoteague" on pages 202–203. Compare Assateague Island with the Black Hills Wild Horse Sanctuary. Use details from both selections to support your answer. Reading/Writing Across Texts

Language Arts

Genre

Tall Tales are stories with events so exaggerated that they are beyond belief. Tall tales are an American form of folklore, or storytelling.

Literary Elements

Hyperbole is the use of exaggeration for emphasis. The author does not expect the reader to believe it. An example is: *I told you a million times to clean your room.*

A **Metaphor** is the comparison of two unlike things without the use of *like* or *as*.

The Tale of Pecos Bill

retold by Gillian Reed

Pecos Bill was the best cowboy and toughest man there ever was. He had bounced out of his family's wagon when he was a baby and landed in the Pecos River. He was raised by coyotes, but he didn't talk about that very much.

One day Bill showed up on the Texas range wearing a blue bandanna and a big Stetson hat. "Hey, partner," Pecos Bill roared at a gold prospector, "I'm lookin' for some real cowhands. Got me a ranch in New Mexico — well, to tell the truth, New Mexico is my ranch. I need some tough guys to work for me. I'm looking for the kind of man who can eat a pot of beans in one gulp and pick his teeth with barbed wire."

Pecos Bill's description of a tough guy is **hyperbole**. It's a humorous exaggeration that the reader is not meant to believe.

The prospector said some tough cowhands were camped out 200 miles down the river. Bill and his horse set off in that direction, and before long a mountain lion leaped from a boulder straight down onto Pecos Bill.

Bill's horse didn't wait around to see what happened next. If he had, all he would have seen was a blur of flying fur. He would have heard nothing but hideous snarls and groans. When the fur settled, the big cat was apologizing to Bill.

"How can I make it up to you?" it asked.

"You can't, but I'm putting this saddle on you," said Bill. "You scared off my horse, and I hate walkin'."

So Pecos Bill rode the cat to the tough guys' campsite. Those tough men took one look at Bill on that mountain lion and made him their new boss. Then the whole crew headed out for New Mexico.

Back on the ranch, Pecos Bill caught a wild black horse for himself and named it Widow-Maker. That crazy horse had the power of twelve horses and wouldn't let anyone but Bill ride him.

Pecos Bill also got himself a spouse. He first spied Slue-Foot Sue on the Rio Grande. She was riding a catfish the size of a boat and whooping at the top of her lungs. Bill admired her fog-horn voice.

The day she married Bill, Slue-Foot Sue wore a dress with one of those old-time bustles. The bustle was a steel-spring contraption that made the back of her dress stick out a mile.

After the wedding, Sue wanted to ride Widow-Maker. Now, Pecos Bill loved Slue-Foot Sue, so he attempted to talk her out of this notion.

"Widow-Maker won't let anybody ride him but me. He'd throw you in a second."

But Sue insisted, and Bill finally let Sue give it a try. Sue got on Widow-Maker, who bucked and jumped and bucked again. Then he threw Slue-Foot Sue, and she sped into the sky like she'd been shot from a cannon. When Sue finished going up, she plummeted down. And when she hit the ground, she bounced on her steel-spring bustle, a giant pogo stick, that sent her up again, even higher than before. She even hit her head on the moon.

Sue's bustle is not a pogo stick, but the comparison helps the reader picture what happened. This is an example of **metaphor**.

For days Pecos Bill watched his bouncing bride. Up and down she went. Every time Sue landed, she bounced up higher, until she came down to Earth only once every few weeks.

It took a long time for Pecos Bill to find another bride as accomplished as Slue-Foot Sue. And he never again allowed a wife of his to ride Widow-Maker.

Connect and Compare

1. Find two examples of hyperbole in the descriptions of Slue-Foot Sue and her adventures. Explain why they are examples of hyperbole. **Hyperbole**
2. Identify the metaphor on page 222 and explain what two things are being compared. **Metaphor**
3. Compare Widow-Maker to the mustangs described in *Wild Horses*. How are they similar? How are they different? **Reading/Writing Across Texts**

LOG ON FIND OUT **Language Arts** Tall tales
www.macmillanmh.com

Reading and Writing Connection

Writing

Trait: Word Choice

Writers include **strong verbs** in their writing to help readers see exactly what is happening.

Read the passage below. Notice how the author Cris Peterson uses strong verbs in her story.

An excerpt from *Wild Horses*

The author uses strong verbs to help us see exactly how the horses moved and looked in this moment. She chose verbs that put specific pictures in our heads so that we can "see" what she wants us to see.

On a miserably cold fall day, huge creaking semi-trailers filled with snorting, stomping steeds finally arrived at the ranch. After hours of coaxing, Dayton succeeded in getting Magnificent Mary to skitter off the trailer. She was a battle-scarred, mean-eyed mare with a nose about twice as long as it should be. The rest of the herd clattered behind her, eyes bulging with fear.

Read and Find

Read Pat's writing below. How did she use strong verbs to help you picture the moment? Use the checklist below to help you.

Flying to Milwaukee

by Pat S.

I gazed out the plane's tiny window. As the plane's engine roared to life, I clutched the armrests and squeezed my eyes shut. The intercom squawked out a final message from our pilot, and the plane picked up speed. As we zoomed down the runway, I felt like a giant hand was pressing me into my seat. I finally peeked out again, and we were soaring high above the city.

Read about Pat's flight.

Writer's Checklist

- [x] Does the writer choose verbs that describe specific actions?
- [x] Does the writer use several **strong verbs** instead of the same verb over and over?
- [ ] Do you get a clear image of the actions as Pat experienced them?

Courage

Talk About It

How are these travelers showing courage?

LOG ON VIEW IT

Oral Language Activities
Courage
www.macmillanmh.com

HISTORY AT YOUR FEET

by *André Melillo*

Vocabulary

sores **amazement**
loosened **midst**
mysterious **responsibility**

Dictionary

Homophones are words that sound the same but have different spellings and meanings. *Sores* and *soars* are homophones. Can you think of other homophones?

"Do I have to go?" Sam asked. "I've got **sores** on my feet from walking so much."

Sam, his sister Kim, and their family were on their way to the Pawnee Indian Village Museum.

Mom gave Sam some bandages to put on his blisters and said, "You'll enjoy learning about the Pawnee nation."

After that, Sam let out a sigh and **loosened** his tight sandal straps. He then dragged himself toward the museum.

Who Were the Pawnee?

The origins of the Pawnee nation are **mysterious** and unknown. In the early 1800s, there were 10,000–30,000 Pawnee living in four separate bands.

"This museum is located where one band of Pawnee settled back in 1820," explained Mom when they got there.

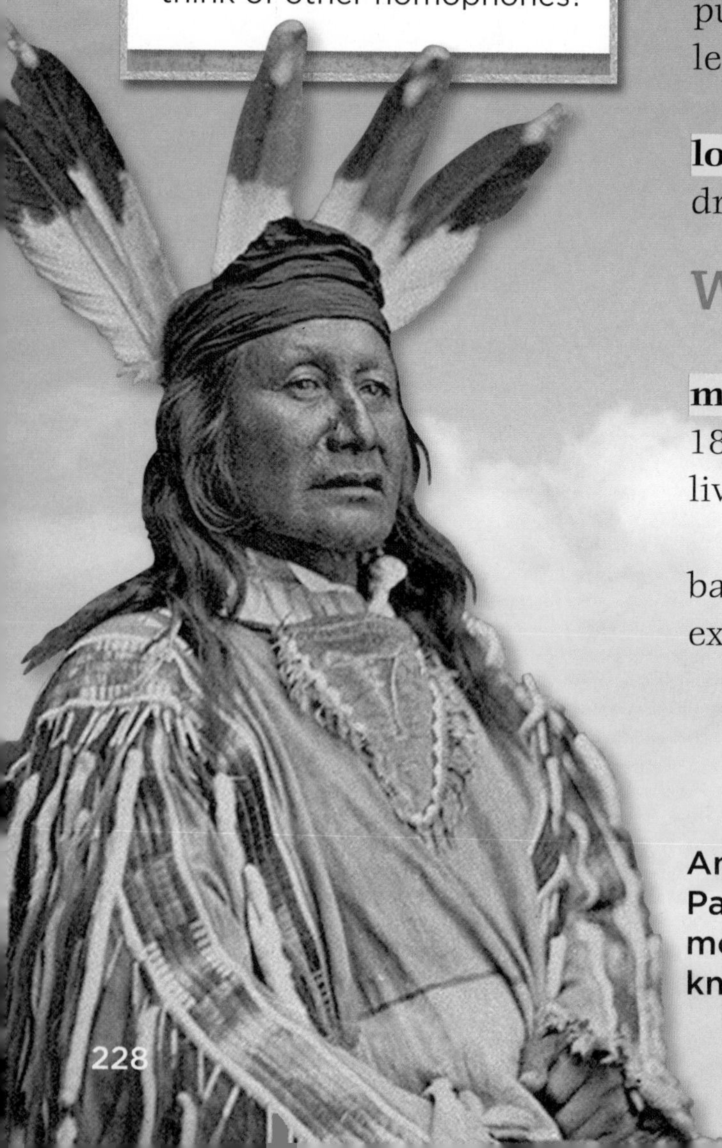

Anikarus Rushing of the Pawnee nation. The Pawnee mostly lived in the area now known as Nebraska.

"And now we're standing exactly where the Pawnee lived!" exclaimed Kim in **amazement**.

"That's right," said Dad. "Here's part of the original floor," he said, pointing. "You can see some burned timbers from the fire that destroyed the village."

What Was Life Like?

Sam had to admit that being in the **midst** of all that history was exciting. "What was it like to live back then?" he wondered aloud.

A museum guide spoke up. "It happens to be my job and **responsibility** to tell you just that. The Pawnee hunted mostly buffalo and used every part of the animals they killed for food or clothing. They let nothing go to waste."

Then Kim said, "Clothing? Buffalo aren't shaped like any clothing I've ever seen."

Everyone chuckled. "They'd sew a patchwork of pieces into warm winter robes and pants," explained the guide.

A battle between the Pawnee and the Konza was painted on this bison hide.

Reread for Comprehension

Analyze Story Structure

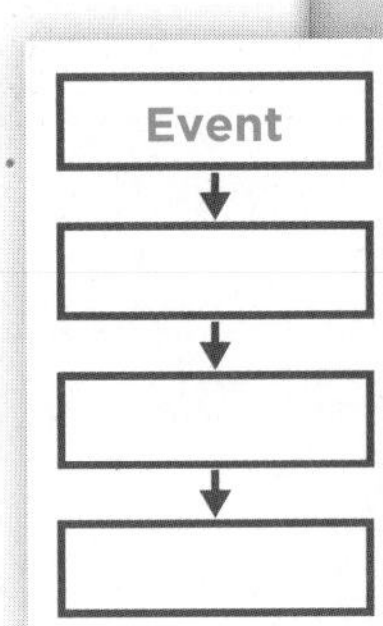

Sequence is the order in which events take place. Time-order words such as *then*, *before*, and *after* are clues to a story's sequence of events. Putting the story's main events in sequence can help you summarize the **plot** and understand the story's structure. Reread the selection. Use your Sequence Chart to help you put events in order.

LOG ON LEARN IT **Comprehension** www.macmillanmh.com

Comprehension

Genre

A **Legend** is a story that has been handed down by people for many years, and that often has some basis in fact.

Analyze Story Structure

Sequence As you read, fill in your Sequence Chart.

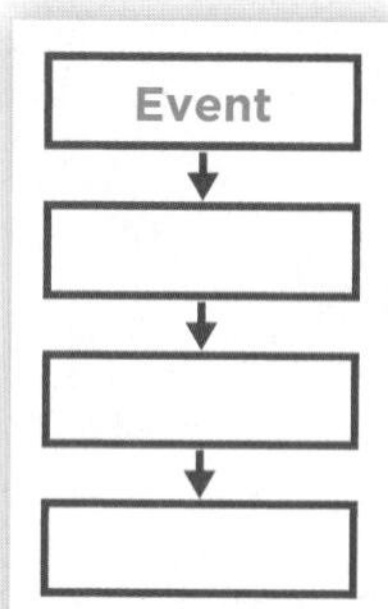

Read to Find Out

What gift does the mystic horse give to the boy and his tribe?

Mystic Horse

written and illustrated by **PAUL GOBLE**

IN THOSE LONG AGO DAYS, when the Pawnee people had harvested their crops of corn and squash, they would leave their earth-lodge villages and travel out on the Great Plains to hunt buffalo. They had horses to ride and to carry their tipis and belongings when they went great distances in search of the wandering herds.

When they were not traveling, and the tipis were pitched, it was the **responsibility** of the older boys, the young men, to look after the herds of horses, and to guard the village. They would stay with the horses at pasture throughout the day, often far away from the camp. All the while they would keep a good lookout for enemies.

Traveling with the people were an old woman and her grandson. They were poor, living alone without any relatives at the edge of the village. Their only shelter was made of sticks and a patchwork of pieces of old tipi covers which people had thrown away. Nobody took much notice of them.

When the people moved from one camping place to another, the old woman and her grandson would stay behind to look for scraps of food, and to pick up discarded clothes. They had no horse. They walked, and what their dogs could not carry, they packed on their own backs. Their life was hard, but they were happy.

One day, as they followed far behind the village, they came upon a sad and sickly worn-out horse standing in the trail. He was terribly thin, with **sores** on his back.

"Grandmother," the boy said, "nobody wants this poor old horse. If we are kind and look after him, he will get well again. He will help us carry our packs! Then I will be able to join the buffalo hunt, and we will have meat, and fresh skins as well!"

And so they led the old horse, limping along behind them. People laughed: "You've got yourself a great warhorse, boy! How will we keep up with you now?"

But the boy loved his horse, and looked after him well.

Sequence
What is the first thing the boy does when he finds the horse?

After some days had passed, the boys who were out on the hills looking after the horses spotted enemies approaching on horseback. They quickly drove the herds back to the safety of the camp. The men grabbed their weapons, mounted their fastest horses, and rode out to meet the enemy.

The boy, riding the poor old horse, followed shyly at a distance. But the men pointed at the horse and laughed: "Look! Here's the one who'll leave us all behind! Boy, that's an old good-for-nothing half-starved horse. You'll be killed. Go back home!"

The boy was ashamed, and rode off to one side where he could not hear their unkind remarks. The horse turned his head and spoke to the boy: "Listen to me! Take me down to the river and cover me with mud." The boy was alarmed to hear him speak, but without hesitation he rode to the river and daubed mud all over his horse.

Then the horse spoke again: "Don't take your bow and arrows. Cut a long willow stick instead. Then ride me, as hard as you can, right into the enemy's **midst** and strike their leader with the stick, and ride back again. Do it four times, and the enemy will be afraid; but do not do it more than four times!"

While the horse was speaking, he was tossing his head, stamping and prancing this way and that, until the boy could hardly hold him back. He **loosened** the reins, and the horse galloped toward the enemy. He was no longer an old sickly worn-out horse! He flew like a hawk, right to where the enemy riders were formed up in line of battle. The boy struck their leader with his willow stick, turned, and rode back to his people with arrows flying past him like angry wasps.

He turned again without stopping, and the horse carried him back to strike another enemy rider. By then his people were cheering loudly. Four times the boy charged back and forth, and each time he hit one of the enemy, just as his horse had told him.

Sequence
Summarize the horse's instructions using time-order words.

The men watched the boy with **amazement**. Now they, too, felt brave enough to follow his example, and they drove the enemy in full retreat from the village. It was like chasing buffalo.

The boy was eager to join the chase. He said to himself: "I have struck four times, and I have not been hurt. I will do it once more." And so, again, he rode after the retreating enemy riders. He whipped another with his stick, but at that very instant his horse was pierced by an arrow, and fell. The horse tried to stand, but he could not.

When the enemy had fled, the men returned and gathered round the boy. His horse was dead. They wanted to touch the horse, for they knew he had been no ordinary one, but a horse with mystic powers.

The leader spoke: "Today this boy has shown that he is braver than all of us. From now on we will call him Piraski Resaru, Boy Chief."

But the boy cried. He was sad for his horse, and angry with himself that he had not done what the **mysterious** horse had told him. He untied the lariat, pulled out the arrow, and carefully wiped away the blood.

He climbed to the top of a nearby hill to mourn. He sat on a rock and pulled his blanket over his head. While he sat there crying, fearsome dark clouds closed across the sky, and it grew dark as if night was falling. Lightning flashed! Thunder shook the hilltop, and it rained with a terrific downpour.

Looking through the downpour, he imagined he saw the dead horse move his legs a little, and that he even tried to lift his head. He wondered if something strange and wonderful was happening. And then he knew it was true: the horse slowly stretched out his front legs, and then stood up!

The boy was a little afraid, but he ran down from the hilltop and clasped his arms round the horse's neck, crying with joy that he was alive again.

The horse spoke softly to him: "Tirawahat, Our Father Above, is good! He has forgiven you. He has let me come back to you."

The storm passed; the rain stopped. All was still and fresh, and the sun shone brilliantly on his beautiful living horse. "Now take me up into the hills, far away from people," the horse told him. "Leave me there for four days, and then come for me."

When the four days had passed, Boy Chief left the village and climbed into the pine tree hills.

A horse neighed, and the mysterious horse appeared, followed by a herd of spirited horses. They surrounded Boy Chief, snorting and stamping excitedly, horses of every color—beautiful bays, chestnuts, shiny blacks, whites, grays, and paints.

Mounted on his mysterious horse, Boy Chief drove the horses round and round the village. He stopped in front of his grandmother's shelter.

"Grandmother," he said, "now you will always have horses! You need never walk again! Choose the ones you want, and give the rest to those who need them most." And so it was done.

After that, the boy and his grandmother rode whenever they moved camp. They lived in a tipi and were not poor any longer. And, just as his grandmother had looked after him when he was young, so he, too, always took good care of her for all her years.

Meet Paul Goble

Paul Goble first became interested in Native Americans when he was a boy growing up in England. He thought their beliefs, art, and tales were wonderful. When Paul grew up, he moved to the western United States to live and learn among the Native Americans. Paul began to write and illustrate books that retold traditional tales. Before writing each book, he carefully researches Native American customs and clothing. He also likes his books to show how people and nature are connected.

Other books by Paul Goble

LOG ON FIND OUT

Author Paul Goble
www.macmillanmh.com

Author's Purpose

Legends often have some basis in fact. Why did Paul Goble write *Mystic Horse*? Use details from the story in your answer.

LOG ON LEARN IT Comprehension
www.macmillanmh.com

Comprehension Check

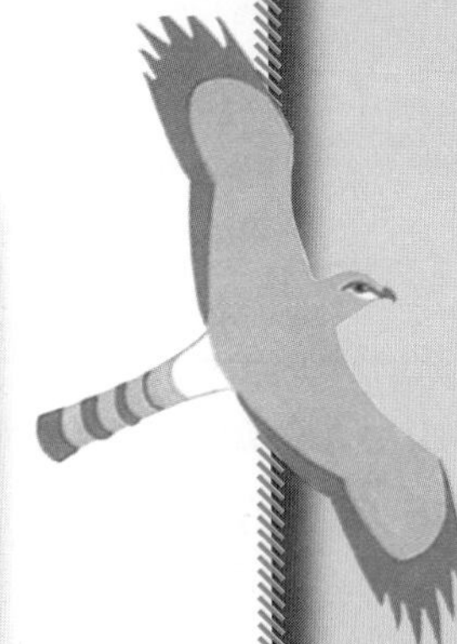

Summarize

To summarize *Mystic Horse* use the most important details from the selection. Information from your Sequence Chart may help you.

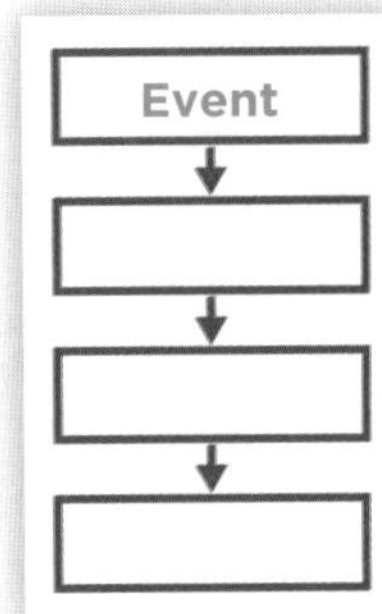

Think and Compare

1. What did the boy find that helped to change his life? Plot
2. Describe the **mysterious** changes that happened to the horse after the boy covered it with mud. Use story details to support your answer. Analyze Story Structure: Sequence
3. Why did the boy ignore the horse's directions? Explain using story details. Make Inferences
4. Is the narrator of this story first or third person? Why did the author choose this point of view? Author's Purpose
5. Read "Who Were the Pawnee?" on pages 228–229 and pages 233–234 of *Mystic Horse*. What do both selections teach the reader about Pawnee life? Reading/Writing Across Texts

Social Studies

Genre

Expository texts, such as **almanacs**, have information, facts, and figures about many different subjects.

Text Feature

Charts present a large amount of information, such as names, places, and numbers, in a compact way.

Content Vocabulary

relays	**frontier**
intervals	**telegraph**

The Pony Express

by Beatriz Santiago

The Pony Express used riders on horseback to deliver mail. Although the Pony Express lasted only a short time, it was one of the most colorful and exciting parts of American history.

A Need for Speed

Many people went west in the late 1800s to seek their fortune. Some of the travelers decided to stay and make their homes there. These new settlers needed a faster way to communicate across the country for both business and pleasure. At this time, the quickest way to move mail west was on John Butterfield's stagecoach line. Butterfield's stagecoaches went west from Missouri, south to El Paso, Texas, then west to San Diego, and north to San Francisco. This route took about 25 days to complete.

The most famous Pony Express rider was Bill Cody, later known as Buffalo Bill.

Ads for Pony Express riders called for young, skinny, expert riders under the age of 18, who were willing to risk death on a daily basis.

A Mail Solution

William Hepburn Russell came up with an idea for a faster way to deliver mail. He believed that young men riding fast horses across the center of the country on **relays** could make the journey in just ten days! Relay stations would provide fresh horses every ten miles. The rider would switch to a fresh horse, taking only his *mochila*, or mail bag. The riders would also switch every 50 to 100 miles.

Russell and his partners mapped out a trail from St. Joseph, Missouri, to Sacramento, California. The route would take riders through Kansas, Nebraska, Colorado, Wyoming, Utah, and Nevada. The founders built 190 stations along the trail at ten-mile **intervals**. They bought over 400 horses and hired about 80 young men as riders.

National Historic Trails

Reading a Chart

Almanacs often have tables and charts that list facts and other information. Use this chart to find the lengths and locations of some of the United States' most famous historic trails.

Name	Location (by state)	Total Mileage
Lewis and Clark	Iowa, Idaho, Illinois, Kansas, Missouri, Montana, Nebraska, North Dakota, Oregon, South Dakota, Washington	3,700
Old Spanish Trail	Arizona, California, Colorado, Nevada, New Mexico, Utah	2,700
Trail of Tears	Alabama, Arkansas, Georgia, Illinois, Kentucky, Missouri, North Carolina, Oklahoma, Tennessee	2,200
Pony Express	California, Colorado, Kansas, Missouri, Nebraska, Nevada, Utah, Wyoming	1,800
El Camino Real de Tierra Adentro	New Mexico, Texas	404

The Pony Express Riders

The average age of the riders was 22. They received a salary of $25.00 a week, which was a lot of money in those days. Pony riders faced many hardships and dangers, such as snowstorms, hot deserts, and flooded rivers. They always rode alone.

Because their job was so dangerous, riders were very much admired. Newspapers published stories about them. People wrote poems and songs about their courage. They became heroes of the **frontier**. Some of the earliest riders were James Randall, Johnny Fry, and Billy Hamilton.

Mail Service in Ten Days

On April 3, 1860, a large crowd gathered in St. Joseph, Missouri. They cheered as the first rider galloped off with the mail pouch that would arrive in California just ten days later. Another mail carrier headed east from Sacramento at the same time.

From the beginning, the Pony Express did exactly what it promised—it delivered the mail in just ten days!

The End of the Pony Express

When the transcontinental **telegraph** lines were completed on October 24, 1861, it marked the end of the Pony Express. The telegraph could send messages across the country in seconds. Even so, people in the west felt sad. The Pony Express connected the young country in newer, faster ways and showed how Americans could work together. It will always be remembered as an important part of our country's past.

Connect and Compare

1. Look at the chart of National Historic Trails on page 254. Which historic trail is shorter than the Pony Express? How long is that trail, and what is its location? **Reading a Chart**
2. Describe how the author organized the information in the article. **Apply**
3. Think about this article and *Mystic Horse*. How were Pony Express riders similar to the grandson in *Mystic Horse*? Use details to support your answer. **Reading/Writing Across Texts**

RESEARCH INQUIRY

Social Studies Activity

Use reference books or the Internet to research and find one of the poems written about Pony Express riders. Use it as a model to create your own poem about a figure from the Old West.

LOG ON FIND OUT **Social Studies** Pony Express
www.macmillanmh.com

Writing

Trait: Word Choice

Writers include **strong verbs and descriptive details** to help readers visualize actions.

Reading and Writing Connection

Read the passage below. Notice how the author Paul Goble uses strong verbs and descriptive details in his story.

An excerpt from *Mystic Horse*

While the horse was speaking, he was tossing his head, stamping and prancing this way and that, until the boy could hardly hold him back. He loosened the reins, and the horse galloped toward the enemy. He was no longer an old sickly worn-out horse! He flew like a hawk, right to where the enemy riders were formed up in line of battle. The boy struck their leader with his willow stick, turned, and rode back to his people with arrows flying past him like angry wasps.

The author uses strong verbs and details to help us see the action. They help us picture exactly how the boy and the horse looked and moved.

Read and Find

Read Darryl's writing below. How did he use strong verbs and descriptive details to help you picture the moment? Use the checklist below to help you.

Read about Darryl's creepy crawler.

Watching a Spider

by Darryl D.

As I lay in bed last night, I saw a spider creeping across my wall. It scurried forward a few inches at a time, froze, then scrambled on a little farther. When it arrived at my desk, it hopped down and began to spin a web. It seemed to slide down an invisible pole as it dropped to the ground.

Writer's Checklist

- [x] Does the writer choose **strong verbs** that describe specific actions?
- [x] Does the writer use **descriptive details** in his writing to help the reader see what is happening?
- [ ] Do you get a clear image of the action as Darryl experienced it?

Review

Cause and Effect
Sequence
Main Idea and Details
Prefixes and Suffixes
Chart

READING FOR MISTER PAREDO

Benito knocked quietly on the door to Mr. Paredo's room. There was no answer.

"Fantastic," thought Benito. "I can just go home." When he turned to leave, a nurse caught his eye.

"You better knock louder than that," she said. "Mr. Paredo has a difficult time hearing."

Benito sighed and knocked again. A gruff voice shouted, "What is it?"

He opened the door. An old man lay in the bed. He looked feeble and exhausted, but his deep blue eyes were still dynamic. "What do you want?" he asked.

"Um, I'm the reader," Benito began. "The school sent me to help you, um, read."

Mr. Paredo didn't say anything for a long time. He just stared. At last he muttered, "Well, what are you going to read?"

Benito took a step closer to the bed. He took off his backpack and started rummaging through it. "I didn't know what you would like," he said. "So I brought a bunch of stuff. I have today's newspaper—"

"I hate the news," said Mr. Paredo. "It's always unpleasant."

"I also have a sports magazine."

"No. My team always loses."

As Benito was taking the books out of his backpack, a magazine fell out. It landed on the bed, hitting Mr. Paredo right on the leg. He flinched and his blue eyes looked furious. "What was that?" he asked.

"I'm sorry," said Benito as he hurried to put it away.

"Wait," said Mr. Paredo, grabbing Benito's wrist before he could take the magazine. "Is that a comic book?"

"I'm sorry," repeated Benito. "It's mine. I just got it. I didn't mean to hit you with it."

"I love comics," said Mr. Paredo, smiling for the first time. He held the cover very close to his face so he could read the title. "I used to read them all the time. Now my eyes won't let me."

"You like comics?" asked Benito. "If you want, I can read it to you." Mr. Paredo was silent. "Don't worry. I'll describe the pictures so you can almost see them."

"Okay," said Mr. Paredo.

At first, Benito felt unprepared. It was hard to read the words and describe the pictures at the same time. Mr. Paredo would interrupt with so many questions. He wanted to know every detail, from the color of someone's hair to the shape of the speech balloons. But soon Benito became an expert. His descriptions grew longer and more elaborate. When he finished, Benito felt like he had never read one of his comic books more thoroughly.

"I can come back on Saturday if you want. I have more comics," he said.

"Great!" said Mr. Paredo. He smiled as Benito left.

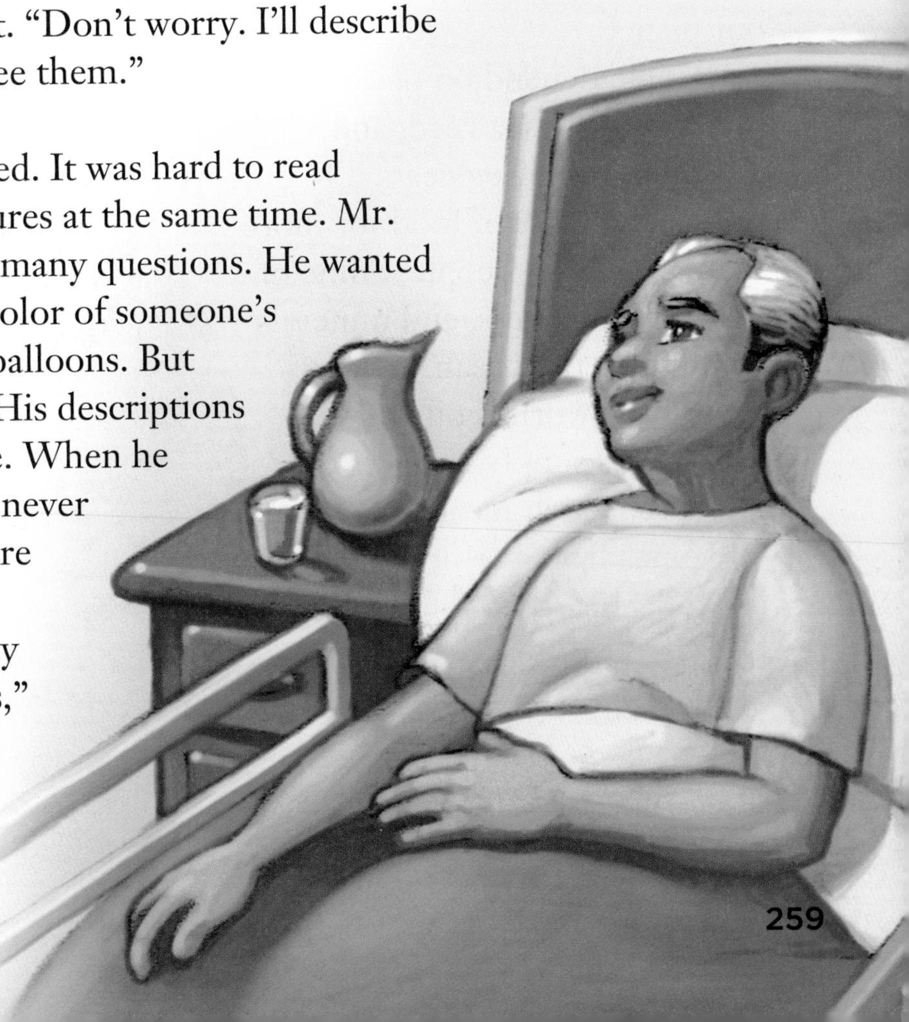

Protect Our Valuable OCEANS

When astronauts look down at Earth from space, they see a beautiful blue world. Oceans cover more than 70% of our planet. Earth has five oceans. They are the Pacific, Atlantic, Indian, Arctic, and Southern oceans. These oceans are important to us and our planet.

People depend on oceans for survival. Fish, seaweed, and shellfish all come from the ocean. They are the main source of food for more than 3.5 billion people. Some of our salt, fertilizers, and minerals come from the ocean. A great deal of the world's oil and natural gas supply is drilled offshore, which means the oil comes from the ocean, beneath the ocean floor.

Oceans also provide us with transportation. Many cities have ferries, which people use to get to work every morning. Freight and fuel also travel by boat. Oil tankers transport 60% of the oil used by the world. Ships also carry clothes, toys, and other goods you see in stores.

About 21 million barrels of oil run into the oceans each year from street runoff, factory waste, and ships flushing their tanks.

Chart of Ocean Facts

Oceans	Area	Length of Coastline	Elevation Lowest Point
Atlantic Ocean	76.762 million sq km	111,866 km	-8,605 m
Pacific Ocean	155.557 million sq km	135,663 km	-10,924 m
Indian Ocean	68.556 million sq km	66,526 km	-7,258 m
Arctic Ocean	14.056 million sq km	45,389 km	-4,665 m
Southern Ocean	20.327 million sq km	17,968 km	-7,235 m

Use this chart to find facts about the different sizes of oceans and their coastlines.

Even though our oceans do so much for us, we have not been taking care of them. Water pollution is a big problem because it kills many kinds of sea creatures. Some of this pollution results from things people dump into the ocean. For example, cruise ships and cargo ships dump waste into the ocean every day. Other pollution comes from factories and power plants dumping their waste into rivers. The rivers carry this waste to the oceans.

It is not just the dumping of waste into oceans that harms them. For example, nitrogen, a chemical in fertilizers, is carried to the oceans as runoff. As water "runs off" the ground, it flows into our streams and rivers, which carry it to the sea.

Pollutants, such as nitrogen, can cause problems in the ocean and serious imbalances in nature. Nitrogen reduces the amount of oxygen in the ocean; less oxygen can kill some sea animals or cause diseases. Too much nitrogen can produce large amounts of algae, tiny plants that grow in the water, which can hurt other plants and animals.

Luckily there are things we can do to protect oceans. A good start is to learn about them. Another thing we can do is get rid of waste properly. Finally, we can ask our government to get involved by passing more laws to help stop pollution. Oceans are an important part of our world, and we have to take care of them.

Show What You Know

Comprehension

Stated or Implied Purpose

- In expository selections, such as magazine articles, an author states or implies his or her purpose.
- Stated purpose: The author states his or her reason for writing the article. You will be able to find a sentence that ties all the ideas of the article together.
- Implied purpose: You will find ideas in the text and see how they are all connected. You will not find a sentence in the text that ties all of these ideas together.
- Read a magazine article. Explain if the purpose is stated or implied. Use details from the article to support your answer.

Genre

Persuasive Writing

- Persuasive writing states the author's point of view. It uses language to influence, or convince, people to think a certain way about something.
- With a partner, reread "The Ride of His Life" on page 191. What is the author's opinion of Alejandro Abor and the handcycles that he builds?
- Identify the persuasive language the author uses to talk about Alejandro Abor. Explain how these words and phrases influence the reader to think a certain way.

Word Study

Idioms

- An idiom is a phrase that cannot be figured out by knowing the meaning of each word. For example: "Stop pulling my leg" has nothing to do with a person's leg. Instead it means, "Stop trying to make me believe something that is not true."
- With a partner, use a dictionary and online resources to help you figure out the meanings of these idioms:

  raining cats and dogs
  break the news
  all in the same boat

- Then use each idiom in a sentence.

Prefixes and Suffixes

- Prefixes added to the beginning of a base word or root change the meaning of the word. Here are the meanings of some common Greek and Latin prefixes that can help you figure out the meanings of unfamiliar words.

  pre- "before"   **sub-** "under"
  post- "after"   **trans-** "across"

- Suffixes added to the end of a base word or root change the meaning of the word. Here are some common Greek and Latin suffixes.

  -able "capable of"   **-fy** "to make or become"
  -logy "science of"   **-ician** "a specialist in"

- Use four of the prefixes and suffixes to form words. Write each word and use a dictionary to look up its definition.

Unit 3
The Power of Words

The Big Question

How can words be powerful?

LOG ON VIEW IT

Theme Video
The Power of Words
www.macmillanmh.com

How can words be powerful?

Most people communicate with one another using words. Think about how often in a day you read, speak, or listen to words. Words, spoken or written, are powerful tools. We can use them to change a person's mind, to explain something, or to entertain others. Throughout history, words have helped create great changes. The words in the Declaration of Independence, the Gettysburg Address, and Martin Luther King, Jr.'s "I Have a Dream" speech have helped change the world.

Learning about the power of words can help you understand how important words and communication have been throughout history. It can help you choose your words more carefully, and it can encourage you to speak up in certain situations.

Research Activities

For this unit you will create a piece of writing that tells about a person whose words inspire you. Your writing needs to tell your audience why this person inspires you. Set your purposes for reading and research people who have made famous speeches. Write about one of them and tell how that person inspired your writing.

Keep Track of Ideas

As you read, keep track of all you are learning about the power of words. Use the **Study Book Foldable** to organize your ideas. On the front panel, write the Unit Theme: *The Power of Words.* On each of the next panels, write the facts you learn each week that will help you in your research and in your understanding of the Unit Theme.

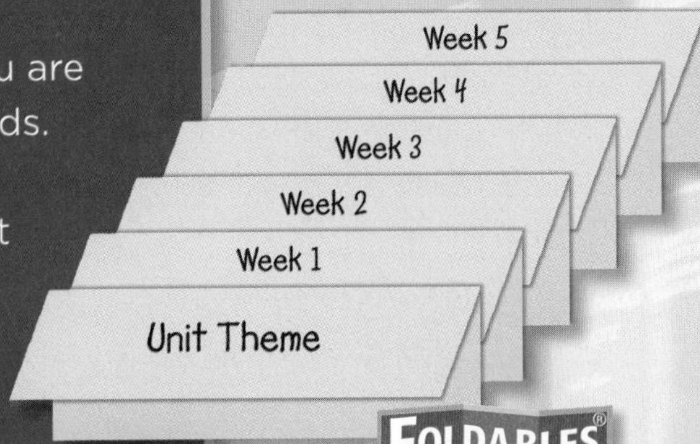

FOLDABLES®
Study Organizer

Digital Learning

LOG ON FIND OUT www.macmillanmh.com

StudentWorks Plus™
Interactive Student Book

- **Research Roadmap**
  Follow a step-by-step guide to complete your research project.

Online Resources

- Topic Finder and Other Research Tools
- Videos and Virtual Field Trips
- Photos and Drawings for Presentations
- Related Articles and Web Resources
- Web Site Links

People and Places

The Franklin Public Library

America's first public library was started in Franklin, Massachusetts, in 1781. Benjamin Franklin donated books to the town and the citizens decided that these books would be lent to the public free of charge.

Letters

Talk About It

In what ways do letters help you express yourself?

LOG ON VIEW IT

Oral Language Activities
Letters
www.macmillanmh.com

Vocabulary

weekdays
slithered
apologize
genuine
harmless
ambulance

Word Parts

Base Words can help you figure out the meaning of a word.

harm = "hurt"; injure

harmless = "without hurt"

NAME THAT REPTILE

by Catherine Lutz

Narrator: Mark and Jean have been studying together **weekdays** after school for a big test on Friday. Jean takes a card from a cardboard box. The card has the name of a reptile on it. Now Mark will ask questions and try to name the reptile. Can you guess the answer before Mark?

Mark: Is it furry?

Jean: No. Remember, reptiles don't have fur.

Mark: That's right. Where does it live?

Jean: Mostly in the southwestern United States.

Mark: What does it eat?

Jean: It eats small birds, rabbits, mice, and squirrels.

Mark: Is it a crocodile?

Jean: No. Crocodiles live near streams, and this reptile lives where it's dry.

Mark: How big is it?

Jean: Some can be 7 feet long. Others are only 2 feet long.

Mark: It's probably not a turtle or a lizard. Is it a snake?

Jean: Yes!

Is it a crocodile?

Mark: Remember when my pet snake got loose? It **slithered** slowly across my mother's foot. As it slid over her foot, she screamed. Then she stood on a chair until I caught it. I had to return it to the pet store.

Jean: Did you **apologize** to your mom and say you were sorry? Was it a sincere and **genuine** apology?

Mark: Yes. I told her I was really sorry, but she didn't change her mind.

Jean: Okay, back to studying.

Mark: Does the snake crush its prey?

Jean: No.

Mark: So it's not a python. Is it **harmless**?

Jean: No. It's dangerous. Its bite can be fatal. If you get bitten, you'd need an **ambulance** to drive you to the hospital!

Mark: Yikes. Does it give a warning before it attacks?

Jean: Its tail shakes and makes noise. Each time the snake sheds, its tail gets a new segment in it.

Mark: I've got it! It's a rattlesnake!

Narrator: Did you guess the reptile before Mark did?

It's a rattlesnake!

Reread for Comprehension

Generate Questions

Make Inferences When you make inferences, you use story clues to understand what is not directly stated in the story. You can also use any prior knowledge you have connected to the story. Generating questions as you read can help you make inferences about the characters and the changes they undergo. Reread the story and fill in your Inferences Web.

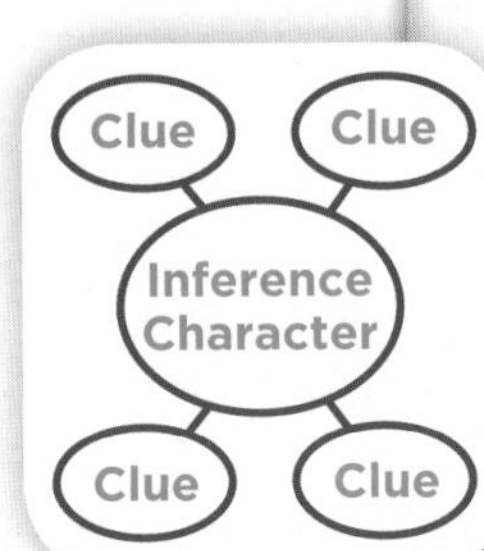

LOG ON LEARN IT **Comprehension**
www.macmillanmh.com

Comprehension

Genre

Humor can be found in both fiction and nonfiction selections. Humorous fiction is a made-up story written to make the reader laugh.

Generate Questions

Make Inferences

As you read, fill in your Inferences Web.

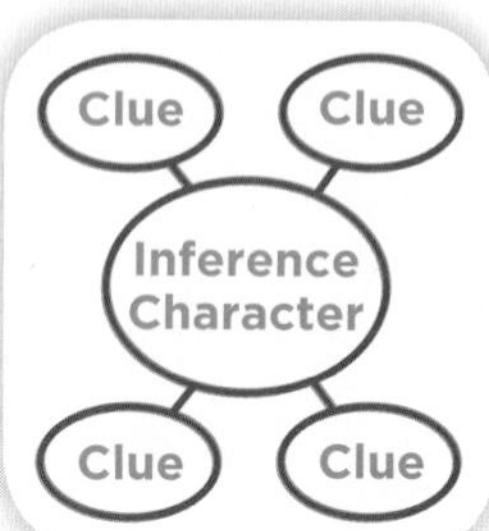

Read to Find Out

What do you learn when you read between the lines?

When I Went to the Library

by Ken Roberts

illustrated by Nicole E. Wong

Dear Mr. Winston,

My parents said that I have to write and **apologize**. Dad says he is going to read this letter before it's sent and that I'd better make sure my apology sounds truly **genuine**. So, I am truly, genuinely sorry for bringing that snake into the library yesterday.

My parents say that what I did was wrong, even though the cardboard box was shut, most of the time, and there was no way that snake could have escaped if you hadn't opened the box and dropped it on the floor.

My parents say it's my fault for having brought that snake into the library and I truly, genuinely apologize but I still don't know how I was supposed to find out what kind of snake I had inside that box without bringing the snake right into the library so I could look at snake pictures and then look at the snake and try to find a picture that matched the snake.

I told my parents something that I didn't get a chance to remind you about before the **ambulance** took you away. I did come into the library without the snake, first. I left the box outside, hidden under a bush and tried to borrow a thick green book with lots of snake pictures. You told me that the big green book was a reference book which meant that it had to stay inside the library and I couldn't take it out, even for ten minutes.

My parents say I still shouldn't have brought that snake into the library and that I have to be truly, genuinely sorry if I ever hope to watch Galactic Patrol on television again. My parents picked Galactic Patrol because it's my favorite show, although I'm not sure what not watching a television program has to do with bringing a snake into the library.

The people at the library say you hate snakes so much that you won't even touch a book with a picture of snakes on the cover and that is why you won't be back at the library for a few more weeks. If you want, you could watch Galactic Patrol. It's on at 4:00 P.M. **weekdays**, on channel 7. There are no snakes on the show because it takes place in space.

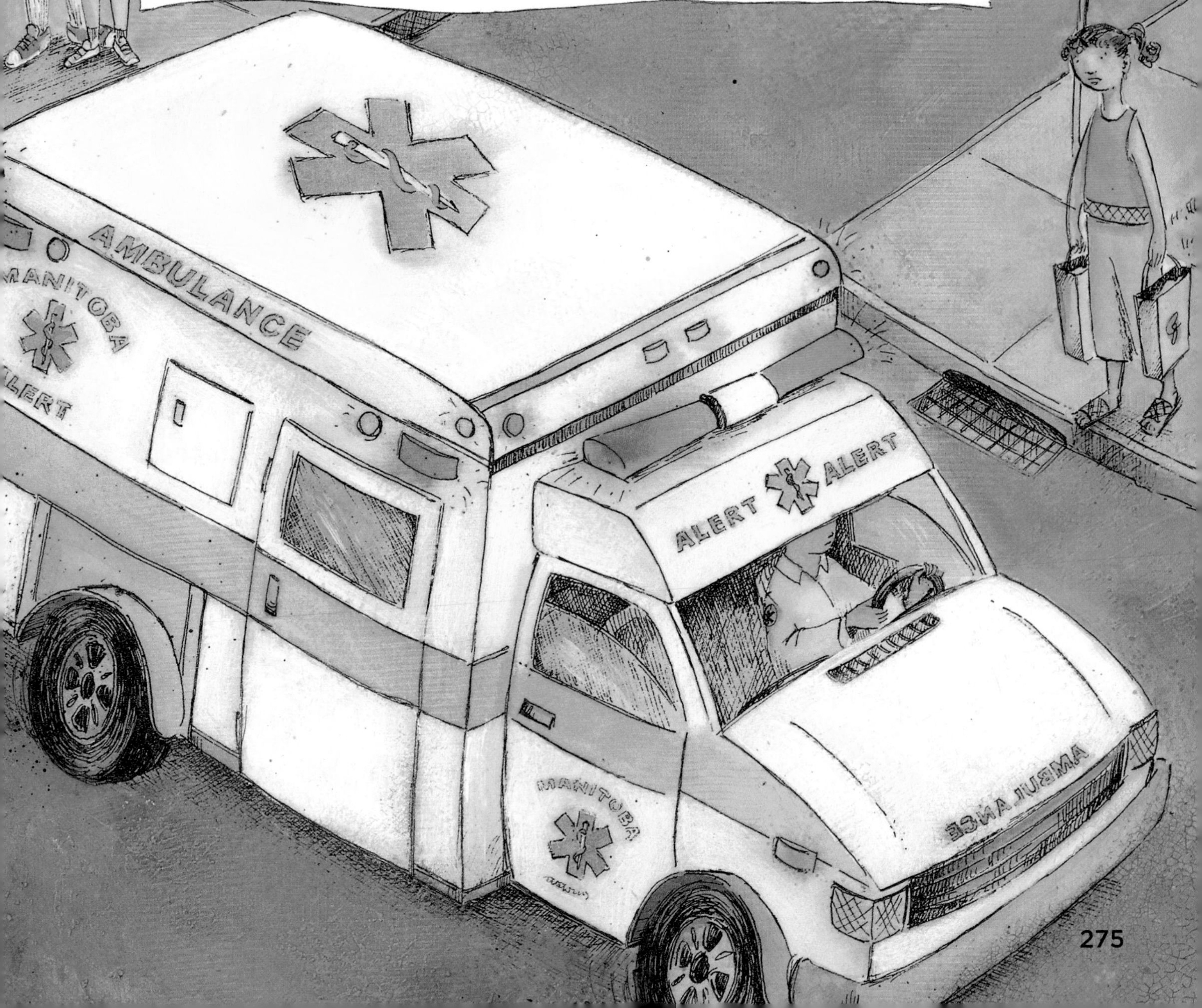

LIBRARY

Did the flowers arrive? Dad picked them out but I have to pay for them with my allowance for the next two months. The flowers are proof that I am truly, genuinely sorry for having brought that snake into the library. I hope the people who work at the library find that snake soon! Did they look under all the chairs?

That snake isn't dangerous. It is a local snake, and there are no poisonous snakes in Manitoba. The people at the library say you know that too because that was one of the reasons you decided to move here. I bought that snake from a friend. I paid one month's allowance for it, which means that snake has cost me a total of three months' allowance and I only owned it for one hour!

Mom says I don't have to tell who sold me that snake so I won't tell you either because Dad says he is going to read this letter. Besides, I don't want you to be mad at anyone else when I am the one who brought that snake into the library yesterday. I am truly, genuinely sorry.

Make Inferences

How can you tell that the girl writing the letter is not truly sorry? Use details from the story to explain your answer.

I want you to know that I didn't plan to show you that snake. I didn't mean to scare you at all. I knew where the big green snake book was kept. I put the box on a table close to the book and tried to find the right picture. I looked at a picture, then at the snake, at another picture, and then the snake. I did that five times and can tell you that the snake inside the library is not a python, a rattlesnake, an anaconda, an asp, or a cobra.

Anyway, I was surprised when you wanted to see what was inside the box because I didn't ask for any help and there were plenty of people in the library who did need help.

Dad says that the fact that I said, "Nothing," instead of "A snake," is proof that I knew I was doing something wrong when I brought that snake into the library. I am truly, genuinely sorry even though my friend Jake Lambert promised me that the snake I bought from him is perfectly **harmless**.

M-N
O-P

I did tell you that I didn't need any help and I did have a snake book open in front of me, so I don't know why you insisted on looking inside the box if you are so afraid of snakes and everything. I don't know why you picked up that box before opening a flap, either. If you had left the box on the table and maybe even sat down next to it, then maybe the box would have been all right when you screamed and fainted. You wouldn't have fallen so far, either, if you were sitting down.

Did you know that you broke out in a rash after you fainted? I thought a person had to touch something like poison ivy to get a rash. I didn't know it was possible to get a rash by just thinking about something but my parents say it really can happen. I think maybe you did touch something. Maybe, when you were lying on the floor, that snake **slithered** over to you and touched you! Did you know that snake skin feels dry, not wet and slimy at all?

Make Inferences
Explain how the girl is not taking responsibility for what happened to Mr. Winston.

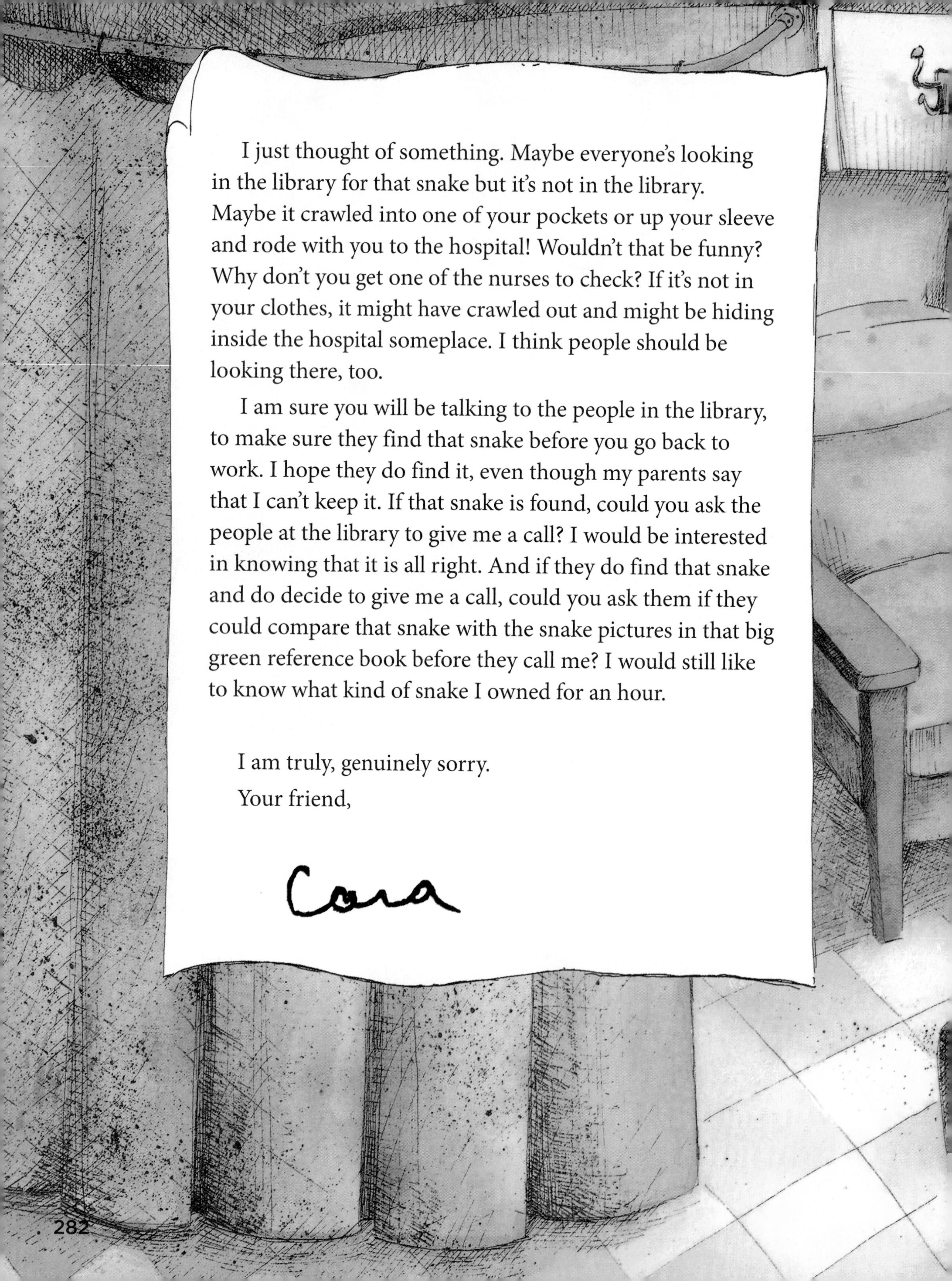

I just thought of something. Maybe everyone's looking in the library for that snake but it's not in the library. Maybe it crawled into one of your pockets or up your sleeve and rode with you to the hospital! Wouldn't that be funny? Why don't you get one of the nurses to check? If it's not in your clothes, it might have crawled out and might be hiding inside the hospital someplace. I think people should be looking there, too.

I am sure you will be talking to the people in the library, to make sure they find that snake before you go back to work. I hope they do find it, even though my parents say that I can't keep it. If that snake is found, could you ask the people at the library to give me a call? I would be interested in knowing that it is all right. And if they do find that snake and do decide to give me a call, could you ask them if they could compare that snake with the snake pictures in that big green reference book before they call me? I would still like to know what kind of snake I owned for an hour.

I am truly, genuinely sorry.

Your friend,

Cara

MR. WINSTON

Identify the Author and Illustrator

Ken Roberts is actually a librarian. He often writes funny stories with unusual characters, like the girl in this piece. Ken has many talents. He is a storyteller, puppeteer, juggler, and magician. He was once a champion runner, too.

Nicole E. Wong has been interested in art all her life and even went to college to study it. She has been very fortunate to have turned her passion and training into her career in illustration. Nicole's artwork has appeared in several books, including Jan Wahl's *Candy Shop*, and various magazines. Nicole lives in Massachusetts with her husband, Dan, and their dog, Sable.

Another book illustrated by Nicole E. Wong

LOG ON ▶ FIND OUT

Author Ken Roberts
Illustrator Nicole E. Wong
www.macmillanmh.com

Author's Purpose

Why did Ken Roberts write this story in the form of a letter? Identify whether he wrote the story using the first- or third-person point of view.

LOG ON LEARN IT Comprehension
www.macmillanmh.com

Comprehension Check

Summarize

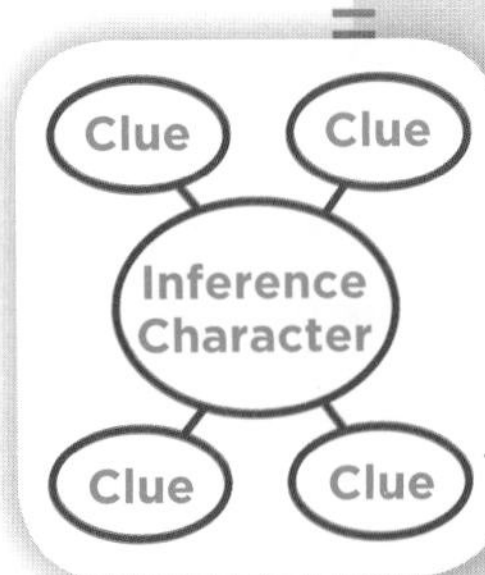

To summarize *When I Went to the Library* use the most important details from the selection. Information from your Inferences Web may help you.

Think and Compare

1. Who told Cara that she had to **apologize** to Mr. Winston? Details
2. According to Cara, what was one of the reasons Mr. Winston decided to move to Manitoba? Cause and Effect
3. Describe how Cara feels about apologizing to Mr. Winston. Explain using details from the story. Generate Questions: Make Inferences
4. Why did the author tell the story from Cara's perspective? Author's Purpose
5. Read "Name That Reptile" on pages 270–271. How do Mark's mother and Mr. Winston feel about snakes? Use details from both selections. Reading/Writing Across Texts

Find Snakes

Science

Genre

Expository selections, such as **electronic encyclopedia articles**, include facts, diagrams, and photographs on many topics.

Text Features

Toolbars and **Guide Words** help you find more information or move to a related topic in an electronic encyclopedia.

Content Vocabulary

reptiles	**hibernate**
camouflage	**digested**

▼ article outline

Snakes

Physical Characteristics

Snakes are **reptiles**. They have flexible skeletons and no legs. Their bodies are covered with scales. Clear scales even cover their eyes. Most snakes are colored to **camouflage** them. For example, the emerald tree boa is green. This helps it hide among tree leaves. Other snakes, like coral snakes, are brightly colored to warn enemies that they are poisonous. Snakes range greatly in size. The dwarf blind snake is 10 cm (about 4 in.) long. The anaconda and reticulated python can be as long as 10 m (about 33 ft).

Timber rattlesnakes (*crotalus horridus*), northeastern United States

Behavior

Like all reptiles, snakes are cold-blooded. They cannot make their own body heat. Snakes need the sun or warm surroundings to keep them warm. In cool weather, many snakes gather underground or in other sheltered places. There they **hibernate**, meaning they stay at rest during the winter.

Printers

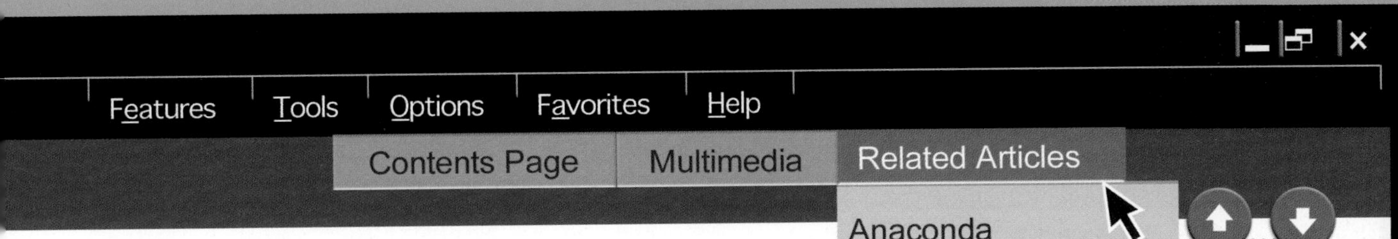

Using a Toolbar

Click on the Related Articles pull-down menu and use the guide words to select the subject about which you want to learn more.

Coral Snake a kind of poisonous snake found in North and South America. There are about 30 species. Coral snakes all have bright bands of color on their bodies and are two to three feet in length. They hunt lizards and other snakes.

Anaconda a member of the boa family living in swamps and rivers in South America. The anaconda, like other boas, wraps itself around its prey to suffocate it. It is one of the longest and thickest snakes. It also bears live young.

Coral snake

Find Snakes

Printers

Hunting and Eating

Egg-eater snake (*Dasyreptis scabra*), savannah, South Africa

Snakes are meat eaters but do not chew their prey. They swallow animals whole. Snakes can stretch their jaws far apart. This lets them eat animals that are bigger than their own heads.

Constrictors, such as boa constrictors, wrap themselves around their prey. These snakes suffocate their prey and then swallow it. Some snakes are venomous and kill their prey with poison. Venomous snakes, such as rattlesnakes, inject the poison through their fangs. Some poisons kill the animal. Others break down the animal's flesh so that it is partly **digested** by the time the snake eats it.

Cobra hatching

Raising Young

Most female snakes lay eggs that have soft, leathery shells. Some females stay close to guard the eggs. Others, such as pythons, coil around the eggs to keep them warm. Some snakes give birth to live babies. Garter snakes can have more than 40 baby snakes at once. Snakes do not usually take care of their young.

Features Tools Options Favorites Help

Contents Page | Multimedia | Related Articles

Boa Constrictor
Garter Snake
Python
Rattlesnake

Garter Snake a common and harmless type of snake in North America. They are fairly small (about two feet long) and usually have dark colors, with stripes running along their bodies. They live in moist areas and feed on toads, frogs, earthworms, and similar animals.

Connect and Compare

1. Look at the Related Articles menu on this page. Explain what guide word you would click on if you were researching venomous snakes. **Using a Toolbar and Guide Words**

2. Constrictors often hunt animals that have sharp teeth, claws, or hooves. Why would they need to kill their prey before swallowing it? **Apply**

3. Think about this article and *When I Went to the Library*. Which of the snakes discussed in this selection would not make a good pet for Cara? Explain using details from both selections. **Reading/Writing Across Texts**

Science Activity

Research a snake's life cycle and its habitat. Write a letter to a friend telling the interesting facts you learned about the snake. Don't forget to include the date on your letter.

LOG ON FIND OUT **Science** Snakes
www.macmillanmh.com

Writing

Trait: Ideas

Good writers use **facts**, **details**, and **explanations** to support their ideas and opinions.

Reading and Writing Connection

Read the passage below. Notice the details the author chose to include in the narrator's explanation.

An excerpt from *When I Went to the Library*

Mom says I don't have to tell who sold me that snake so I won't tell you either because Dad says he is going to read this letter. Besides, I don't want you to be mad at anyone else when I am the one who brought that snake into the library yesterday. I am truly, genuinely sorry.

I want you to know that I didn't plan to show you that snake. I didn't mean to scare you at all.

The author uses supporting details to explain why Cara is not saying who sold her the snake. These details show Cara does not want anyone to get into trouble.

Read and Find

Read Becky's writing below. What supporting details does she use to describe her dinner? Use the checklist below to help you.

Yuck!

by Becky L.

I didn't want to hurt my aunt's feelings. She had cooked my favorite recipe for pasta primavera. I took a big bite. It was awful—a mushy mass in my mouth! I drank a big gulp of milk and managed to swallow it. Luckily, Scampy, her round little dog, came waddling by. I put a forkful in my napkin and offered it to him under the table. Scampy sniffed the pasta and then waddled away.

Read about Becky's mushy mass.

Writer's Checklist

- ☑ What is the writer's opinion or idea?
- ☑ What supporting **details** does the writer give?
- ☐ What descriptive words show her opinion?

The Art of Persuasion

Talk About It

How is this dog using persuasion?

LOG ON VIEW IT

Oral Language Activities
The Art of Persuasion
www.macmillanmh.com

Vocabulary

neglected **desperate**
appreciated **endured**
misunderstood **obedience**

Word Parts

Prefixes are added to the beginnings of words to change their meanings.
mis- = "badly" or "wrongly"
misunderstood = "wrongly understood"

Puppy Trouble

by Lana Engell

We got back from the grocery store and found the house a mess. I had **neglected** to close the bathroom door again, and because of my forgetfulness, our Saint Bernard, Bernie, had left chewed toilet paper all over the house. Bernie was happily running in circles. He had no idea that what he had done while we were away was not liked or **appreciated**.

Bernie had already chewed Mom's favorite handbag and my new shoes. He had spread garbage throughout the house and pawed the furniture. Mom didn't like that, because she's very neat. Mom was also concerned about Bernie jumping on people when I took him out for walks. She was afraid he might scare somebody.

Mom said that if Bernie didn't start behaving, we couldn't keep him, and I knew Mom wasn't bluffing. I could also tell she wasn't kidding. Her message was clear, so there was no way it could be **misunderstood**. Bernie was in trouble again.

I was **desperate**. If I didn't think of something really fast, I was going to lose my dog!

Then I had a really wonderful idea. It meant I would have to give up watching some of my favorite TV shows to spend more time with Bernie. In the end, though, if I could keep him, it was worth a try.

Just then Mom finished putting the groceries away. She came into the living room and saw the mess.

"I've had it with this puppy," Mom said in a tired voice. "I'm just about out of patience, Lin."

"I know, Mom," I said. "You've **endured** Bernie's chewing and messes for three long months now. But I've never had a pet before. If I'm not training him correctly, then it's not Bernie's fault. Can we take him to **obedience** school?" I asked.

And that's just what we did.

Reread for Comprehension

Generate Questions

Draw Conclusions Generating questions can help you draw conclusions about what happens in the **plot** of a story. When you draw conclusions, you use information from the story as well as your own experiences connected to the story to understand the characters and events of the plot. Reread the story and use your Conclusions Chart to keep track of your conclusions.

Text Clues	Conclusion

LOG ON LEARN IT **Comprehension** **www.macmillanmh.com**

Dear

Comprehension

Genre

A **Fantasy** is a story about characters and settings that could not exist in real life.

Generate Questions

Draw Conclusions

As you read, fill in your Conclusions Chart.

Text Clues	Conclusion

Read to Find Out

How close to reality are the events Ike is describing in his letters to Mrs. LaRue?

Mrs. LaRue

Letters from Obedience School

Written and Illustrated by

Mark Teague

Award Winning Selection

The Snort City Register/Gazette

September 30

LOCAL DOG ENTERS OBEDIENCE SCHOOL

"Ike LaRue"

Citing a long list of behavioral problems, Snort City resident Gertrude R. LaRue yesterday enrolled her dog, Ike, in the Igor Brotweiler Canine Academy.

Established in 1953, the Academy has a history of dealing with such issues.

"I'm at my wit's end!" said Mrs. LaRue. "I love Ike, but I'm afraid he's quite spoiled. He steals food right off the kitchen counter, chases the neighbor's cats, howls whenever I'm away, and last week while I was crossing the street he pulled me down and tore my best camel's hair coat! I just don't know what else to do!"

School officials were unavailable for comment . . .

Dear Mrs. LaRue,

October 1

How could you do this to me? This is a PRISON, not a school! You should see the other dogs. They are BAD DOGS, Mrs. LaRue! I do not fit in. Even the journey here was a horror. I am very unhappy and may need something to chew on when I get home. Please come right away!

Sincerely,

Ike

BROTWEILER
IGOR
BROTWEILER
CANINE
ACADEMY
"WE AIM TO TAME"
WARNING!
PRISONERS
ON BOARD
BADDOG
KEEP OUT
IGOR
BROTWEILER
CANINE
ACADEMY

October 2

Dear Mrs. LaRue,

Were you really upset about the chicken pie? You know, you might have discussed it with me. You could have said, "Ike, don't eat the chicken pie. I'm saving it for dinner." Would that have been so difficult? It would have prevented a lot of hard feelings.

Needless to say, I am being horribly mistreated. You say I should be patient and accept that I'll be here through the term. Are you aware that the term lasts TWO MONTHS? Do you know how long that is in dog years?

Sincerely,

Ike

Draw Conclusions
What can you conclude about Ike from his letters?

October 3

Dear Mrs. LaRue,

I'd like to clear up some misconceptions about the Hibbins' cats. First, they are hardly the little angels Mrs. Hibbins makes them out to be. Second, how should I know what they were doing out on the fire escape in the middle of January? They were being a bit melodramatic, don't you think, the way they cried and refused to come down? It's hard to believe they were really sick for three whole days, but you know cats.

Your dog,

Ike

October 4

Dear Mrs. LaRue,

You should see what goes on around here. The way my teach — I mean WARDEN, Miss Klondike, barks orders is shocking. Day after day I'm forced to perform the most meaningless tasks. Today it was "sit" and "roll over," all day long. I flatly refused to roll over. It's ridiculous. I won't do it. Of course I was SEVERELY punished.

And another thing: Who will help you cross the street while I'm away? You know you have a bad habit of not looking both ways. Think of all the times I've saved you. Well, there was that one time, anyway. I must say you weren't very grateful, complaining on and on about the tiny rip in your ratty old coat. But the point is, you need me!

Yours,

Ike

Dear Mrs. LaRue,

October 5

The GUARDS here are all caught up in this "good dog, bad dog" thing. I hear it constantly: "Good dog, Ike. Don't be a bad dog, Ike." Is it really so good to sit still like a lummox all day? Nevertheless, I refuse to be broken!

Miss Klondike has taken my typewriter. She claims it disturbs the other dogs. Does anybody care that the other dogs disturb ME?

Yours,

Ike

Dear Mrs. LaRue,

October 6

Were the neighbors really complaining about my howling? It is hard to imagine. First, I didn't howl that much. You were away those nights, so you wouldn't know, but trust me, it was quite moderate. Second, let's recall that these are the same neighbors who are constantly waking ME up in the middle of the afternoon with their loud vacuuming. I say we all have to learn to get along.

My life here continues to be a nightmare. You wouldn't believe what goes on in the cafeteria.

Sincerely,

Ike

P.S. I don't want to alarm you, but the thought of escape has crossed my mind!

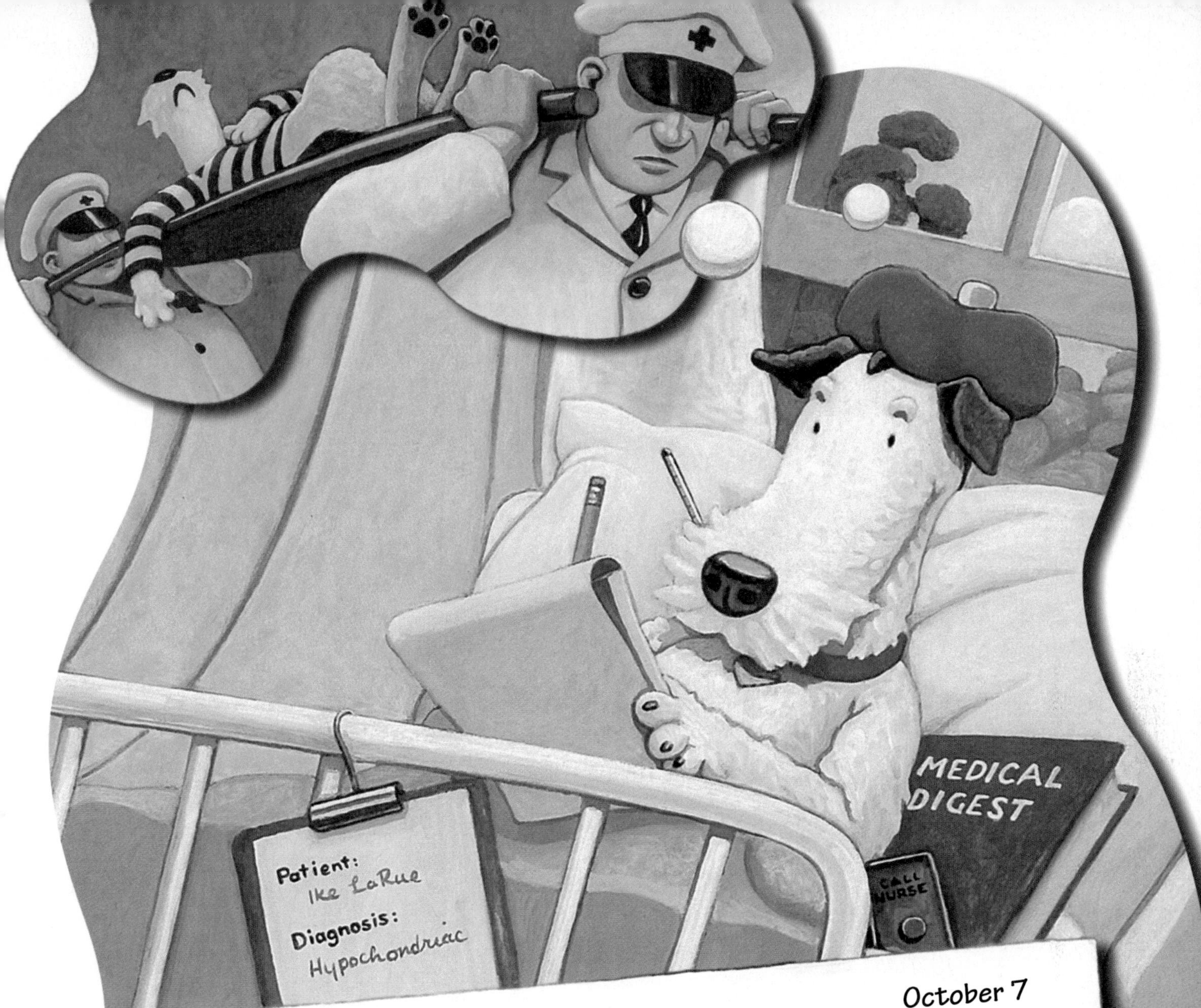

October 7

Dear Mrs. LaRue,

I hate to tell you this, but I am terribly ill. It started in my paw, causing me to limp all day. Later I felt queasy, so that I could barely eat dinner (except for the yummy gravy). Then I began to moan and howl. Finally, I had to be taken to the vet. Dr. Wilfrey claims that he can't find anything wrong with me, but I am certain I have an awful disease. I must come home at once.

Honestly yours,

Ike

Draw Conclusions
Is Ike's illness real? Explain using details from the story.

BROTWEILER
PUMPKIN FESTIVAL
THE
BIRDMAN
OF
ALCATRAZ

October 8

Dear Mrs. LaRue,

Thank you for the lovely get well card. Still, I'm a little surprised that you didn't come get me. I know what Dr. Wilfrey says, but is it really wise to take risks with one's health? I could have a relapse, you know.

With fall here, I think about all the fine times we used to have in the park. Remember how sometimes you would bring along a tennis ball? You would throw it and I would retrieve it EVERY TIME, except for once when it landed in something nasty and I brought you back a stick instead. Ah, how I miss those days.

Yours truly,

Ike

P.S. Imagine how awful it is for me to be stuck inside my tiny cell!

P.P.S. I still feel pretty sick.

October 9

Dear Mrs. LaRue,

By the time you read this I will be gone. I have decided to attempt a daring escape! I'm sorry it has come to this, since I am really a very good dog, but frankly you left me no choice. How sad it is not to be **appreciated**! From now on I'll wander from town to town without a home — or even any dog food, most likely. Such is the life of a **desperate** outlaw. I will try to write to you from time to time as I carry on with my life of hardship and danger.

Your lonely fugitive,

Ike

The Snort City Register / Gazette

October 10

LARUE ESCAPES DOGGY DETENTION

Former Snort City resident Ike LaRue escaped last night from the dormitory at the Igor Brotweiler Canine Academy. The dog is described as “toothy” by local police. His current whereabouts are unknown.

“To be honest, I thought he was bluffing when he told me he was planning to escape,” said a visibly upset Gertrude R. LaRue, the dog’s owner. “Ike tends to be a bit melodramatic, you know. Now I can only pray that he’ll come back.” Asked if she would return Ike to Brotweiler Academy, Mrs. LaRue said that she would have to wait and see. “He’s a good dog basically, but he can be difficult. . . .”

October 11 — Somewhere in America

Dear Mrs. LaRue,

I continue to suffer horribly as I roam this barren wasteland. Who knows where my wanderings will take me now? Hopefully to someplace with yummy food! Remember the special treats you used to make for me? I miss them. I miss our nice, comfy apartment. But mostly, I miss you!

Your sad dog,

Ike

P.S. I even miss the Hibbins' cats, in a way.

October 12 — Still Somewhere

Dear Mrs. LaRue,

The world is a hard and cruel place for a "stray" dog. You would scarcely believe the misery I've **endured**. So I have decided to return home. You may try to lock me up again, but that is a risk I must take. And frankly, even more than myself, I worry about you. You may not know it, Mrs. LaRue, but you need a dog!

Your **misunderstood** friend,

Ike

GET U2

The Snort City Register/Gazette

October 13

HERO DOG SAVES OWNER!

Ike LaRue, until recently a student at the Igor Brotweiler Canine Academy, returned to Snort City yesterday in dramatic fashion. In fact he arrived just in time to rescue his owner, Gertrude R. LaRue of Second Avenue, from an oncoming truck. Mrs. LaRue had made the trip downtown to purchase a new camel's hair coat. Apparently she **neglected** to look both ways before stepping out into traffic.

The daring rescue was witnessed by several onlookers, including patrolman Newton Smitzer. "He rolled right across two lanes of traffic to get at her," said Smitzer. "It was really something. I haven't seen rolling like that since I left the police academy."

Mrs. LaRue was unhurt in the incident, though her coat was badly torn. "I don't care about that," she said. "I'm just happy to have my Ike back home where he belongs!"

LaRue said she plans to throw a big party for the dog. "All the neighbors will be there, and I'm going to serve Ike's favorite dishes. . . ."

“. . . I’ll bet he can’t wait to taste the chicken pie. . . .”

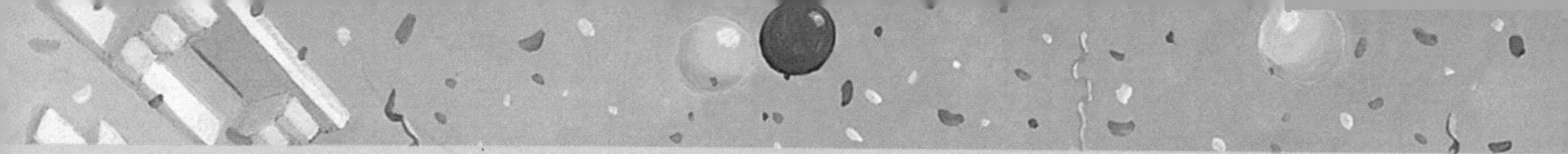

Write Home About Mark Teague

Mark Teague says that this story is one of his favorites. He had lots of fun pretending he was Ike and writing from a dog's point of view. Mark based Ike on two dogs he and his brother had. One dog loved to eat, the other dog liked to play tricks. Now Mark has cats. He put them in this story, too. Mark gets ideas for many of his books from things he did as a boy. Then he adds a twist or two to make his stories really funny.

Other books by Mark Teague

LOG ON FIND OUT

Author Mark Teague
www.macmillanmh.com

Author's Purpose

What experiences from his real life did Mark Teague use to write *Dear Mrs. LaRue*? Explain if he wrote the story using the first-person or third-person point of view.

LOG ON LEARN IT Comprehension
www.macmillanmh.com

Comprehension Check

Text Clues	Conclusion

Summarize

To summarize *Dear Mrs. LaRue* use the most important details from the selection. Information from your Conclusions Chart may help you.

Think and Compare

1. Who took Ike's typewriter away? **Details**
2. Mrs. LaRue's coat is torn twice. How is her reaction the first time it is torn different from her reaction the second time it is torn? **Compare and Contrast**
3. Why did Ike decide to escape from **obedience** school? Explain using details from the story. **Generate Questions: Draw Conclusions**
4. The author tells the story from Ike's point of view. What clues does the author give to show the reader that Ike's letters are full of exaggeration? **Author's Craft**
5. Compare the events and characters in "Puppy Trouble" and *Dear Mrs. LaRue*. Use details from both selections in your answer. **Reading/Writing Across Texts**

Science

Genre

Expository selections, such as **news stories**, give information about events.

Text Feature

Line Graphs show changes over time.

Content Vocabulary

intelligent
impressive
demonstrated
exposure
phrases

DOG AMAZES SCIENTISTS!

Rico the border collie has a knack for learning words.

by Kim Christopher

GERMANY — A border collie named Rico is amazing scientists with his knowledge of human language. Rico recognizes at least 200 words and quickly learns and remembers even more.

Rico began his training when he was ten months old. His owner, Susanne Baus, put toys in different places and had Rico fetch them by name. She rewarded Rico with food or by playing with him. Rico continued to learn more and more new words. Scientists first noticed Rico when he showed off his talent on a popular German game show.

Border collies are **intelligent** medium-size dogs that have a lot of energy and are easily trained. They like to stay busy, and they like to please their owners.

Even though nine-year-old Rico knows 200 words, he doesn't know as many words as even the average two-year-old person does. Human nine-year-olds know thousands and thousands of words, and they learn about ten new words a day. Still, Rico's ability to find objects by name is so **impressive** that scientists wanted to study him.

Number of Words a Child Understands

Reading a Line Graph

This line graph shows an increase in number. It shows how many words a child understands at different ages.

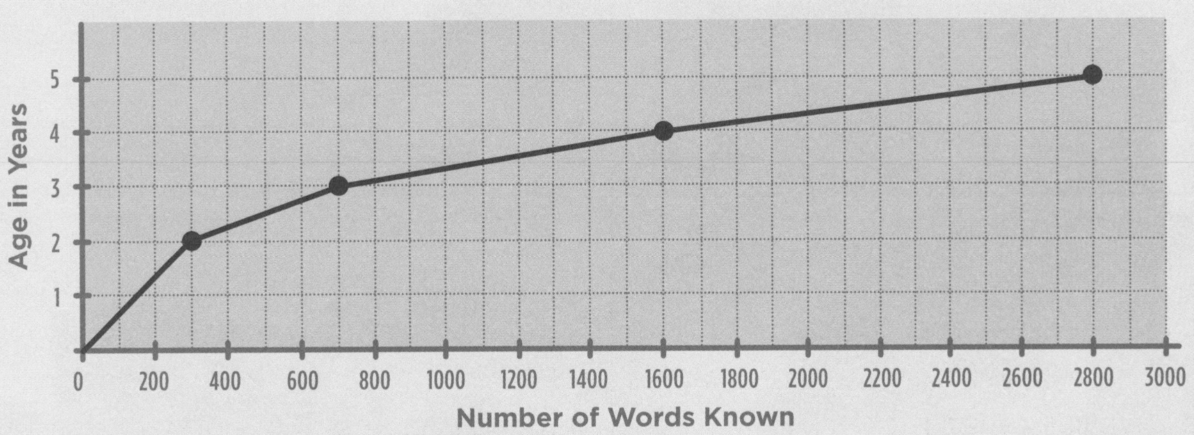

Humans have the ability to learn words far more quickly than even the smartest dog.

Scientists learned a lot about Rico as they watched him fetch familiar toys by name. Then Rico **demonstrated** something amazing. He showed scientists that he could pick out by name toys he had never seen before! Scientists put some familiar toys in a room. They added a new toy. Rico's owner asked him to fetch the new toy. Rico picked out the right toy most of the time in these tests.

Scientists think that Rico connects new words to new things. Since Rico already knows the names of old toys, he knows he should pick out a new toy when he hears a new word.

Rico can also remember the name of a new toy after just one **exposure**, or experience, with that toy. This shows scientists that even though animals are unable to talk, they can understand words. Rico's vocabulary seems to be as large as that of animals that have been trained in language. Those animals include apes, sea lions, dolphins, and parrots.

Most dog owners will tell you that their pets are very smart. But just how smart is Rico? Is he an outstanding dog in a breed known to be very intelligent? Or is Rico a "dog genius"?

Scientists are now studying Rico to learn more. They want to know if Rico can understand **phrases** such as "put the toy in the box." Rico's owner thinks that he can. The answers to questions about Rico's intelligence are still to come. The outcome of the study will be interesting to both scientists and dog owners all over the world.

Connect and Compare

1. Look at the line graph on page 321. How many words does a four-year-old understand? **Reading a Line Graph**

2. According to the graph, at what age does a child understand 2,800 words? **Apply**

3. Think about this article and *Dear Mrs. LaRue*. What would Rico say if he wrote a letter to his owner? Explain using details from both selections. **Reading/Writing Across Texts**

RESEARCH INQUIRY

Science Activity

Research how dogs became pets. Use online sources and information from graphs to write a research report to explain how dogs have become pets over time.

LOG ON FIND OUT **Science** Border collies
www.macmillanmh.com

Writing

Trait: Ideas

Writers provide **good reasons** that explain their ideas or opinions.

Reading and Writing Connection

Read the passage below. Notice how the author Mark Teague has Mrs. LaRue give her reasons for sending Ike to school.

The author gives reasons why Mrs. LaRue is "at her wit's end." Each reason is a strong one that explains why she is feeling upset.

An excerpt from
Dear Mrs. LaRue

"I'm at my wit's end!" said Mrs. LaRue. "I love Ike, but I'm afraid he's quite spoiled. He steals food right off the kitchen counter, chases the neighbor's cats, howls whenever I'm away, and last week while I was crossing the street he pulled me down and tore my best camel's hair coat! I just don't know what else to do!"

Read and Find

Read Jaden's writing below. What reasons did she provide for her opinion? Use the checklist below to help you.

At My Grandmother's House

by Jaden S.

I think Nana's living room is the most comfortable place in the world. She has a huge tan armchair and two couches. The couches are so puffy that when you sit on them, you sink down! I also love her blue and green rug which is as soft as a fleece blanket. I can lie on it for hours. It's even better than lying on grass or sand.

Read about how Jaden feels about Nana's living room.

Writer's Checklist

- [x] What is the writer's opinion?
- [x] Does the writer give **good reasons** to explain her opinion?
- [ ] Does each reason support her opinion?

Talk About It

How can powerful words move us to act?

LOG ON VIEW IT

Oral Language Activities
From Words to Action
www.macmillanmh.com

From Words to ACTION

TIME FOR KIDS®

Vocabulary

dismiss **interact** **motivate** **conceived** **definition**

The writer Langston Hughes was part of the Harlem Renaissance.

A Renaissance in Harlem

During the early 1920s, many African Americans moved from rural areas to cities. They were in search of jobs and a better life. In New York City, many people headed to the neighborhood of Harlem. Many African American musicians, poets, artists, and entertainers also came to Harlem at that time. The talented people gathered here gave birth to a period of artistic growth, known as the Harlem Renaissance.

Writers such as Langston Hughes, Zora Neale Hurston, and Claude McKay wrote poems and stories about the African American experience. Musicians such as Louis Armstrong, Duke Ellington, and Bessie Smith sang about what life was like for African Americans. The Harlem Renaissance was a chance for African Americans to use art to talk about their culture and to **dismiss** racism.

Before this time, many white people did not want to **interact** with black people. But during the Harlem Renaissance, many Americans started to take notice of African American culture. For the first time, white publishers printed poems and stories by African Americans. This helped **motivate** many other African Americans to become writers and artists. The Harlem Renaissance helped to boost pride in African American history and culture.

A Speech with Reach

Great speeches use powerful words to move people. Throughout history, speeches have caused people to think and to act. Here are some famous lines from well-known speeches.

"General Secretary Gorbachev, if you seek peace, if you seek prosperity..., if you seek liberalization: Come here to this gate! Mr. Gorbachev, open this gate! Mr. Gorbachev, tear down this wall!"

— President Ronald Reagan, delivered in West Berlin on June 12, 1987

"Fourscore and seven years ago our fathers brought forth on this continent a new nation, **conceived** in liberty, and dedicated to the proposition that all men are created equal."

— President Abraham Lincoln, Gettysburg Address, 1863

The Top 5 Most-Searched Words on the Internet

When you don't know the **definition** of a word, do you look it up? Over the past 10 years, people have most often looked up on an online dictionary the following words:

1. effect (i-fekt) noun: an event, condition, or state of affairs that is produced by a cause
2. affect (a-fekt) verb: to produce a significant influence upon or change in
3. love (luhv) noun: a quality or feeling of strong or constant affection for and dedication to another being or thing
4. blog (blawg) noun: [short for "weblog"] a Web site that contains an online personal journal often with hyperlinks provided by the writer
5. integrity (in-te-gruh-tee) noun: the condition of being free from damage or defect

Source: merriam-webster.com

Comprehension

Genre

An **Expository** selection, such as a magazine article, presents facts about a person, place, or event.

Monitor Comprehension

Fact and Opinion

A fact is something that can be proven true. An opinion is a belief that does not have to be supported by facts.

Words Add Up to Success

Jaime Escalante was a math teacher at Garfield High School in East Los Angeles. However, he quickly became a national figure.

On his first day, he knew his students were in trouble. "They were using their fingers adding stuff at the board," he says. "They came in without supplies, with nothing."

Escalante wanted to help them. His first challenge was to get their attention. Many of the students at Garfield didn't care about education. They were involved in gangs and violence. Math wasn't an important subject for most of them. Escalante needed to make math real and interesting to them. He had to find a way to **interact** with his students.

So one day in 1974, Escalante came to school wearing a chef's hat. He carried a meat cleaver and apple into his classroom. With one swift chop, he cut the apple in two. "Let's talk about percentages," he said. With one quick action, he had the students' attention.

Working Wonders

From that day forward, Escalante used his imagination to reach students. He **conceived** of different ways to keep them interested in the lessons. He wanted the students to understand that school and math were important to their lives.

Escalante believed that his job was to **motivate** as well as teach students. He used jokes and real-life examples to keep their interest. He also made sure his students took class seriously.

If someone wasn't paying attention, Escalante would nudge him or her with a little red pillow. If students were late, they had to sit in a chair built for a kindergartener. The students felt embarrassed. As a result, they got to class on time and focused on their work.

Escalante sometimes used tough words to shake up his class. However, he also gave his students plenty of encouragement. He often told them, "You are the best, you are our hope for the future. Remember that." Those words inspired his students to try harder and do better.

Jaime Escalante speaks to audiences, such as this one at Lyon College, about his experiences.

Making an Impact

Escalante's words and determination made his students want to do well—and they did. Many of his students studied hard and passed an advanced math test. The test was so difficult, only two percent of all high school seniors passed it each year. About 80 percent of Escalante's students passed the test. The students' attitudes changed when they got good grades. They knew the **definition** of hard work and now, success. They felt better about themselves, and they wanted to do well in school.

The people in charge of the test thought the students from Garfield had cheated. They didn't believe students from an urban school, like Garfield, could do so well. Escalante's students took the test again and did just as well the second time. Through their scores the students were able to **dismiss** any doubt, and the testers had to admit they were wrong! A movie director heard this story and decided to make a movie about Escalante and his students. He knew other people would also be inspired by them.

From the Classroom to the Big Screen

The film *Stand and Deliver* was a box office hit in 1988, and it made Escalante famous. The movie also brought attention to Garfield High School. Companies gave hundreds of thousands of dollars to improve the school's many programs. Students and teachers were helped by the movie's success.

Escalante no longer teaches at Garfield, but his words and actions live on. Maria Torres is one example of his influence. She was a student of Escalante's at Garfield. When she graduated from high school, she entered college at UCLA. "Many teachers merely instruct you," reports Torres. "Mr. Escalante's secret is he really cares. He made us feel powerful, that we could do anything."

Actor Edward James Olmos played Escalante in *Stand and Deliver*.

Think and Compare

1. What percentage of Escalante's students passed the advanced math test?
2. Identify an opinion in the article and explain why it is an opinion.
3. What is this article mainly about? Use details from the text to support your answer.
4. What do the speech makers in "A Speech with Reach" have in common with Jaime Escalante?

Test Practice

Answering Questions

Right There answers are found in one place in the text.
Think and Search answers are found in more than one place.
Author and Me answers ask the reader to look for clues.

The Latest Lingo

1 Are you a mouse potato? If you don't know what that means, look it up in Merriam-Webster's Collegiate Dictionary. The phrase was added to the dictionary in 2006, along with nearly 100 other words.

2 Thousands of new words and their meanings enter the English language each year. Some go into the dictionary. Others fade from use. "Our language is a living thing," Jim Lowe, an editor at Merriam-Webster, told TFK. "It keeps growing."

3 In other words, as the world changes, we always need new terms to describe it. Each year, the dictionary's editors look in everything from catalogs to comic books for the latest lingo. What happens when a new word or phrase is spotted? New words go on index cards. The cards note when and where the words first appeared. For a word to be added to the dictionary, it must show up regularly in a lot of places. Every 10 years the dictionary gets a total makeover. Lowe and the other editors review the new terms they have found. About 10,000 new ones make it into the dictionary.

New Words

Here are some words that were recently added to the dictionary. How many of these words do you use?

mouse potato	manga
ringtone	ollie
spyware	wave pool
supersize	bling-bling
unibrow	google

Use "The Latest Lingo" to answer questions 1–4.

1 What new phrase was added to the dictionary in 2006?

- **A** latest lingo
- **B** mouse potato
- **C** bling-bling
- **D** wave pool

2 Paragraph 2 is mostly about —

- **F** new words on index cards
- **G** Jim Lowe's job
- **H** the idea that language is a living thing
- **J** a dictionary makeover

3 For a new word to be added to the dictionary it must —

- **A** show up in a lot of places
- **B** appear on a Web site
- **C** be in a catalog and comic book
- **D** be in the dictionary already

4 Which is the best summary of this article?

- **F** Jim Lowe has a great job. He is an editor of Merriam-Webster's Collegiate Dictionary. He thinks that language is a living thing. He likes to look for new words in catalogs and comic books.
- **G** Every 10 years, all the editors at Merriam-Webster decide to look for new words. They write new words and phrases like "mouse potato" and "spyware" on index cards.
- **H** Every year, new words enter the English language. The editors of Merriam-Webster's Collegiate Dictionary keep track of these new words. If a word is used regularly in enough places, it will eventually make it into the dictionary.
- **J** The words "supersize" and "manga" were added to Merriam-Webster's Collegiate Dictionary. The dictionary is revised every 10 years. Lowe and his editors review about 10,000 new words.

Write to a Prompt

Write a composition about starting a new project.

Think about how to clearly express your ideas and opinions.

As you write, think about what makes an effective sentence.

Below, see how one student begins a response to the prompt above.

The writer included an opinion to express a point of view.

Sometimes, it is hard for kids in our class to relate to what they read. That is why I have started a magazine only for kids. I call it Kids Today. The magazine will be written and run by kids. It will talk about topics that are important and interesting to us.

First, I am looking for kids my age who want to write for the magazine. I have decided to arrange the writing by subject: school, news, sports, music, and movies. Second, I need kids to edit the articles.

This magazine is such a great way to reach our classmates and to talk about what interests us and is important to us. Come join Kids Today and help make it a success!

Writing Prompt

Respond in writing to the prompt below. Review the hints below before and after you write.

Write a composition about how you could help your classmates.

Writing Hints

- ☑ Remember to write about helping your classmates. Think about the genre.
- ☑ Form an opinion about a topic.
- ☑ Plan your writing by organizing your ideas.
- ☑ Include important details.
- ☑ Use correct spelling and grammar.
- ☑ Review and edit your writing.

Talk About It

Why is it important to keep promises?

LOG ON VIEW IT

Oral Language Activities
Keeping Promises
www.macmillanmh.com

Keeping Promises

Vocabulary

selfish
cranky
commotion
exasperated
specialty
famished

Analogies

Analogies compare two pairs of words usually using **Synonyms** or **Antonyms**. *Cranky* is to *mad* as *thin* is to *slim*.

The Frog Prince

by Maryn Stevens

Narrator: There once was a beautiful princess whose favorite object was a golden ball. One day the princess tossed the ball too high, and it landed in the well. As the princess cried over her lost treasure, she heard someone ask a question.

Frog: Why are you crying, princess?

Narrator: The princess looked around and saw only a frog.

Princess: I am crying because my favorite golden ball fell into the well.

Frog: I can retrieve it for you, but first you must agree to one condition. You must promise to take me home and be my friend.

Narrator: The princess had no intention of being friends with a frog, but she promised anyway. When the frog brought her the ball, the princess snatched it from him and scampered home.

Frog: What a **selfish** princess. She only cares about herself. I'm certain she has forgotten her promise. I'll just hop over to the castle to remind her.

Narrator: The frog hopped through the meadow and knocked on the heavy door of the castle.

Princess: What are you doing here, you bumbling frog?

Frog: My, aren't we grouchy and **cranky**? Bumbling? I wasn't the one who dropped the ball into the well. I am here to remind you of the promise you made.
Narrator: The princess slammed the door in the frog's face with a big BANG.
King: I heard a door slam. What's all the **commotion**? If you made a promise, you must honor it.
Narrator: A frustrated and **exasperated** princess obeyed her father. The king, the princess, and the frog ate dinner together. It was beef stew, the cook's favorite recipe, his famous **specialty**.
Frog: I was **famished**, but now I'm full. Thank you for dinner. Kindly show me to my bed now.
Narrator: The princess did as she was asked, but the frog looked sad.
Frog: You have welcomed me into your home, but I can tell that you don't want to be my friend.
Narrator: The princess blushed, for what the frog said was true. She bent down to kiss the frog, but ended up kissing a prince.
Frog: I am a prince who was turned into a frog, and your kiss turned me back. Thank you, dear friend!
Narrator: The prince and princess were wonderful friends from that day on and lived happily ever after.

Reread for Comprehension

Monitor Comprehension

Theme The theme of a selection is the lesson or message about life an author wants to communicate to readers in a story. One way to identify the theme is to pay attention to the characters' words, actions, and what happens as a result of their actions.

Use the Theme Chart to help you monitor your comprehension and identify clues in the text about the theme of "The Frog Prince."

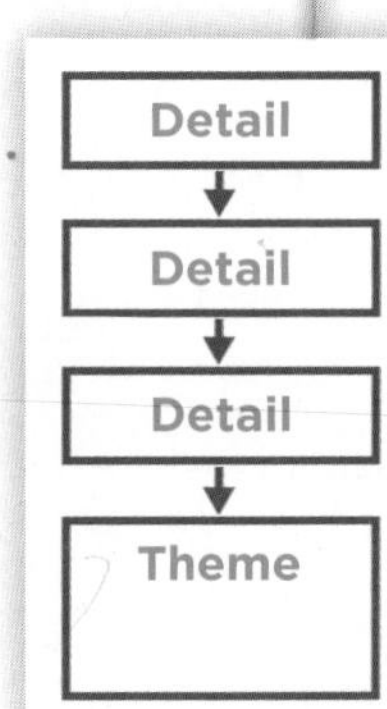

LOG ON LEARN IT **Comprehension**
www.macmillanmh.com

Comprehension

Genre

A **Play** is a story that is intended to be performed and has features such as dialogue, stage directions, and scene descriptions.

Monitor Comprehension

Theme

As you read, use your Theme Chart.

Detail
↓
Detail
↓
Detail
↓
Theme

Read to Find Out

What is the lesson or message of this play?

Ranita
The Frog Princess

by Carmen Agra Deedy
illustrated by Renato Alarcão

SETTING

Long ago in Mexico. The Viceroy's hunting lodge in Chapultapec forest.

PLAYERS

FELIPE, the Viceroy's rotten son

PEPE, Felipe's mistreated servant

RANITA, a little frog with a mysterious past

VIEJA SABIA, a wise but **cranky** old woman

VICEROY, the representative of the Spanish throne

VICEROY'S WIFE

COOK

MAN ONE

MAN TWO

SERVANT ONE

SERVANT TWO

MAN THREE

EXTRAS: Members of hunting party, servants attending dinner, noblemen and ladies

Scene 1

In a forest clearing, men are frantically searching the ground. From a nearby stone well, Ranita watches but remains unnoticed.

Man One: *(Frustrated)* Keep looking! If we don't find that golden arrow—

Man Two: —we'll be on *tortillas* and water for the next month!

(Men, grumbling, all agree.)

(Enter Felipe.)

Felipe: *(Loud and demanding)* Well? Have you found my golden arrow yet?

Man Three: Not yet, Señor!

Felipe: *(Sweetly, hand over heart)* It was a gift from my dear mother. *(Turning suddenly and hissing)* Find it or I will feed you to the jaguars—starting with my bumbling servant, Pepe. It's his fault I missed my mark. Now, out of my sight, all of you!

(Men exit hurriedly.)

Felipe: *(Stomping foot and whining)* I want my golden arrow back!

Ranita: *(Sitting on top of well, holding the golden arrow)* You mean, *this* golden arrow?

Felipe: *(Joyously)* My golden arrow! You found it! You—*(Stops cold)*—you're a frog.

Ranita: You were expecting a Mayan princess, perhaps?

Felipe: *(Rolls eyes)* Well, I wasn't expecting a talking frog!

Ranita: *(Sighs)* I'm under a spell. I don't like to talk about it.

Felipe: *(Pauses to think)* Not my problem. Hand over the arrow.

Ranita: *(Plink! Drops it back down the well)* Hmm, looks like it's your problem now.

Felipe: N-n-noooo! *(Threateningly)* What have you done, you foolish frog?

Ranita: If I am so foolish, how come I am the one with the arrow while you are the one standing there talking to a *rana*, a frog?

Felipe: I would squish you right now—*(Sniffs)*—but you are only a frog.

Ranita: *(Warningly)* You want that golden arrow?

Felipe: *(Suspicious)* In exchange for what?

Ranita: A promise.

Felipe: *(Relieved)* Oh, is that all?

Ranita: A promise is a very serious thing.

Felipe: *(Coughing)* Yes, yes, of course—go on.

Theme
Think about Felipe's character. Does he take promises seriously?

Ranita: IF I rescue your golden arrow, you must promise to let me eat from your *plato*, sleep in your *cama*, and give me a *beso* when the sun comes up.

Felipe: *(Just stares)* Eat from my plate? Sleep in my bed? KISS you? *That* is disgusting!

Ranita: No promise, no golden arrow.

Felipe: *(Crossing his fingers behind his back)* I promise.

(Ranita fetches the arrow. Felipe bows and runs off.)

Ranita: *Espera*! Wait! I can't hop that fast! *(Hangs her head and begins to cry)* He's gone. Now I'll never break this evil spell.

(Enter wise woman, leaning on two canes.)

Vieja Sabia: It doesn't feel very good, does it?

Ranita: *(Blows nose)* Please, no lectures today, old woman.

Vieja Sabia: My name is Vieja *Sabia*.

Ranita: Sorry, *Wise* Old Woman. *(Sadly)* You've already turned me into a frog. Isn't that enough?

Vieja Sabia: You wouldn't be a frog if you hadn't refused to give me a drink from this well, so long ago.

Ranita: I was a **selfish** child then. I have paid for that, haven't I? I have learned what it is like to be alone and forgotten.

Vieja Sabia: Perhaps you have . . .

Ranita: *(Brightening)* Then, you will turn me into a girl again?

Vieja Sabia: No. But I will take you as far as the Viceroy's hunting lodge. You must make the leap from there.

(Exit Vieja Sabia and Ranita.)

Scene 2

Hunting lodge with Viceroy, his wife, noblemen and women, all seated at long banquet table. Servants scurry in and out with bowls of food.

Servant One: *(Placing bowl of soup before Viceroy) Sopa*, Señor?

Viceroy: (***Exasperated***) *Sí, sí*. Where is Felipe?

Viceroy's Wife: *(Wistfully)* Dear boy. He is probably feeding the birds.

Servant Two: *(Aside)* To the cat.

Servant One: *(Muffles laugh)*

(Enter Felipe.)

Felipe: I am **famished**. What a day I've had today. First, I lost my golden arrow—

(Shouting from the kitchen can be heard.)

Felipe: *(Louder)*—then I met this ridiculous, demanding—

(Enter Ranita, running from the kitchen chased by cook and servants.)

Felipe: *(Slack-jawed)*—frog.

Cook: You hop back here! *(To servant)* Stop her, right now!

Servant One: *(Tries to catch frog)* Aaaaayyyy! She's a slippery one!

Servant Two: Oooooeeeeee! She bit me!

Cook: Get her, Pepe. *(Pepe catches Ranita under the table, smiles, and lets her go. A* ***commotion*** *follows as the cook and servants chase Ranita.)*

Theme
How does Felipe feel about his promise to Ranita?

Viceroy: *Basta!* Enough! Who *is* this creature?

Felipe: *(Sneering)* She's the nasty little frog who rescued my golden arrow.

Ranita: And in return he promised to let me eat from his *plato*, sleep in his *cama*, and give me a *beso* when the sun came up.

Viceroy: Did you make this promise?

Felipe: *(Sullen)* I don't remember.

Viceroy's Wife: *(Indignant)* Even if he did—he is the Viceroy's son!

Viceroy: *(Grave) Sí*. And THE VICEROY'S SON KEEPS HIS PROMISES. Pepe! Set a place for our guest.

Felipe: But, Father—

Viceroy's Wife: Ernesto!

Viceroy: *(Slams fist on table.) Silencio!* Silence!

(Ranita hops on table. Felipe is too stunned to speak. Viceroy's Wife is glaring.)

Viceroy: Everyone—and I mean *everyone*—EAT!

(Pepe puts bowl down in front of Felipe.)

Felipe: *(Gives a yelp)* Pepe!

Pepe: *(Innocently) Sí?*

Felipe: *(Disgusted)* There is a fly in my soup!

Pepe: It's for the frog.

Viceroy: Excellent. Eat up, Felipe.

Viceroy's Wife: *(Revolted)* Arggh.

Scene 3

(Felipe's bedroom)

Felipe: *(On bed)* I refuse to sleep next to a FROG. Pepe!!!!!!!!

Pepe: *(Enters immediately)* *Sí*, Señor?

Felipe: *(Snappish)* What took you so long? Hurry—tell my father I can't do this. *(Desperate)* Tell him I'll get warts.

(Enter Viceroy.)

Viceroy: *(Annoyed)* With any luck, you will get one on your oath-breaking tongue, boy.

Felipe: *(Whining)* Father—

Viceroy: You made a promise, Felipe. *(To Pepe)* Help him keep his word, eh, Pepe?

(Exit Viceroy.)

Felipe: *(Throws pillow at Pepe. Falls on bed and begins to wail.)* AAAAAAAYYYYYYYY!

Pepe: *(Blows out candle and sits in chair.) Hasta mañana . . .* until tomorrow. Sweet dreams, Felipe.

Felipe: *(Growls)* I will dream of roasted frog legs.

Ranita: I'm telling.

Felipe: Bug breath!

Ranita: Big baby!

Pepe: *(Sighs)* It's going to be a long night.

(Next morning)

Ranita: *(Cheerful) Despierta,* wake up! It's "beso time!"

[Felipe rubs eyes, sees Ranita, and shrieks.]

Felipe: *(Whimpers, clutching his blanket)* It wasn't a bad dream, after all. Forget it, frog! I am not kissing you!

Ranita: *(Stubbornly)* You promised.

Felipe: Well, *(Smiles slowly)* I've just had a better idea. *(Kicks chair to wake his servant)* Pepe!

Pepe: *(Groggy)* Señor!

Felipe: You are sworn to obey me in all things, *sí*?

Pepe: *(Confused) Sí,* Señor.

Felipe: *(Smug)* KISS . . . THE . . . FROG.

[Pepe shrugs and kisses Ranita's cheek.]

(No longer a frog, Ranita is now a beautiful Mayan Princess.)

Felipe: *(Dazzled)* I—but who? *(Bowing)* Allow me to introduce myself, I am—

Ranita: —the Spanish Viceroy's Rotten Son. And I am . . . the Mayan Emperor's Lucky Daughter.

(Felipe and Pepe fall on their knees.)

Ranita: I have been enchanted for 200 years.

Felipe: *(Looks up)* You've been a frog for 200 years? What's so LUCKY about that?

Ranita: I'll tell you. As a princess, I could have ended up the wife of a spoiled brat like you. Instead, I found myself a prince . . . *(Takes Pepe's hand)* a prince of a husband, that is.

(Pepe kisses the Princess's hand, while Felipe has a screaming tantrum.)

Epilogue

The same clearing in the forest as in Scene 1

Felipe: *(Kicks a stone)* If they think I'm going to their ridiculous wedding . . . ha! May they have a dozen ugly tadpole children!

(Enter Vieja Sabia.)

Vieja Sabia: *Agua!* Water from the well, my son, before I die of thirst.

Felipe: *(Snarling)* I'm no water boy. I'm the Viceroy's son! Get your own water, you old *cucaracha!*

Vieja Sabia: *(With gentle concern)* Cockroach? It's very rude to speak to your elders that way. Has no one taught you manners?

Felipe: *(Puzzled)* No.

Vieja Sabia: *(Smiling wickedly)* Well *(pointing finger at Felipe)*, that is my **specialty**.

*(**POOF** Felipe the Frog hops onto the top of the well.)*

Vieja Sabia: *(to audience)* And now you know how the Frog Prince ended up in that well.

Once Upon a Time . . .

Carmen Agra Deedy came to the United States from Cuba in 1960, after a revolution made it dangerous for her family to live there. Hoping for a more peaceful life, Carmen and her family settled in Georgia. Carmen has not forgotten her Cuban heritage. She combines it with the heritage of the southern United States when writing her stories.

Other books by Carmen Agra Deedy

Renato Alarcão was born, raised, and currently lives in Rio de Janeiro, Brazil. Among his many art projects was the creation of 13 murals around Paterson and Passaic, New Jersey, all done with a team of artists and local teens.

Author's Purpose

Why did the author write *Ranita, The Frog Princess* as a play?

LOG ON FIND OUT

Author Carmen Agra Deedy
Illustrator Renato Alarcão
www.macmillanmh.com

LOG ON LEARN IT **Comprehension**
www.macmillanmh.com

Comprehension Check

Summarize

To summarize *Ranita, The Frog Princess* use the most important details from the play. Information from your Theme Chart may help you.

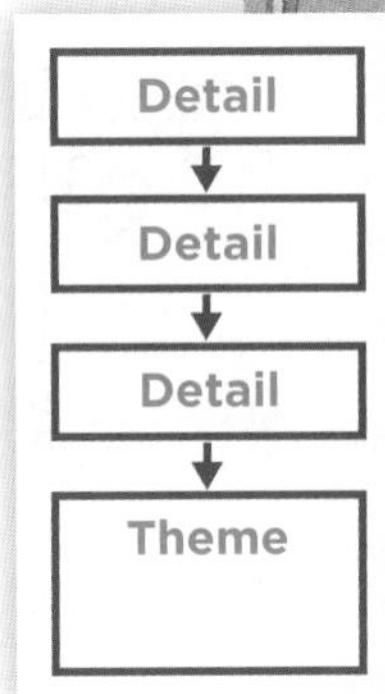

Think and Compare

1. Why did Vieja Sabia turn Ranita into a frog? **Details**
2. Reread the epilogue of the play. What is Vieja Sabia's **specialty**? **Make Inferences**
3. Why does the Viceroy believe that Felipe should keep the promise he made to Ranita? **Monitor Comprehension: Theme**
4. What other structural elements of a play besides dialogue does the author use to help tell the story of Ranita? **Author's Craft**
5. How are the characters and events in "The Frog Prince" and *Ranita, The Frog Princess* similar? Use details from both texts to explain your answer. **Reading/Writing Across Texts**

Language Arts

Genre

Expository texts such as magazine articles give facts and information about a topic. They often include graphic aids, such as maps.

Literary Element

Theme is the main message of a story. Sometimes, the same theme can be found in different texts throughout the world.

And Still More Tales

by Eric Michaels

You are reading a fairy tale or folktale for the first time. Suddenly you think: *This character is familiar! And so is the story!* Don't be surprised. Many tales have different versions. The settings may change, but the characters and the events can be very similar. For example, the fairy tale Cinderella is enjoyed by many different people around the world. Each culture tells the tale in its own way. However, the tales all share the same theme.

Cinderella

A Fairy Tale by the Brothers Grimm

Jacob and Wilhelm Grimm were two storyteller brothers from Germany. Their version of the Cinderella story is familiar to many people. In this tale, Cinderella lives with her wicked stepmother and stepsisters. They make her work very hard and give her nothing but ragged clothes to wear. When the king decides to have a ball, Cinderella cannot go because she does not have a gown.

A bird throws a beautiful dress and a pair of slippers to Cinderella from a special tree. The clothes must be returned by midnight. Cinderella goes to the ball looking like a princess. Of course, the king's son falls in love with her. In her rush to get home, Cinderella loses one of the slippers. The prince finds the slipper and searches for its owner. He tries the slipper on every girl in the kingdom. Finally, he tries it on Cinderella, and the slipper fits! Cinderella and the prince live happily ever after.

Yeh-Shen

A Cinderella Story from China

Yeh-Shen is often called the Chinese Cinderella and is considered by some to be the earliest version of the story. Yeh-Shen also lives with a mean stepmother who mistreats her. Like Cinderella, Yeh-Shen loses a slipper at a spring festival. This time the king is the one who realizes that Yeh-Shen is the slipper's owner. Yeh-Shen and the king marry and live happily ever after.

The Rough-Face Girl

A Native American Tale from Canada

The Native American culture also has a Cinderella tale. In this Algonquin tale, a beautiful, gentle girl is mistreated by her sisters. They are jealous of her and scar her face to make it rough. A warrior named Strong Wind, who has the power to make himself invisible, says he will marry the first girl who can see him. Of course, this is a test. The village girls pretend they can see him, but the rough-face girl does not. Her truthfulness is rewarded, and her goodness wins out. Her face is healed. She becomes Strong Wind's bride, and her sisters are punished.

Trickster Tales

Like "Cinderella," versions of trickster tales are told around the world. In a trickster tale, the main character is a clever animal. Each culture has a favorite trickster.

All tricksters share common traits. They are smart and quick. They can outwit everyone, even those who are bigger, stronger, and more powerful. Once you read a few trickster tales, you'll understand why these clever characters are favorites around the world.

Brer Rabbit appears in many folktales from the American South. He is smart and always gets the best of others.

Coyote appears in tales from Mexico and the American Southwest. You can count on Coyote to be cunning and smart.

In parts of Africa, many people say that all stories belong to Anansi, the spider. Anansi uses his wits to capture the other animals, so that he can own all of the stories. How does Anansi accomplish this? He is a trickster!

Connect and Compare

1. What theme do all three Cinderella tales share? **Theme**

2. Use the map to identify the cultures that have trickster tales. Use details from the article to explain what common traits characters in trickster tales share. **Apply**

3. Think about the Cinderella tales in this article and *Ranita, The Frog Princess*. How are they alike? How are they different? **Reading/Writing Across Texts**

4. Read two trickster tales such as an Anansi tale and a Coyote tale. Use a Venn diagram to compare the adventures of the characters in the two tales. **Apply**

Writing

Trait: Word Choice

Good writers use **descriptive language** to make their ideas clear for readers.

Reading and Writing Connection

Read the passage below. Notice how the author Carmen Agra Deedy uses stage directions to add descriptive detail.

A play is told through dialogue, the lines characters say to each other. In a play the author adds descriptive detail using stage directions. The stage directions give details about how the characters act and feel.

An excerpt from *Ranita, The Frog Princess*

Ranita: No promise, no golden arrow.

Felipe: (*Crossing his fingers behind his back*) I promise.

(Ranita fetches the arrow. Felipe bows and runs off.)

Ranita: *Espera*! Wait! I can't hop that fast! *(Hangs her head and begins to cry)* He's gone. Now I'll never break this evil spell.

Read and Find

Read John's writing below. What descriptive details does he include to make his opinion clear for readers? Use the checklist below to help you.

Read about John's lunch disaster.

Lunch Disaster

by John P.

Dropping a lunch tray in front of everyone is really embarrassing! My lunch tray hit the tile floor with a loud clatter. Everyone started clapping, as I stood in a puddle of warm spaghetti sauce and noodles. My sneakers felt damp from the splatters of oily red sauce on them.

Writer's Checklist

- [x] What is the writer's feeling or opinion?
- [x] What **descriptive details** does he use?
- [ ] What words appeal to a sense of touch?

Expression Through Art

Talk About It

What do you think the artist was trying to express through this mural?

LOG ON VIEW IT

Oral Language Activities
Expression Through Art
www.macmillanmh.com

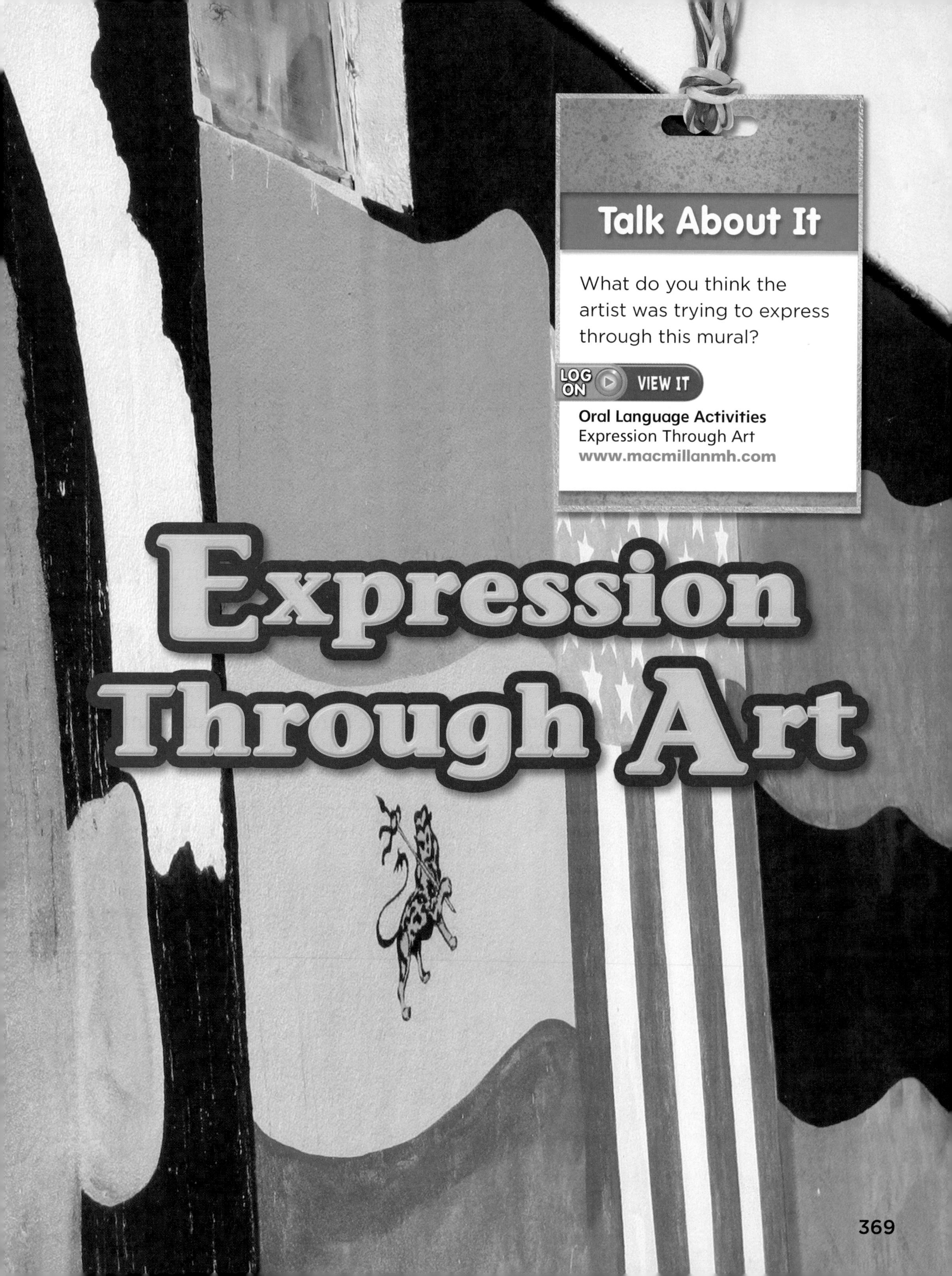

Vocabulary

skyscrapers **glorious**
collage **strutting**
barbecue **swarms**

Context Clues

Examples and **Definitions** can help you figure out the meaning of unfamiliar words. Use the example in the story to figure out the meaning of *skyscrapers*.

SECONDHAND ART

by Amir Ferry

Danny and Emma are working together on their project for the school art contest. They still have not decided what to make.

"Danny, maybe we should make models of those really tall buildings called **skyscrapers**. The Empire State Building is a skyscraper. I know how much you love tall buildings. Isn't it your dream to design the world's tallest building?" Emma asked.

"Yes, it is. That's a great idea, Emma, but it might be too hard for us," said Danny. "We could make a **collage**."

"We could," said Emma, "but lots of kids will make collages. Let's try to be different!"

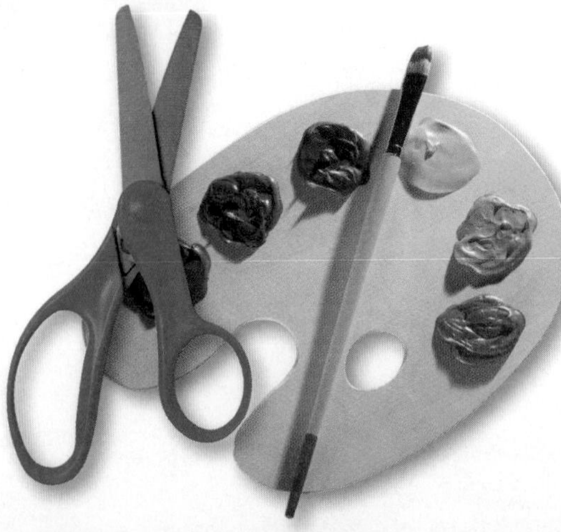

Danny's mom came into the kitchen to remind Danny to put the recycling bin in her car. Danny's eyes lit up.

"I've got it!" he said. "Emma, we can use the recycling. Let's make a papier-mâché city out of that stuff!"

"Great idea," agreed Emma.

They got right to work. There were tons of cans from last week's outdoor grilled chicken **barbecue**.

They cut strips of newspaper and made a paste from flour and water. Then they used the strips of paper and paste to cover the cans and make papier-mâché buildings. At last Danny and Emma were ready to paint.

"Let's use bright yellow," Emma suggested. "It's such a **glorious** color, isn't it?"

Danny giggled. "You're so dramatic, Emma."

He started **strutting** around like a rooster. "Yellow is such a *glorious* color," he teased. Emma flicked her paintbrush at him.

The next day Danny and Emma presented their art project. Everyone loved their "recycled city." Danny and Emma won first prize. **Swarms** of people came up to congratulate them.

"I always told you recycling could be a lot of fun!" Emma exclaimed.

"You were right, Emma. And the best part was that I didn't have to haul everything into Mom's car," said Danny.

Reread for Comprehension

Visualize

Character, Setting, Plot Identifying and visualizing the setting of a story can help readers think about how the setting affects both the characters and the main events of the plot. For example, a change in setting is a main event that can influence future events in the story. A Story Flowchart can help you keep track of the setting, plot events, and a character's reactions in a story. Reread "Secondhand Art" and fill in the Story Flowchart.

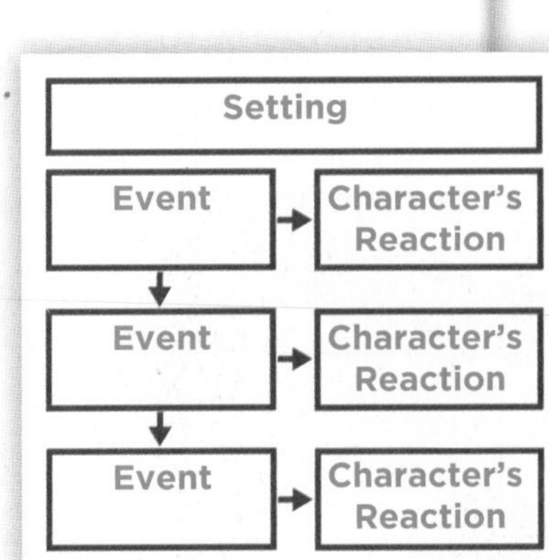

LOG ON LEARN IT **Comprehension** www.macmillanmh.com

Comprehension

Genre

Historical Fiction has real and fictional characters taking part in actual historical events.

Visualize

Character, Setting, Plot
As you read, fill in your Story Flowchart.

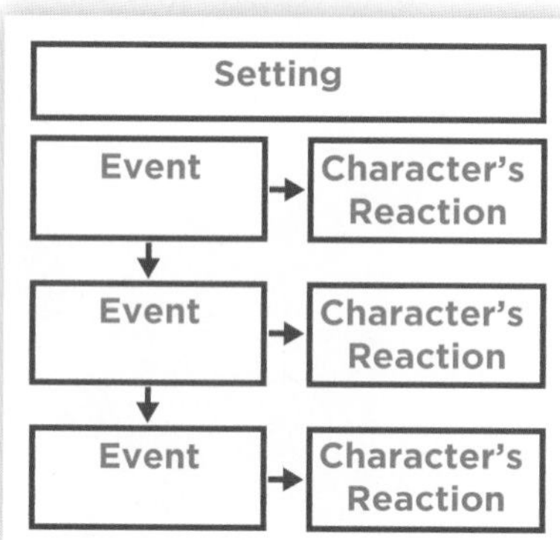

Read to Find Out

How does James's summer in New York change him?

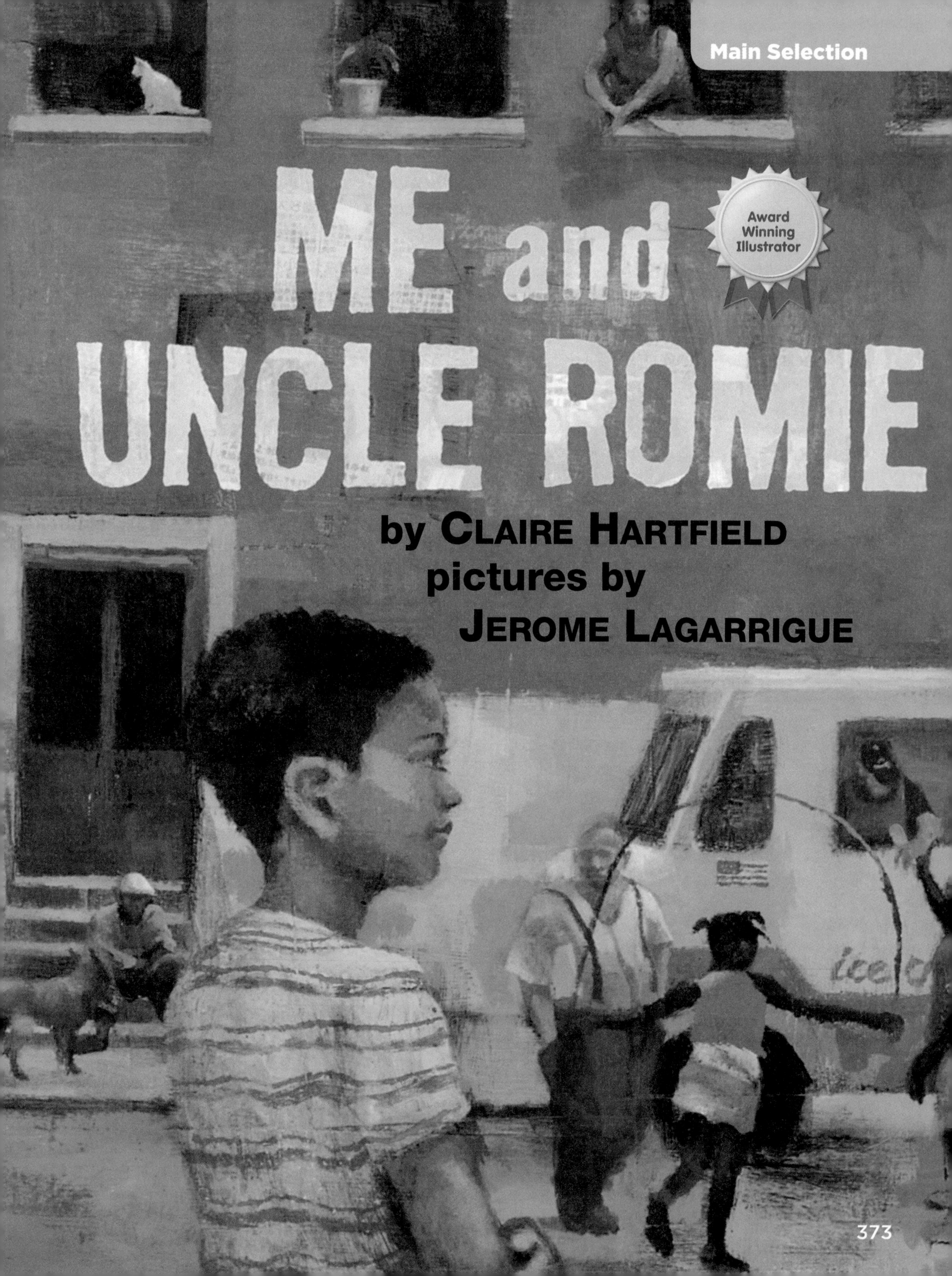

ME and UNCLE ROMIE

Award Winning Illustrator

by Claire Hartfield
pictures by
Jerome Lagarrigue

It was the summer Mama had the twins that I first met my uncle Romie. The doctor had told Mama she had to stay off her feet till the babies got born. Daddy thought it was a good time for me to visit Uncle Romie and his wife, Aunt Nanette, up north in New York City. But I wasn't so sure. Mama had told me that Uncle Romie was some kind of artist, and he didn't have any kids. I'd seen his picture too. He looked scary—a bald-headed, fierce-eyed giant. No, I wasn't sure about this visit at all.

The day before I left home was a regular North Carolina summer day. "A good train-watching day," my friend B.J. said.

We waited quietly in the grass beside the tracks. B.J. heard it first. "It's a'coming," he said. Then I heard it too—a low rumbling, building to a roar. *WHOOO—OOO!*

"The *Piedmont*!" we shouted as the train blasted past.

"I'm the greatest train-watcher ever," B.J. boasted.

"Yeah," I answered, "but tomorrow I'll be *riding* a train. I'm the lucky one."

Lucky, I thought as we headed home. *Maybe*.

That evening I packed my suitcase. Voices drifted up from the porch below.

"Romie's got that big art show coming up," Mama said quietly. "I hope he's not too busy for James, especially on his birthday."

"Romie's a good man," Daddy replied. "And Nanette'll be there too."

Character, Setting, Plot
How does James feel about visiting Uncle Romie in New York City?

The light faded. Mama called me into her bedroom. "Where's my good-night kiss?" she said.

I curled up next to her. "I'll miss the way you make my birthday special, Mama. Your lemon cake and the baseball game."

"Well," Mama sighed, "it won't be those things. But Uncle Romie and Aunt Nanette are family, and they love you too. It'll still be a good birthday, honey."

Mama pulled me close. Her voice sang soft and low. Later, in my own bed, I listened as crickets began their song and continued into the night.

The next morning I hugged Mama good-bye, and Daddy and I headed for the train. He got me seated, then stood waving at me from the outside. I held tight to the jar of pepper jelly Mama had given me for Uncle Romie.

"ALL A-BOARD!" The conductor's voice crackled over the loudspeaker.

The train pulled away. *Chug-a-chug-a-chug-a-chug.* I watched my town move past my window—bright-colored houses, chickens **strutting** across the yards, flowers everywhere.

After a while I felt hungry. Daddy had packed me a lunch and a dinner to eat one at a time. I ate almost everything at once. Then my belly felt tight and I was kind of sleepy. I closed my eyes and dreamed about Mama and Daddy getting ready for those babies. Would they even miss me?

Later, when I woke up, I ate the last bit of my dinner and thought about my birthday. Would they make my lemon cake and take me to a baseball game in New York?

The sky turned from dark blue to black. I was getting sleepy all over again.

"We're almost there, son," the man next to me said.

Then I saw it . . . New York City. Buildings stretching up to the sky. So close together. Not like North Carolina at all.

"Penn Station! Watch your step," the conductor said, helping me down to the platform. I did like Daddy said and found a spot for myself close to the train. **Swarms** of people rushed by. Soon I heard a silvery voice call my name. This had to be Aunt Nanette. I turned and saw her big smile reaching out to welcome me.

She took my hand and guided me through the rushing crowds onto an underground train called the subway. "This will take us right home," she explained.

Home was like nothing I'd ever seen before. No regular houses anywhere. Just big buildings and stores of all kinds—in the windows I saw paints, fabrics, radios, and TVs.

We turned into the corner building and climbed the stairs to the apartment—five whole flights up. *Whew!* I tried to catch my breath while Aunt Nanette flicked on the lights.

"Uncle Romie's out talking to some people about his big art show that's coming up. He'll be home soon," Aunt Nanette said. She set some milk and a plate of cookies for me on the table. "Your uncle's working very hard, so we won't see much of him for a while. His workroom—we call it his studio—is in the front of our apartment. That's where he keeps all the things he needs to make his art."

"Doesn't he just paint?" I asked.

"Uncle Romie is a **collage** artist," Aunt Nanette explained. "He uses paints, yes. But also photographs, newspapers, cloth. He cuts and pastes them onto a board to make his paintings."

"That sounds kinda easy," I said.

Aunt Nanette laughed.

"Well, there's a little more to it than that, James. When you see the paintings, you'll understand. Come, let's get you to bed."

Lying in the dark, I heard heavy footsteps in the hall. A giant stared at me from the doorway. "Hello there, James." Uncle Romie's voice was deep and loud, like thunder. "Thanks for the pepper jelly," he boomed. "You have a good sleep, now." Then he disappeared down the hall.

The next morning the door to Uncle Romie's studio was closed. But Aunt Nanette had plans for both of us. "Today we're going to a neighborhood called Harlem," she said. "It's where Uncle Romie lived as a boy."

Harlem was full of people walking, working, shopping, eating. Some were watching the goings-on from fire escapes. Others were sitting out on stoops greeting folks who passed by—just like the people back home calling out hellos from their front porches. Most everybody seemed to know Aunt Nanette. A lot of them asked after Uncle Romie too.

We bought peaches at the market, then stopped to visit awhile. I watched some kids playing stickball. "Go on, get in that game," Aunt Nanette said, gently pushing me over to join them. When I was all hot and sweaty, we cooled off with double chocolate scoops from the ice cream man. Later we shared some **barbecue** on a rooftop way up high. I felt like I was on top of the world.

As the days went by, Aunt Nanette took me all over the city—we rode a ferry boat to the Statue of Liberty . . . zoomed 102 floors up at the Empire State Building . . . window-shopped the fancy stores on Fifth Avenue . . . gobbled hot dogs in Central Park.

But it was Harlem that I liked best. I played stickball with the kids again . . . and on a really hot day a whole bunch of us ran through the icy cold water that sprayed out hard from the fire hydrant. In the evenings Aunt Nanette and I sat outside listening to the street musicians playing their saxophone songs.

On rainy days I wrote postcards and helped out around the apartment. I told Aunt Nanette about the things I liked to do back home—about baseball games, train-watching, my birthday. She told me about the special Caribbean lemon and mango cake she was going to make.

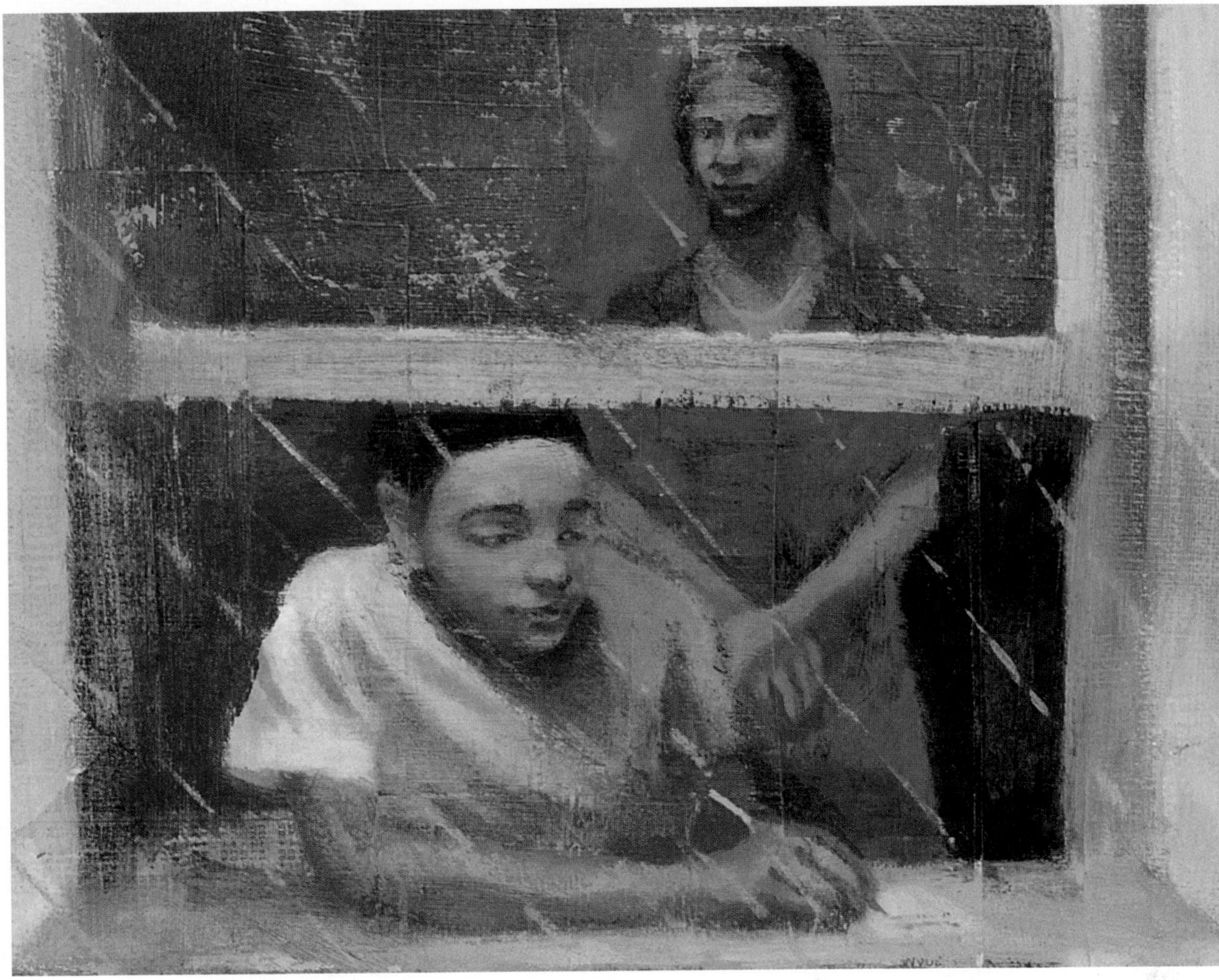

My uncle Romie stayed hidden away in his studio. But I wasn't worried anymore. Aunt Nanette would make my birthday special.

4 . . . 3 . . . 2 . . . 1 . . . My birthday was almost here!

And then Aunt Nanette got a phone call.

"An old aunt has died, James. I have to go away for her funeral. But don't you worry. Uncle Romie will spend your birthday with you. It'll be just fine."

That night Aunt Nanette kissed me good-bye. I knew it would not be fine at all. Uncle Romie didn't know about cakes or baseball games or anything except his dumb old paintings. My birthday was ruined.

When the sky turned black, I tucked myself into bed. I missed Mama and Daddy so much. I listened to the birds on the rooftop—their songs continued into the night.

The next morning everything was quiet. I crept out of bed and into the hall. For the first time the door to Uncle Romie's studio stood wide open. What a **glorious** mess! There were paints and scraps all over the floor, and around the edges were huge paintings with all sorts of pieces pasted together.

I saw saxophones, birds, fire escapes, and brown faces. *It's Harlem*, I thought. *The people, the music, the rooftops, and the stoops.* Looking at Uncle Romie's paintings, I could *feel* Harlem—its beat and bounce.

Then there was one that was different. Smaller houses, flowers, and trains. "That's home!" I shouted.

"Yep," Uncle Romie said, smiling, from the doorway. "That's the Carolina I remember."

"Mama says you visited your grandparents there most every summer when you were a kid," I said.

"I sure did, James. *Mmm.* Now that's the place for pepper jelly. Smeared thick on biscuits. And when Grandma wasn't looking . . . I'd sneak some on a spoon."

"Daddy and I do that too!" I told him.

We laughed together, then walked to the kitchen for a breakfast feast—eggs, bacon, grits, and biscuits.

"James, you've got me remembering the pepper jelly lady. People used to line up down the block to buy her preserves."

"Could you put someone like that in one of your paintings?" I asked.

"I guess I could." Uncle Romie nodded. "Yes, that's a memory just right for sharing. What a good idea, James. Now let's get this birthday going!"

He brought out two presents from home. I tore into the packages while he got down the pepper jelly and two huge spoons. Mama and Daddy had picked out just what I wanted—a special case for my baseball cards, and a model train for me to build.

"Pretty cool," said Uncle Romie. "I used to watch the trains down in North Carolina, you know."

How funny to picture big Uncle Romie lying on his belly!

"B.J. and me, we have contests to see who can hear the trains first."

"Hey, I did that too. You know, it's a funny thing, James. People live in all sorts of different places and families. But the things we care about are pretty much the same. Like favorite foods, special songs, games, stories . . . and like birthdays." Uncle Romie held up two tickets to a baseball game!

It turns out Uncle Romie knows all about baseball—he was even a star pitcher in college. We got our mitts and set off for the game.

Way up in the bleachers, we shared a bag of peanuts, cracking the shells with our teeth and keeping our mitts ready in case a home run ball came our way. That didn't happen—but we sure had fun.

Aunt Nanette came home that night. She lit the candles and we all shared my Caribbean birthday cake.

After that, Uncle Romie had to work a lot again. But at the end of each day he let me sit with him in his studio and talk. Daddy was right. Uncle Romie is a good man.

The day of the big art show finally came. I watched the people laughing and talking, walking slowly around the room from painting to painting. I walked around myself, listening to their conversations.

"Remember our first train ride from Chicago to New York?" one lady asked her husband.

"That guitar-playing man reminds me of my uncle Joe," said another.

All these strangers talking to each other about their families and friends and special times, and all because of how my uncle Romie's paintings reminded them of these things.

Later that night Daddy called. I had a brand-new brother and sister. Daddy said they were both bald and made a lot of noise. But he sounded happy and said how they all missed me.

This time Aunt Nanette and Uncle Romie took me to the train station.

"Here's a late birthday present for you, James," Uncle Romie said, holding out a package. "Open it on the train, why don't you. It'll help pass the time on the long ride home."

I waved out the window to Uncle Romie and Aunt Nanette until I couldn't see them anymore. Then I ripped off the wrappings!

And there was my summer in New York. Bright sky in one corner, city lights at night in another. Tall buildings. Baseball ticket stubs. The label from the pepper jelly jar. And trains. One going toward the **skyscrapers**. Another going away.

Character, Setting, Plot
Explain how James's feelings about Uncle Romie change during the story.

Back home, I lay in the soft North Carolina grass. It was the first of September, almost Uncle Romie's birthday. I watched the birds streak across the sky.

Rooftop birds, I thought. *Back home from their summer in New York, just like me.* Watching them, I could still feel the city's beat inside my head.

A feather drifted down from the sky. In the garden tiger lilies bent in the wind. *Uncle Romie's favorite flowers.* I yanked off a few blossoms. And then I was off on a treasure hunt, collecting things that reminded me of Uncle Romie.

I painted and pasted them together on a big piece of cardboard. Right in the middle I put the train schedule. And at the top I wrote:

Visit the Studios of Claire and Jerome

Claire Hartfield based this story on African American artist Romare Bearden. She likes his collages because they seem to tell stories. Claire wrote her story to show how we can use art to share ideas. She's been expressing herself through art since she was young. Claire was a shy child, and she found that dance and art helped her share her feelings.

Jerome Lagarrigue comes from a family of artists. He grew up in France, but came to the United States to study art. Jerome illustrates books and magazines. He also teaches art.

Other books by Jerome Lagarrigue

LOG ON ▶ FIND OUT

Author Claire Hartfield
Illustrator Jerome Lagarrigue
www.macmillanmh.com

Author's Purpose

Why did Claire Hartfield write this story? How did the author's own love of art affect her purpose for writing? Explain using details from the story.

LOG ON LEARN IT Comprehension
www.macmillanmh.com

Comprehension Check

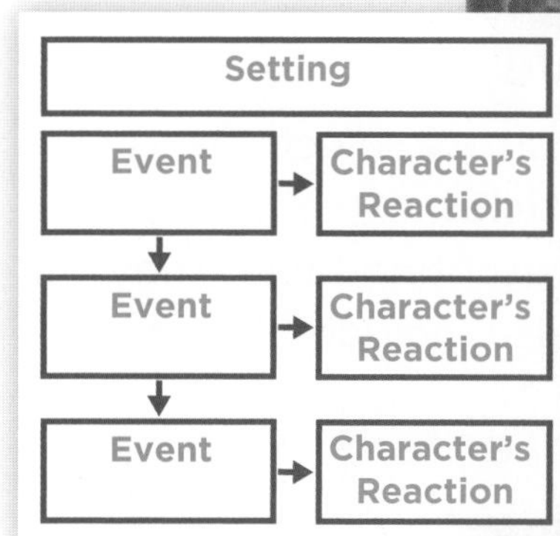

Summarize

To summarize *Me and Uncle Romie* use the most important details from the selection. Information from your Story Flowchart may help you.

Think and Compare

1. What kind of artist is Uncle Romie? Details
2. How does James's **glorious** birthday experience change his relationship with Uncle Romie? Cause and Effect
3. What can you tell about James from the birthday card he makes for Uncle Romie? Explain using details from the story. Visualize: Character, Setting, Plot
4. What point of view is the story told from? Explain why the author chose this point of view. Author's Purpose
5. Read "Secondhand Art" on pages 370–371. Compare the artwork with the artwork in *Me and Uncle Romie*. How is it alike? How is it different? Use details from both selections to explain. Reading/Writing Across Texts

Science

Genre

Expository selections, such as **articles**, explain a topic by presenting facts. They can also include photos.

Text Feature

Multiple-Step Instructions are the steps you follow in order to do or make something.

Content Vocabulary

technology **drawbacks**
software

COMPUTERS

THE FUTURE OF ART

by Lynn Boulanger

What do you think of when you hear the word *artist*? Most people picture someone painting or drawing on a canvas. Others see a person using a hammer to create a sculpture. Today, **technology** allows artists to express themselves using new and exciting tools.

Reading Multiple-Step Instructions

The following instructions tell how to install a software program like CAD:

Instructions:

1. Check that your computer meets the requirements of the software.
2. Close other programs.
3. Follow the exact instructions in the manual.
4. Install other necessary programs if prompted to do so.

Art and Technology

Computers are the latest tool artists are using to create new art. Computer-assisted design (CAD) is a **software** program sculptors can use to plan their art. At one time, artists sketched plans for a new piece on paper. Now many of them bring their ideas to life by using computer programs such as these. With CAD, artists can play around with the size of their creations. CAD can even produce images of three-dimensional shapes. These images can help artists plan or change their work before they actually create it.

Even though this new technology has many benefits, it also has some **drawbacks**. Computer-assisted programs are expensive. An artist has to buy the program in order to use it. Also, some of these programs can be hard for artists to understand. Other programs require artists to take a class, so that they can learn the programs' special features. In spite of the drawbacks, computers are changing the way artists create art!

Connect and Compare

1. Look at the Reading Multiple-Step Instructions box on page 392. What should you do after you close all other programs on your computer? **Reading Multiple-Step Instructions**
2. How does the author feel about artists using technology to create art? Explain using details from the article. **Apply**
3. Think about this article and *Me and Uncle Romie*. How might computer-assisted programs, such as CAD, help Uncle Romie in his work? Explain using details from both selections. **Reading/Writing Across Texts**

RESEARCH INQUIRY

Science Activity

On your own, research another form of technology artists are using today. Give an oral report and restate the steps that are needed to use this technology.

LOG ON FIND OUT **Science** Computers
www.macmillanmh.com

Writing

Trait: Ideas

Good writers use **strong reasons and details** to convince readers.

Reading and Writing Connection

Read the passage below. Notice how Claire Hartfield uses strong reasons and details in her story.

The author gives three reasons why James likes Harlem. Each reason is made stronger by the rich details that she uses to describe what James did, saw, felt, and heard.

An excerpt from
Me and Uncle Romie

But it was Harlem that I liked best. I played stickball with the kids again . . . and on a really hot day a whole bunch of us ran through the icy cold water that sprayed out hard from the fire hydrant. In the evenings Aunt Nanette and I sat outside listening to the street musicians playing their saxophone songs.

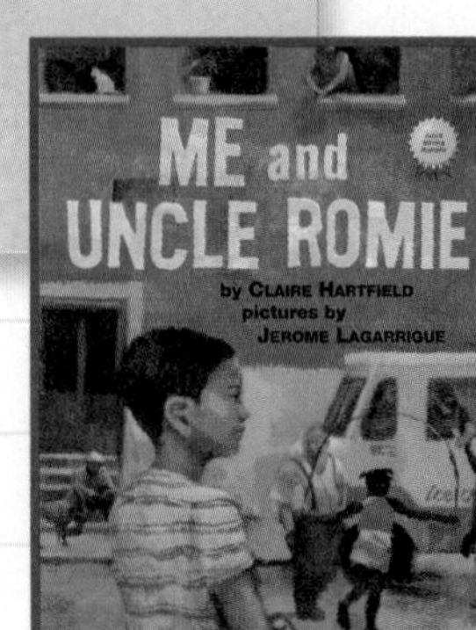

Read and Find

Read Krysta's writing below. What reasons and details does she give for feeling great? Use the checklist below to help you.

Read about a big game.

Go Kyle!

by Krysta D.

Even though I was sitting on a hard wooden bench and the cold December air was biting my cheeks, I felt great. My brother's football team was playing under the bright lights at the high school and was about to win! I could smell mud and crushed grass as they lined up near the end zone. "Go Kyle! Go! Woo hoo!" I shouted to my brother.

Writer's Checklist

- [x] Does the writer state her opinion or feelings?
- [x] Does she support her statement with **convincing reasons**?
- [ ] What words does Krysta use to convince the reader to agree with her opinion or argument?

Review

Make Inferences
Draw Conclusions
Fact and Opinion
Prefixes
Line Graph

Diary of a Scarecrow's Helper

March 15

Oh no! They're getting rid of Jack Patches! Mom and I planned a visit to the community garden today to help clean up for spring. When we arrived, something felt peculiar. At first I couldn't figure it out. Then, as I was putting some old planting ties on the garbage pile, I saw a familiar old hat. Our wonderful scarecrow was lying in pieces in the trash.

I talked to Mr. Collins, the garden supervisor. He told me that there was a terrible storm this winter. The metal pole that Jack used to hang on snapped in two because it was rusty and old. Mr. Collins thinks it would be dangerous to try to put Jack back up, so he's getting rid of him.

I'm really unhappy and I'm going to miss him.

March 16

I keep thinking about Jack Patches lying in the garbage pile. I've got to do something. I can't let him stay there! But what can I do? I called Mr. Collins. He keeps saying that it is not safe to put Jack back up because the metal post is sharp and rusty. Besides, Jack's shirt is a mess. It practically rotted away. And his face is ruined, too. His button eyes fell off and his nose is coming loose.

March 17

I had a dream about Jack Patches. He was holding his nose in his hands and asked me to help him. What can I do?

March 18

I called Mr. Collins again. He agreed to keep Jack for at least a week. Then I talked to my uncle, who is really good with tools and wood. He says it won't be hard to fabricate a new support for Jack.

March 22

Uncle Jorge and I went back to the garden with a brand new post. Mr. Collins agreed that the new post looked very safe and sturdy. Uncle Jorge taught me how to plant a post safely. We placed the post into the concrete and held it there until it hardened, or set, enough that we could remove our hands. Tomorrow the concrete will be set, and we can put Jack back together. I brought his face home with me so I can redo it.

March 23

Jack Patches is back! He looks better than ever. Uncle Jorge donated a new shirt to replace the old one that was threadbare and faded. I finished sewing his face together this morning. His shiny new blue button eyes look terrific. He's so happy to be back that he's smiling. Well, he sort of has to, because I sewed him that way. But I'm sure everyone who visits the garden and sees him will smile, too!

Silent Spring No Longer: RACHEL CARSON

RACHEL CARSON WAS BORN on a farm in Springdale, Pennsylvania, in 1907. It was here, through the gentle encouragement of her mother, that she learned to love nature. When Carson went to college, she took her love of nature with her. She majored in marine biology, the study of life in the sea.

After college Carson taught for five years before joining the U.S. Bureau of Fisheries. She wrote for a radio show that explored life in the seas. It was called "Romance Under the Waters." Carson's writing was wonderful and made the sea come alive. She also wrote three books about the sea: *Under the Sea Wind*, *The Sea Around Us*, and *The Edge of the Sea*.

These books all became bestsellers and won many awards. Carson soon left her job so she could become a full-time writer.

In the late 1940s and 1950s, people used chemicals called pesticides to kill unwanted insects. One of these pesticides was DDT. Scientists began to learn that DDT did kill harmful insects, but it also killed birds. Birds took the chemical into their bodies when they ate insects infected with it. The chemicals made the birds' eggs very frail. The delicate eggs broke easily, and many baby birds did not hatch. Birds such as peregrine falcons and bald eagles began to die out.

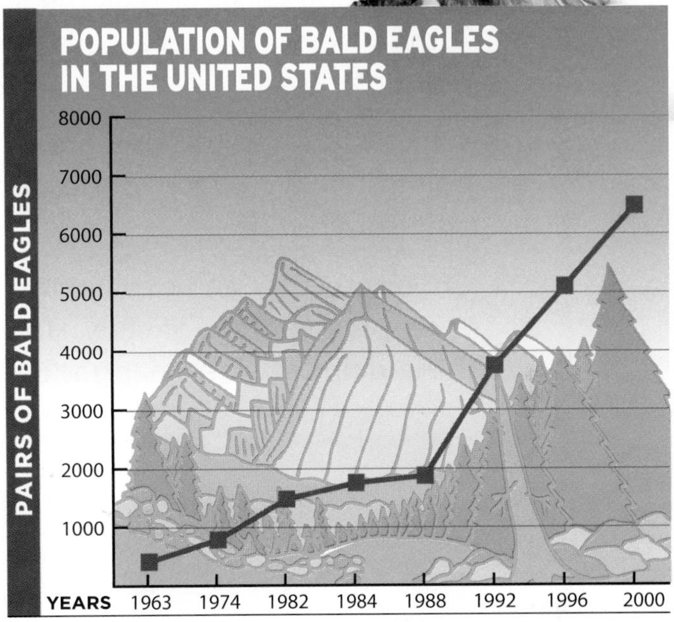

This line graph shows how the population of bald eagle pairs increased after DDT was banned in the United States.

Rachel Carson became concerned about this problem. She spent a lot of time gathering facts. Then she wrote a book called *Silent Spring*. In the book she wrote about how birds were dying because of DDT.

Companies that made the chemicals tried to say that Carson was mistaken. President John F. Kennedy called for testing of chemicals used as pesticides. Tests showed that Carson was right. Pesticides were harming the environment and causing birds to die out.

Rachel Carson published *Silent Spring* in 1962. Carson did not get to see her work change history because she died in 1964. The use of DDT in the United States was banned in 1972. Since then birds that were in danger of dying out were saved and have come back. Now each spring you can hear these wonderful birds singing in the trees. Thanks to Rachel Carson, spring is not silent.

Show What You Know

Comprehension

Point of View

- Point of view refers to the way a narrator tells a story. A first-person narrator tells the story in his or her own words. A third-person narrator tells the story from one character's point of view.
- Which stories in this unit are written from a first-person point of view? Which stories are written from a third-person point of view?
- Choose a story and explain the difference between first- and third-person point of view. How would the story be different if the point of view changed?

Genre

Elements of a Play

- A play is a story that is intended to be performed. It has features such as a prologue or epilogue, stage directions, scene descriptions, and dialogue.
- With a partner look at the play *Ranita, The Frog Princess* on page 342. Identify the setting, characters, stage directions, and dialogue.
- Think of a story that both of you know such as "The Three Little Pigs." Pick a scene from the story and make it into a scene from a play by adding: setting, characters, stage directions, and dialogue.

Word Study

Analogies Using Synonyms and Antonyms

- An analogy shows how two pairs of words are related. For an analogy to make sense, the words in each pair must be related in the same way. If the words in one pair are synonyms then the words in the second pair must be synonyms.
- The following analogies use either synonyms or antonyms.

  slender is to thin as big is to ________
  quiet is to loud as whisper is to ________
- Write these analogies on a separate sheet of paper, identify if they are synonyms or antonyms, and choose the word that best completes each analogy.

Context Clues

- Context clues, such as definitions, can help you figure out the meaning of an unfamiliar word. For example: *That car runs on solar energy which is energy that comes from the sun.*
- Sometimes there is an example in a sentence that will help you figure out the meaning of an unfamiliar word. For example: *A popular national monument, such as the Liberty Bell, has thousands of visitors each year.*
- Write the following three words in sentences: *island*, *shellfish*, *predator*. Include context clues that provide either a definition or an example to help make the meaning of each word clear. Then trade papers with a partner.

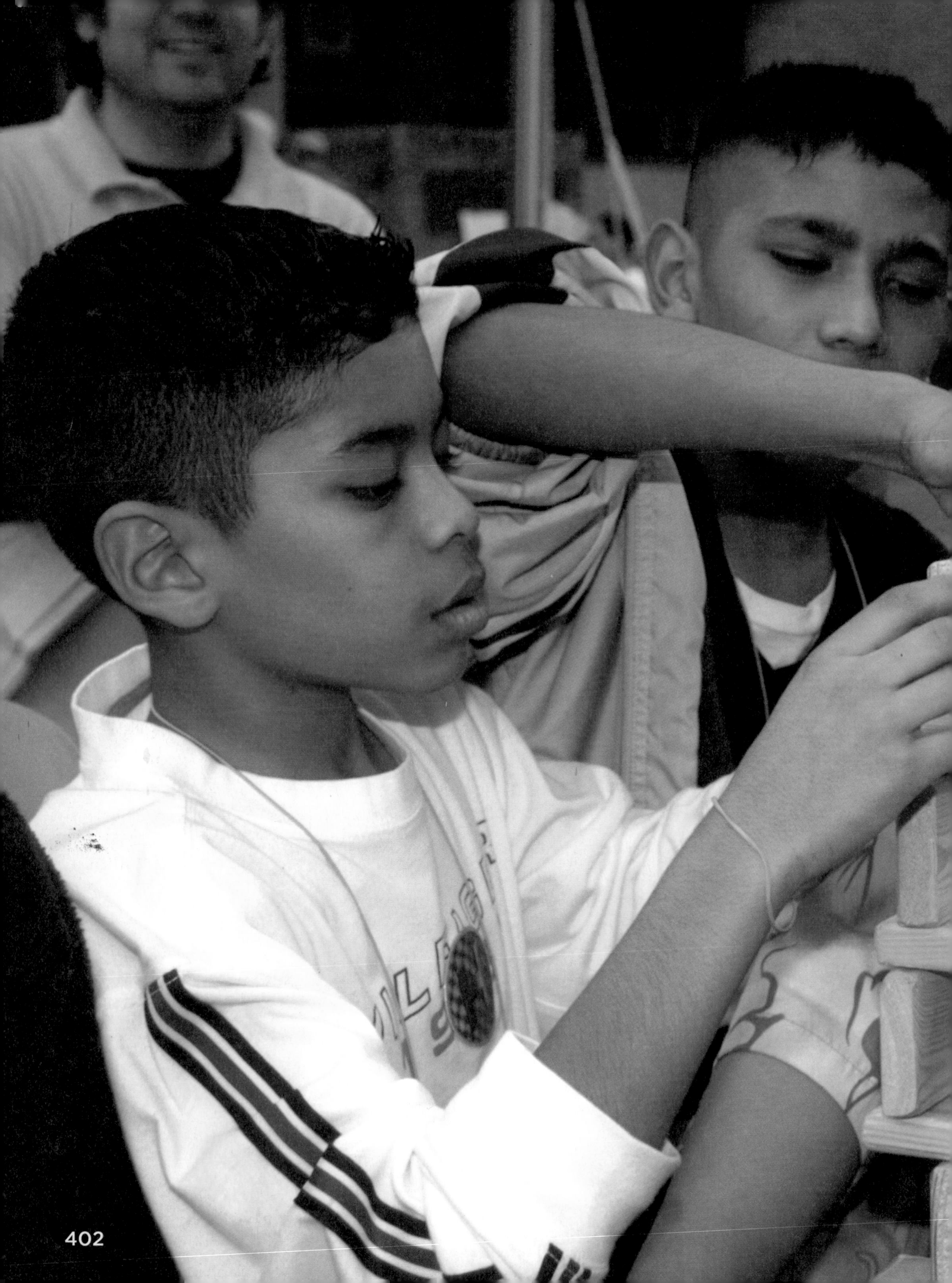

Unit 4
Working Together

The Big Question

Why do people work in teams?

LOG ON VIEW IT

Theme Video
Working Together
www.macmillanmh.com

Why do people work in teams?

One person can make a big difference. However, sometimes, that one person needs the help of other people. There are many situations where people need to work together to accomplish a goal, to help others, or to change something. For example, rescue teams work together to help others or to clean up after natural disasters. Sports teams must work together to be successful. NASA is an example of a group in which many people work together to accomplish a single goal.

Learning why teamwork is so valuable can help you understand how large tasks get finished and also help you work better with others.

Research Activities

Throughout the unit, you will be gathering information about projects that were successful because of teamwork. Choose one project to focus your research on and create a process booklet. A process booklet shows how something develops, from beginning to end. Use graphic aids in your booklet.

Keep Track of Ideas

As you read, keep track of all you are learning about teamwork and how it affects large projects. Use the **Chart Foldable**. In the first column, write the Unit Theme: *Working Together.* On each of the following columns, write facts you learn each week that will help you in your research and in your understanding of the Unit Theme.

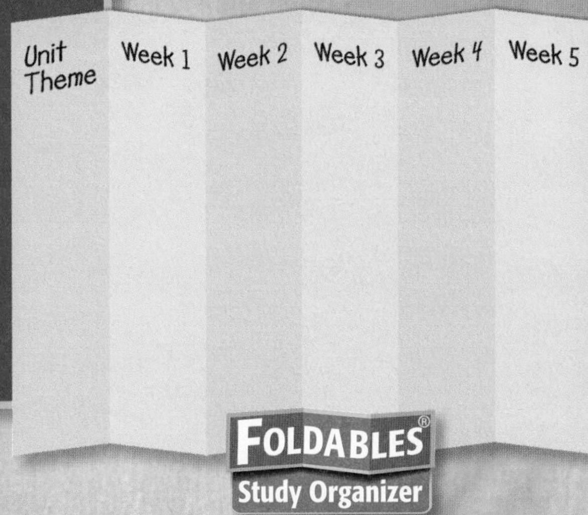

Digital Learning

LOG ON FIND OUT www.macmillanmh.com

StudentWorks Plus™

Interactive Student Book

- **Research Roadmap**
  Follow a step-by-step guide to complete your research project.

Online Resources

- Topic Finder and Other Research Tools
- Videos and Virtual Field Trips
- Photos and Drawings for Presentations
- Related Articles and Web Resources
- Web Site Links

People and Places

David Crockett 1786–1836

Frontiersman, soldier, politician, and legendary figure, Colonel David Crockett was a symbol of the American Frontier. He died in 1836 while defending the Alamo during the Texas Revolution.

Value of Friendship

Talk About It

In what ways do friends work together and help one another?

LOG ON VIEW IT

Oral Language Activities
Value of Friendship
www.macmillanmh.com

Vocabulary

eavesdropping	jumble
acquaintance	scornfully
route	logical

Context Clues

Paragraph Clues can help you figure out the meaning of unfamiliar words and multiple-meaning words.

Use clues within the paragraph to figure out the meaning of the word *second* in the story.

The Country Mouse and the City Mouse

retold by Jeff Banner

One day Country Mouse invited an old friend from the city to visit her. Country Mouse welcomed City Mouse with a delicious meal of fresh barley and corn. City Mouse was very quiet, so Country Mouse asked her whether anything was wrong.

"I was just missing the city," she replied wistfully. "You must come visit one day. There are lots of good things to eat."

Country Mouse thought this was a very good idea, so a few weeks later she traveled to the city. City Mouse invited her friend for dinner at her favorite restaurant. Country Mouse followed City Mouse as she tiptoed quietly into a cupboard and listened.

"So, what are we doing?" asked Country Mouse.

"Shhh. We're doing a bit of **eavesdropping**," City Mouse whispered. "When the cook leaves for the night, we can help ourselves to that second bag of sugar over there. The first one is too high up."

A light went out, and it grew quiet. City Mouse nibbled a hole in the bag, and Country Mouse took the tiniest taste.

"I've never tasted anything so wonderful in all my life!" she cried.

Just then the mice heard a scuffling sound coming from behind the cupboard door. "Run for your life!" screamed City Mouse.

"That's Esperanza, the cook's rotten cat," City Mouse explained when they were safe. "You don't ever want to meet or make her **acquaintance**. One swipe from her claws and it's over. When she's asleep again, we can go back for more sugar."

But Country Mouse was too frightened to go back, so they followed a new **route** down to the basement instead. There they found a **jumble** of grain bags stacked randomly against the wall. Country Mouse happily nibbled this and that. Then she saw something that made her mouth water—a hunk of cheese! Country Mouse was about to bite it when . . .

"STOP!" yelled City Mouse. "Can't you see that's a trap?" she said **scornfully**. "One nibble and that big metal thing comes crashing down."

Country Mouse was horrified. The city was not the safest, most **logical** place for a mouse to live—or visit! So Country Mouse went home and never visited the city again.

Reread for Comprehension

Visualize

Theme In a fable, the theme may be expressed as the moral of a story. To identify the theme, look for **clues** in the story about the characters. Visualize and think about what the characters say and do and what happens as a result. Then, think about what lesson, or message, the author wants readers to learn. Reread the selection and use your Theme Chart to help you analyze the theme.

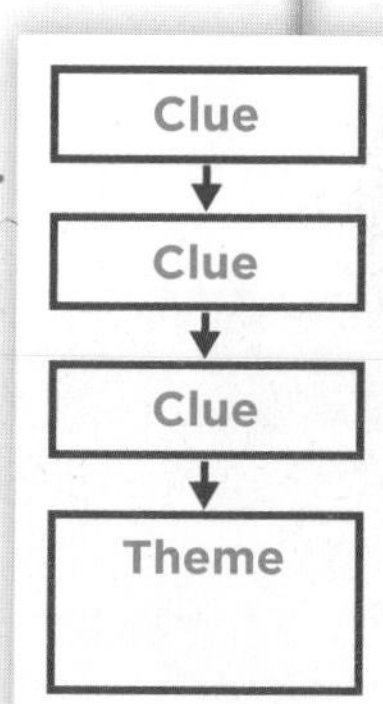

LOG ON LEARN IT **Comprehension** www.macmillanmh.com

Comprehension

Genre

Fantasy is a story with invented characters, settings, or other elements that could not exist in real life.

Visualize

Theme As you read, fill in your Theme Chart.

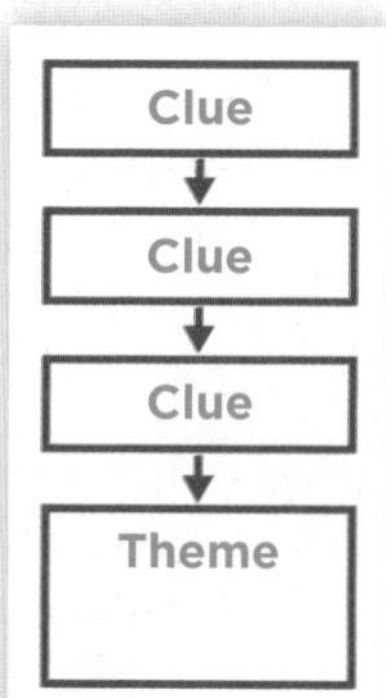

Read to Find Out

What happens when a country cricket winds up in a big city?

THE CRICKET IN TIMES SQUARE
By George Selden
NEWBERY HONOR BOOK
DRAWINGS BY
Garth Williams

Chester

Tucker Mouse had been watching the Bellinis and listening to what they said. Next to scrounging, **eavesdropping** on human beings was what he enjoyed most. That was one of the reasons he lived in the Times Square subway station. As soon as the family disappeared, he darted out across the floor and scooted up to the newsstand. At one side the boards had separated and there was a wide space he could jump through. He'd been in a few times before—just exploring. For a moment he stood under the three-legged stool, letting his eyes get used to the darkness. Then he jumped on it.

"Psst!" he whispered. "Hey, you up there—are you awake?"

There was no answer.

"Psst! Psst! Hey!" Tucker whispered again, louder this time.

From the shelf above came scuffling, like little feet feeling their way to the edge. "Who is going 'psst'?" said a voice.

"It's me," said Tucker. "Down here on the stool."

A black head, with two shiny black eyes, peered down at him. "Who are you?"

"A mouse," said Tucker, "Who are *you*?"

"I'm Chester Cricket," said the cricket. He had a high, musical voice. Everything he said seemed to be spoken to an unheard melody.

"My name's Tucker," said Tucker Mouse. "Can I come up?"

KLEENEX
WHITE

"I guess so," said Chester Cricket. "This isn't my house anyway."

Tucker jumped up beside the cricket and looked him all over. "A cricket," he said admiringly. "So you're a cricket. I never saw one before."

"I've seen mice before," the cricket said. "I knew quite a few back in Connecticut."

"Is that where you're from?" asked Tucker.

"Yes," said Chester. "I guess I'll never see it again," he added wistfully.

"How did you get to New York?" asked Tucker Mouse.

"It's a long story," sighed the cricket.

"Tell me," said Tucker, settling back on his haunches. He loved to hear stories. It was almost as much fun as eavesdropping—if the story was true.

"Well it must have been two—no, three days ago," Chester Cricket began. "I was sitting on top of my stump, just enjoying the weather and thinking how nice it was that summer had started. I live inside an old tree stump, next to a willow tree, and I often go up to the roof to look around. And I'd been practicing jumping that day too. On the other side of the stump from the willow tree there's a brook that runs past, and I'd been jumping back and forth across it to get my legs in condition for the summer. I do a lot of jumping, you know."

"Me too," said Tucker Mouse. "Especially around the rush hour."

"And I had just finished jumping when I smelled something," Chester went on, "liverwurst, which I love."

"You like liverwurst?" Tucker broke in. "Wait! Wait! Just wait!"

In one leap, he sprang down all the way from the shelf to the floor and dashed over to his drain pipe. Chester shook his head as he watched him go. He thought Tucker was a very excitable person—even for a mouse.

Inside the drain pipe, Tucker's nest was a **jumble** of papers, scraps of cloth, buttons, lost jewelry, small change, and everything else that can be picked up in a subway station. Tucker tossed things left and right in a wild search. Neatness was not one of the things he aimed at in life. At last he discovered what he was looking for: a big piece of liverwurst he had found earlier that evening. It was meant to be for breakfast tomorrow, but he decided that meeting his first cricket was a special occasion. Holding the liverwurst between his teeth, he whisked back to the newsstand.

"Look!" he said proudly, dropping the meat in front of Chester Cricket. "Liverwurst! You continue the story—we'll enjoy a snack too."

"That's very nice of you," said Chester. He was touched that a mouse he had known only a few minutes would share his food with him. "I had a little chocolate before, but besides that, nothing for three days."

"Eat! Eat!" said Tucker. He bit the liverwurst into two pieces and gave Chester the bigger one. "So you smelled the liverwurst—then what happened?"

Theme
What message about friendship does the author want readers to understand?

"I hopped down from the stump and went off toward the smell," said Chester.

"Very **logical**," said Tucker Mouse, munching with his cheeks full. "Exactly what I would have done."

"It was coming from a picnic basket," said Chester. "A couple of tuffets away from my stump the meadow begins, and there was a whole bunch of people having a picnic. They had hard boiled eggs, and cold roast chicken, and roast beef, and a whole lot of other things besides the liverwurst sandwiches which I smelled."

Tucker Mouse moaned with pleasure at the thought of all that food.

"They were having such a good time laughing and singing songs that they didn't notice me when I jumped into the picnic basket," continued Chester. "I was sure they wouldn't mind if I had just a taste."

"Naturally not," said Tucker Mouse sympathetically. "Why mind? Plenty for all. Who could blame you?"

"Now, I have to admit," Chester went on, "I had more than a taste. As a matter of fact, I ate so much that I couldn't keep my eyes open—what with being tired from the jumping and everything. And I fell asleep right there in the picnic basket. The first thing I knew, somebody had put a bag on top of me that had the last of the roast beef sandwiches in it. I couldn't move!"

"Imagine!" Tucker exclaimed. "Trapped under roast beef sandwiches! Well, there are worse fates."

"At first I wasn't too frightened," said Chester. "After all, I thought, they probably come from New Canaan or some other nearby town. They'll have to unpack the basket sooner or later. Little did I know!" He shook his head and sighed. "I could feel the basket being carried into a car and riding somewhere and then being lifted down. That must have been the railroad station. Then I went up again and there was a rattling and roaring sound, the way a train makes. By this time I was pretty scared. I knew every minute was taking me farther away from my stump, but there wasn't anything I could do. I was getting awfully cramped too, under those roast beef sandwiches."

"Didn't you try to eat your way out?" asked Tucker.

"I didn't have any room," said Chester. "But every now and then the train would give a lurch and I managed to free myself a little. We traveled on and on, and then the train stopped. I didn't have any idea where we were, but as soon as the basket was carried off, I could tell from the noise it must be New York."

"You never were here before?" Tucker asked.

"Goodness no!" said Chester. "But I've heard about it. There was a swallow I used to know who told about flying over New York every spring and fall on her way to the North and back. But what would I be doing here?" He shifted uneasily from one set of legs to another. "I'm a country cricket."

"Don't worry," said Tucker Mouse. "I'll feed you liverwurst. You'll be all right. Go on with the story."

"It's almost over," said Chester. "The people got off one train and walked a ways and got on another—even noisier than the first."

"Must have been the subway," said Tucker.

"I guess so," Chester Cricket said. "You can imagine how scared I was. I didn't know *where* I was going! For all I knew they could have been heading for Texas, although I don't guess many people from Texas come all the way to Connecticut for a picnic."

"It could happen," said Tucker, nodding his head.

"Anyway I worked furiously to get loose. And finally I made it. When they got off the second train, I took a flying leap and landed in a pile of dirt over in the corner of this place where we are."

"Such an introduction to New York," said Tucker, "to land in a pile of dirt in the Times Square subway station. Tsk, tsk, tsk."

"And here I am," Chester concluded forlornly. "I've been lying over there for three days not knowing what to do. At last I got so nervous I began to chirp."

"That was the sound!" interrupted Tucker Mouse. "I heard it, but I didn't know what it was."

"Yes, that was me," said Chester. "Usually I don't chirp until later on in the summer—but my goodness, I had to do *something*!"

The cricket had been sitting next to the edge of the shelf. For some reason—perhaps it was a faint noise, like padded feet tiptoeing across the floor—he happened to look down. A shadowy form that had been crouching silently below in the darkness made a spring and landed right next to Tucker and Chester.

"Watch out!" Chester shouted, "A cat!" He dove headfirst into the matchbox.

Harry Cat

Chester buried his head in the Kleenex. He didn't want to see his new friend, Tucker Mouse, get killed. Back in Connecticut he had sometimes watched the one-sided fights of cats and mice in the meadow, and unless the mice were near their holes, the fights always ended in the same way. But this cat had been upon them too quickly: Tucker couldn't have escaped.

There wasn't a sound. Chester lifted his head and very cautiously looked behind him. The cat—a huge tiger cat with gray-green eyes and black stripes along his body—was sitting on his hind legs, switching his tail around his forepaws. And directly between those forepaws, in the very jaws of his enemy, sat Tucker Mouse. He was watching Chester curiously. The cricket began to make frantic signs that the mouse should look up and see what was looming over him.

Very casually Tucker raised his head. The cat looked straight down on him. "Oh, him," said Tucker, chucking the cat under the chin with his right front paw, "he's my best friend. Come out from the matchbox."

Chester crept out, looking first at one, then the other.

"Chester, meet Harry Cat," said Tucker. "Harry, this is Chester. He's a cricket."

"I'm very pleased to make your **acquaintance**," said Harry Cat in a silky voice.

"Hello," said Chester. He was sort of ashamed because of all the fuss he'd made. "I wasn't scared for myself. But I thought cats and mice were enemies."

NO SALE
Musical America

"In the country, maybe," said Tucker. "But in New York we gave up those old habits long ago. Harry is my oldest friend. He lives with me over in the drain pipe. So how was scrounging tonight, Harry?"

"Not so good," said Harry Cat. "I was over in the ash cans on the East Side, but those rich people don't throw out as much garbage as they should."

"Chester, make that noise again for Harry," said Tucker Mouse.

Chester lifted the black wings that were carefully folded across his back and with a quick, expert stroke drew the top one over the bottom. A *thrumm* echoed through the station.

"Lovely—very lovely," said the cat. "This cricket has talent."

"I thought it was singing," said Tucker. "But you do it like playing a violin, with one wing on the other?"

"Yes," said Chester. "These wings aren't much good for flying, but I prefer music anyhow." He made three rapid chirps.

Tucker Mouse and Harry Cat smiled at each other. "It makes me want to purr to hear it," said Harry.

"Some people say a cricket goes 'chee chee chee,'" explained Chester. "And others say, 'treet treet treet,' but we crickets don't think it sounds like either one of those."

"It sounds to me as if you were going 'crik crik crik,'" said Harry.

"Maybe that's why they call him a 'cricket,'" said Tucker.

They all laughed. Tucker had a squeaky laugh that sounded as if he were hiccupping. Chester was feeling much happier now. The future did not seem nearly as gloomy as it had over in the pile of dirt in the corner.

"Are you going to stay a while in New York?" asked Tucker.

"I guess I'll have to," said Chester. "I don't know how to get home."

"Well, we could always take you to Grand Central Station and put you on a train going back to Connecticut," said Tucker. "But why don't you give the city a try. Meet new people—see new things. Mario likes you very much."

"Yes, but his mother doesn't," said Chester. "She thinks I carry germs."

"Germs!" said Tucker **scornfully**. "She wouldn't know a germ if one gave her a black eye. Pay no attention."

"Too bad you couldn't have found more successful friends," said Harry Cat. "I fear for the future of this newsstand."

"It's true," echoed Tucker sadly. "They're going broke fast." He jumped up on a pile of magazines and read off the names in the half-light that slanted through the cracks in the wooden cover. "*Art News—Musical America*. Who would read them but a few long-hairs?"

"I don't understand the way you talk," said Chester. Back in the meadow he had listened to bullfrogs, and woodchucks, and rabbits, even a few snakes, but he had never heard anyone speak like Tucker Mouse. "What is a long-hair?"

Tucker scratched his head and thought a moment. "A long-hair is an extra-refined person," he said. "You take an Afghan hound—that's a long-hair."

"Do Afghan hounds read *Musical America*?" asked the cricket.

"They would if they could," said Tucker.

Chester shook his head. "I'm afraid I won't get along in New York," he said.

"Oh, sure you will!" squeaked Tucker Mouse. "Harry, suppose we take Chester up and show him Times Square. Would you like that, Chester?"

"I guess so," said Chester, although he was really a little leery of venturing out into New York City.

The three of them jumped down to the floor. The crack in the side of the newsstand was just wide enough for Harry to get through. As they crossed the station floor, Tucker pointed out the local sights of interest, such as the Nedick's lunch counter—Tucker spent a lot of time around there—and the Loft's candy store. Then they came to the drain pipe. Chester had to make short little hops to keep from hitting his head as they went up. There seemed to be hundreds of twistings and turnings, and many other pipes that opened off the main **route**, but Tucker Mouse knew his way perfectly—even in the dark. At last Chester saw light above them. One more hop brought him out onto the sidewalk. And there he gasped, holding his breath and crouching against the cement.

They were standing at one corner of the Times building, which is at the south end of Times Square. Above the cricket, towers that seemed like mountains of light rose up into the night sky. Even this late the neon signs were still blazing. Reds, blues, greens, and yellows flashed down on him. And the air was full of the roar of traffic and the hum of human beings. It was as if Times Square were a kind of shell, with colors and noises breaking in great waves inside it. Chester's heart hurt him and he closed his eyes. The sight was too terrible and beautiful for a cricket who up to now had measured high things by the height of his willow tree and sounds by the burble of a running brook.

"How do you like it?" asked Tucker Mouse.

"Well—it's—it's quite something," Chester stuttered.

"You should see it New Year's Eve," said Harry Cat.

Gradually Chester's eyes got used to the lights. He looked up. And way far above them, above New York, and above the whole world, he made out a star that he knew was a star he used to look at back in Connecticut. When they had gone down to the station and Chester was in the matchbox again, he thought about that star. It made him feel better to think that there was one familiar thing, twinkling above him, amid so much that was new and strange.

Theme
How does the author express the story's theme through his characters?

HOTEL
ASTOR
STATE
CHEVROLET
KINSEY
BO
CRITE
SHE

On a Journey with George and Garth

George Selden wrote this story after he heard a cricket chirping in the Times Square subway station. Chester's whole story came to George immediately. The cricket reminded George of his home in the countryside where he used to live.

Other books by George Selden and Garth Williams

Garth Williams worked very hard to make the creatures in this story look and act like real people. First, he started with an actual photograph of the animal. Then he drew and redrew until the animal seemed to have human qualities.

LOG ON ▶ FIND OUT

Author George Selden
Illustrator Garth Williams
www.macmillanmh.com

Author's Purpose

Why did George Selden write *The Cricket in Times Square*? What details help you figure out what his main purpose was?

LOG ON LEARN IT **Comprehension** www.macmillanmh.com

Comprehension Check

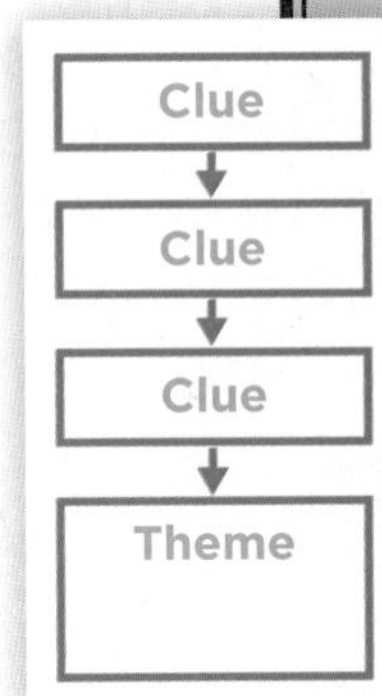

Summarize

To summarize *The Cricket in Times Square* use the most important details from the selection. Information from your Theme Chart may help you.

Think and Compare

1. Where did Chester live before he found himself in New York City? Details
2. What is the sequence of events that led to Chester coming to New York City? Retell the events in the order in which they happened. Sequence
3. What can you tell about Chester's new **acquaintance**, Tucker? Use details from the story to support your answer. Character
4. What message is the author trying to communicate to the reader by making a cricket, a cat, and a mouse his main characters? Explain using story details. Visualize: Theme
5. Read "The Country Mouse and the City Mouse" on pages 408–409. How is Country Mouse's experience similar to Chester's on pages 419–420? How is it different? Use details from both selections to explain. Reading/Writing Across Texts

Science

Genre

Persuasive writing, such as **editorials**, expresses the opinion of the writer and tries to influence the reader to think a certain way about an issue.

Text Feature

Advertisements try to persuade consumers to buy a product.

Content Vocabulary

colony **echolocation** **insecticides**

The Chance of a Lifetime

by Patrick West

What words come to mind when you see or think of a bat? People who know very little about this creature might answer with "creepy," "dark," or "dangerous." Those who know bats would use words such as "fascinating," "amazing," even "beautiful."

All of us here in Austin, Texas, have an incredible opportunity to take a first-hand look at the Mexican free-tailed bat. A **colony** of bats has settled under the Congress Avenue Bridge.

I urge all of you to come out to see these bats. They tend to come out around sunset. Depending on the size of a colony, bats can eat tens of thousands of insects during their nightly flights. That, my friends, is a lot of mosquitoes.

cont. on page 432

Advertisement

Reading an Advertisement

The purpose of an advertisement is to persuade people to buy a product. Look for ways in which the author motivates customers to come to Kramer's.

Our Best Bat House Just Went On Sale!

Now Only $40.00

(Regularly $55.00)

Designed by the Bat Society
Slanted roof for better run-off
Weather-resistant red cedar
Made in the USA

Special: Hammocks–Up to 50% off!

Wheelbarrows–10% off when you bring this ad

For a limited time only. Sales end 6/30.

KRAMER'S LAWN AND GARDEN

555 Main Street, Cedar Park, Texas • (555) 555-5555

Open daily 10–6

cont. from page 430

Unfortunately, bat populations are falling all around the country. This decline is due to several factors. **Insecticides** have killed many bats. People have disturbed bat roosts. Sadly, people who mistakenly think that bats are dangerous or carry disease have intentionally destroyed them. Scientists, however, believe that fewer than one bat in 200 is sick. Sick bats are too weak to fly, so they rarely come in contact with people. We need to spread the word.

Dr. Markus Rivera, a scientist who studies bats, has some helpful advice to pass along. Here are his bat-viewing suggestions.

Tips on Viewing Bats

- Look for bats at dawn or dusk.
- Pick an open spot to see bats against the sky.
- Look for bats near water or streetlights.
- Never touch a bat.
- Do not disturb bats during the day when they sleep.

Did You Know?

Did you know that bats do not rely on their eyes when they fly and hunt insects? They use **echolocation**. They emit high-pitched sounds. When the sound waves bounce off objects and return to the bat's ears, it can tell how far away the object is.

Connect and Compare

1. What are some persuasive techniques used in the ad on page 431? Are these techniques successful? Use details from the ad to support your answer. **Reading an Advertisement**

2. According to "Tips on Viewing Bats," where are some places you might go to look for bats? **Apply**

3. Think about this **editorial** and *The Cricket in Times Square*. How have the bats in Austin, and Tucker and Harry in New York, adapted to living in a city? **Reading/Writing Across Texts**

RESEARCH INQUIRY

Science Activity

Use reference texts and online searches to find out the importance of bats in an ecosystem. Using your research, predict what might happen to the ecosystem if bats became extinct. Present your findings and prediction to the class.

LOG ON FIND OUT **Science** Bats
www.macmillanmh.com

Writing

Trait: Voice

Writers use **dialogue** to show what characters say and to show what is happening in the story.

Reading and Writing Connection

Read the passage below. Notice how the author George Selden integrates dialogue to show what is happening in the story.

An excerpt from
The Cricket in Times Square

“I’m Chester Cricket,” said the cricket. He had a high, musical voice. Everything he said seemed to be spoken to an unheard melody.

“My name’s Tucker,” said Tucker Mouse. “Can I come up?”

“I guess so,” said Chester Cricket. “This isn’t my house anyway.”

Tucker jumped up beside the cricket and looked him all over. “A cricket,” he said admiringly. “So you’re a cricket. I never saw one before.”

The author helps us see the meeting between Chester and Tucker by writing exactly what they said to each other. We learn more about the characters by what they say.

Read and Find

Read Jackie's writing below. How did she use dialogue to show what was happening? Use the checklist below to help you.

Salmon on Board

by Jackie D.

"Help me pull in the net!" I shouted to my brother. You always had to yell on the boat or no one could hear you over the hum of the motor.

"You're doing it all wrong," he yelled back. "You're supposed to put your right hand on top!"

"Oh yeah!" I remembered. Just then, my brother Peter helped me pull in pounds and pounds of fresh, wiggly, Pacific salmon.

Read about a fishing trip.

Writer's Checklist

- [x] Did the author use **dialogue** instead of telling statements?
- [x] Does the author show what is happening through the characters' words?
- [ ] Does it feel like you're listening to people talking as you read?

ANIMAL TEAMS

Talk About It

How do these ants work together, as a team?

LOG ON VIEW IT

Oral Language Activities
Animal Teams
www.macmillanmh.com

Vocabulary

investigates
solitary
territory
communication
nutrients
prehistoric

Word Parts

Greek and Latin Roots can help you figure out the meaning of unfamiliar words. The Greek root *astron* = "star" and an *astronomer* = "one who studies the stars." The Latin root *terr* = "land" and *territory* is a "large tract of land."

Amazing Ants

by Tara Rosati

What do you want to be when you grow up? Perhaps an astronomer who studies the stars? How about a scientist who **investigates** ants? Find out how interesting these misunderstood insects really are!

Social Insects

There are about 10,000 kinds of ants. Most are not **solitary** but live in groups called colonies. Ants are everywhere, but they prefer their **territory** to be in warm climates and never in very cold areas.

Communication among ants varies. For example, some tap the outside of their nest to alert the ants inside that food or enemies are nearby. Other ants make squeaking or buzzing sounds. Ants also make chemicals that other ants in the colony can smell. Each chemical communicates different information to the colony.

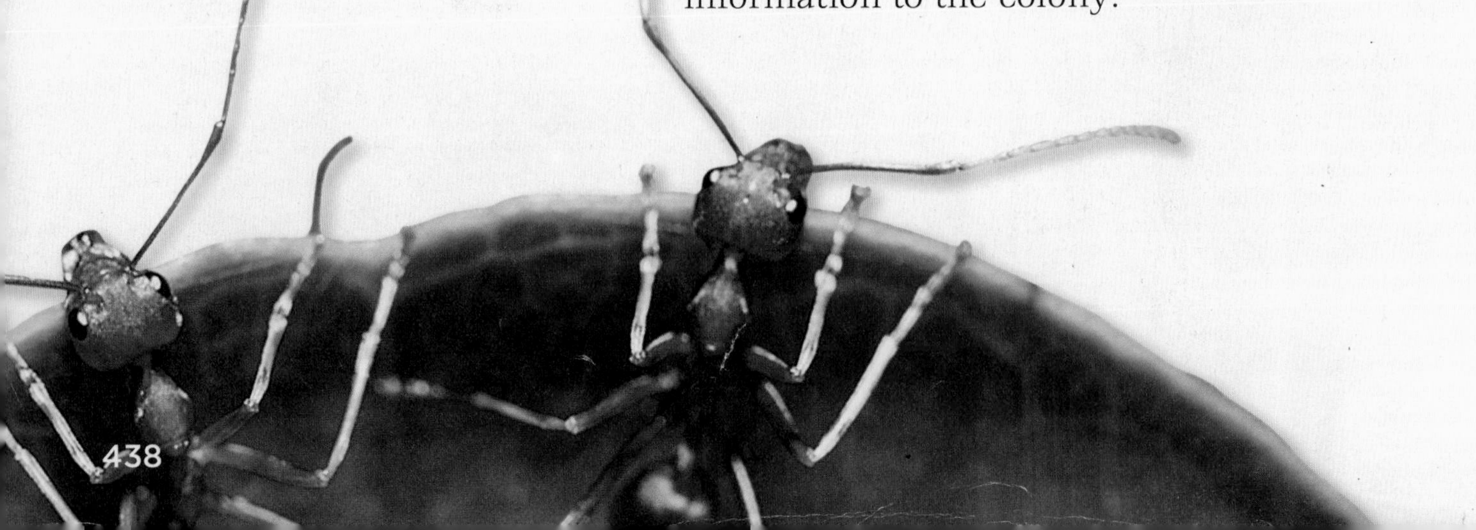

Dairying Ants

These ants got their name from the way they get most of their food or **nutrients**. Dairying ants "milk" insects called aphids. In exchange for the juice, dairying ants protect the aphids against other insects.

Some dairying ants are also baby-sitters. They keep aphids' eggs in their nests during the winter. When the eggs hatch, the ants place the baby aphids on plants.

Fungus Growers

Some ants are gardeners. They grow fungi that the colony can eat. These ants gather leaves, flower petals, and other things from outside the nest. Then they bring them inside to use as fertilizer in their fungi gardens.

Ant Survival

Ants have lived on Earth for a long time. They have been found in **prehistoric** pieces of amber. This is material from the time of the dinosaurs! These tiny, but complex and intelligent, creatures have overcome many challenges in order to survive. Ants are here to stay.

A black garden ant caught in sundew

Reread for Comprehension

Generate Questions

Description Generating questions as you read can help you understand how information is being presented. Authors often use description to present information. Description defines or classifies information by describing its characteristics or details. Authors often use signal words such as *for example*, *is like*, *such as*, or *include* to alert readers to an upcoming list of details. Use your Description Web to classify information in "Amazing Ants."

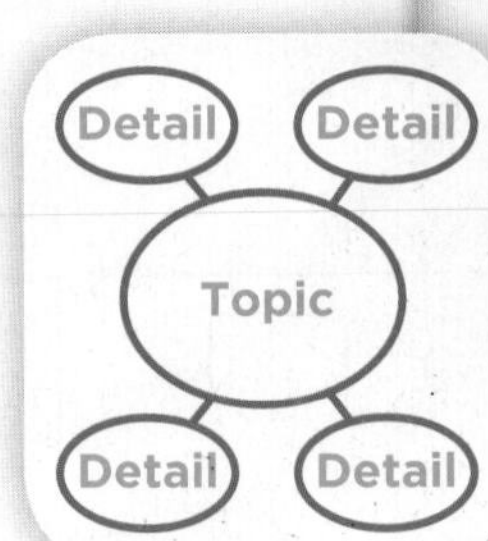

LOG ON LEARN IT **Comprehension**
www.macmillanmh.com

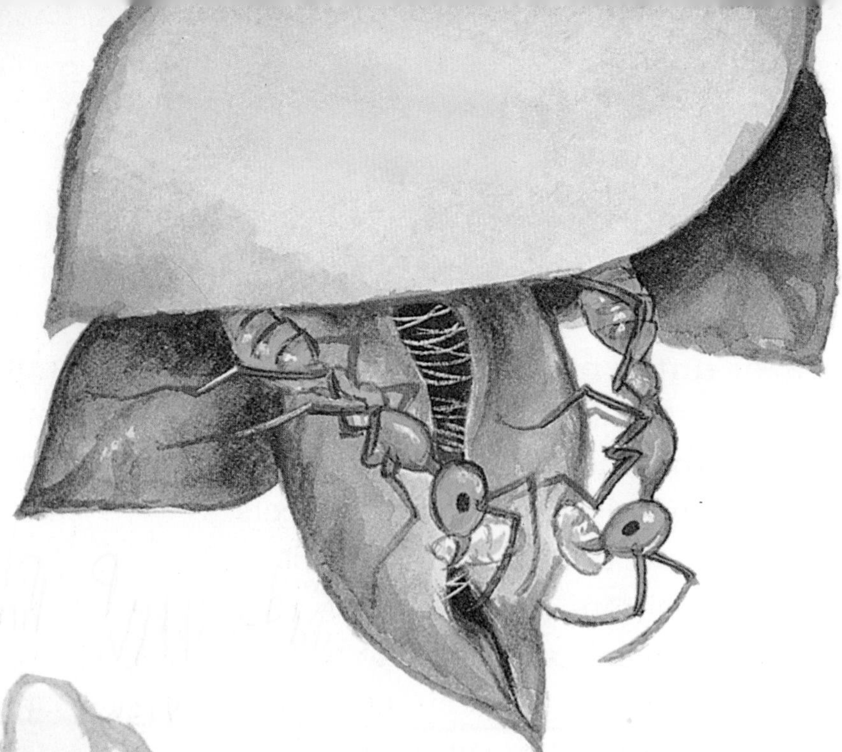

Comprehension

Genre

Expository selections are detailed compositions that explain something by presenting facts and illustrations about it.

Generate Questions

Description

As you read, fill in your Description Web.

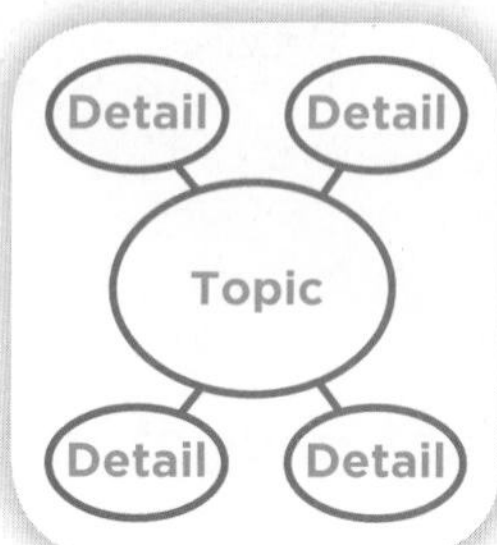

Read to Find Out

What characteristics do ants have?

The Life and Times of the Ant

written and illustrated by

Charles Micucci

Masters of the Earth

Ants are one of the world's most important insects. They plow more soil than beetles, eat more bugs than praying mantises, and outnumber many insects by 7 million to 1.

Tunneling out of jungles and forests and into back yards on every continent except Antarctica, ants ramble on as if they own the Earth. Perhaps they do.

Ounce for ounce, an ant is one of the strongest animals on earth. An ant can lift a seed five times its weight, while an elephant can lift a log only one fifth of its weight.

Each year, the world's ants dig up more than 16 billion tons of dirt— enough to fill 3 billion dump trucks.

Ants are frequently compared with people because they live in social communities and work together to solve their problems.

Great Dynasties on Earth

Ants have been digging through dirt for more than 100 million years. Their dynasty stretches from the time of dinosaurs to today.

Friends in Low Places

There are more than a million kinds of insects. Most of them are **solitary** insects. Their survival depends on only one being—themselves.

An ant is different; it is a social insect. It cannot survive by itself for long periods of time. Ants need other ants to help build a nest, gather food, and protect themselves from enemies. This need for other ants is not a weakness but a strength that enables the ant to overcome its small size.

When an ant is threatened by a larger insect, it emits a scent called an alarm pheromone. Other ants smell the odor and rush to help.

Description

In "Friends in Low Places," describe the ways in which ants are social insects.

Ant Talk

Successful teamwork requires effective **communication**. Ants express themselves by using four senses.

Smell

Ants emit pheromones that other ants smell through their antennae. These scents warn of danger, say hello to friends, and inspire fellow ants to work harder.

Touch

Ants tap one another with their antennae to announce the discovery of food and to ask for food.

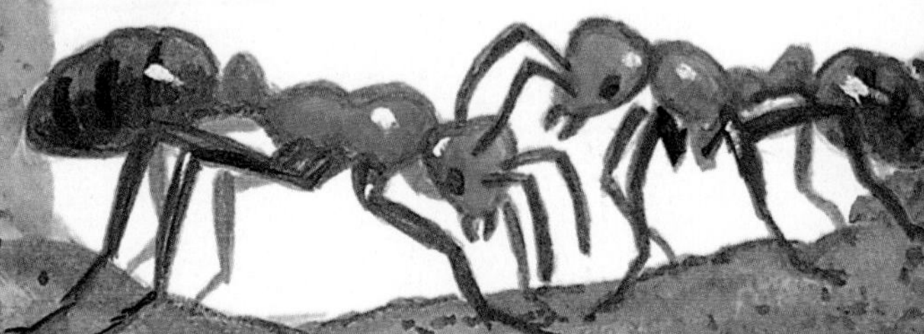

Taste

Ants exchange food with other ants mouth to mouth. These ant "kisses" are a way to share nutrition and chemicals that says "We're family."

Sound

When some ants are trapped in a cave-in, they rub the joint between their waist and abdomen to produce a squeaky sound that other ants "hear" through their legs.

Because it is dark underground, most ants do not rely on sight for communication. In fact, many ants can see only a couple of inches, and some army ants are blind.

The Ant Family

Ants live in social groups called colonies. A small colony may contain only 12 ants, while a large colony overflows with more than 7 million ants. Each colony has three types of ants: workers, male ants, and the queen ant.

Worker Ants

Most of the colony's ants are workers. They are all female, but they do not lay eggs. Although they are the smallest ants, they do all of the chores: clean the nest, gather food, and defend the colony. When you see an ant dragging a crumb of food, you are looking at a worker.

Male Ants

All males have wings and can be seen for only a few weeks in the summer. They mate with the queen but do no work in the colony.

Queen Ants

The queen ant lays eggs and is the mother of all the ants. Young queens have wings, but old queens do not. All queens have large abdomens to produce eggs. Some queens lay millions of eggs per year.

How an Ant Colony Starts

After a hot summer rain, a young queen takes off on her mating flight. The queen flies into a cloud of male ants and mates in the air.

Afterward, all the males die, and the queen returns to the earth. She breaks her wings off by rubbing them on the ground.

Then she digs a hole in the soft, moist earth and starts laying eggs. She will never leave the nest again.

During the next three months, the eggs develop through four stages: egg, larva, pupa, and adult ant.

After they have hatched, the first workers assume the duties of the colony. They search for food and protect the queen. As the queen lays more eggs, the workers enlarge the nest.

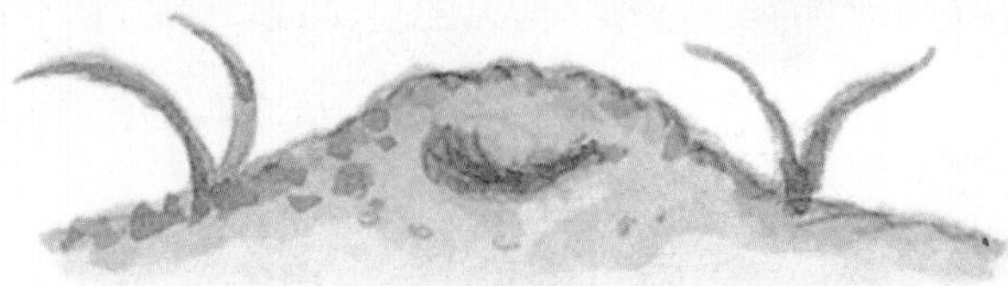

Inside an Anthill

Most ants build their homes underground. Ants dig by scooping dirt with their mandibles (jaws). As they chew the dirt, it mixes with their saliva to form little bricks. Then they pack the little bricks together to reinforce the tunnels. Finally, the ants carry the excess dirt outside with their mandibles, and it gradually forms an anthill.

Beneath the anthill lies the ant nest. Small nests have only one chamber just inches below the surface, while large nests may have thousands of chambers and may be as deep as twenty feet. All nests provide shelter from the weather and a safe environment for the queen ant to lay eggs.

An anthill absorbs the sun's rays and transfers the heat down into the nest. An anthill can be ten degrees warmer than the surrounding area.

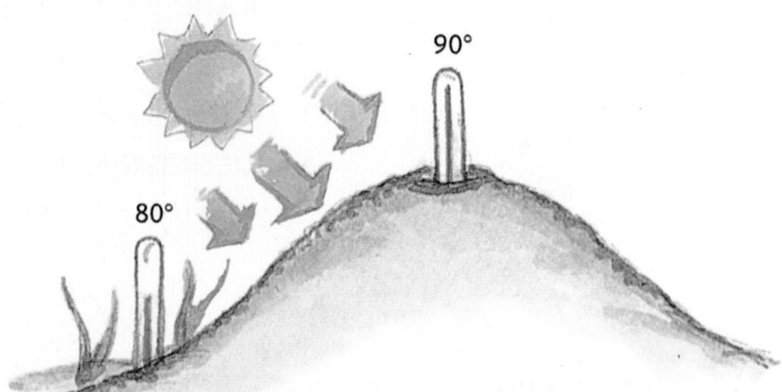

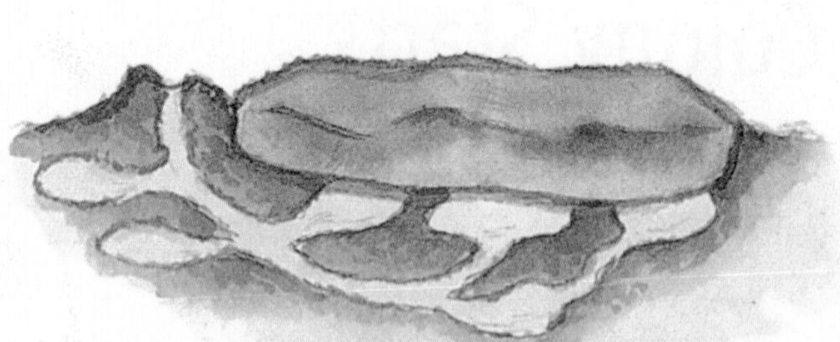

Ants often nest beneath a rock or log, which protects the nest and traps moisture in the dirt. Ants require moisture so that their bodies do not dry out.

Ants dig their nests deep enough to reach damp dirt. As air dries out the nest, they dig new tunnels into the damp dirt.

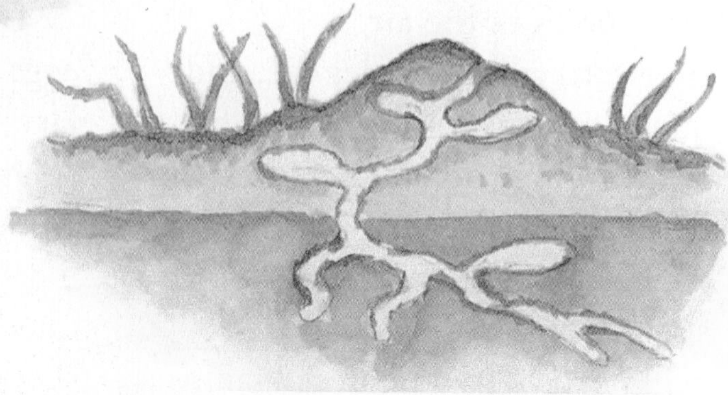

As ants bring up dirt, they recycle **nutrients** that help plants grow.

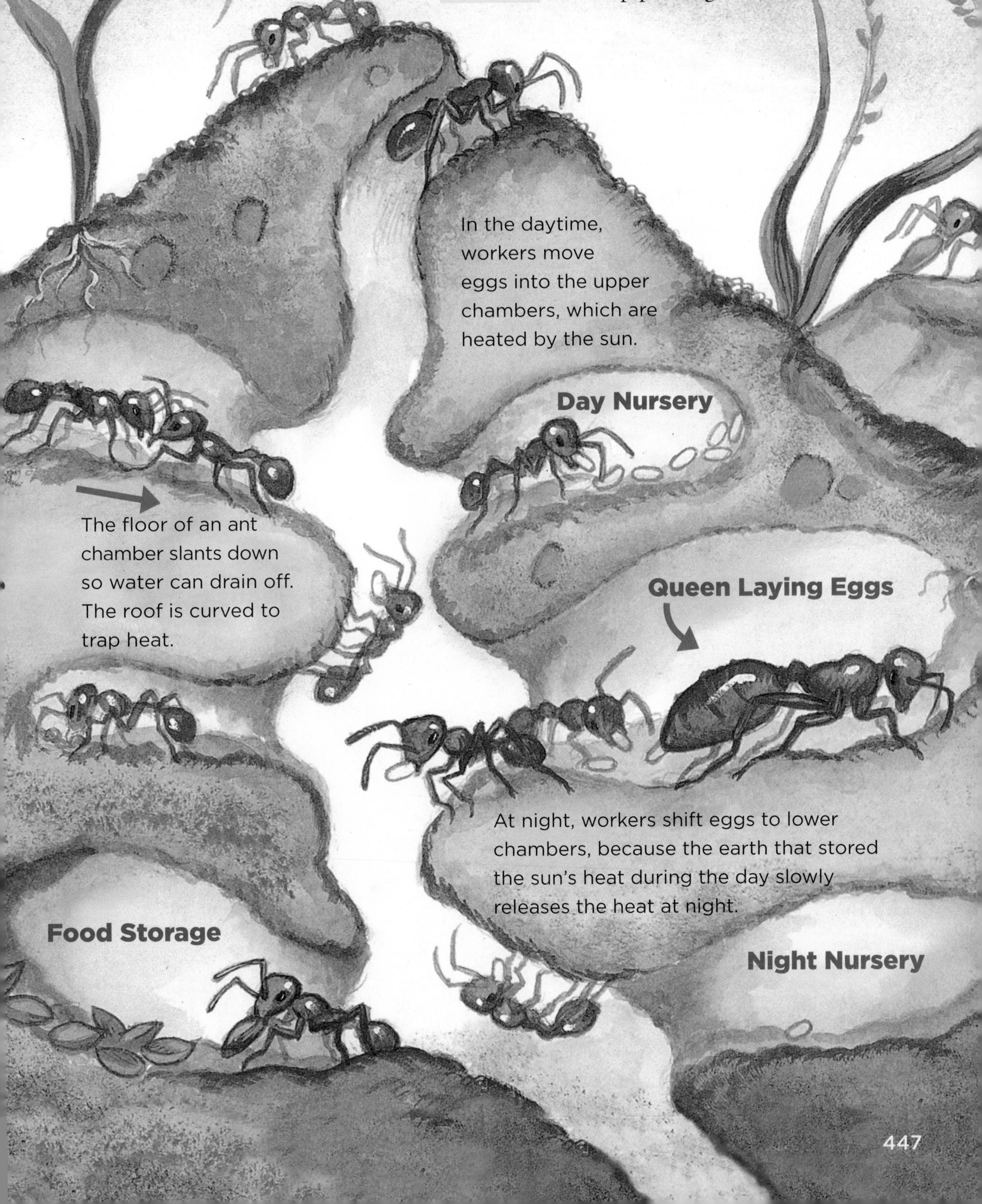

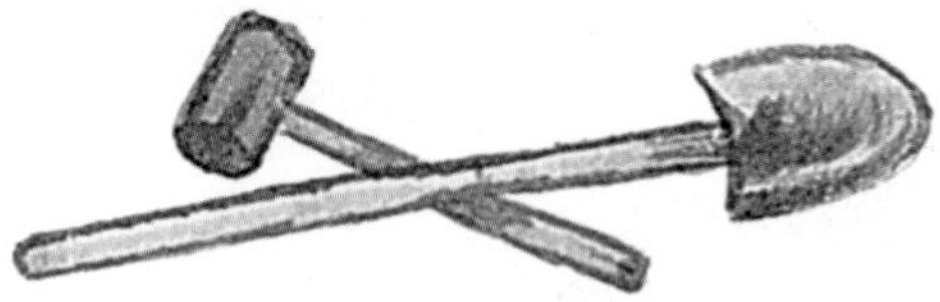

A Life of Work

Ants begin their working lives by cleaning themselves. In a couple of days they start sharing food and licking each other. These food exchanges bond the colony together. There is no boss ant, but active ants usually begin doing chores and then other ants join in.

Younger ants work in the nest — tending the queen ant, feeding larvae, and digging tunnels. After a couple of months, the ants leave the nest to search for food. There is no retirement; worn out or battle-scarred, ants work until they die.

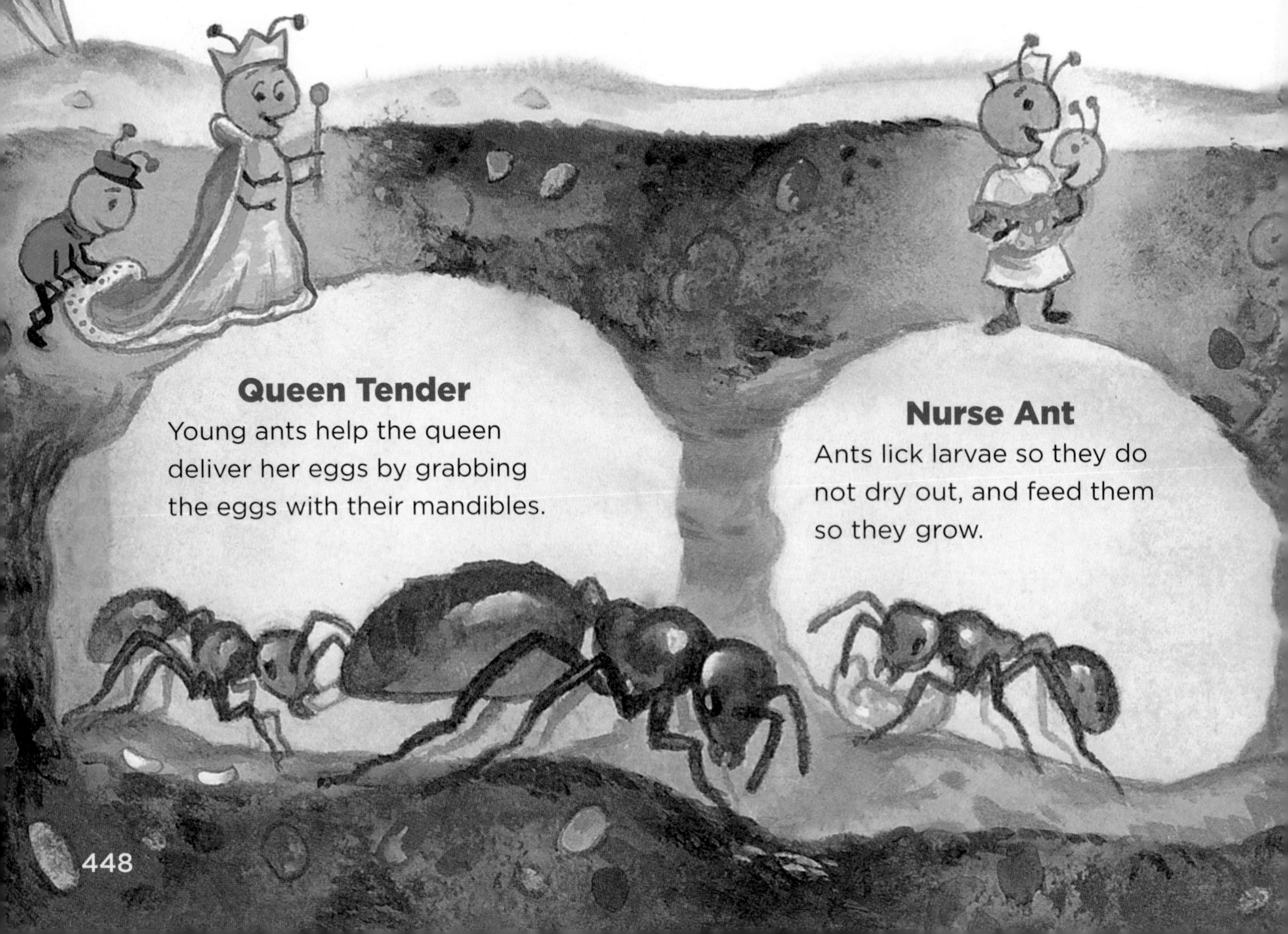

Foragers

The oldest ants search for food. Most foragers search within fifty feet of the nest, but if food is scarce, they may travel thousands of feet.

Guard

When ants first leave the nest, they stand near the entrance, blocking strange ants from entering.

Tunnel Diggers

As the population grows, ants dig more tunnels for the increased traffic and new chambers to store the eggs and larvae.

Digging holes can be hard work. To remove a pile of dirt 6 inches high, 6 inches wide, and 6 inches long requires 500,000 loads of dirt.

Show Me the Way

Every warm day, foraging ants patrol the colony's **territory**. They are not just wandering; they are searching for food. When an ant finds food, she rushes back to the colony while laying a scent trail. It is the scent trail that leads the other ants to the food source.

Each forager moves out in a different direction. One of the ants discovers a cookie crumb. She **investigates** it with her antennae. Then she tries to drag it home, but it's too big.

So she rushes home to get help. Every couple of steps she bumps her abdomen against the ground and her scent gland releases an invisible vapor, which forms a scent trail.

Back inside the colony, the forager alerts other ants about the cookie by tapping them with her antennae. Suddenly, several ants rush out and follow the scent trail to the food.

Each of the new ants harvests part of the cookie and transports it back to the colony while laying a scent trail of her own.

Soon the vapors of the scent trail are so thick that many more ants join the harvest. As they return, the foraging ants share their feast with the ants inside the nest. Within twenty-four hours, every ant in the colony has tasted the cookie.

Harlow Shapley, an astronomer whose hobby was ants, tested their speed. He discovered that they run faster on hot days.

Temperature	78°F	85°F	92°
Speed (inches per second)	1	$1\frac{3}{8}$	$1\frac{5}{8}$

Description
Explain how an ant gets a large cookie crumb back to the colony.

Tunneling Through Time

Ants evolved from wasps more than 100 million years ago. They have been dodging footsteps ever since. As dinosaurs thundered above ground, ants dug out a home below. The mighty dinosaurs are long gone, but the little ant has survived.

Today, myrmecologists search for the secrets of the ants' long existence and how those traits may benefit our society. They study ant fossils in **prehistoric** amber and observe the daily habits of ant colonies.

100,000,000 B.C.
Ants dug tunnels under dinosaurs.

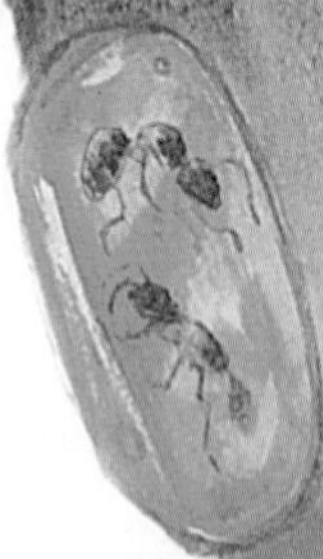

90,000,000 B.C.
Two ants were sealed in amber. Millions of years later, the amber was found in New Jersey.

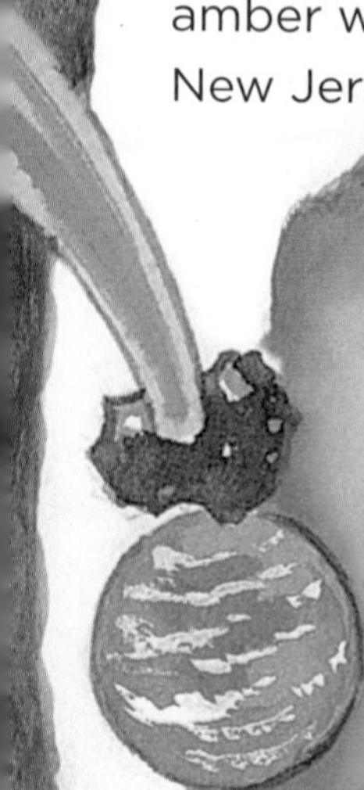

65,000,000 B.C.
Some scientists think a giant meteorite crashed into Earth, killing the dinosaurs. But ants, which could hide underground, survived the disaster.

2000 B.C.
Aborigines in Australia ate the honey of honeypot ants. Their modern descendants call these sweet ants *yarumpa*.

400 B.C.
Herodotus, a Greek historian, wrote about ants that mined gold. Today, some miners sift through anthills to learn what minerals lie underground.

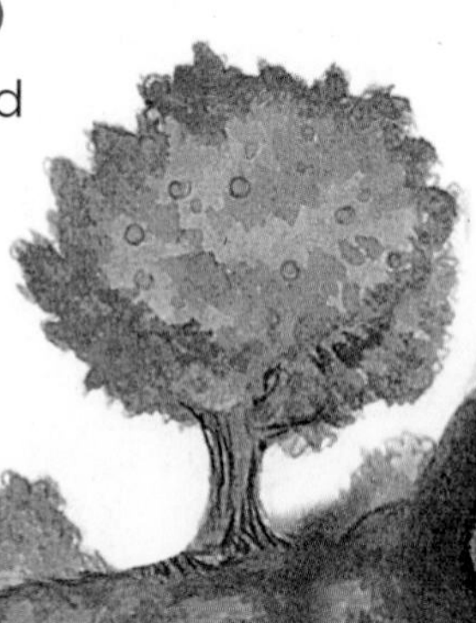

A.D. 1200–1300
Chinese farmers used ants to keep their orange trees free of insect pests.

1500s–1800s
When Europeans conquered the Caribbean islands, their forts were frequently invaded by ants. They offered rewards and prayed to Saint Saturnin to stop the six-legged armies.

1687
Anton von Leeuwenhoek, who invented the microscope, discovered ant eggs and pupae.

1991
Bert Hölldobler and Edward O. Wilson, two myrmecologists, won the Pulitzer Prize for their book *The Ants*.

1859
The biologist Charles Darwin wrote about ant intelligence and teamwork in his classic work *The Origin of Species*.

1880
Germany passed a law protecting wood ants because they kept trees free of pests.

1890s–1930s
William Wheeler, one of America's first myrmecologists, traveled around the world collecting ants and ant fossils.

2000
Scientists applied ant behavior as a model for computer networks. Computer systems based on ant behavior rerouted around problems quicker than previous systems did.

The tunnel of time continues for ants. Their hard work inspires people today, as it has for many centuries. Look down on a warm day and you will probably find an ant. Drop a piece of food . . . and an ant will probably find you.

The Life and Times of Charles Micucci

Charles Micucci often fills his nature books with amusing illustrations, just as he does in this selection. Once he even drew the planet Earth wearing red sneakers. Charles carefully researches his science topics. Sometimes he does experiments to help him write. When he was working on a book about apples, he planted 23 apple seeds and cared for them in his apartment.

Other books by Charles Micucci

LOG ON FIND OUT

Author Charles Micucci
www.macmillanmh.com

Author's Purpose

What was Charles Micucci's purpose for writing *The Life and Times of the Ant*? Was that purpose stated or implied?

LOG ON LEARN IT **Comprehension**
www.macmillanmh.com

Comprehension Check

Summarize

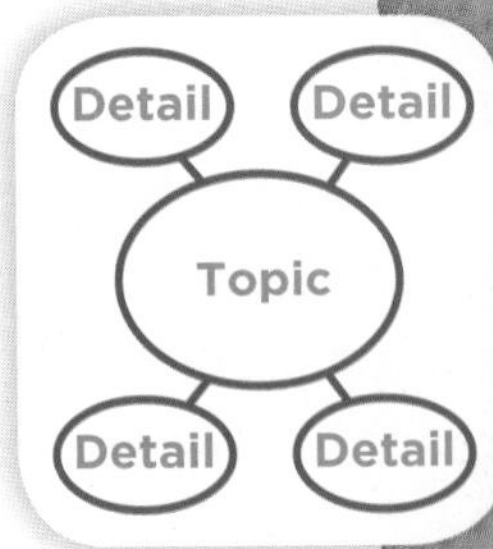

To summarize *The Life and Times of the Ant* use the most important details from the selection. Information from your Description Web may help you.

Think and Compare

1. In a colony, what type of ant lays eggs? Details
2. When ants build their homes underground, what happens before the ants pack the little bricks to reinforce the tunnels? Sequence
3. Describe the different forms of **communication** that ants use. Include details from the text. Generate Questions: Description
4. Reread "Show Me the Way" on pages 450–451. What kind of information do the illustrations add to the text? Author's Purpose
5. Reread "Amazing Ants" on pages 438–439 and *The Life and Times of the Ant*. What do readers learn about how ants get their food? Reading/Writing Across Texts

Language Arts

Fables are stories that have animal characters that talk and act as people do. A moral, or lesson, usually appears at the end of a fable.

Literary Elements

Personification is a literary device where human characteristics such as feelings are given to animals or things.

A **Moral** is a lesson taught by a fable or a story.

THE Ant AND THE Grasshopper

retold and illustrated by Amy Lowry Poole

A LONG TIME AGO, in the old Summer Palace at the edge of the Emperor's courtyard, there lived a grasshopper and a family of ants.

The ants awoke every day before dawn and began their endless tasks of rebuilding their house of sand, which had been washed down by the evening rains, and searching for food, which they would store beneath the ground. They carried their loads grain by grain, one by one, back and forth, all day long.

The grasshopper liked to sleep late into the morning, rising as the sun stretched toward noon.

"Silly ants," he would say. "You work too hard. Come follow me into the courtyard, where I will sing and dance for the great Emperor."

The ants kept on working.

"Silly ants," the grasshopper would say. "See the new moon. Feel the summer breeze. Let us go together and watch the Empress and her ladies as they prepare for midsummer's eve."

But the ants ignored the grasshopper and kept on working.

Soon the days grew shorter and the wind brought cooler air from the north. The ants, mindful of the winter to come, worked even harder to secure their home against the impending cold and snow. They foraged for food and brought it back to their nest, saving it for those cold winter months.

Comparing the words of the grasshopper and the ants will help you identify the moral.

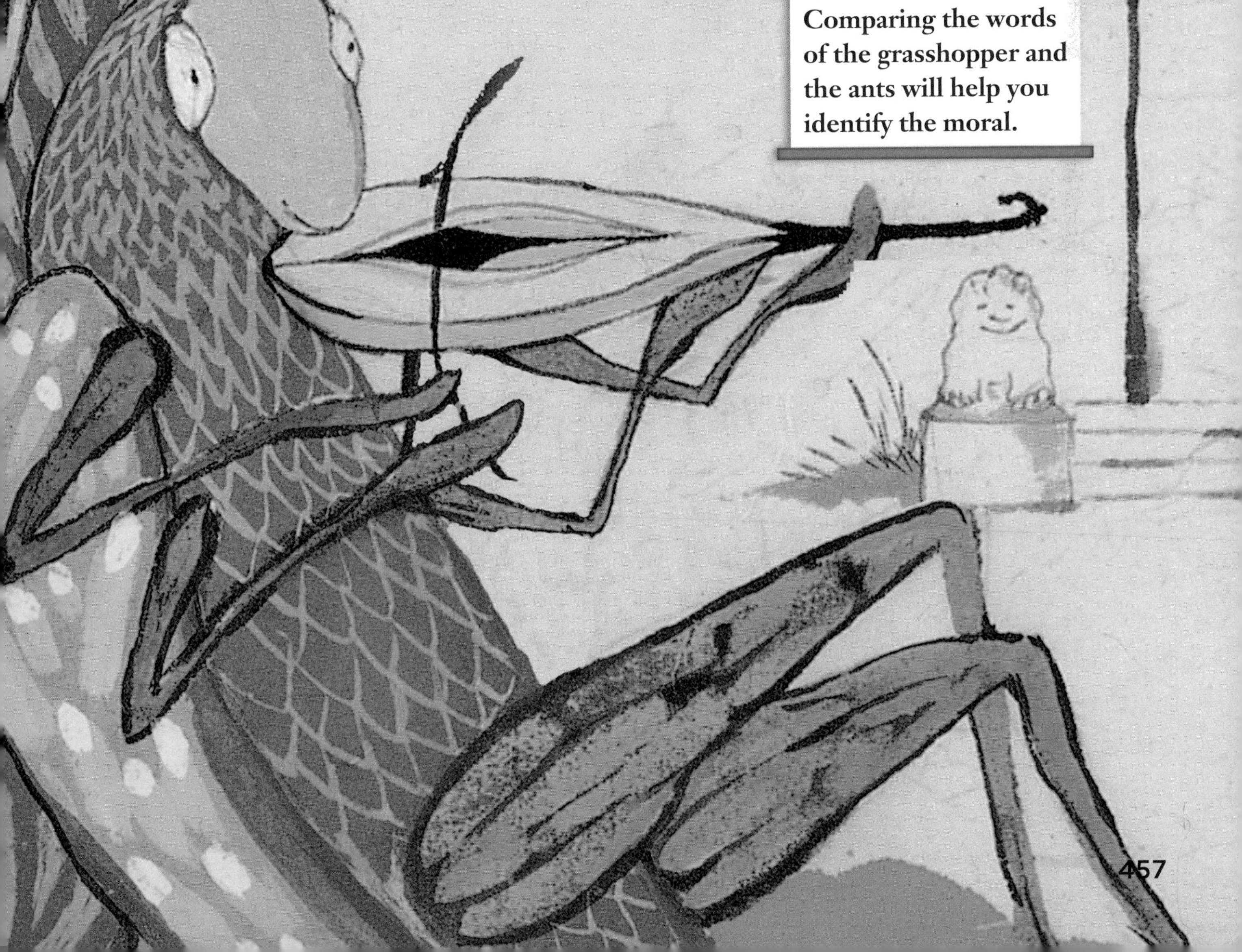

"Silly ants," said the grasshopper. "Don't you ever rest? Today is the harvest festival. The Emperor will feast on mooncakes and sweet greens from the fields. I will play my music for him until the moon disappears into the smooth lake water. Come and dance with me."

"You would do well to do as we do," said one of the ants. "Winter is coming soon and food will be hard to find. Snow will cover your house and you will freeze without shelter."

But the grasshopper ignored the ant's advice and continued to play and dance until the small hours of the morning.

Winter arrived a week later and brought whirls of snow and ice. The Emperor and his court left the Summer Palace for their winter home in the great Forbidden City. The ants closed their door against the ice and snow, safe and warm, resting at last after their long days of preparation.

And the grasshopper huddled beneath the palace eaves and rubbed his hands together in a mournful chirp, wishing he had heeded the ant's advice.

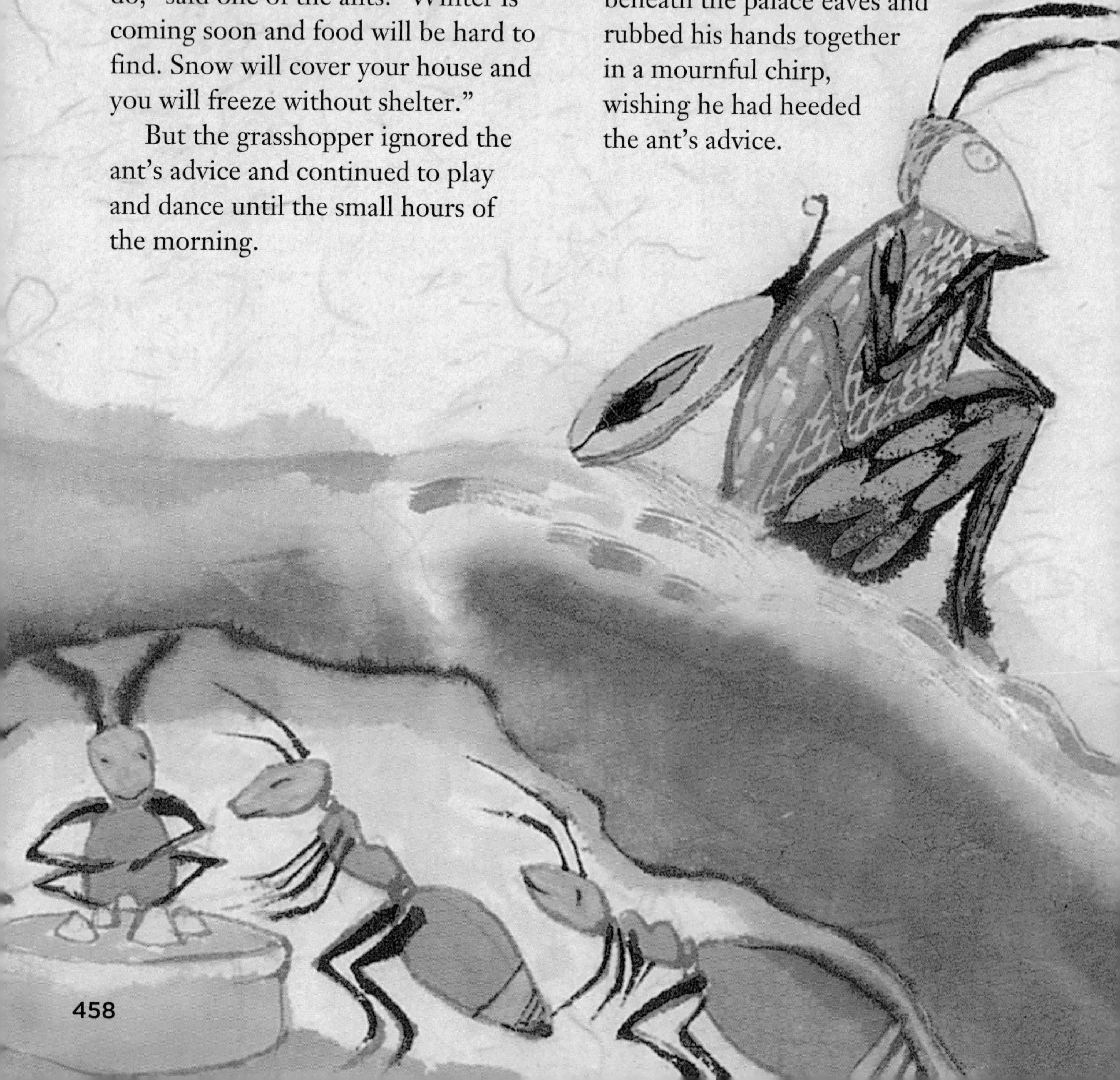

Connect and Compare

1. Summarize and explain the moral of "The Ant and the Grasshopper." **Moral**

2. Why does personification work well in fables? **Apply**

3. Think about *The Life and Times of the Ant*. How are the ants in this fable similar to the ants in that selection? How are they different? **Reading/Writing Across Texts**

4. On your own, choose two different fables to read. Use a Venn diagram to compare and contrast the adventures of the characters in each fable. **Apply**

Writing

Trait: Word Choice
Good writers use **dialogue and description** to show what happens in a story.

Reading and Writing Connection

Read the passage below. Notice how Amy Lowry Poole uses dialogue and description to show what is happening.

An excerpt from
The Ant and the Grasshopper

The author uses dialogue between the grasshopper and the ant to show why each thinks he is right. The author also describes how the grasshopper dances all night instead of preparing for winter.

"Silly ants," said the grasshopper. "Don't you ever rest? Today is the harvest festival. . . . Come and dance with me."

"You would do well to do as we do," said one of the ants. "Winter is coming soon and food will be hard to find. Snow will cover your house and you will freeze without shelter."

But the grasshopper ignored the ant's advice and continued to play and dance until the small hours of the morning.

Read and Find

Read Jeff's writing below. How did he use dialogue and description to show what was happening? Use the checklist below to help you.

Pond Adventure

by Jeff P.

"Get ready!" I yelled to my cousin Colleen. I let go of the rope and let the weight carry it to her on the other side.

"Okay, I'm kind of nervous," she fumbled.

"Just hang on and when you can, jump off. The water's warm, so don't worry!"

Suddenly, she was gliding through the air. "That was awesome!" she laughed from the sparkling water.

Read about Colleen's plunge.

Writer's Checklist

- [x] Did the author use **dialogue** instead of telling statements?
- [x] Does the author show what is happening through the **descriptive details**?
- [ ] Does it feel like you're listening to people talking as you read?

Talk About It

How many different kinds of energy are being used here? Why does it matter what kind of energy we use?

LOG ON VIEW IT

Oral Language Activities
Energy
www.macmillanmh.com

ENERGY

Clean as a Breeze

Vocabulary

electrical globe
fuels decayed

A windmill farm uses clean technology to turn wind energy into electricity.

High wind speeds in the San Gorgonio Pass make conditions just right for delivering clean electricity to homes. Since 1998 Californians have been able to choose the source of their electricity. I am proud to say that my parents switched to a clean source of **electrical** power.

Though it costs a bit more to generate electricity from wind than from fossil **fuels**, my parents decided to help the environment. They knew that burning fossil fuels always releases pollutants into the air.

"Choosing wind or solar power is the key to making sure that Earth's future is bright," says Nancy Hazard. Part of an organization that promotes the use of non-polluting energy sources, Ms. Hazard also says, "Creating that vision and really going for it—that's how we'll get energized!"

Around the **globe**, more people than ever are willing to pay extra for clean sources of energy. If you live in a place where power might be generated with a clean technology, get things rolling by talking to your parents and teachers. Remember: "Clean Energy for a Bright, Pollution-Free Future!"

Tiayana Banks, Palm Springs, CA

U.S. Energy Sources

Nuclear power plants generate some of the energy we use, but most of our energy comes from fuels such as oil, natural gas, and coal. These fuels are called fossil fuels. Over millions of years, heat and pressure from deep within Earth have reacted with the remains of plants and animals that have **decayed** to form fuel. Once these natural resources are used up, they are gone forever.

Nuclear power plant

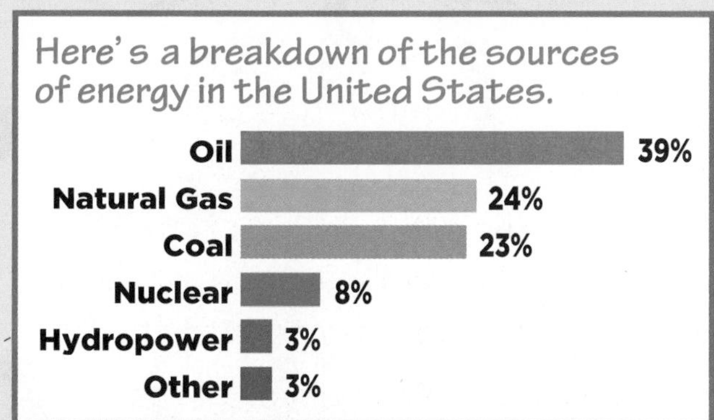

Renewable energy sources can be reused, and they create much less pollution than fossil fuels.

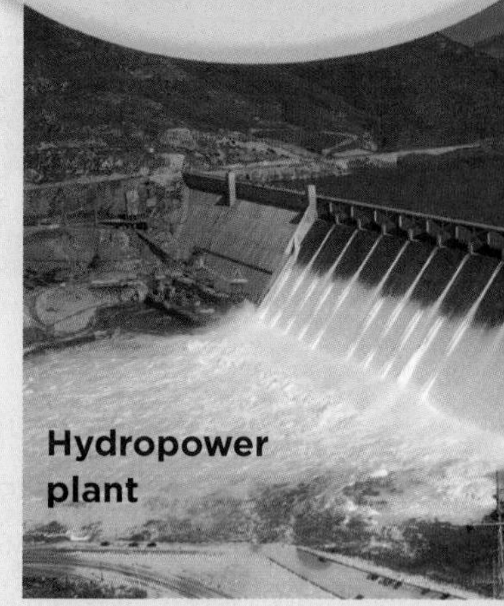

Hydropower plant

- Hydropower uses the force of flowing water to create electricity.
- Solar energy comes from the sun.
- Wind turbines are machines that look like giant windmills. They use the force of the wind to create electricity.
- Geothermal energy comes from heat in Earth's core that is used to create electricity.
- Biomass includes natural products such as wood and corn. These materials are burned and used for heat.

Top 5 Oil Users

Worldwide, people use more than 80 million barrels of oil per day. A barrel contains 42 gallons. These countries are the biggest oil guzzlers. China's oil consumption is growing faster than that of any other country.

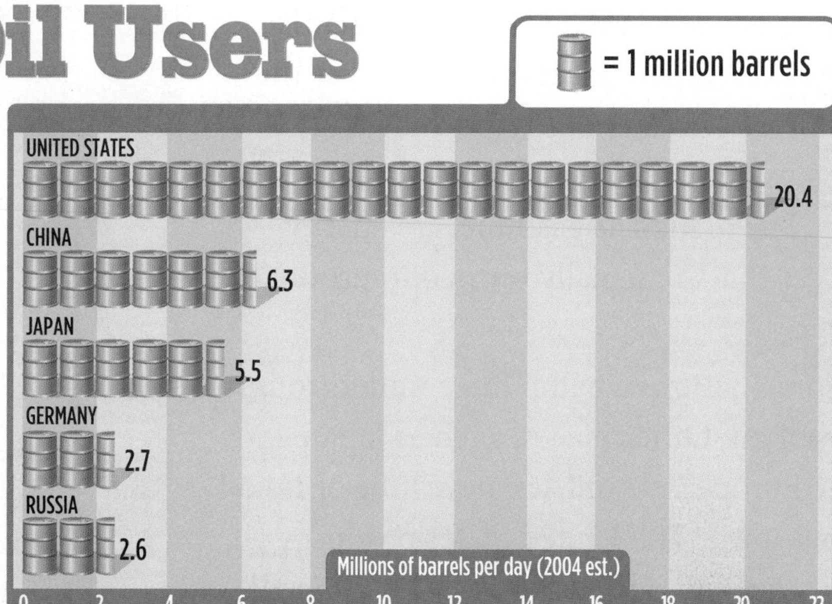

Comprehension

Genre

Expository writing such as a magazine article presents facts and information about a topic.

Generate Questions

Author's Purpose

An author's purpose is the reason the author wrote the selection. Authors write to entertain, inform, or persuade.

THE POWER OF OIL

WHAT MAKES OIL SO VALUABLE AND SO CHALLENGING?

Oil field worker

What can you find deep beneath Earth's surface? Here's a hint: it's shiny, sticky, slick, and very powerful. It's oil.

Oil began forming hundreds of millions of years ago as plant and animal remains were covered with layers of rock. Over the ages those remains **decayed**. They turned into a mighty black brew that we use to make **fuels**. Fuels, such as gasoline, are energy sources that are usually burned to produce power.

Some nations sit atop huge underground lakes of oil. Other places, such as Japan and some European countries, have little or no oil of their own. The United States produces oil, but it also buys about 59% of what it needs.

Oil is a very important fuel because it helps power cars, planes, trains, factories, and **electrical** plants. Oil changed the American economy. The discovery of oil created many new jobs, and allowed farmers to use machines that produced and shipped food more quickly. The United States was transformed into an industrial nation. At the same time, it became a nation dependent on oil.

Although the world depends on oil, scientists are working together to look for alternate forms of energy because oil is a nonrenewable energy source. Once this resource is used up, it is gone forever. Another problem with oil is that when it is burned to produce power it creates carbon dioxide and other polluting gases that are bad for our health and our planet.

HOOKED ON OIL

The United States uses more oil than any other country on the **globe**. Most is pumped into our 200 million cars in the form of gasoline. On average an American burns through 25 barrels of oil each year. Compare this with 15 barrels for a citizen of Japan or 12 for a person living in France.

Some of the 200 million cars on American roads

WHERE DOES ALL THE OIL GO?

The answer is . . . directly into our vehicles mostly. Traffic on U.S. highways grows heavier every year. Cars, trucks, airplanes, trains, and other forms of transportation burn the most fossil fuel. As you can see, the other uses for oil don't begin to measure up.

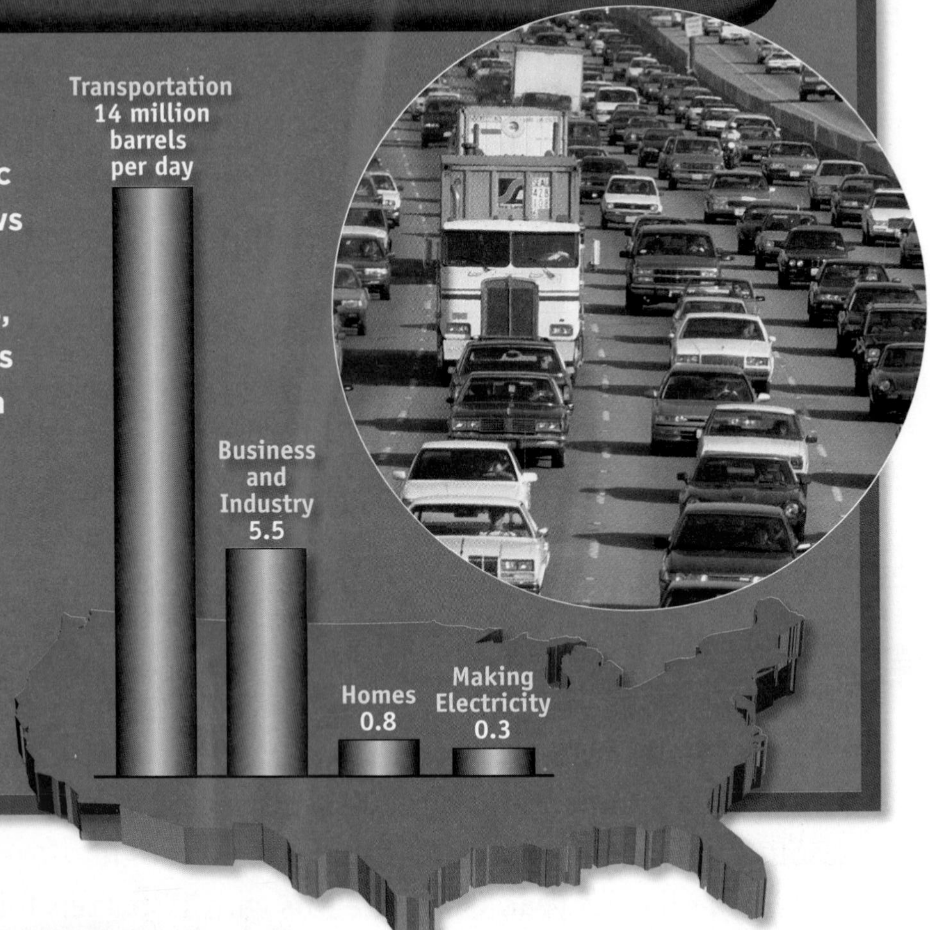

Source: Department of Energy 2008

IS THERE ANOTHER WAY?

If oil causes so many problems, why do we depend on it? For starters, nearly all of our cars and factories are designed to use oil and gas. Changing them to use other fuels would be very costly.

Still, there are ways we can use less oil. We can all work together to figure out ways to conserve oil. New technology has made it possible to build cars that use less gas. In 1975, the average car could go just 12 miles on one gallon of gas. By 1990, some cars could travel 30 miles on just one gallon. Since then, car makers have begun to make cars that can use other, alternative, fuels, such as electricity, natural gas, and fuels made from plants such as corn.

In the twenty-first century, hybrid cars powered by gas and electricity are becoming more and more popular as people look for new ways to conserve oil.

ADVERTISEMENT

WHAT ARE YOU WAITING FOR?

The Facts Are In

Research says roughly 353,000 hybrids were sold in the United States in 2007. That total will climb to 760,000 hybrids per year by 2012. Hybrids use electric motors and battery packs to improve fuel efficiency.

A hybrid engine gets better gas mileage than one that runs on gasoline. Hybrid owners save money at the pumps, and through 2010 they can also get up to a $3,150 tax break. Best of all, hybrid drivers are cutting their annual emission levels by a whopping 90%!

What Hybrid Drivers Are Saying

- Bill says, "I'd have to throw an anchor out of my window to get mileage less than 40 mpg."
- Dennis says, "I have 60,000 miles on my hybrid. Love it! My lifetime mileage is 53 mpg!"

Celebrities Are Joining the Bandwagon

Many actors and professional athletes are driving hybrids. They are raving about the performance of their cars and feeling good about making the responsible choice.

Come See for Yourself!

In celebration of Earth Day, alternative energy groups across the nation will be hosting at least one presentation of hybrid vehicles in every state. Find the location of the one near you by logging on to www.earthdayevents.example.com. See for yourself! "The Hybrid—It's the Future Now."

Hybrid cars shut off to save power when stopped in traffic. Their engines restart when traffic starts moving again!

Think and Compare

1. Where is oil found?
2. How did the problems with oil affect the design of American cars?
3. What techniques does this advertisement use to influence how readers feel about hybrid cars?
4. Compare the information in "U.S. Energy Sources" and "The Power of Oil." How is the information alike? How is it different?

Test Practice

Answering Questions

Right There answers are found in one place in the text.
Think and Search answers are found in more than one place.
Author and Me answers ask the reader to look for clues.

Windmills on the Prairies

A windmill farm uses clean technology to turn wind energy into electricity.

1 Mackenzie Burkhart, a sixth-grader from Park Ridge, Illinois, worries that nuclear reactors threaten the prairies in his state. A dozen reactors produce nearly three quarters of all the electricity for the state. Mackenzie believes nuclear reactors have the potential to be extremely dangerous. In an accident at a nuclear power plant, nuclear waste could leak out. Radioactive steam and debris could have devastating effects on the plants and animals of the prairies and their surrounding communities.

2 Burkhart's proposed solution: Provide energy from a more environmentally safe source—a windmill! Big, colorful windmills caught Burkhart's eye while he was on vacation in Denmark with his family. "Windmills were everywhere, and they provided power for much of the country," he says.

During the 1800s windmills played an important role as people began settling in the West. Windmills were used to pump water, grind grain, and generate electricity. Now, with energy prices rising, windmills are slowly being restored and becoming a popular topic of conversation. Many of the midwestern states are discovering the advantages of wind power and have started building more wind farms. 3

Not only would windmills be environmentally safer, but, as Burkhart points out, they are also a renewable source of power. Unlike fossil fuels or even nuclear fuels, he says, "wind is endless." 4

Use "Windmills on the Prairies" to answer questions 1–3.

1 Look at the following web of information from the article.

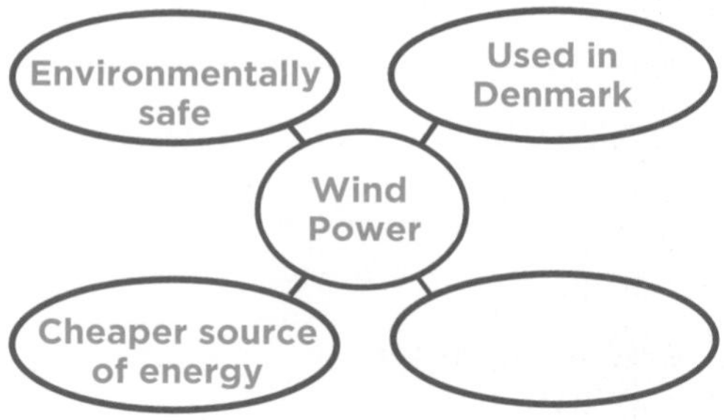

Which information belongs in the empty oval?

A Nuclear waste
B Renewable source of power
C Fossil fuels
D Radioactive steam

---

2 The reader can tell from paragraph 1 that Mackenzie Burkhart —

F likes living in Illinois
G approves of nuclear energy
H cares about the environment
J thinks fossil fuels are better than wind power

3 The author wrote this article most likely to —

A give information about wind power
B persuade readers to use nuclear power
C tell a funny story about Mackenzie Burkhart
D encourage readers to visit Denmark

Write to a Prompt

Write a composition about going on a trip with friends.

Think about how to clearly express your ideas.

Develop your ideas in a logical order.

Below, see how one student begins a response to the prompt above.

The writer included important details.

Kea's mother was driving their new hybrid car. Kea, Bo, and I were talking in the back seat about our camping trip. We were really excited about getting a camping spot at Lake Heron. Bo had brought along his new solar-powered camping stove. Then Kea looked out the window at the big gray clouds.

"What if it stays cloudy and we don't have enough solar power to get Bo's camping stove to work? Did anyone think to bring matches?" Kea asked. Bo and I shook our heads.

Luckily, Kea's mother came to the rescue.

TIME FOR KIDS

Writing Prompt

Respond to the prompt below. Review the hints below before and after you write.

Write a composition about something you like to do.

Writing Hints

- ☑ Remember to write about something you like to do. Think about the genre.
- ☑ Plan your writing by organizing your ideas.
- ☑ Include important details to support your ideas.
- ☑ Check that each sentence you write helps the reader to understand your story.
- ☑ Use correct spelling, capitalization, punctuation, grammar, and sentences.
- ☑ Review and edit your writing.

Teaming Up

Talk About It

How do this team of dogs and the sled driver work together?

LOG ON VIEW IT

Oral Language Activities
Teaming Up
www.macmillanmh.com

Vocabulary

anticipation **slender**
enormous **released**
encouraged **glanced**

Analogies: Synonyms and Antonyms

Analogies compare two pairs of words. Sometimes analogies use **Antonyms** or **Synonyms** to compare words. An analogy that uses antonyms is: *enormous* is to *tiny* as *loud* is to *quiet*.

Tony and Shadow

by Carolina Cisneros

"All ready to help on the ranch, Tony?" Grandpa asks, smiling at the eager **anticipation** in my brown eyes.

"You bet. Can I ride Shadow?" I ask.

Grandpa laughs. "Good choice. That horse knows more about running a ranch than I do."

We walk out to the red barn as the sun comes up over the hill. Grandpa saddles the horses. Shadow looms in front of me. I feel like a tiny speck standing next to this huge animal. Grandpa helps me up onto the **enormous** gray horse. Then he hands me my lariat.

"Tony, I'd like you and Shadow to ride along the fence on the west side. Check the fence for holes and look for stray cattle. We'll meet back here in two hours," Grandpa says.

I turn Shadow toward the fence. Even though I'm really nervous about riding Shadow, I'm **encouraged** by Grandpa's confidence in me. This is the first time he's let me ride Shadow and check the fence without him.

All of a sudden, Shadow puts up his head and starts walking toward a clump of trees and rocks. I pull on the reins but he ignores me. As we get closer, I see a calf struggling under a big tree branch. One of the calf's **slender**, delicate legs is trapped under the branch.

Shadow neighs gently at the calf. I'm worried that if I get off Shadow, I won't be able to get back on. But I know I have to help the calf even if it means walking all the way back. I dismount and try lifting the branch off. It's too heavy. I put the loop of my lariat over the end of the branch and pull at it.

I feel Shadow's big nose nudging me in the back. Then he walks over to a big rock and stands next to it.

"You're a genius!" I tell Shadow as I climb the rock, and use it to get back up on his back. I wrap the end of the rope around the saddle horn as Shadow starts moving backward. The branch shifts forward. The calf suddenly realizes his leg has been **released** and scrambles up, freed from the weight of the branch.

"Shadow, we make a great team," I say patting the big horse's neck.

Later, when I told Grandpa about what Shadow had done, he **glanced** at the horse and then looked back at me.

"Like I said, Shadow knows more about running a ranch than I do."

Reread for Comprehension

Visualize

Draw Conclusions Readers must often visualize and look for text clues to draw conclusions about a **character** in a story. To draw conclusions, you think about various pieces of information in the story to arrive at a new understanding about a character or story event. A Conclusions Chart can help you analyze what you read.

Text Clues	Conclusion

LOG ON LEARN IT **Comprehension** www.macmillanmh.com

Comprehension

Genre

Fiction is an invented story that could have happened in real life.

Visualize

Draw Conclusions
As you read, fill in your Conclusions Chart.

Text Clues	Conclusion

Read to Find Out

What can you conclude about Ima by the end of the story?

Ima and The Great Texas Ostrich Race

Words by Margaret McManis
Pictures by Bruce Dupree

Papa told me not to brag too much. I promised I wouldn't. Papa says a real lady knows her own worth and doesn't have to tell everyone. People listen to Papa all over the state of Texas.

I listen too . . . most times.

But I didn't when the Union Pacific locomotive lumbered into the station on my tenth birthday. Papa pointed to the last car on the line.

"Happy birthday, Ima!" he hollered as two men lowered a yellow ramp from the side of the caboose.

I stood at the end of the ramp, my feet hopping with curiosity. Even my toes were curious. "What is it? What *is* it, Papa?" I jumped with **anticipation**.

The wobbly ramp hit the ground with a crash, and out raced the biggest, ugliest bird thing I had ever seen. And boy, could that thing run! It headed down Main Street, black and white feathers flapping, and long legs stirring up a trail of dust. That crazy-looking bird thing outran every last one of Papa's wranglers! By the time the boys rounded him up to put him in a cage, my mind had already hatched a mighty fine plan.

"Governor Hogg, that there bird thing just ain't natural, sir," coughed a tired wrangler as he slid the bolt shut on the cage.

Papa just laughed. "Ima, girl, you got yourself one fast bird . . . I mean ostrich."

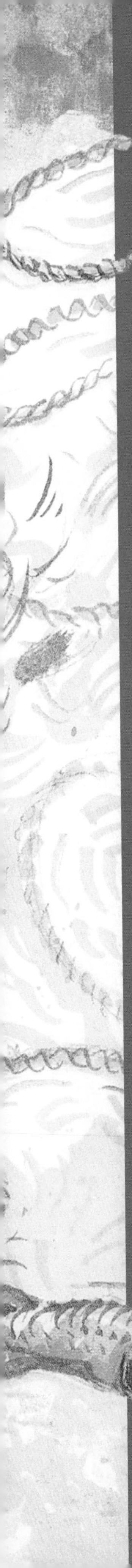

I smiled back at Papa and hugged his round body. An ostrich was something I hadn't reckoned on. What would my brothers think of my bird, my Ossy?

Will whooped with laughter at the sight of Ossy. "Why, little sister, that's the silliest-looking bird in the whole state of Texas!"

Brother Tom joined in. "*He-he-he-he-haw*, wh-why, Ima, that ole bird can't even fly! And would you take a gander at those drumsticks?" he bellowed.

I sort of broke my no-bragging promise to Papa when I shouted, "Ossy may be silly looking, but he's the fastest racing bird in all of Texas!"

"*Pshaw!* Fast he may be, but who ever heard of an ostrich that could race?" Will snickered. "Anyway, who's gonna saddle that ornery-looking thing?"

"And I don't see no teeth in that mouth of his. What about a bridle?" Tom roared.

My feet were not curious now, not curious at all! They were mad. Even my toes were mad!

"I'll ride Ossy, and beat both of you! I'll show you!" I shouted as I stamped off, my feet stirring up a storm of Texas dust.

The next morning a wrangler helped me up to Ossy's tall, black-and-white-feathered back. Papa handed me the reins.

"Hang on, Ima!" he shouted as he **released** the bird.

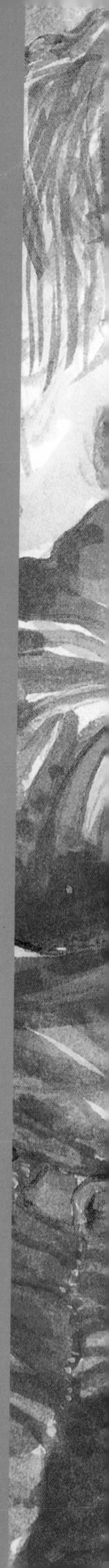

Boy, could that bird buck! He whirled his **slender** brown neck around like a wrangler lassoing a heifer. His big eyes rolled back and forth, and he hissed like a rock rattler. I flew over the top of the corral and buried my face in the hard, dry sand.

"Hold him, Papa, hold him!" I cried. I scrambled under the fence, wiped the dirt from my eyes, and took the reins once more. Ossy blinked in my direction. He leaped into the air. Then he flapped his enormous wings and ran in circles while hissing mightily.

Draw Conclusions
What can you conclude about Ima's character?

This time I stayed put like sorghum syrup.

"Why, Ima!" Papa shouted proudly. "Girl, you've got mettle!"

A great race was planned for the next day, and news of it spread like a West Texas prairie fire.

"Hey, little sister, are you and that overstuffed turkey thinking about winning this race?" Will hooted from the back of his horse.

Tom snickered at my bird. "Gobble, gobble!" he mocked.

"Now, Ima girl, don't let those boys hornswoggle ya," **encouraged** Papa. "You're the best—and I'm not bragging!"

Papa could always make me feel better, even when I was down real low.

The next morning Tom and Will grinned at me from the starting line. They had the best quarter horses money could buy, but there was something they didn't have. A thing Papa told me that I have—METTLE!

Draw Conclusions
What can you conclude about Ima's relationship with her father?

When the gun sounded, their horses raced forward. Ossy leaped wildly into the air. His big eyes rolled from side to side and his neck swung around. He ran in circles. I tried to remember what Papa had said: *Show him your mettle, Ima!* I pulled on the reins firmly and talked to Ossy soothingly.

The wind snapped my hair around as the brush-covered hills whooshed past. Tom and Will were far ahead, their horses' hooves stirring up the dusty road. Ossy pumped his gigantic drumsticks and sped ahead. I smelled the sweat of Tom's gelding as we streaked past. My brother's eyes nearly popped out of his head.

"Gobble, gobble, big brother!" I shouted.

Now brother Will turned his head and **glanced** back in my direction. I rounded the last corner and saw Papa standing by a sorghum barrel that marked the finish line. His grin was as wide as the Brazos River. Will stared in disbelief at the strange bird coming alongside his prize-winning horse. The pounding of hooves and claws filled my ears. Dirt clogged my throat and eyes, but mettle filled my heart.

Ossy's gait was smooth as buttermilk. His four **enormous** claws pulled at the hard-packed dirt. I pressed my knees into his feathered sides, and Ossy slowly pulled ahead.

Now it was *my* turn to look back and smile at my brother. It felt good! I watched him wipe grit and dust from his tight mouth. His horse would not give up so easily. To be defeated by a bird was no joke to him either!

Then Ossy stuck out his long neck and streaked past that sorghum barrel. We were only one inch ahead!

The whole state seemed to be sitting on Papa's corral fence that day, watching in amazement as my Ossy came roaring across the finish line, black and white feathers and long legs stirring up a curious Texas dust storm.

Papa looked up into my smiling, dirt-covered face and winked. I knew for sure the worth of a real lady—especially a lady with lots of mettle. I decided to keep my promise to Papa, and didn't brag once about winning.

People listen to Papa all over the state of Texas. After all, he *is* the governor. I listen, too, and it sure feels good!

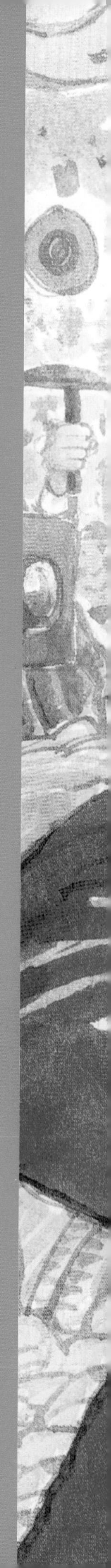

Off to the Races

with Margaret and Bruce

Margaret McManis loves books, and has been a librarian for more than 30 years. She also loves writing about Texas history, and as luck would have it she lives near where Ima grew up! *Ima and The Great Texas Ostrich Race* was her first book. Ms. McManis also wrote *The Wild Texas Stampede* and a musical about Ima and her adventures with Ossy the Ostrich.

Bruce Dupree is an artist and professor of art. Other books he has illustrated include *Hernando de Soto*, *Coming Home Auburn!*, and *Homecoming Alabama!* In addition to teaching and illustrating, Mr. Dupree also enjoys playing the drums.

LOG ON FIND OUT

Author Margaret McManis
Illustrator Bruce Dupree
www.macmillanmh.com

Author's Purpose

Is the narrator of this story first or third person? Why did the author choose this point of view?

LOG ON LEARN IT Comprehension www.macmillanmh.com

Comprehension Check

Text Clues	Conclusion

Summarize

To summarize *Ima and The Great Texas Ostrich Race* use the most important details from the story. Information from your Conclusions Chart may help you.

Think and Compare

1. Ima's father was governor of which state? Details

2. What happened after Ima got on Ossy's back and the wrangler **released** Ossy? Sequence

3. What can you conclude about the relationship between Ima and her father? Use details from the story to support your answer. Visualize: Draw Conclusions

4. Identify the two similes in the first paragraph on page 489. How does the author's use of simile help you visualize the events taking place? Author's Craft

5. Read "Tony and Shadow" on pages 476–477. How are Tony and Ima the same? How are they different? Use evidence from the text to support your answer. Reading/Writing Across Texts

Social Studies

Genre

Expository articles, such as **encyclopedia entries**, give facts and information about people, places, or things.

Text Feature

Multiple Text Features such as guide words found at the top of the page, headings, and typefaces provide an overview of the text and help readers to locate information.

Content Vocabulary

reform **specialized** **charity**

ENCYCLOPEDIAS

An encyclopedia contains factual articles about people, places, and events. Encyclopedias come in different formats, including sets of books, CD-ROMs, and online.

Encyclopedia articles in book format are arranged alphabetically by subject in volumes. Each volume is labeled with one or more letters or guide words. The label shows the first letter or guide word of subjects covered in that volume.

Article titles are in boldface type. Unless they are proper nouns, article titles may not be capitalized. Encyclopedia entries sometimes provide cross-references, often in capital letters.

Locating Information

When searching for information on a person in a set of encyclopedias, search by using the last name and then the first name. When searching for information in CD-ROM or online encyclopedias, type the name or keywords into the search box.

Jane Addams was a leader in social reform.

Addams, Jane *(1860–1935)*

Jane Addams was born in Cedarville, Illinois, on September 6, 1860. Her father, who was a state senator, was a friend of President Abraham Lincoln. He taught Jane the importance of hard work, social justice, leadership, and compassion for others.

Early Challenges

All her life Jane suffered from a medical problem with her back. Along with this physical challenge, Jane also faced the challenge that women did not have the same opportunities as men. She wanted to become a doctor, but her family did not approve of her choice.

Later Achievements

After a trip to Europe, Addams returned home with new ideas. She became a leader in social **reform** and worked to make people's lives better. She created Hull House in Chicago to provide educational, legal, and medical assistance to poor people.

Addams gave many speeches and wrote many books on peace, freedom, and social justice. She was a founding member of the American Civil Liberties Union (ACLU) and the National Association for the Advancement of Colored People (NAACP). For these efforts and more, she was awarded the Nobel Peace Prize in 1931.

See also NOBEL PEACE PRIZE

Ima Hogg helped to promote the arts.

Hogg, Ima *(1882–1975)*

Ima Hogg was born in Mineola, Texas, on July 10, 1882. Her father, James Stephen Hogg, became governor of Texas when Ima was eight years old. Ima's parents named her after the heroine of a Civil War poem written by her uncle.

Early Years

Together with her three brothers, Ima enjoyed an exciting childhood. She learned to play the piano at the age of three. She also cared for her pet ostriches. Her family made a great deal of money after oil was discovered on their ranch.

A Life of Travel and Charity

Ima's love of music lasted her entire life. She studied in both the United States and Europe. When she returned to Texas, she helped to create the Houston Symphony Orchestra in 1913.

"Miss Ima," as Ima was known, believed in the power of **charity**. She used her family's money to help others. In addition to donating to the arts, she helped to create education and health programs. She worked with President Dwight Eisenhower to plan what is now the Kennedy Center for the Performing Arts in Washington, D.C.

In 1969, Ima Hogg, along with Oveta Culp Hobby and Lady Bird Johnson, was elected to the Academy of Texas, an organization founded to honor persons who "enrich, enlarge, or enlighten" knowledge in any field. They were the first three women members to be elected to the Academy.

See also LADY BIRD JOHNSON

Johnson, Claudia Taylor "Lady Bird" *(1912–2007)*

Married to the 36th President of the United States, Lyndon B. Johnson, Claudia Taylor Johnson was First Lady from 1963 to 1969. As First Lady she became involved in the development of the Head Start program for preschool children. She also worked hard to protect the environment and preserve natural plant species.

Early Life

Born in Karnack, Texas, Claudia was given the nickname "Lady Bird" when she was five years old. In 1930, she entered the University of Texas at Austin, graduating with degrees in history and journalism. She married Lyndon B. Johnson in 1934.

Wildflower Research Center

Lady Bird **specialized** in making people aware of the importance of native plants. She wanted people to understand that wildflowers provide food and homes for birds and animals. In 1982, she opened the National Wildflower Research Center near Austin, Texas. The Center teaches visitors how to protect the environment and how to grow their own gardens full of native plants. See also WILDFLOWERS

Connect and Compare

1. What is the cross-reference that appears at the end of the entry for Jane Addams? **Using Text Features**
2. In what ways have these women improved people's lives? **Apply**
3. What facts might the writer of *Ima and The Great Texas Ostrich Race* have used from the encyclopedia entry on Ima Hogg? **Reading/Writing Across Texts**

Social Studies Activity

Research a woman who is an important historical figure in your state's history. Write a report of your findings.

LOG ON FIND OUT Women's History **www.macmillanmh.com**

Writing

Trait: Ideas

Writers use detail, dialogue, and description to **develop characters**.

Reading and Writing Connection

Read the passage below. Notice how the author, Margaret McManis, provides clues about Ima's character.

An excerpt from
Ima and The Great Texas Ostrich Race

The author shows us something about Ima through her actions and through the dialogue between Ima and her father.

"Hold him, Papa, hold him!" I cried. I scrambled under the fence, wiped the dirt from my eyes, and took the reins once more. Ossy blinked in my direction. He leaped into the air. Then he flapped his enormous wings and ran in circles while hissing mightily.

This time I stayed put like sorghum syrup.

"Why, Ima!" Papa shouted proudly. "Girl, you've got mettle!"

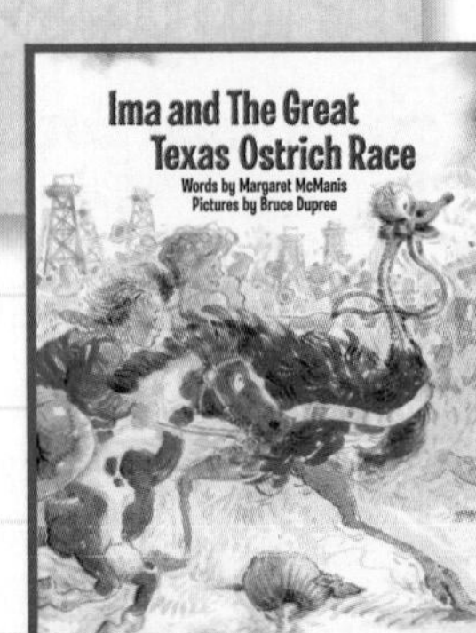

Read and Find

Read Christina's writing below. How does she use dialogue and description to show you what Omar is like? Use the checklist below to help you.

Omar's Painting

by Christina M.

Omar spills his little cup of mud right onto the paper. "I'm Picasso!" announces Omar. He smacks his bamboo sticks in the mud and creates a piece of art—actually, a paper with mud on it. I'm trying to ignore him but he keeps bumping my arm to try to get my attention. I look over and don't see anything worthy of praise. But he's so full of joy over his artistic experiment that I say, "Wow!" and smile at him.

Read about Omar's painting.

Writer's Checklist

- ☑ Does the author use dialogue and description to show you what the **characters** are like?
- ☑ Does the author make Omar's actions believable?
- ☐ Does it feel like Omar could be a real person?

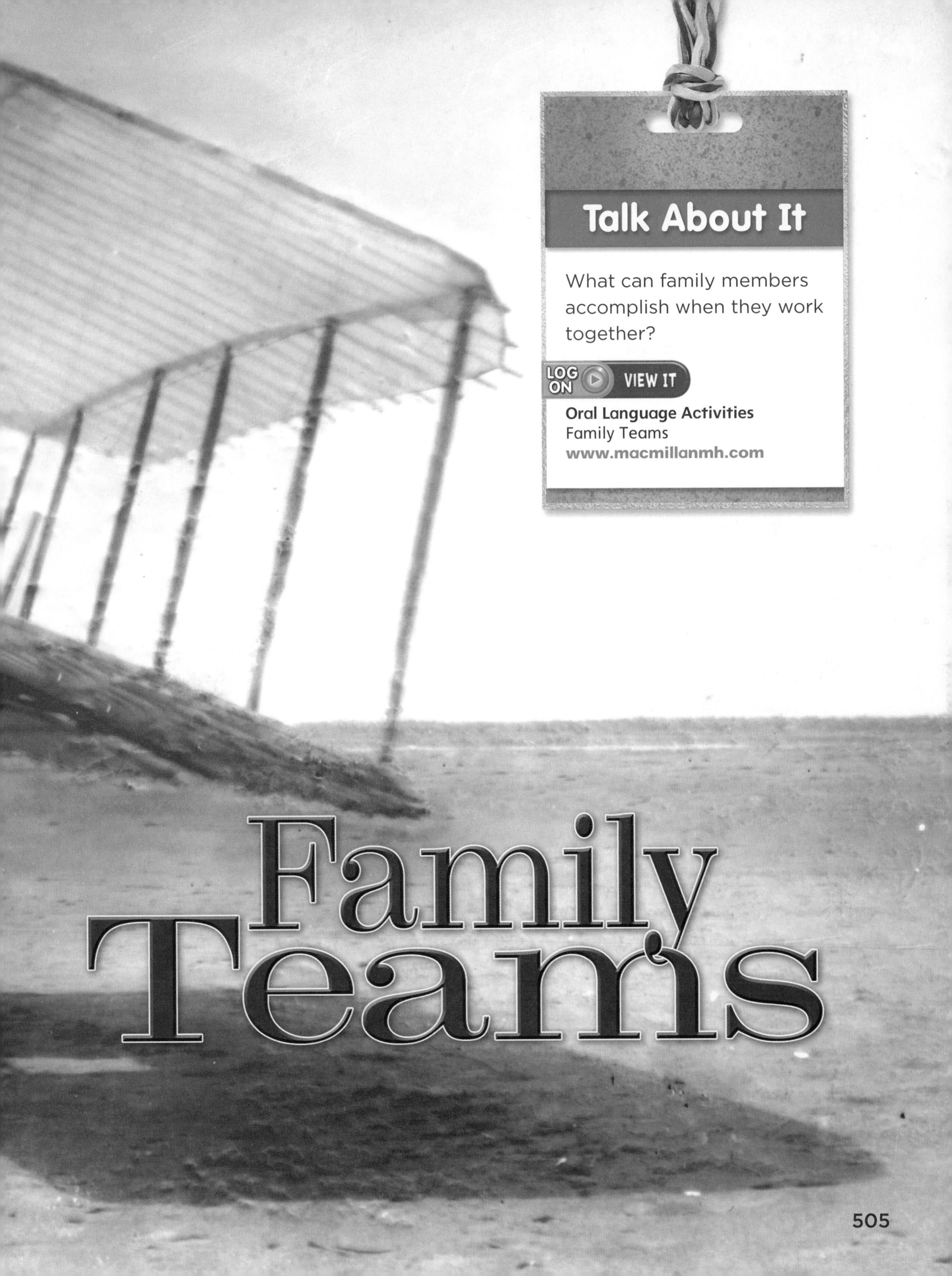

Family Teams

Talk About It

What can family members accomplish when they work together?

LOG ON VIEW IT

Oral Language Activities
Family Teams
www.macmillanmh.com

Vocabulary

assembled
unstable
applauded
headlines
hoisting
assured

Word Parts

Suffixes such as *-er* and *-or* are word parts added to the end of words. Suffixes can change words' meanings.

-or = one who
inventor = one who invents

Take Off

by Terry Eager

Every day thousands of people fly in airplanes. It is easy to take flying for granted, but it is important for us to remember that it took many years and several inventors to master flight.

Early Ideas

About 1500, Leonardo da Vinci, an Italian artist and inventor, made sketches of flying machines with wings that flapped like a bird's. In 1783 the Montgolfier brothers made a balloon out of linen cloth and paper. A controlled fire filled the balloon with hot air, which made it rise. Other inventors tried using hydrogen to make their balloons rise. Hydrogen is a gas that is lighter than air.

In 1804, Sir George Cayley made the first successful glider. A glider is an aircraft without engines. Although Cayley's first glider could not carry a passenger, his later gliders could.

Over time, better gliders were made and **assembled**. They were still **unstable**, though, and hard to control. It was the Wright brothers who figured out how to steer a glider.

Great Developments

In 1903, the Wright brothers built their first airplane. It had a gasoline engine and a wingspan of 40 feet, 4 inches. Only a few inventors praised and **applauded** the Wright brothers' success. Other inventors continued working to perfect the flying machine.

Newspaper **headlines** cheered Charles "Lucky" Lindbergh in 1927. He was the first to fly alone across the Atlantic Ocean. Amelia Earhart became the first woman to do the same thing, in 1932.

Jets

In the 1950s, American engineers designed passenger jet planes. By 1970 the world's first jumbo jet could carry more than 400 people. Today jets can fly farther and faster than ever.

Flight has come a long way since the days of **hoisting** a glider to the top of a sand dune. We owe our thanks to those who risked their lives when no one was **assured** or certain of success.

Reread for Comprehension

Visualize

Author's Perspective An author's perspective is how he or she feels about a subject. To identify an author's perspective, look for clues about how the author presents events and information. Descriptive details can help you visualize events and help you identify the author's perspective. Use the Author's Perspective Map to help you identify clues about the author's perspective as you reread the selection.

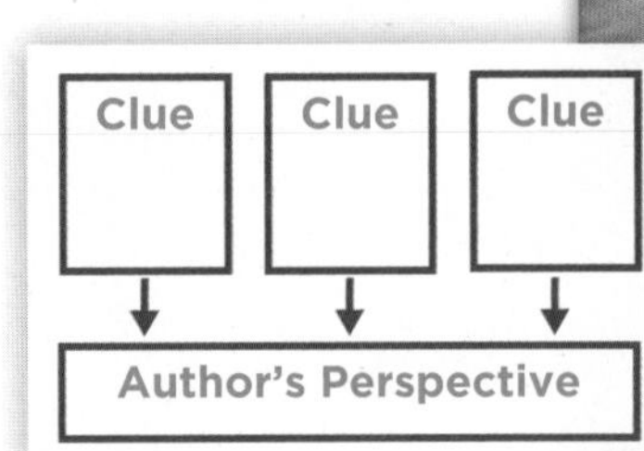

LOG ON LEARN IT **Comprehension**
www.macmillanmh.com

Comprehension

Genre

A **Biography** is the story about the life of a real person told by somebody else.

Visualize

Author's Perspective

As you read, fill in your Author's Perspective Map.

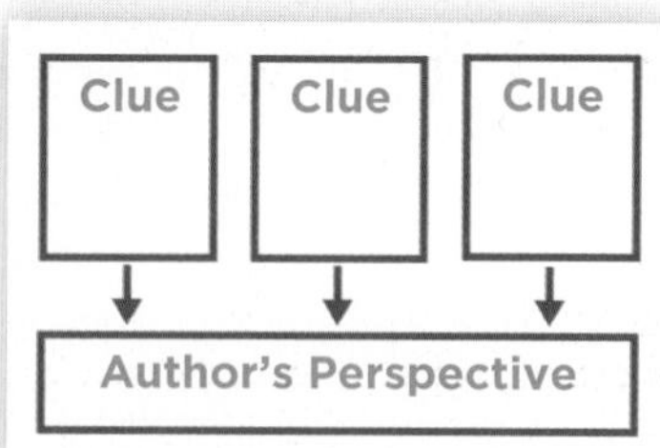

Read to Find Out

How does the author feel about the Wright brothers' attempts to fly?

My Brothers' Flying Machine

by
JANE YOLEN
paintings by
JIM BURKE

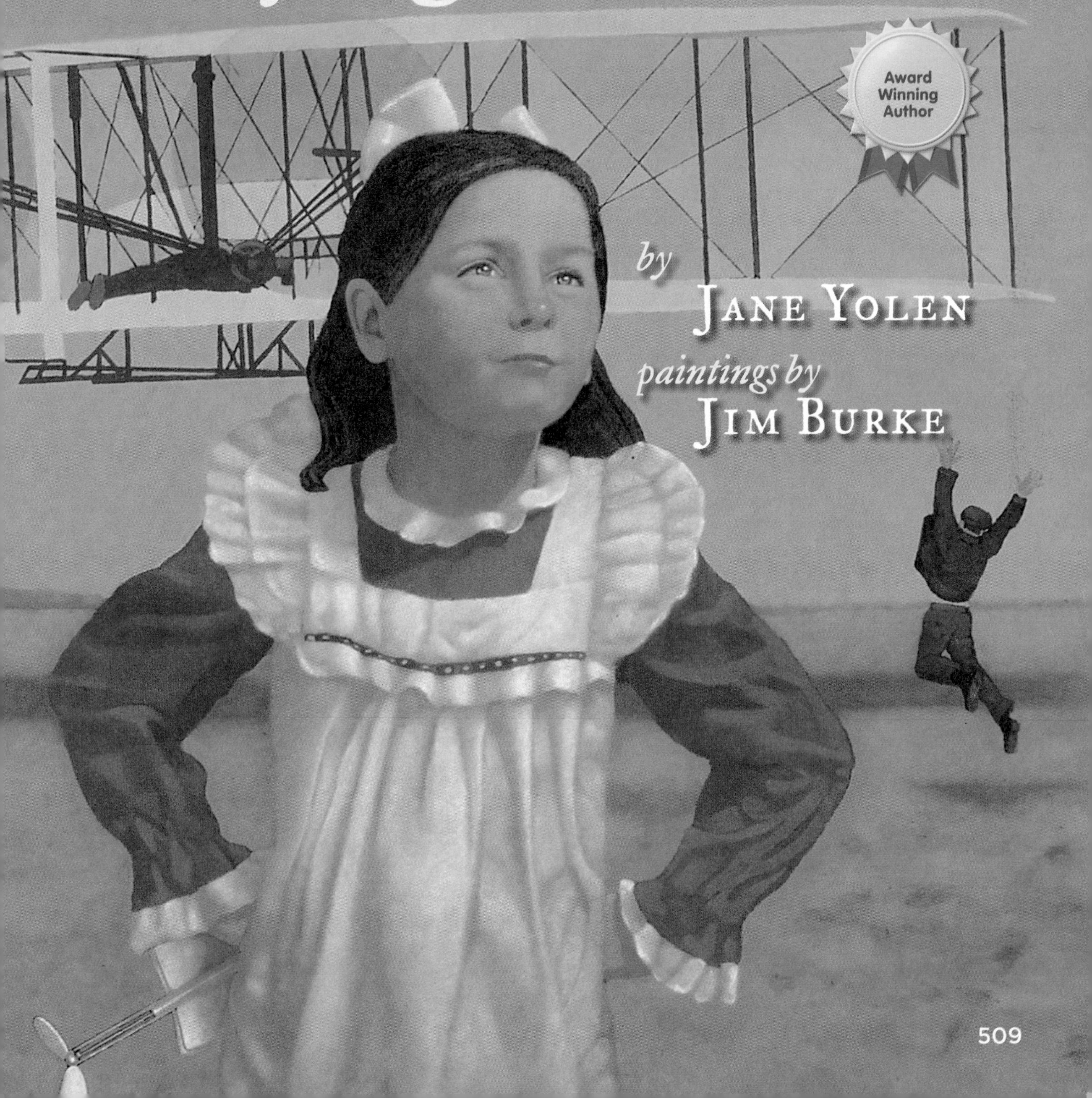

I was four years old when Papa brought home a little flying machine. He tossed it into the air right in front of Orv and Will. They leaped up to catch it.

"Is it a bat?" Orv asked. Or maybe it was Will.

When at last the "bat" fell to the floor, they gathered it up like some sultan's treasure, marveling at its paper wings, admiring the twisted rubber band that gave it power. I wanted to touch it, too, but they would not let me, saying I was too little, though I was but three years younger than Orv, to the very day.

When the "bat" broke, they fixed it together, Will directing Orv—with his busy hands—tinkering till the toy worked better than when Papa first brought it home.

Our older brothers, Reuchlin and Lorin, looked down on childish activity, but Will was not put off. He made one, and two, and three more "bats," each one bigger than the last. Orv was his constant helper. I stood on tiptoe by the table, watching them work.

Will shook his head. "On a much larger scale," he said, "the machine fails to work so well."

They both were puzzled. They did not know yet that a machine twice as big needs eight times the power to fly.

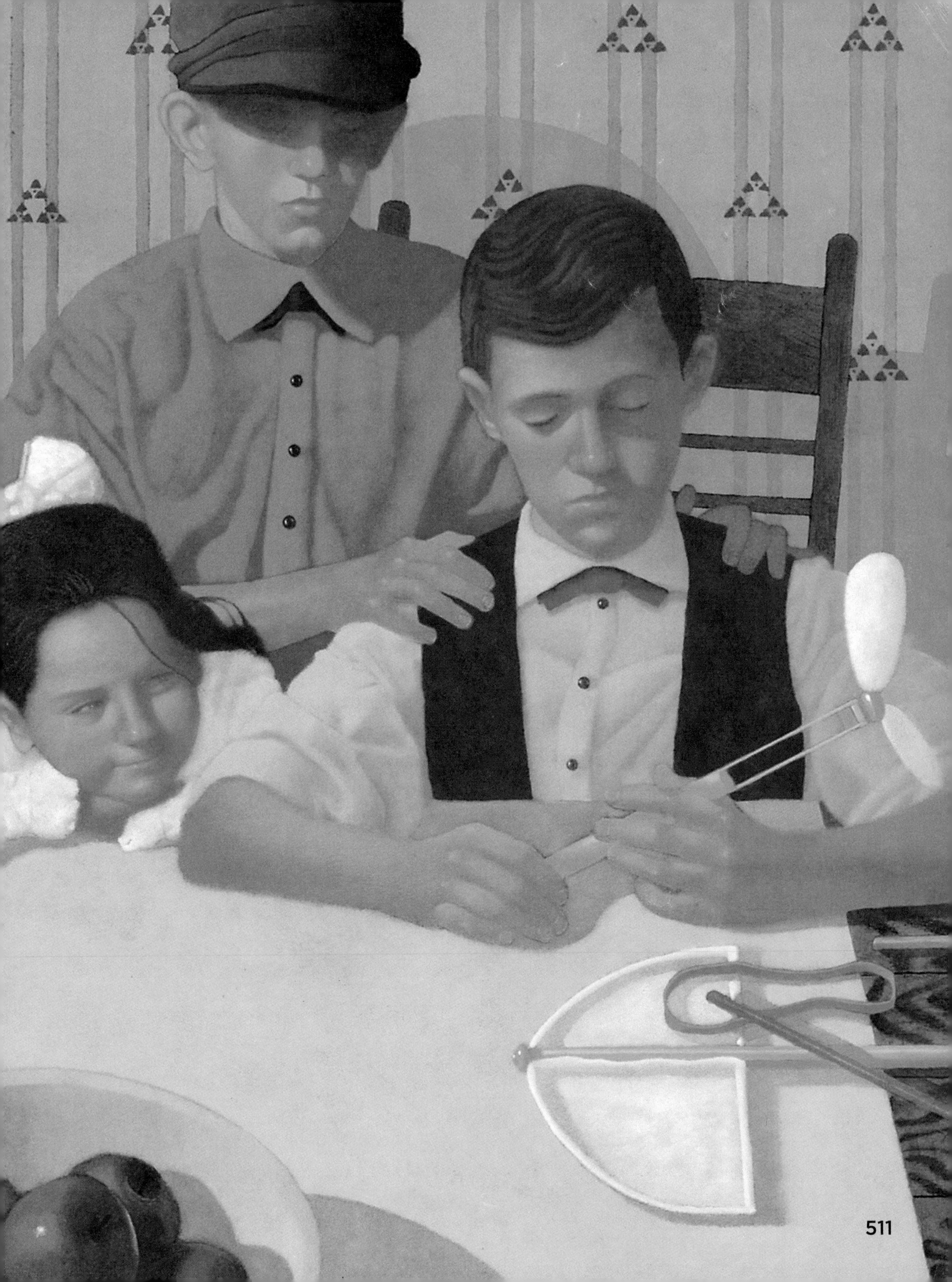

After that, Will built sturdy kites, which he sold to his pals in school. Orv made a printing press, with an old tombstone for a press bed, wheels and cogs from a junkyard, and the folding top of my old baby buggy that he had found in the barn. My, it made me smile to see it.

Papa and Mama **applauded** their efforts. Orv's press could print a thousand pages an hour. A printer from the great city of Denver came to visit and climbed under and over Orv's baby-buggy press. At last he laughed, amazed. "Well it works," he said, "but I certainly don't see how."

Orv and Will made many messes, but Mama never complained. She'd always been the one who gave them a hand building things when they were boys. Poor Papa. He knew God's word well enough, but not how to drive a nail.

When dear Mama died of tuberculosis, I took over her role: keeping the house, making the meals, and always giving the boys applause, even after I graduated from college and worked as a teacher.

West Side News

Will and Orv never went on in school. They ran a print shop, then a bicycle shop, repairing and making custom-built models they called the Van Cleve and the St. Clair. Theirs was not the biggest bicycle shop in Dayton, but I like to think it was the best.

Will and Orv. Orv and Will. They worked side by side in the bicycle shop, whistling at the same time, humming the same tune. They even—so Will said—*thought* together.

Some folks mistook them for twins, though they looked nothing alike. Will had a hawk's face, and Orv a red mustache. Orv was the neat one. He wore special cuffs for his sleeves and a blue-and-white-striped apron to protect his clothes. But Will—land's sake, he was a mess. I had to remind him when his suit needed pressing and when his socks did not match, or find him one of Orv's shirts when he was ready to go off to give a speech.

The newspapers and magazines were full of stories about people trying to fly. Lilienthal, Pilcher, Chanute, MEN INTO BIRDS, the **headlines** read. I wondered if such a thing were really possible. Orv said: "insects, birds, and mammals fly every day at pleasure, it is reasonable to suppose that man might also fly."

Will wrote off to the Smithsonian for all their books and pamphlets on flight. He and Orv studied page after page. The first question they asked was: *How can we control the flight?*

They knew that a bicycle is **unstable** by itself, yet it can be controlled by a rider. *How much more control would an aeroplane need?*

Overhead, buzzards wheeled in the sky, constantly changing the positions of their wings to catch the flow of air. "If birds can do it," Orv mused out loud, "so can men." He seemed so certain, I began to believe it could be done. I began to believe it could be done by Will and Orv.

Author's Perspective
What have you learned about Will and Orv from the information presented so far?

They built their first aircraft right in the bicycle shop. I took over running the place, as Mama would have, so they might make their flying machine.

That first aircraft's wings spanned a full five feet. I measured it out myself. The craft was of pinewood covered with fabric and sealed with shellac. Like a kite, it was controlled by a set of cords.

When it was finished, Orv and I went off on a camping trip with a group of friends. While we were gone, Will did a sneak. He marched out to a nearby field and he flew the glider, watched only by some boys. The thing suddenly swooped down on them. The boys ate dust that day, I'll tell you.

Their first aircraft was a big kite. But a kite is not an aeroplane. So Will and Orv set about to build it bigger—sixteen or seventeen feet, large enough to carry a man but still open to all the elements.

Will lay facedown on the lower wing, showing me how he planned to fly. I tried to imagine the wind in his face, the dirt and grass rushing up to greet him like an old bore at a party.

"Is it safe?" I whispered.

He winked at me, smiled, and said, "If you are looking for perfect safety, sit on the fence and watch the birds."

Dayton, Ohio, where we lived, was not the place to fly the craft. Will and Orv needed somewhere with open spaces and strong, regular breezes. They thought about San Diego, about St. James, Florida, about the coasts of South Carolina and Georgia.

At last they settled on Kitty Hawk on the Outer Banks, a two-hundred-mile strip of sand with the ocean at its face and North Carolina at its back. Will called it "a safe place for practice." Only sand and hearty breezes. Only sun and a moon so bright Orv could read his watch all hours. I kept the store. Will and Orv kept the sky.

Weeks, months went by in practice. The boys sent me letters almost every day so that I might follow their every move. When they were home, I was in their closest confidence.

At Kitty Hawk they flew the aircraft with a man—and without one—but always controlled the craft from the ground. We had thought: *Stand on the shoulders of giants, and you are already high above the ground*, but success did not come as quickly as we hoped. Finally Will made a big decision: "We cast the calculations of others aside."

Back in Dayton they would start anew. This time when they left Kitty Hawk for home, when they left the wind, the sand, the mosquitoes that left lumps like hen's eggs, they came home with a new idea.

Author's Perspective
What clues reveal how the author feels about the Wright brothers? Use details from the text to explain your answer.

Now they worked dawn to dusk, so absorbed in what they were doing, they could hardly wait for morning to come to begin again. They built a small wind tunnel out of an old starch box and used a fan to make the wind. Then they built a larger tunnel.

They learned about lift and drag. They tried out many different kinds of wings. And three years, almost to the day, after Will had written to the Smithsonian, they were ready for *powered* flight. They built the *Flyer*, with a wingspan of just over forty feet.

Our friend Charlie Taylor made a twelve-horsepower engine for the *Flyer*, a motor both light and powerful. Gasoline was gravity-fed into the engine from a small tank just below the upper wing. The *Flyer* was so big—over six hundred pounds of aeroplane—it could not be **assembled** whole in our shop.

Back to Kitty Hawk they went at the tag end of September 1903, carrying crates filled with aircraft parts. It took weeks to put the *Flyer* together, weeks more to prepare for the flight.

Winter came blustering in early. It was cold in camp, each morning the washbasin was frozen solid, so they wrote in their letters. They kept fiddling, tinkering, changing things.

Finally, on December 14, they were ready. They flipped a coin to see who would be pilot. Will won, grinned, climbed into the hip cradle, and off the *Flyer* went, rattling down the sixty-foot starting track, then sailing fifteen feet into the air, where it stalled, crashed. But they were encouraged nonetheless. The telegram they sent to Papa and me read: *Rudder only injured. Success* **assured**. *Keep quiet.*

On December 17, a cold and windy day, the *Flyer* repaired and ready, they decided to try again. **Hoisting** a red flag to the top of a pole, they signaled the lifesaving station for witnesses. Four men and a teenage boy appeared.

The men helped them get the *Flyer* onto the starting track. Orv lay down on the lower wing, his hips in the padded cradle. Will shook Orv's hand.

"Now you men," Will called out, "laugh and holler and clap and try to cheer my brother."

The motor began: *Cough, cough, chug-a-chug-a-chug*. Orv released the wire that held the plane to the track. Then the plane raced forward into the strong wind and into history.

The boys sent a telegram home to Papa and me.

After that, the world was never the same. Many men went into the air. Women, too. I was not the first woman to fly. That honor went to the wife of one of our sponsors, Mrs. Hart O. Berg, with a rope around her skirt to keep it from blowing about and showing her legs. She flew for two minutes and seven seconds, sitting stiffly upright next to Will.

A Parisian dressmaker who watched the flight invented the hobble skirt, which for a short time was quite smart. Such is fashion.

But how I laughed when I had my turn at last, flying at Pau in France on February 15, 1909. Will took his seat beside me. Orv waved from the ground. The plane took off into the cold blue. Wind scoured my face till my cheeks turned bright red. Then I opened my arms wide, welcoming all the sky before me.

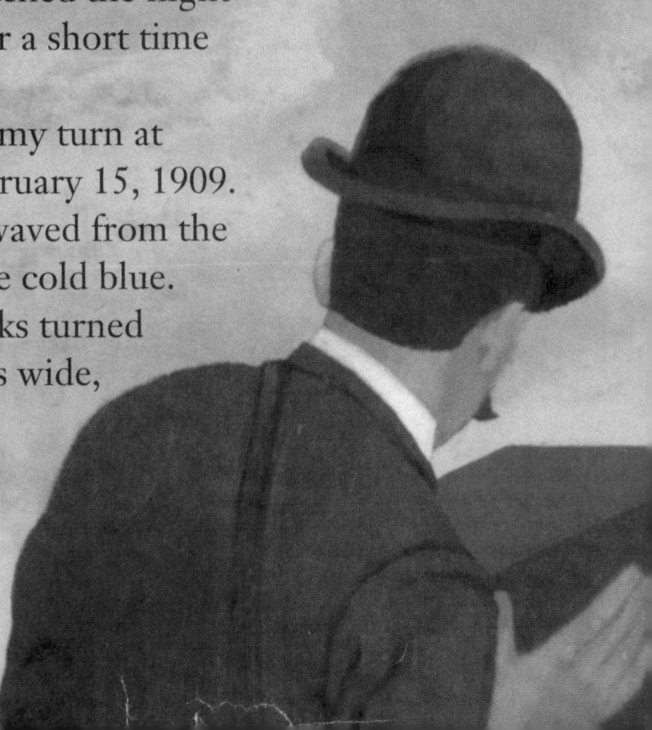

Soar with Jane and Jim

Jane Yolen was asked by her editor to write a book about the Wright brothers for the 100th anniversary of their first flight. Jane wanted her book to be different from all the other books about the Wrights. She did a lot of research until she came across an interesting note about the Wright brothers' sister. Jane knew she had found her story.

Other books by Jane Yolen

Jim Burke has been an award-winning artist for many years, but this is his first book for children. Jim currently lives in New York City.

Another book by Jim Burke

Author's Purpose

Identify whether the narration of the story in *My Brothers' Flying Machine* is first- or third-person. Why did the author tell the story from the sister's point of view?

LOG ON FIND OUT

Author Jane Yolen
Illustrator Jim Burke
www.macmillanmh.com

LOG ON LEARN IT **Comprehension**
www.macmillanmh.com

Comprehension Check

Summarize

To summarize *My Brothers' Flying Machine* use the most important details from the selection. Information from your Author's Perspective Map may help you.

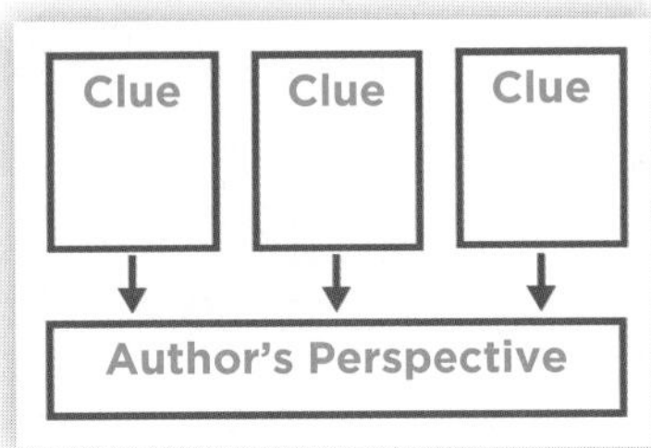

Think and Compare

1. Where did the Wright brothers build their first aircraft? **Details**
2. Find an example of a fact and an opinion in this selection. Explain how you would prove the fact. **Fact and Opinion**
3. How does the narrator feel about her two brothers? Use details from the selection to support your answer. **Make Inferences**
4. Identify the simile the author uses on page 521. What does this tell you about the author's opinion of the conditions at Kitty Hawk? **Visualize: Author's Perspective**
5. What do readers learn about the Wright brothers' first airplane in the selection "Take Off" on page 507 and in the story *My Brothers' Flying Machine*? **Reading/Writing Across Texts**

Poetry

A **Narrative Poem** tells a story or gives an account of fictional or real events.

Literary Elements

Repetition happens when a word or phrase is repeated throughout a poem.

Personification is a literary device in which human characteristics are given to an animal, a thing, or an idea.

Brave New Heights

I hear Amelia Earhart
took a plane
and flew it like a bullet
straight up through clouds
into an atmosphere
we can't see

and when the engine
cut
(the plane being pushed
as high as it would go)

I hear Amelia Earhart
turned that plane
straight back
down into a blanket
of foggy cloud lying thick
and nearly to the ground

only with the clouds gone
could she pull back on the stick
the ground screaming in her face
Amelia tacked that plane
back into the sky
saving herself and breaking
another flying record

— *Monica Kulling*

The first line of the poem is **repeated** in the third stanza.

The phrase "the ground screaming in her face" is an example of **personification**. The poet describes the ground as if it were a human being.

Connect and Compare

1. The author repeats the phrase "I hear Amelia Earhart" in the first and third stanzas of the poem. How are these two stanzas the same? How are they different? **Repetition**

2. What is an example of a simile used in the first stanza of the poem? **Apply**

3. Compare Amelia Earhart with the Wright brothers as they are described in *My Brothers' Flying Machine*. How are they similar? How are they different? **Reading/Writing Across Texts**

LOG ON FIND OUT **Poetry** Narrative Poems
www.macmillanmh.com

Writing

Trait: Word Choice
Writers include **sensory details** to appeal to the reader's sense of taste, touch, smell, or sound.

Reading and Writing Connection

Read the passage below. Notice how the author Jane Yolen uses sensory details in her story.

An excerpt from
My Brothers' Flying Machine

The author uses sensory details to help us experience this moment. The author chooses details to show what people in the plane hear, see, and feel.

But how I laughed when I had my turn at last, flying at Pau in France on February 15, 1909. Will took his seat beside me. Orv waved from the ground. The plane took off into the cold blue. Wind scoured my face till my cheeks turned bright red. Then I opened my arms wide, welcoming all the sky before me.

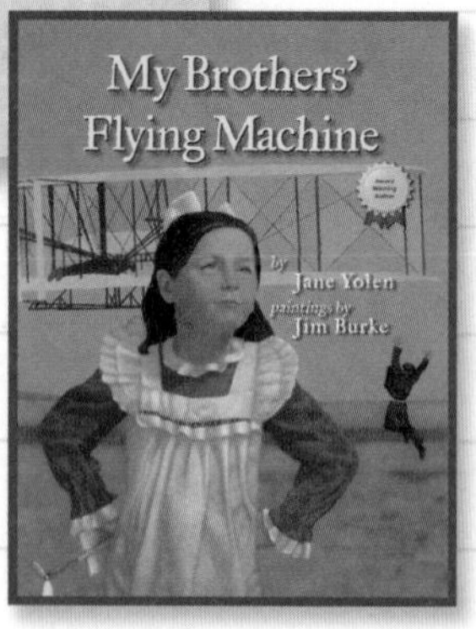

Read and Find

Read Linda's writing below. How did she use details to show what was happening? Use the checklist below to help you.

Did I Mention I Hate Flying?

by Linda L.

The microphone crackled as the flight attendant told us to buckle our seat belts. My seat was comfortable, but I wasn't relaxed. Mom handed me gum to keep my ears from popping as the plane took off. I focused on the sweet cinnamon flavor.

Suddenly, the plane's engine roared loudly. I nervously looked out the window as the plane lifted up. To my delight, the buildings and cars looked like toys!

Read about an airplane flight.

Writer's Checklist

- [x] Did the writer give you more than just "seeing" **details**?
- [x] Does the writer help you hear, touch, or taste the moment she is describing?
- [ ] Can you picture what it is like to be there?

Review

Theme
Draw Conclusions
Description
Latin and Greek Roots
Multiple-Step Directions

Mouse and Crow

Mouse had a beautiful collection of 10 glittering crystals. She loved looking at the way they sparkled, so she displayed each one on a shiny metal bottle cap.

One day she brought a sparkling green crystal to the river to wash it. Crow was perched in a tree nearby. The gleam of the crystal caught his eye.

"That's beautiful," called out Crow as he eyed the crystal jealously.

"Yes it is," said the innocent Mouse, "but it's not my prettiest. I have nine others at home that are more beautiful."

Crow didn't respond. He knew he would have to be patient.

A few days later, as Mouse was walking in the field, Crow began performing flying tricks. He soared up and down and zigzagged across the sky to get her attention. Mouse watched him in amazement.

"What fun it is to fly!" Crow laughed. "You cannot imagine how wonderful it feels!"

"Oh! I wish I could fly," said Mouse.

"I can take you," volunteered Crow. "All I ask in return is one crystal. I pick that green one. You said you have others."

Mouse happily agreed. She ran home and got the crystal. She brought it back to Crow and they flew off. Mouse was astonished. She giggled as they soared into the air. It was a thrilling feeling! Crow flew for miles. The sky seemed limitless! After several hours Crow landed on a large rock.

"That was amazing!" Mouse said excitedly.

"I'm glad you had fun!" smiled Crow. He then got up and started to fly away.

"Wait!" shouted Mouse helplessly. "I need to go home."

"Oh dear," said Crow. "I'm afraid that will cost you more. You will have to pay me nine more crystals. Otherwise you have to find your own way home."

Upset, Mouse realized she didn't know how to get home. She would have to go home with Crow. As she rode back with Crow, Mouse felt angry. The more she thought about it, the angrier she got. "How can he be so greedy?" she wondered. The question made her think, and suddenly she knew how she could save her crystals.

As she handed over her crystals to Crow, she sighed sadly and said, "Well, that's the last one. Except…oh, never mind." She pretended to be nervous.

"Except what?" Crow said angrily.

"N-n-n-nothing," stammered Mouse.

"TELL ME!" shouted Crow.

"Well, I was saving them for me. I mean, you won't like them. They're not that special."

"Bring whatever it is out here right away," Crow said threateningly.

Mouse brought out the 10 bottle caps. Crow thought that Mouse was trying to keep them for herself. "They must be extremely precious," thought Crow. "I'll take those instead of those boring crystals."

And he did.

Mouse still has her beautiful crystals. She loves her collection more than ever, but she no longer boasts about them. She now knows not everyone can be trusted.

How to Change a Flat Tire on a Bike

If YOU RIDE A BIKE, chances are you're going to get a flat tire. Sometimes the smallest piece of glass or even a piece of gravel can ruin a ride on your bike. Other times an encounter with a pothole can put an end to your ride.

To fix a flat tire, you need a new tube, a pump, and three tire levers. Then, follow these multiple-step directions from a technical manual:

1. Take the bicycle wheel off the frame of the bike. If the tire is not completely flat, release the rest of the air from it.

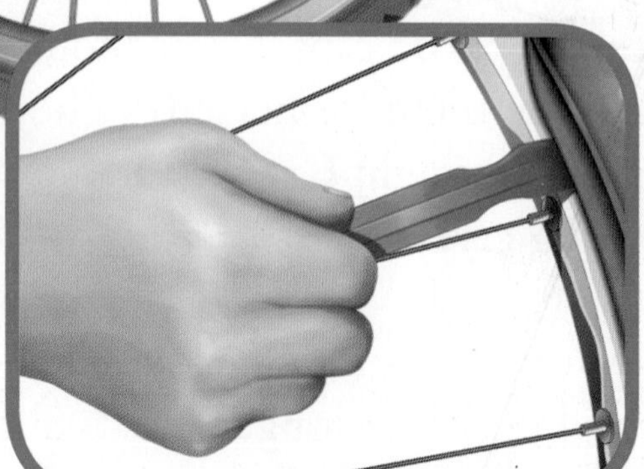

2. Place the thin end of the tire lever between the tire and the rim of the wheel.

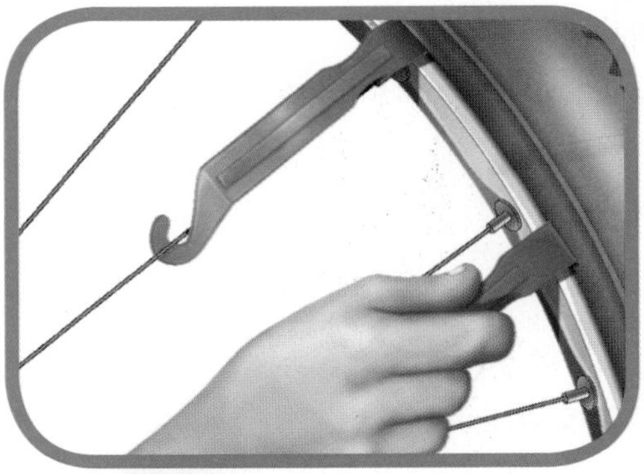

3

Find a spot on the wheel about two spokes over from the last lever. Place the second lever there. Continue to place levers around the rim, removing the first levers as you go.

4

Stop when the tire is free from the wheel. Remove the old tube. Carefully check the tire. Remove any objects. Use your bike pump to put just a little air in your tube. Put the tube into your old tire. Be sure it does not have twists or kinks.

5

Find the hole in the rim of your wheel for the tire valve. Put the tire valve in the tube through the hole as you pull the tire and tube over the wheel. Use your fingers to ease the tire onto the wheel.

6

Use the pump to blow up the tire. The tire should feel firm to the touch. Then put the wheel back on the bicycle frame.

Show What You Know

Comprehension

Theme

- Theme is the message or overall idea that the author wants to communicate to the reader.
- To identify the theme of a story, think about what the characters say and do. Look at the events in the story that happen because of the characters' words and actions. Then decide what message the author is trying to get across to the reader.
- On your own, read a folktale, fairy tale, or fable. Identify and explain the theme of the story. Write a brief paragraph that summarizes the theme and provide details and examples from the story to support your summary.

Genre

Persuade Me

- Persuasive writing tries to get the reader to think or act in a certain way. An advertisement is an example of persuasive writing. Advertisements use different techniques to try to persuade you to buy a product.
- Some ads use loaded words such as *famous* or *best-selling* to sell their product. Others use testimonials. These ads feature someone, usually a celebrity, praising a product. Some ads are informational. These ads rely on facts to convince the reader that their product is the best.
- Work with a partner to find an advertisement from a newspaper or magazine. Identify and write down examples of persuasive language and techniques that the ad uses. Explain why you would or would not buy the product.

Word Study

Words with Roots in Other Languages

- Many words that we use in English come from different countries around the world. For example, the word "brick" comes from the Dutch word *bricke*.
- You can learn about the root and origin, or history, of a word in the dictionary.
- Use a dictionary to look up the following words: *bazaar*, *algebra*, *plateau*. Write down the definition of each word, its root, and its origin. Then think of another word that may have come from another language. Look it up in the dictionary to find its root and origin.

Greek and Latin Roots

- Knowing even a few Greek and Latin roots can help you to figure out the meaning of many words.
- Write the following words and look them up in a dictionary: *telephoto*, *graphics*, *construct*, *audible*. Underline the root of each word and label it "Latin" or "Greek."
- Create flashcards with each of the Latin and Greek roots. On one side put a Latin or Greek root, for example, *graph*, and on the other side write its meaning.

Unit 5
Habitats

The Big Question

What makes a habitat unique?

LOG ON VIEW IT **Theme Video** Habitats
www.macmillanmh.com

What makes a habitat unique?

Every creature has a habitat, or a place where it lives. There are a variety of habitats in the world. Habitats are special and different, and the animals that live there have adapted to life in these areas. An animal's habitat can tell you a lot about its size, its food, its intelligence, and its purpose on Earth. For example, the spotted owl lives in the forests of western America. The nocturnal spotted owl usually nests in tree holes, rock cracks, or existing nests in large trees.

Learning about unique habitats will help you understand animal life better, as well as the larger natural world around you.

Research Activities

Throughout the unit, you will be gathering information about natural habitats and what makes them unique. Choose one habitat to focus your research on and create a poster about that habitat. Use diagrams and photographs in your poster.

Keep Track of Ideas

As you read, keep track of all you are learning about natural habitats and what makes them unique. Use the **Accordion Book Foldable**. In the first column, write the Unit Theme: *Habitats*. On each of the following columns, write facts you learn each week that will help you in your research and in your understanding of the Unit Theme.

Digital Learning

LOG ON FIND OUT www.macmillanmh.com

StudentWorks Plus™

Interactive Student Book

- **Research Roadmap**
  Follow a step-by-step guide to complete your research project.

Online Resources

- Topic Finder and Other Research Tools
- Videos and Virtual Field Trips
- Photos and Drawings for Presentations
- Related Articles and Web Resources
- Web Site Links

People and Places

The Great Plains

The Great Plains is a vast region in western North America. It extends from Canada to Texas and includes parts of North Dakota, South Dakota, Montana, Wyoming, Colorado, Nebraska, Kansas, Oklahoma, and New Mexico.

Adapting to Survive

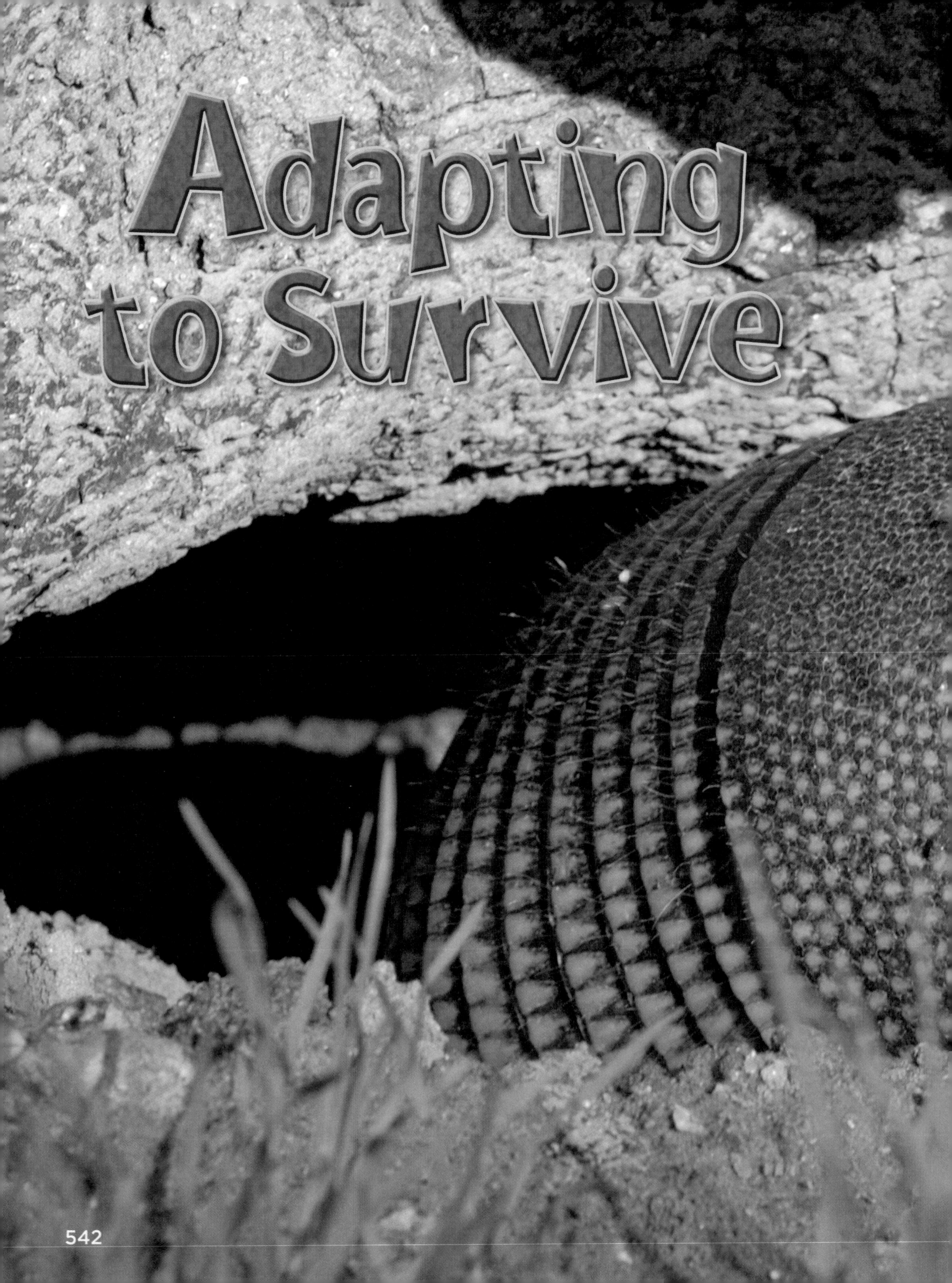

Talk About It

How does this animal adapt to survive?

LOG ON VIEW IT

Oral Language Activities
Adapting to Survive
www.macmillanmh.com

Vocabulary

shimmer **climate**
eerie **silken**
lurk **lumbering**

Context Clues

Surrounding Words can help you figure out the meanings of unfamiliar words. Read the story and find the sentence where the word *shimmer* appears. Use the surrounding words in the sentence to help you figure out the meaning of *shimmer*.

Living in Alaska

by Marsha Adams

Another World

In some ways, living in Alaska is like living in another world. Winter lasts for about nine months. For more than two months each year, the northern lights that shine and **shimmer** in the sky are the only source of light.

For the people there, it can be strange and **eerie** to go so long without seeing the sun. For the animals, it can be dangerous. Such dim light makes it difficult to see whether predators **lurk** in the shadows, waiting for their next meal. It may be a snowy owl that swoops down on silent wings and swallows its prey whole!

Winter Coats

Beavers, sea otters, and other mammals adapt to survive in the cold Alaskan **climate**. They grow two layers of fur. The thick bottom layer is soft, **silken** fur that helps trap body heat. The longer, coarse hairs that form the outer layer act as a barrier against water, snow, and wind.

The ptarmigan, Alaska's state bird, has a special way to keep warm. It grows feathers down its legs, over its toes, and on the soles of its feet!

A Winter Nap

You won't find **lumbering** black or brown bears when the frigid weather arrives. Bears, mice, and other animals hibernate, or go into a deep sleep, during the winter. When they hibernate, their bodies don't need food or water. Other animals, such as some caterpillars, fish, and houseflies, actually freeze during the winter. Then they thaw out in the spring!

A Low Profile

Arctic plants have their own special traits that help them survive. During the summer months, the dark soil absorbs the sun's heat. So plants grow close to the ground, where it's warmer. When snow falls, it protects the plants from the cold winds above.

Reread for **Comprehension**

Summarize

Main Idea and Details The main idea is the most important point that an author makes about a topic. The main idea is supported by details that help to explain or describe it. As you read, ask yourself what the sentences in the selection have in common, tell about, explain, or describe. Use the Main Idea Chart to help you classify and summarize these details and to determine the main idea.

Detail
Detail
Detail
Main Idea

LOG ON LEARN IT Comprehension
www.macmillanmh.com

Comprehension

Genre

Expository writing sets out to explain something by presenting verifiable facts about it.

Summarize

Main Idea and Details
As you read, fill in your Main Idea Chart.

Detail
Detail
Detail
Main Idea

Read to Find Out

What characteristics allow desert animals to live in such a hot, dry place?

A Walk in the Desert

by Rebecca L. Johnson

with illustrations by Phyllis V. Saroff

Biomes of North America

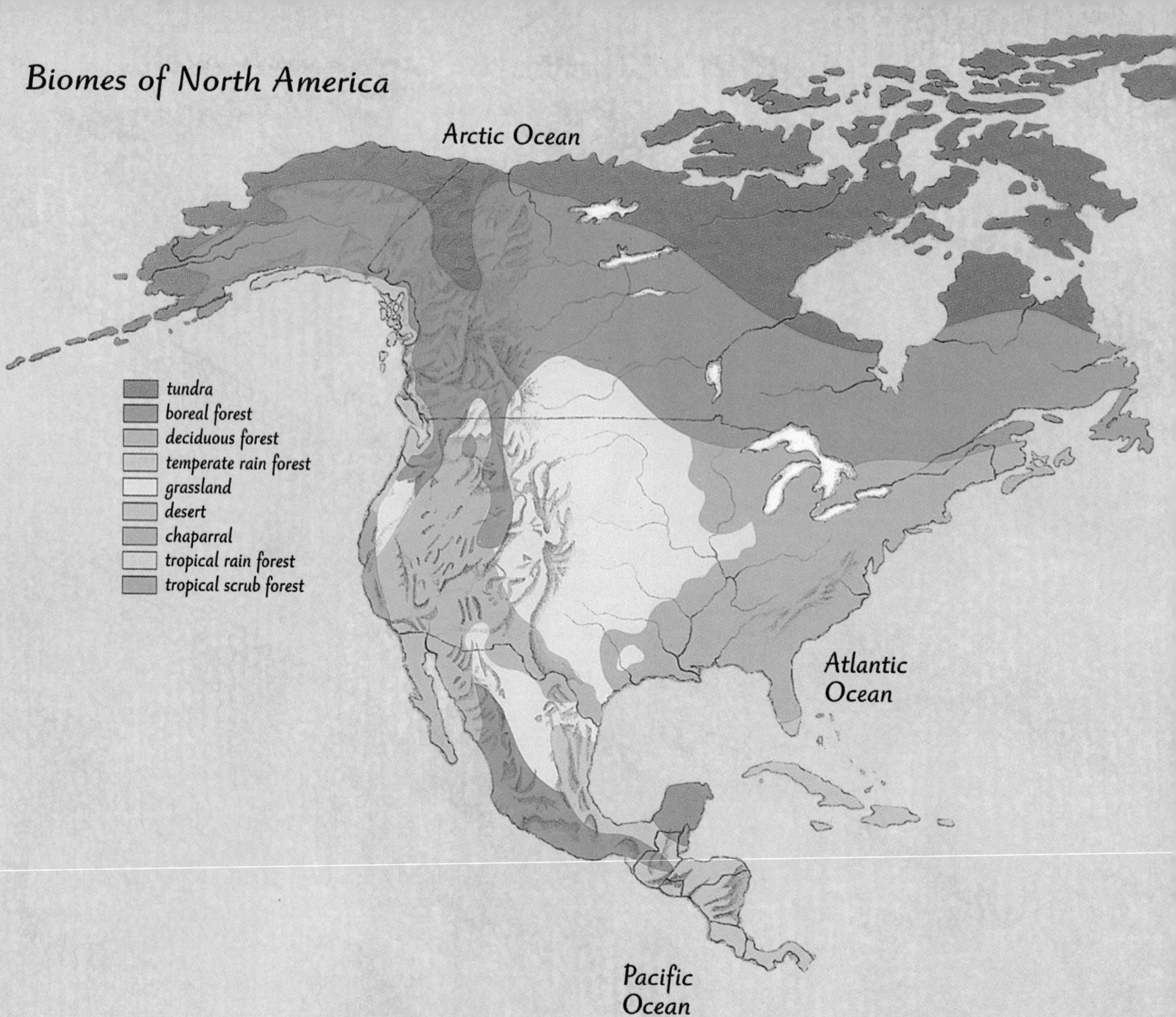

Sunbeams are flickering over the landscape as the sun rises. A kit fox heads for her den as another day in the desert begins.

Deserts are surrounded by other kinds of landscapes. Scientists call these different land zones biomes. All the plants and animals in a biome form a community. In that community, every living thing depends on other community members for its survival. A biome's **climate**, soil, plants, and animals are all connected this way.

Deserts have a very dry climate. They do get a little rain, but it doesn't come regularly. One storm might drench a desert with several inches of rain in just a few hours. It might not rain again for months—even years.

A mother desert tortoise lays her eggs in sandy soil. The sun warms the eggs until they hatch.

Desert plants provide many animals with food and water. Here comes a desert tortoise. It shuffles slowly along and stops often to rest. The tortoise stretches its long neck to nibble a wildflower. Tortoises rarely drink. They get nearly all the water they need from the plants they eat.

Cacti also provide homes for desert animals. Halfway down a nearby saguaro's thick stem, a Gila woodpecker pecks a hole in the juicy flesh. It is making a nest for its eggs. Woodpeckers have nested in this cactus for many years, so they've made many holes in it.

Other creatures have moved into some of the old woodpecker holes. A pair of flycatchers lives in one. Another is home to a hive of honeybees. And peeking out of still another hole is an elf owl. It has white eyebrows and fierce yellow eyes.

Saguaro cacti grow very slowly. But they may live for 200 years.

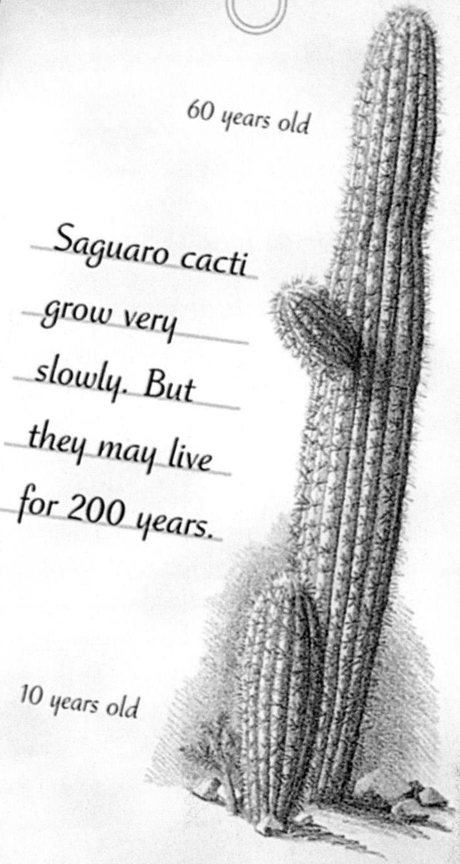

A wood rat nibbles
on the sweet fruit
of a prickly pear cactus.

Not far from the saguaro, you see a very different kind of desert home. Jammed between a dead cactus and a fallen tree is a huge mound of tangled twigs. It's the nest of a wood rat.

Wood rats are also called pack rats. They use anything they can find to build enormous nests. A wood rat's nest might be made of sticks, rocks, leaves, cactus spines, or even bones. It may be as tall as a person and just as wide. The nest protects the wood rat from foxes, hawks, and other predators. It is also a cool place to hide from the hot sun.

Main Idea and Details
What is the second paragraph mainly about?

Many desert animals are nocturnal. They are active only at night, when it is cooler. Nocturnal desert-dwellers spend their days in burrows, dens, and other sheltered places. The kangaroo rat and the kit fox are nocturnal. They stay underground until the sun goes down.

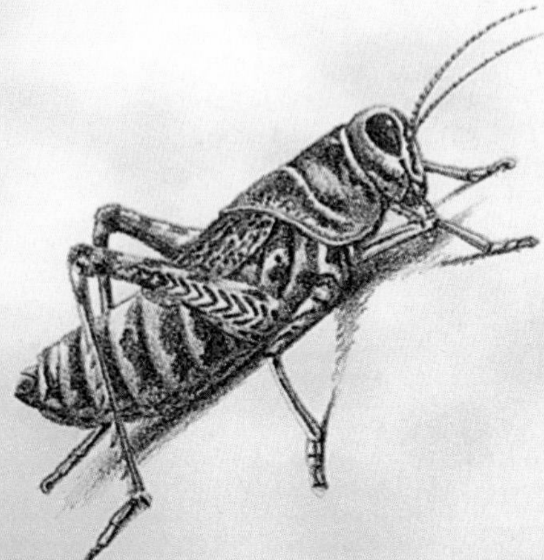

A painted grasshopper uses its long legs to hop from plant to plant—and to escape being eaten.

But some desert animals are active during the day. Insects are on the move everywhere. Columns of ants march across the ground. Colorful beetles crawl up and down stems. Grasshoppers spring from leaf to leaf. Insect-eating spiders are busy, too. They spin **silken** webs among cactus spines.

The sun has climbed higher in the clear blue sky. Can you feel the heat? Desert lizards don't seem to mind. Their tough, scaly skin seals water inside their bodies and keeps them from drying out. Lizards rest on rocks, hunt insects, and cling to cactus stems. In one small patch of desert, you could see tiny skinks, chunky chuckwallas, spiny horned lizards, and **lumbering** Gila monsters.

A horned lizard's spiny scales are a good defense against desert predators.

A roadrunner's feet have two toes that point forward and two that point backward. This shape helps the bird grip the ground when it runs.

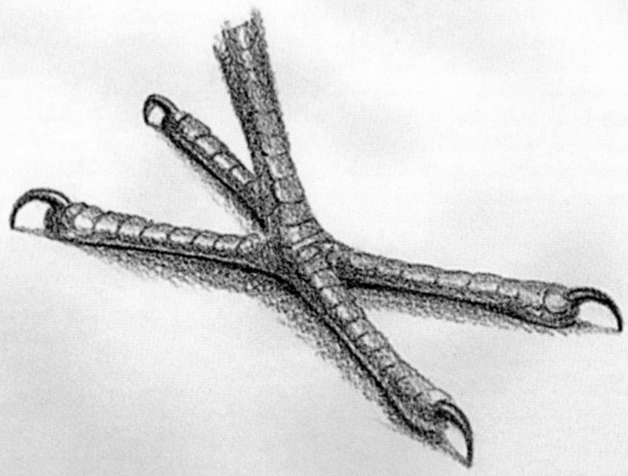

Suddenly, something streaks across your path. It's a speedy lizard, and right on its heels is a roadrunner. Roadrunners can fly. But these desert birds prefer to run after lizards and the other small animals they hunt.

Roadrunners have long, strong legs. They can run as fast as many lizards can. In fact, this time the bird is faster. The roadrunner catches the lizard by its tail and swallows it in one gulp.

Nearby, a jackrabbit looks for plants to nibble. Jackrabbits are even faster than roadrunners. They can outrun almost everything in the desert. They can even outrun coyotes—most of the time!

Coyotes eat rabbits when they can catch them. But they will eat just about anything, from birds and lizards to berries. To find underground water, they dig holes in dry streambeds. Coyotes can survive almost anywhere.

A mother scorpion carries her babies around on her back until they can survive on their own.

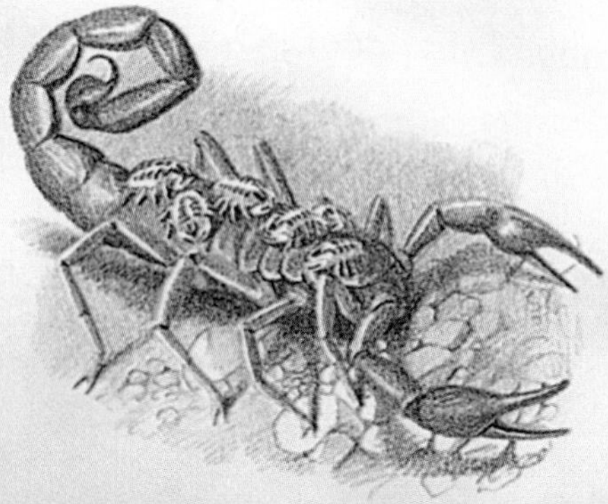

By noon, even the coyotes are panting. It's well over 100 degrees. The sun is a fireball overhead. Nearly all the daytime animals move into the shade of rocks and cacti during the hottest part of the day.

A rattlesnake's rattle is made up of a row of large, dry scales.

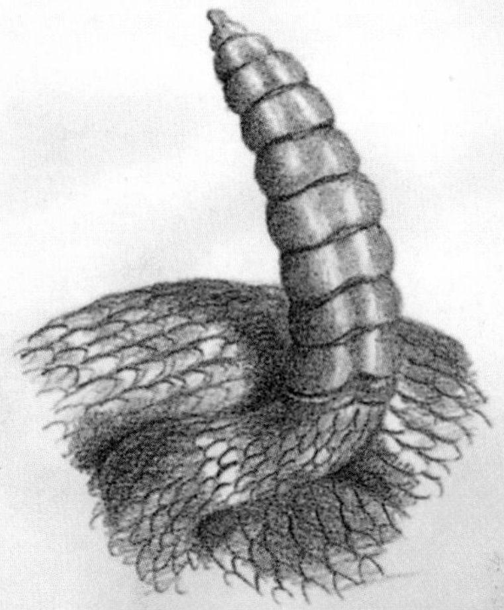

Take a tip from the animals. Find a place out of the sun to rest. Just be careful where you sit. Scorpions often **lurk** in crevices or under rocks during the day. A scorpion's tail has a stinger filled with poison. Few kinds of scorpions can kill a person. But the sting of any scorpion is very painful.

Watch out for hiding rattlesnakes and coral snakes, too. Their poison is deadly. You don't want to get within striking distance of either one.

Heat waves **shimmer** above the landscape. The leaves of the mesquite trees curl up. Curled leaves lose less water to the hot, dry air. The desert is very quiet. Most of the birds are silent. They seem to be waiting for the sun's fierce heat to fade.

Gradually, the sun moves lower in the sky. As shadows grow longer, the temperature starts to drop. Desert birds begin to sing again. At sunset, coyotes call to each other, barking and yelping. They join voices in an **eerie**, wailing song.

Main Idea and Details
What are these two pages mainly about? Use details to support your answer.

The hot desert day is over. The cool night is about to begin. Birds, lizards, and other daytime animals retreat to snug nests and safe hiding places. There they

Take a Walk with Rebecca

Rebecca L. Johnson grew up in South Dakota. Harsh prairie winters helped her prepare for working with scientists in Antarctica. Ms. Johnson has traveled to Antarctica twice and has written three books on the experience: *Braving the Frozen Frontier*, *Investigating the Ozone Hole*, and *Science on the Ice* (winner of the *Scientific American* Young Readers Award). She has also "walked" in several other biomes—the tundra, the rain forest, the prairie, and others—for the "Biomes of North America" series.

Rebecca studied Biology at Augustana College and has worked as a teacher and a museum curator. She enjoys scuba diving, watercolor painting, and cross-country skiing, and lives in South Dakota with her husband.

LOG ON FIND OUT

Author Rebecca L. Johnson
www.macmillanmh.com

Author's Purpose

The author uses photos, drawings, and captions in the selection. How do these text features help you locate information in the selection?

LOG ON LEARN IT **Comprehension**
www.macmillanmh.com

Comprehension Check

Summarize

To summarize *A Walk in the Desert* use the most important details from the selection. Information from your Main Idea Chart may help you.

Detail
Detail
Detail
Main Idea

Think and Compare

1. What is an example of a desert animal that is nocturnal? Details
2. Why do wood rats build enormous nests? Explain your answer using details from the selection. Cause and Effect
3. Reread the two paragraphs on page 556. Summarize the main idea and details. Summarize: Main Idea and Details
4. Is the author's purpose stated or implied? Explain your answer using details from the text. Author's Purpose
5. Read "Living in Alaska" on pages 544–545. Compare the plants and animals that live in Alaska's **climate** with those that live in a desert climate. How are they similar? Use details from both selections to explain your answer. Reading/Writing Across Texts

Science

Genre

Expository writing presents facts about a topic. It can also include photographs, captions, and graphic aids such as diagrams.

Text Feature

A **Process Diagram** shows an entire process from start to finish.

Content Vocabulary

defend **disrupt**
absorbed

Food Chains

PREDATOR vs. PREY

by Chisulo Lingenvelder

A food chain shows how living things get the food they need to survive. Food chains are made up of producers, consumers, and decomposers. Plants are producers because they use energy from the sun to make their own food. Animals are consumers because they cannot make their own food. They have to depend on the other living things in the food chain to eat. There are three kinds of consumers. Herbivores are animals that eat only plants. Carnivores are animals that eat other animals. Animals that eat both plants and other animals are called omnivores. Living things, like fungi, are decomposers. They return minerals to Earth's soil by breaking down plants and animals that have died.

Some predators hunt only a certain kind of prey. Other predators will hunt anything.

Rabbits are herbivores. They are also popular prey for many predators.

A food chain illustrates the way in which energy moves from one living thing to another. For example, energy from sunlight beams down on Earth. That energy is then **absorbed** by green plants. The green plants are eaten by herbivores. Herbivores are then eaten by carnivores or omnivores. When that animal dies, a decomposer breaks down its body and returns the energy to the soil.

Predators and their prey are important to the food chain. Carnivores are hunters. They are also predators. A predator hunts weaker animals to eat. These weaker animals are prey. Prey must hide to keep from being eaten. Nature has given these animals different ways to protect themselves. Some animals can hide by using their color or shape to blend into their surroundings. Other animals are born with hard shells or sharp teeth that they use to **defend** themselves.

Armadillos have thick body armor to protect themselves from being attacked.

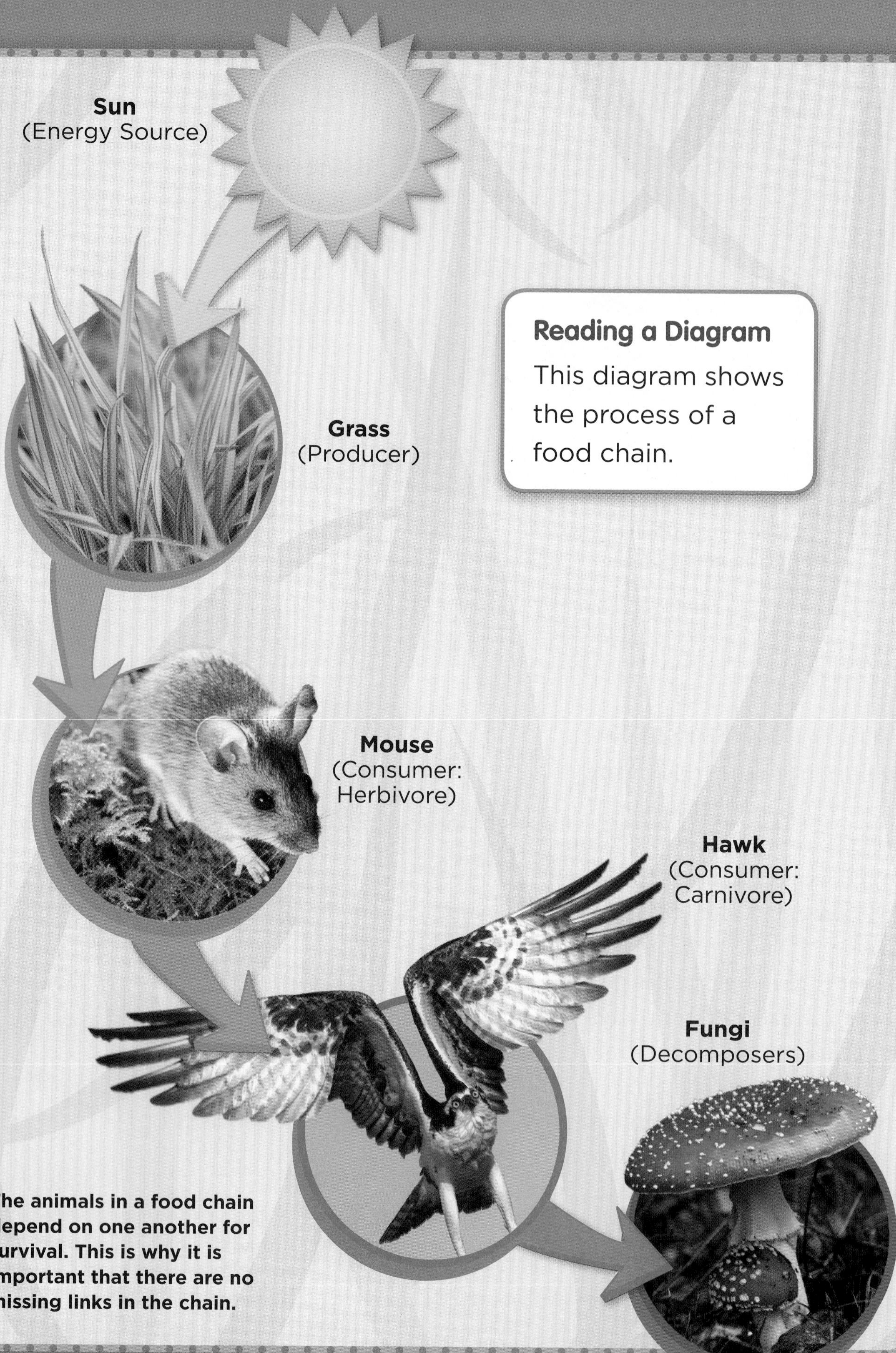

Reading a Diagram

This diagram shows the process of a food chain.

The animals in a food chain depend on one another for survival. This is why it is important that there are no missing links in the chain.

Keeping a Balance

Each living thing in the food chain plays an important role in keeping nature balanced. If one piece of the food chain gets too big, the other animals will have to compete for survival. For example, if there were too many giraffes, there would not be enough plants for all of them to eat. This imbalance could cause giraffes to starve and die and affect the animals that depend on giraffes for food. Changes such as these would **disrupt** the food chain and destroy the world's natural order.

Male giraffes eat from different parts of the tree than the female giraffes. This way there is enough food for all!

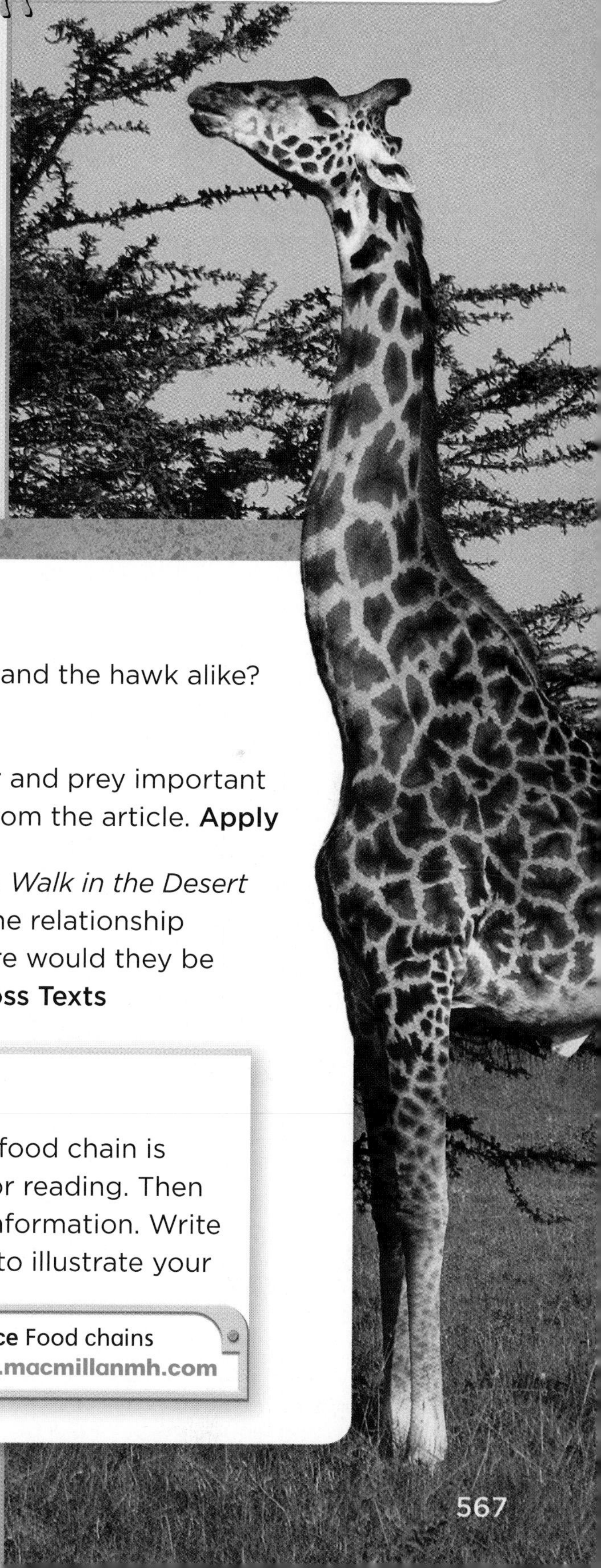

Connect and Compare

1. Look at the diagram. How are the mouse and the hawk alike? **Reading a Diagram**
2. Why is the relationship between predator and prey important to the food chain? Explain using details from the article. **Apply**
3. Connect what happens to the animals in *A Walk in the Desert* to the food chain in this article. What is the relationship between a jackrabbit and a coyote? Where would they be on the food chain? **Reading/Writing Across Texts**

RESEARCH INQUIRY

Science Activity

Research what happens if one part of a food chain is removed. First establish your purpose for reading. Then use different reference sources to find information. Write a report and include a process diagram to illustrate your report.

LOG ON FIND OUT **Science** Food chains
www.macmillanmh.com

Reading and Writing Connection

Writing

Trait: Word Choice

Good writers use **descriptive details** to create a clear image for the reader.

Read the passage below. Notice how the author Rebecca L. Johnson uses descriptive details.

An excerpt from
A Walk in the Desert

The author uses descriptive details to create a picture of a hot desert day coming to an end.

The hot desert day is over. The cool night is about to begin. Birds, lizards, and other daytime animals retreat to snug nests and safe hiding places. There they will sleep the night away.

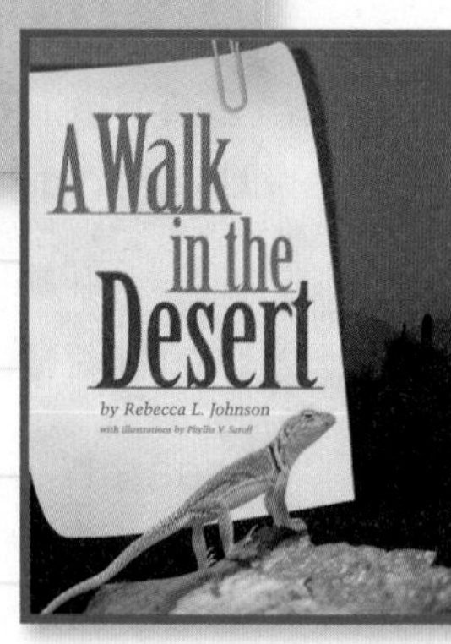

Read and Find

Read Afifa's writing below. What descriptive details does she include to create a picture for the reader? Use the checklist below to help you.

Read about an adventure.

Rappelling

by Afifa B.

I waited for a long time for someone to go down. Finally, it was my turn. I got myself hooked on and then I was off. I went one foot at a time and once I got closer to the bottom, I went a little slow so I could show off. Then I started jumping. I vaulted off as if I was a track star going over a hurdle. At last, I touched down. I unbuckled and took a deep breath. That felt good.

Writer's Checklist

- [x] Does the author use strong verbs to describe what she did?
- [x] What **descriptive details** does the author include to help you picture how she looked as she rappelled?
- [ ] Can you picture what happened to Afifa?

DESERT
ANIMALS

Talk About It

What do you think makes this desert animal unique?

LOG ON VIEW IT

Oral Language Activities
Desert Animals
www.macmillanmh.com

Vocabulary

interfere
convinced
awkward
proclaimed
agile
guardian

Thesaurus

Synonyms are words that have the same, or nearly the same, meanings. You can use a thesaurus to find synonyms.

Use a thesaurus to find a synonym for the word *agile*.

ROADRUNNERS: SURPRISING BIRDS

by Adam Savage

"Today we will hear from Pam," said Mr. Sanders.

Pam stood. "I'm going to talk about roadrunners," she said, smiling.

Someone snickered, but Pam didn't let a little noise **interfere** with her presentation. She was **convinced** that her topic was interesting. Now she had to prove to her classmates that roadrunners were interesting.

Pam was prepared, so she didn't feel **awkward**, or uncomfortable. Holding up her photo album, Pam began her report. "This is a roadrunner." She looked around the room. Nobody was looking at her. Pam knew she had to get everyone's attention.

Holding up the next photo, Pam **proclaimed** with confidence, "This amazing bird is so fast and **agile** it can catch a rattlesnake!"

"Whoa, that's cool!" called Pedro from the back row. "What else can it do?"

Now every eye was on Pam. "Roadrunners can run up to 15 miles per hour!" she continued.

"Do they fly?" someone asked.

"They can fly when they sense danger. But not very far."

Pam held up the next photo. It showed the roadrunner's black-and-white spotted feathers and the crest on its head.

"Where did you get the photos?" asked Mr. Sanders.

"I took these while I was visiting my grandmother in Arizona," explained Pam.

"I see," said Mr. Sanders. "Is there anything else you'd like to tell us?"

"I learned that a roadrunner is a very clever **guardian** of its young. Let's say an enemy comes near a roadrunner's nest. The roadrunner pretends to have a broken leg, and leads the enemy away. I watched a roadrunner as it tottered along. It was so brave!"

Someone asked another question, but Mr. Sanders said to save it for next time. When the class groaned, "Awww," Pam knew her report was a winner.

Reread for Comprehension

Summarize

Problem and Solution A Problem and Solution Chart can help you to summarize the events, or **plot** of a story. Identifying the problems and solutions in a story and how they influence future events in the plot will help you to understand the story better. Reread the story and use the Problem and Solution Chart to help you identify the important events in the story.

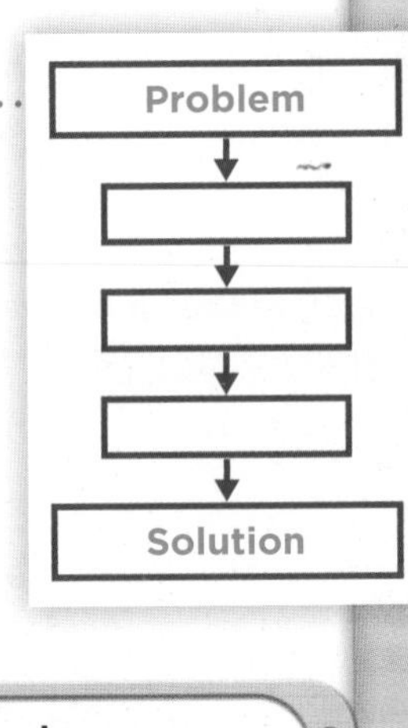

LOG ON LEARN IT **Comprehension**
www.macmillanmh.com

Comprehension

Genre

A **Folktale** is a story based on the traditions of a people or region. They are passed down from generation to generation orally.

Summarize

Problem and Solution
As you read, fill in your Problem and Solution Chart.

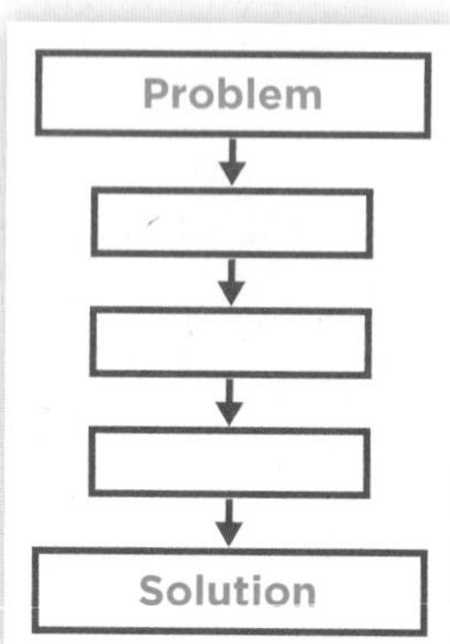

Read to Find Out

What does this folktale teach you about life?

ROADRUNNER'S DANCE

by Rudolfo Anaya • Illustrated by David Diaz

"*Ssss*," hissed Snake as he slithered out of his hole by the side of the road. He bared his fangs and frightened a family walking home from the cornfield.

The mother threw her basketful of corn in the air. The children froze with fright.

"Father!" the children called, and the father came running.

"*Ssss*," Snake threatened.

"Come away," the father said, and the family took another path home.

"I am king of the road," Snake boasted. "No one may use the road without my permission."

That evening the people of the village gathered together and spoke to the elders.

"We are afraid of being bitten by Snake," they protested. "He acts as if the road belongs only to him."

The elders agreed that something should be done, and so the following morning they went to Sacred Mountain, where Desert Woman lived. She had created the desert animals, so surely she could help.

"Please do something about Snake," the elders said. "He makes visiting our neighbors and going to our fields impossible. He frightens the children."

Desert Woman thought for a long time. She did not like to **interfere** in the lives of the people and animals, but she knew that something must be done.

"I have a solution," she finally said.

Dressed in a flowing gown, she traveled on a summer cloud across the desert to where Snake slept under the shade of a rocky ledge.

"You will let people know when you are about to strike," Desert Woman said sternly. And so she placed a rattle on the tip of Snake's tail.

"Now you are Rattlesnake. When anyone approaches, you will rattle a warning. This way they will know you are nearby."

Convinced she had done the right thing, Desert Woman walked on the Rainbow back to her home in Sacred Mountain.

However, instead of inhibiting Rattlesnake, the rattle only made him more threatening. He coiled around, shaking his tail and baring his fangs.

"Look at me," Rattlesnake said to the animals. "I rattle and hiss, and my bite is deadly. I am king of the road, and no one may use it without my permission!"

Problem and Solution
Explain if Desert Woman's solution of putting a rattle on Snake was successful.

Now the animals went to Desert Woman to complain.

"Who, who," Owl said, greeting Desert Woman with respect. "Since you gave Rattlesnake his rattle, he is even more of a bully. He will not let anyone use the road. Please take away his fangs and rattle!"

"What I give I cannot take away," Desert Woman said. "When Rattlesnake comes hissing and threatening, one of you must make him behave."

She looked at all the animals assembled. The animals looked at one another. They looked up, they looked down, but not one looked at Desert Woman.

"I am too timid to stand up to Rattlesnake," Quail whispered.

"He would gobble me up," Lizard cried and darted away.

"We are all afraid of him," Owl admitted.

Desert Woman smiled. "Perhaps we need a new animal to make Rattlesnake behave," she suggested.

"Yip, yip," Coyote barked. "Yes, yes."

"If you help me, together we can make a **guardian** of the road," Desert Woman said. "I will form the body, and each of you will bring a gift for our new friend."

She gathered clay from the Sacred Mountain and wet it with water from a desert spring. Working quickly but with great care, she molded the body.

"He needs slender legs to run fast," said Deer. He took two slender branches from a mesquite bush and handed them to Desert Woman.

She pushed the sticks into the clay.

"And a long tail to balance himself," said Blue Jay.

"Caw, Caw! Like mine," croaked Raven, and he took long, black feathers from his tail.

"He must be strong," cried the mighty Eagle, and he plucked dark feathers from his wings.

"And have a long beak to peck at Rattlesnake," said Heron, offering a long, thin reed from the marsh.

"He needs sharp eyes," said Coyote, offering two shiny stones from the riverbed.

As Desert Woman added each new gift to the clay body, a strange new bird took shape.

"What is your gift?" Owl asked Desert Woman.

"I will give him the gift of dance. He will be **agile** and fast," she answered. "I will call him Roadrunner."

Then she breathed life into the clay.

Roadrunner opened his eyes. He blinked and looked around.

"What a strange bird," the animals said.

Roadrunner took his first steps. He tottered forward, then backward, then forward, and fell flat on his face.

The animals sighed and shook their heads. This bird was not agile, and he was not fast. He could never stand up to Rattlesnake. He was too **awkward**. Disappointed, the animals made their way home.

Desert Woman helped Roadrunner stand, and she told him what he must do. "You will dance around Rattlesnake and peck at his tail. He must learn he is not the king of the road."

"Me? Can I really do it?" Roadrunner asked, balancing himself with his long tail.

"You need only to practice," Desert Woman said.

Roadrunner again tried his legs. He took a few steps forward and bumped into a tall cactus.

"Practice," he said. He tried again and leaped over a sleeping horned toad.

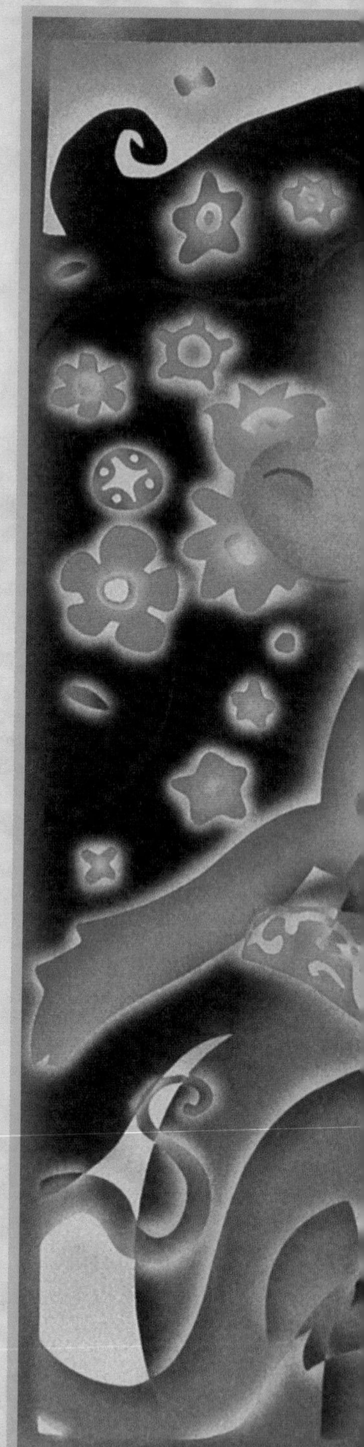

He tried jumping over a desert tortoise, but landed right on her back. The surprised turtle lumbered away, and Roadrunner crashed to the ground.

"I'll never get it right," he moaned.

"Yes, you will," Desert Woman said, again helping him to his feet. "You need only to practice."

So Roadrunner practiced. He ran back and forth, learning to use his skinny legs, learning to balance with his tail feathers.

"Practice," he said again. "Practice."

With time, he was swirling and twirling like a twister. The once awkward bird was now a graceful dancer.

"I've got it!" he cried, zipping down the road, his legs carrying him swiftly across the sand. "Thank you, Desert Woman."

"Use your gift to help others," Desert Woman said, and she returned to her abode on Sacred Mountain.

"I will," Roadrunner called.

He went racing down the road until his sharp eyes spied Rattlesnake hiding under a tall yucca plant.

"*Sssss*, I am king of the road," Rattlesnake hissed and shook his tail furiously. "No one may use *my* road without *my* permission."

"The road is for everyone to use," Roadrunner said sternly.

"Who are you?"

"I am Roadrunner."

"Get off my road before I bite you!" Rattlesnake glared.

"I'm not afraid of you," Roadrunner replied.

The people and the animals heard the ruckus and drew close to watch. Had they heard correctly? Roadrunner was challenging Rattlesnake!

"I'll show you I *am* king of the road!" Rattlesnake shouted, hissing so loud the desert mice trembled with fear. He shook his rattle until it sounded like a thunderstorm.

He struck at Roadrunner, but Roadrunner hopped out of the way.

"Stand still!" Rattlesnake cried and lunged again.

But Roadrunner danced gracefully out of reach.

Rattlesnake coiled for one more attempt. He struck like lightning, but fell flat on his face. Roadrunner had jumped to safety.

Now it was Roadrunner's turn. He ruffled his feathers and danced in circles around Rattlesnake. Again and again he pecked at the bully's tail. Like a whirlwind, he spun around Rattlesnake until the serpent grew dizzy. His eyes grew crossed and his tongue hung limply out of his mouth.

"You win! You win!" Rattlesnake cried.

"You are not king of the road, and you must not frighten those who use it," Roadrunner said sternly.

"I promise, I promise," the beaten Rattlesnake said and quietly slunk down his hole.

The people cheered and praised the bird.

"Now we can visit our neighbors in peace and go to our cornfields without fear!" the elders **proclaimed**. "And the children will no longer be frightened."

"Thank you, Roadrunner!" the children called, waving as they followed their parents to the fields.

Then the animals gathered around Roadrunner.

"Yes, thank you for teaching Rattlesnake a lesson," Owl said. "Now you are king of the road."

"No, now there is no king of the road," replied Roadrunner. "Everyone is free to come and go as they please. And the likes of Rattlesnake had better watch out, because I'll make sure the roads stay safe."

Problem and Solution
What problem did Roadrunner solve?

Dancing with Rudolfo and David

Rudolfo Anaya did not have to do any research on roadrunners to write this story. The birds run free all around his home in the southwestern United States. When Rudolfo was a boy in New Mexico, he heard lots of Mexican American folktales called *cuentos*. Now he writes his own tales to share his Mexican/Native American heritage.

Other books by Rudolfo Anaya and David Diaz

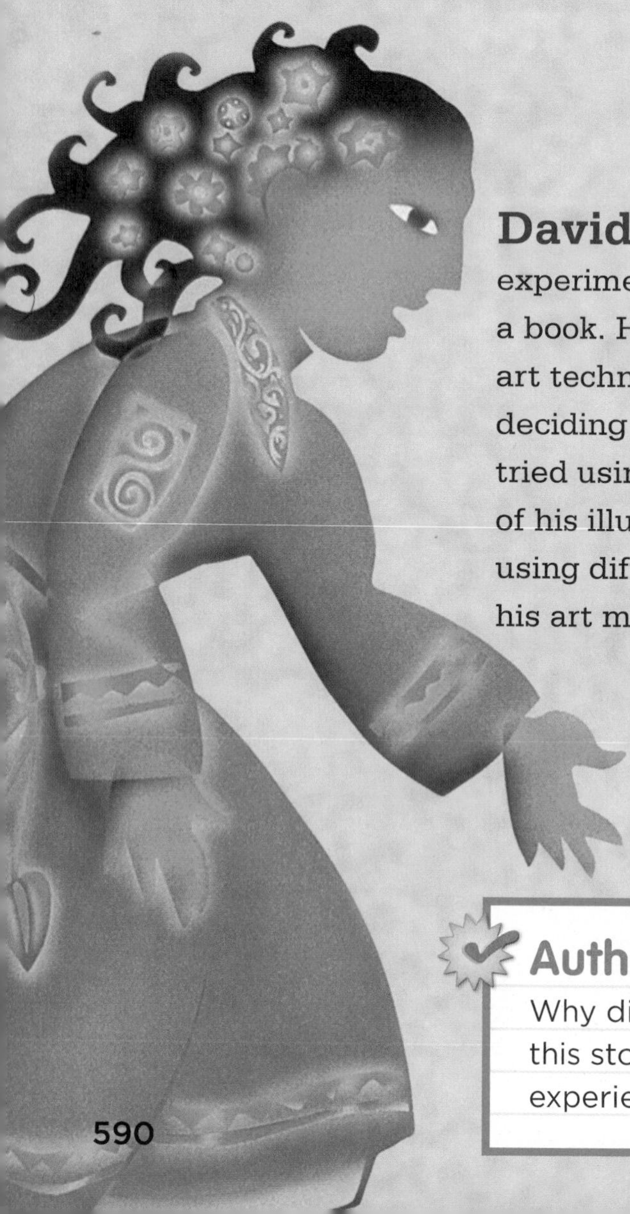

David Diaz likes to experiment when he illustrates a book. He always tries different art techniques for a story before deciding on one. David has even tried using a computer to do some of his illustrations. He believes that using different techniques makes his art more interesting.

LOG ON FIND OUT

Author Rudolfo Anaya
Illustrator David Diaz
www.macmillanmh.com

Author's Purpose

Why did Rudolfo Anaya write this story? How did his childhood experiences influence his writing?

LOG ON LEARN IT Comprehension www.macmillanmh.com

Comprehension Check

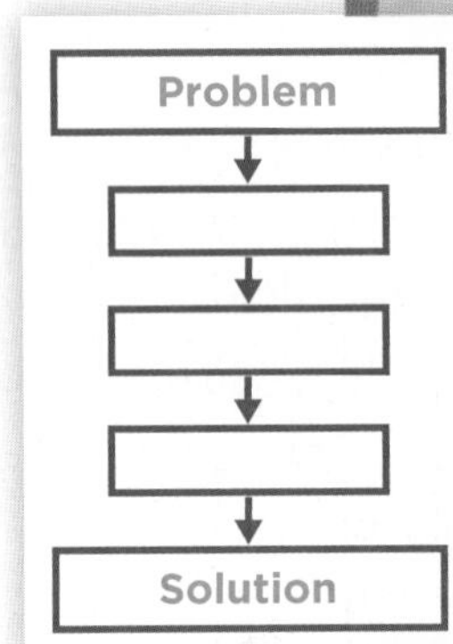

Summarize

To summarize *Roadrunner's Dance* use the most important details from the selection. Information from your Problem and Solution Chart may help you.

Think and Compare

1. What gift did **agile** Deer give to Roadrunner? Details
2. What was Roadrunner's problem when he took his first few steps? Summarize: Problem and Solution
3. Summarize the gifts that the animals gave to Roadrunner and explain what effect they had on future events in the plot. Plot
4. Identify the similes on page 586. How does the author's use of similes help the reader visualize the fight between Roadrunner and Rattlesnake? Author's Craft
5. What information about roadrunners was in "Roadrunners: Surprising Birds" that was not provided in *Roadrunner's Dance*? Reading/Writing Across Texts

Language Arts

Genre

Trickster Tales are folktales, usually about animals, in which one character tries to trick another. Sometimes, the trickster ends up looking foolish.

Literary Elements

Foreshadowing is the use of clues to hint at what is going to happen.

Symbolism is the use of an object to represent an idea, such as love, pride, or strength.

Flycatcher and Coyote

by Gillian Reed

Many years ago, Flycatcher visited a lake whose water was a spectacular shade of blue. At that time, Flycatcher's feathers were dull, gray, and ugly, and so the bird loved to look at the beautiful blue water. Coyote hid nearby to watch Flycatcher.

Flycatcher loved the blue of the lake so much that she swooped down from the tree to bathe in the lake. She did this four times every morning for four days in a row. Each time the bird bathed in the water, she sang this song:

Lovely lake,
So pure and blue,
Let me dip myself,
So I'll be blue, too.

Coyote is hiding at the start of the story. His appearance **foreshadows** the important role Coyote will have in the story.

On the fifth morning that Flycatcher went bathing, something amazing happened. When she flew out of the water, her feathers had become a dazzling blue. Flycatcher was now the same color as the lake.

This whole time, Coyote had been watching the bird. Coyote didn't admire the bird or want to learn more about her. No, Coyote was trying to think of a way to trick the bird and eat her. But Coyote was afraid of the water and could never get close enough to Flycatcher.

On the day that Flycatcher turned blue, Coyote was so impressed that he forgot all about catching it. He called up to Flycatcher, who was perched safely in a tree, "How did your ugly gray feathers turn that wonderful blue? Tell me how you did it, so that I can be blue, too."

Flycatcher was so happy that she was feeling generous. She remained safely on her branch, but she told Coyote, "This is what you must do. Jump in the lake four times every morning for four mornings. Then jump in the lake on the fifth morning, and you will turn blue. You might try singing my song, too." Flycatcher taught Coyote her song and then flew merrily on her way.

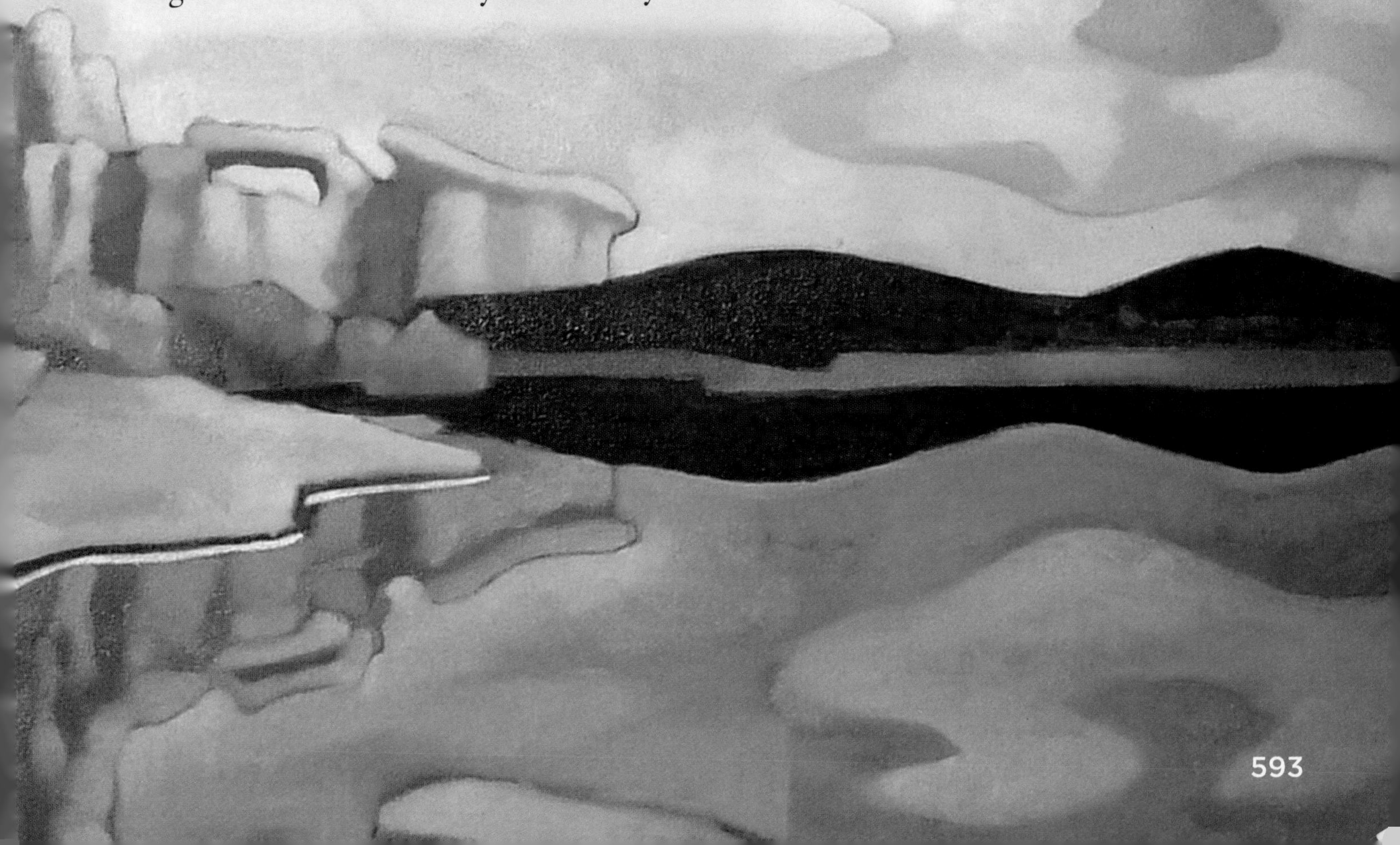

Well, Coyote really wanted to be blue. So even though he hated the water, he jumped into the lake four times the next morning.

He sang the bird's song, and he shivered as he sang. He did this for four days. On the fifth morning, Coyote emerged from his lake bath with lovely blue fur. Coyote whistled to himself. "I'm blue and beautiful."

Coyote couldn't wait to show off his new color. He thought his fine blue fur would make him the envy of all the desert creatures. He strolled along, looking left and right for someone to admire him. Coyote walked for hours, but he didn't find any admirers. He grew impatient. Then Coyote remembered a canyon where many animals and people lived. They would notice him, but he would have to hurry to reach the canyon before sundown.

As Coyote ran, he noticed the late afternoon shadows around him. He wondered if his shadow was as blue as he was. He twisted his blue head around to take a look. Coyote got a good look at his shadow, which was not blue. But he failed to see the big boulder directly ahead of him. Coyote ran smack into the boulder and fell to the ground.

He rolled over and over in the dirt, his blue legs flying. When he finally stopped and stood up, Coyote was the color of the dusty desert earth. Coyote shook himself, but the dusty color stayed on him. To this day, all coyotes are the color of the dusty desert. And to this day, because her intentions were pure, the flycatcher is the color of the beautiful blue lake.

Coyote decided not to go to the canyon after all. No one would be impressed by his color now. He headed for home, stopping only to give the boulder a good, swift kick.

The dull, dusty color of his fur is a **symbol** of his hurt pride.

Connect and Compare

1. The flycatcher turns blue. What does the color blue symbolize in the story? **Symbolism**
2. What effect did Flycatcher's turning blue have on the future events of the plot? **Apply**
3. Compare and contrast Coyote's adventures with Rattlesnake's in *Roadrunner's Dance*. Use details from both stories to support your answer. **Reading/Writing Across Texts**

LOG ON FIND OUT **Language Arts** Trickster tales
www.macmillanmh.com

Writing

Trait: Ideas

Good writers often **make comparisons** to create a clear picture for readers.

Reading and Writing Connection

Read the passage below. Notice how the author uses comparisons to show what Rattlesnake's actions are like.

An excerpt from *Roadrunner's Dance*

The author compares Rattlesnake's rattle to a thunderstorm and his strike to lightning.

"I'll show you I *am* king of the road!" Rattlesnake shouted, hissing so loud the desert mice trembled with fear. He shook his rattle until it sounded like a thunderstorm.

He struck at Roadrunner, but Roadrunner hopped out of the way.

"Stand still!" Rattlesnake cried and lunged again.

But Roadrunner danced gracefully out of reach.

Rattlesnake coiled for one more attempt. He struck like lightning, but fell flat on his face. Roadrunner had jumped to safety.

Read and Find

Read Rob's writing below. What comparisons does he use? Use the checklist below to help you.

Pens and Pencils

by Rob M.

We do a lot of writing in school, so I have a big supply of pens and pencils. Both pens and pencils are used to write on paper. They are both long and skinny with a pointed tip. However, you can erase letters and numbers you make with a pencil. Marks you make with a pen can't be erased.

In math class, we use pencils to write. In my other classes, we use pens. You need both pens and pencils to be prepared for school, so you should always have a few of each in your backpack or supply pouch.

Read about pens and pencils.

Writer's Checklist

- [x] Does the author explain how pens and pencils are alike?
- [x] Does the writer explain how they are different?
- [ ] Does the writer use words that signal a **comparison** or contrast?

Talk About It

National parks are full of history and life. What things can you learn about at a national park?

LOG ON VIEW IT

Oral Language Activities
National Parks
www.macmillanmh.com

NATIONAL PARKS

Vocabulary

roamed
relocated
completed
journey
natural

A Prehistoric Park

More than 200 million years ago, dinosaurs **roamed** freely over the Earth. Have you ever wondered what the land was like or what kind of trees were there? You can see some of these trees today in Arizona! Throughout 28 miles of desert in Petrified Forest National Park, you can see 225-million-year-old fossil trees. Visitors are amazed to see these trees that have turned to stone.

How did it happen? Millions of years ago, water filled with minerals flowed into the area. Over time the minerals seeped into fallen trees and turned them into rock-hard logs. Some of these logs are 100 feet long! Today they create a colorful and amazing sight in Arizona. The petrified logs look like wooden rainbows **relocated** to Arizona's desert. The colors range from red, to yellow, to green, to blue, and black and white.

Petrified Forest National Park is one of the world's biggest displays of petrified wood. Nearly one million people visit the park every year to get an up-close look at these fossils of prehistoric trees.

These logs were trees 225 million years ago. Now they are stone in the Petrified Forest National Park in Arizona.

King of the Mountain

By the time Scott Cory was 13 years old, he had already scaled two major peaks in California's Yosemite National Park. One was the 2,900-foot "Nose" of El Capitan. The other was the 2,000-foot face of Half Dome. The first time Scott climbed the Nose, it took him three days and two nights. One month later he **completed** that climb in one day! Scott later became the youngest person to climb Half Dome in only one day. The **journey** to the top usually takes three days!

Scott started climbing when he was seven years old. When he's not on the peaks, he hits the gym for push-ups and pull-ups. What's next for this peak pro? Scott wants to climb to the top of the Nose and Half Dome together in just 24 hours. You could say this kid really sets a goal and then climbs for it!

The Top 5 Most Visited National Parks

In 1872 Yellowstone National Park became the first national park in the United States. Since then more than 383 parks have been added to the list. More than three million people visit these natural, unspoiled places every year. Visitors take thousands of photos of the wildlife. Which parks recently brought in the most visitors in a year? Here's how they ranked.

1. **Great Smoky Mountains National Park, North Carolina and Tennessee**
2. **Grand Canyon National Park, Arizona**
3. **Yosemite National Park, California**
4. **Olympic National Park, Washington**
5. **Rocky Mountain National Park, Colorado**

Real World Reading

Comprehension

Genre

An **Expository** article presents information about a person, place, or event.

Summarize

Main Idea and Details

To find the main idea of an article, first identify the most important details. Then decide what these details have in common.

A male and female elk graze in the Great Smoky Mountains National Park. Female elk are called cows.

Animals Come Home to Our National Parks

How did the return of elk to one national park and gray wolves to another affect the ecosystems of those parks?

National parks protect wildlife, history, and culture. Still, hundreds of plants and animals have disappeared from our national parks. That's because their environment has changed, mostly because of human activities.

Today park rangers work to restore the balance of each park ecosystem. They are bringing plants and animals back into their **natural** environments. So far the programs are working—especially for elk and wolves.

Long Journey Home

It was a cold morning in January when 28 elk had finally **completed** a long **journey**. They had traveled 2,500 miles by truck from Elk Island National Park in Canada to the Great Smoky Mountains National Park in North Carolina. They were the first of 52 elk to be reintroduced into the park.

Ten million elk once **roamed** all over North America. Now there are only about one million. Elk disappeared from North Carolina more than 150 years ago. Many were killed by hunters. Others died as people built farms, towns, and roads where elk once grazed.

Elk munch on trees and bushes, allowing more sunlight into the park so ground-level plants can grow. Smaller animals, like chipmunks, can then flourish. Chipmunks are food for larger animals, like wolves. Without the elk, the park's ecosystem didn't function as well. "We are trying to restore the ecosystem to what it was 200 years ago," said Lawrence Hartman of the National Park Service.

Park workers watch as the elk dash for freedom.

Have they achieved their goal? So far, so good. Researchers have been studying the **relocated** elks' progress. Jennifer Murrow is leading the research. She tracks the elk using special radio collars that are placed around the elks' necks. The collars send signals that show researchers where the elk are and how they are doing.

Researchers also keep track of the number of elk calves that are born each year. In the first year, 11 calves were born in the park. Eight survived, but some were preyed upon by bears. It's all part of the natural balance—and that's exactly what wildlife researchers like to see.

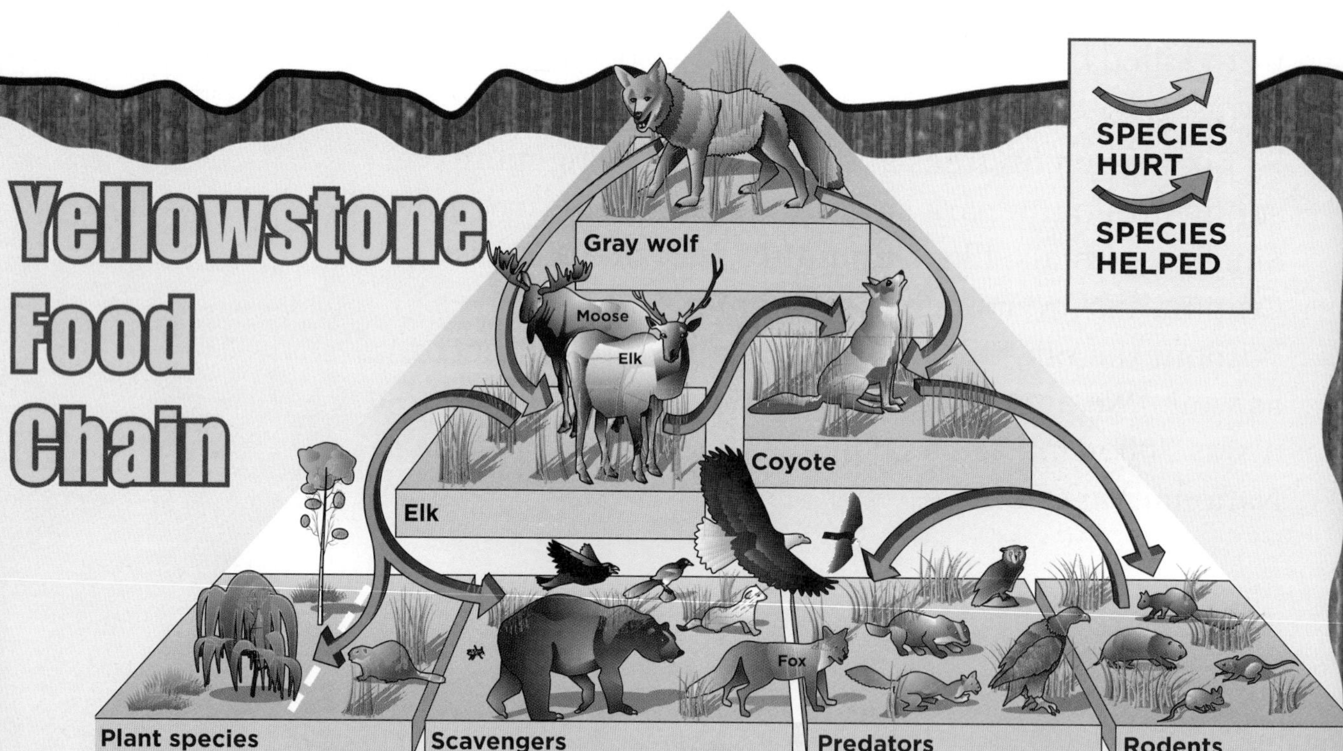

The disappearance of wolves left a big hole in Yellowstone's ecosystem. Coyotes and elk, which are hunted by wolves, became too numerous. Plants began to disappear because the elk population had grown so large. Foxes, which eat the same rodents as coyotes, were starving because the coyotes were catching most of the prey. The ecosystem of the park was badly out of balance.

The government wanted to fix the park's ecosystem. They decided to bring back the wolves. The goal was to put nature back into balance. Now Yellowstone is howling with life once again, and nature is taking its course.

Gray wolves live in packs that can have as few as 8 members or as many as 35.

Howling Back to Life

For centuries, packs of wolves lived in the West. When settlers came in the 1800s, they hunted these wild animals. By the 1970s, the wolves had completely disappeared from Yellowstone National Park. They had also become endangered in much of the United States.

In 1995, 31 gray wolves were released into the park. Now, more than a decade later, there are more than five times as many wolves roaming through Yellowstone.

Think and Compare

1. What animal was returned to the Great Smoky Mountains National Park?
2. Why was Yellowstone's ecosystem out of balance? Use details from the text to support your answer.
3. What is the text on page 605 mainly about? Use details from the text in your answer.
4. Compare the problems a park ranger at Yellowstone might face with those of a ranger at Arizona's Petrified Forest National Park.

Test Practice

Answering Questions

Right There answers are found in one place in the text.
Think and Search answers are found in more than one place.
Author and Me answers ask the reader to look for clues.

Saving a National Park

The Florida Panther is on the endangered species list. Human development in Florida destroyed much of its habitat.

1 The early settlers of Florida's Everglades declared the area a worthless swamp. In fact the Everglades is a unique paradise that is home to thousands of species of plants and animals. The plants and animals living in the Everglades form a delicate food chain where they rely on each other—and a steady supply of precious water—for survival. However, human development in the Everglades has threatened to disrupt the water supply and the ecosystem.

2 In order to develop within the Everglades, people needed dry land to build homes and plant farms. A small portion of the Everglades was dedicated as a national park in 1947, which meant people could not develop on this land. The rest of the Everglades was not protected from human development, so people began draining water from many different areas. This began a chain reaction that upset the delicate ecosystem of the Everglades.

3 The Everglades wetlands are now only half their original size. From 1900 to 2000, the number of wading birds decreased by 90 percent. Human development had a major effect on the national park. It is now considered one of the ten most endangered parks in the United States.

4 Now there is a plan to save the Everglades. Engineers have designed wells and pumps to capture water before it flows out of the Everglades. Many canals built to support human development are being removed. The removal of the canals allows water to follow its natural course. The plan may take as many as 50 years to complete. However, saving this unique ecosystem is an important goal, no matter how long it takes.

TIME FOR KIDS

Use "Saving a National Park" to answer questions 1–4.

1 What do plants and animals rely on for survival in the Everglades?

- **A** Dry land to build homes
- **B** Canals that support development
- **C** Wells and pumps that capture water
- **D** Each other and a steady supply of water

2 Human development upset the ecosystem of the Everglades because people —

- **F** created Everglades National Park
- **G** thought it was a worthless swamp
- **H** drained water from many different areas
- **J** removed the canals that had been built there

3 The plan that was developed to save the Everglades shows that —

- **A** engineers will replace the park with wells and pumps
- **B** people want to save the park no matter how long it takes
- **C** engineers keep wasting natural resources, such as water
- **D** people keep valuing new homes over national parks

4 Which is the best summary of the selection?

- **F** Everglades National Park was dedicated in 1947. The park is a unique paradise, but the food chain upset its ecosystem. People developed the park with houses and canals.
- **G** Plants and animals form a delicate food chain in the Everglades. The number of wading birds decreased by 90% from 1900 to 2000. It may take 50 years to save the Everglades.
- **H** The Everglades is home to many plant and animal species. However, human development has endangered the area. Now a plan is in place to save the Everglades.
- **J** People drained the Everglades to build homes and farms. This affected the ecosystem. Engineers built pumps to get water. Today this wetlands area is Everglades National Park.

Write to a Prompt

Write a composition about how your family gets ready for a trip.

Think about the purpose of your composition.

Think about how to clearly express your ideas. Develop your ideas in a logical order.

Below, see how one student begins a response to the prompt above.

The writer included specific details to tell what each sister does.

On Saturdays my family goes to our city park. We always have a lot of things to do before we are ready to go.

First I help my sister make sandwiches. We always make two different sandwiches for each person. That is a total of twelve sandwiches for the whole family.

Then I pack my backpack. My sister puts in an extra sweater so we won't be cold. If it's warm she packs my softball and mitt. This way we can play catch. The last thing I do before we leave is put the leash on my dog, Chief.

Writing Prompt

Respond to the prompt below. Review the hints below before and after you write.

Write a composition comparing what you do before and after a trip.

Writing Hints

- ☑ Remember to write about what you do before and after a trip. Think about genre.
- ☑ Plan your writing by organizing your ideas.
- ☑ Include important details to support your ideas.
- ☑ Check that each sentence you write helps the reader understand your composition.
- ☑ Use correct punctuation and grammar.
- ☑ Review and edit your writing.

OCEANS

Talk About It

How are oceans different from other habitats?

LOG ON VIEW IT

Oral Language Activities
Oceans
www.macmillanmh.com

Coral Reefs

by Sato Akiki

Vocabulary

reef	**eventually**
partnership	**brittle**
current	**suburbs**

Context Clues

Multiple-Meaning Words are words that have more than one meaning. Use context clues to find out the relevant meaning for the word *current*.

Coral comes in a variety of shapes, colors, and sizes. It can be the size of the head of a pin, or a foot in diameter. Although corals are often mistaken for rocks or plants, they are actually very small animals. When thousands of these animals are grouped together to form a mound or a tree shape, it is called a coral colony. Thousands of these colonies make up a **reef**.

There are more than 700 kinds of coral but only two main types. Each kind of coral is either a soft coral or a hard coral.

The easiest way to identify a hard coral is by its appearance. A colony of hard corals can resemble a vase, a plate, a little tree, a boulder, a brain, or the antlers of an elk. Hard corals have groups of six smooth tentacles around their mouths. They get their name from the hard, cuplike skeletons of limestone that they produce out of seawater.

Soft corals always have eight feathery tentacles around their mouths. They have names like sea fan, sea whip, or sea fingers and are as soft and bendable as plants or tree branches. Soft corals do not have hard skeletons. They have woody cores that support them instead. Soft corals often live on coral reefs along with hard corals, but soft corals can also live in cool, dark regions where hard corals would die.

Hard corals cannot live as far from the surface as soft corals because hard corals have plants, called algae, living inside of them. Through this **partnership**, the algae provide most of the coral polyp's food and the polyp gives the algae protection from the predators that eat them. The algae, though, require sunlight in order to live.

Hard corals begin their lives as fertilized eggs. These develop into soft larvae which drift with the **current** of the waves until they attach themselves to a part of the existing coral reef. **Eventually** the coral polyps die and other living larvae attach themselves to their skeletons.

Scientists believe that the existing coral reefs began to grow more than 50 million years ago. When seaweed, sponges, giant clams, oysters, starfish, and **brittle** stars die, they serve as the foundations upon which another generation of hard coral polyps will attach and grow. In this way the hard corals are the architects of the community—from the downtown area out to the **suburbs**.

The sprawling structures of the coral reefs support a quarter of all known sea animals. This includes over 4,000 different kinds of fish, along with mollusks, octopus and squid, sponges, algae, seaweed, shrimp, sea turtles, and sharks.

Reread for Comprehension

Analyze Text Structure

Compare and Contrast Authors use text structure to organize the information they present in a selection. Comparison is one kind of text structure. Authors who use this text structure show the similarities and differences between two or more things. Sometimes they use clue words such as *also* and *but* to show explicit comparisons. Other times the comparisons are implicit and there are no clue words. Reread the selection and use your Venn diagram to help you learn how things are alike and different.

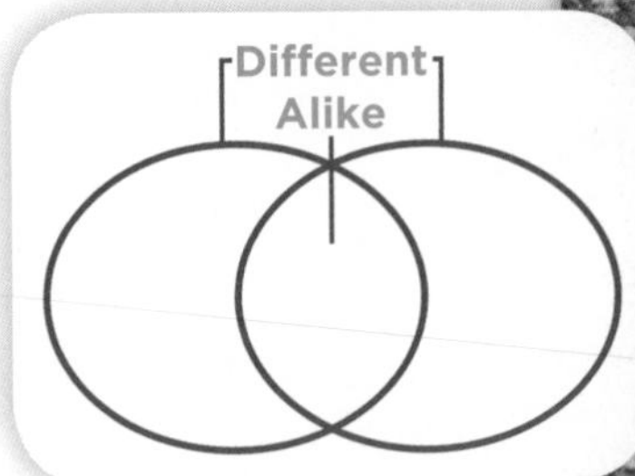

LOG ON LEARN IT **Comprehension** www.macmillanmh.com

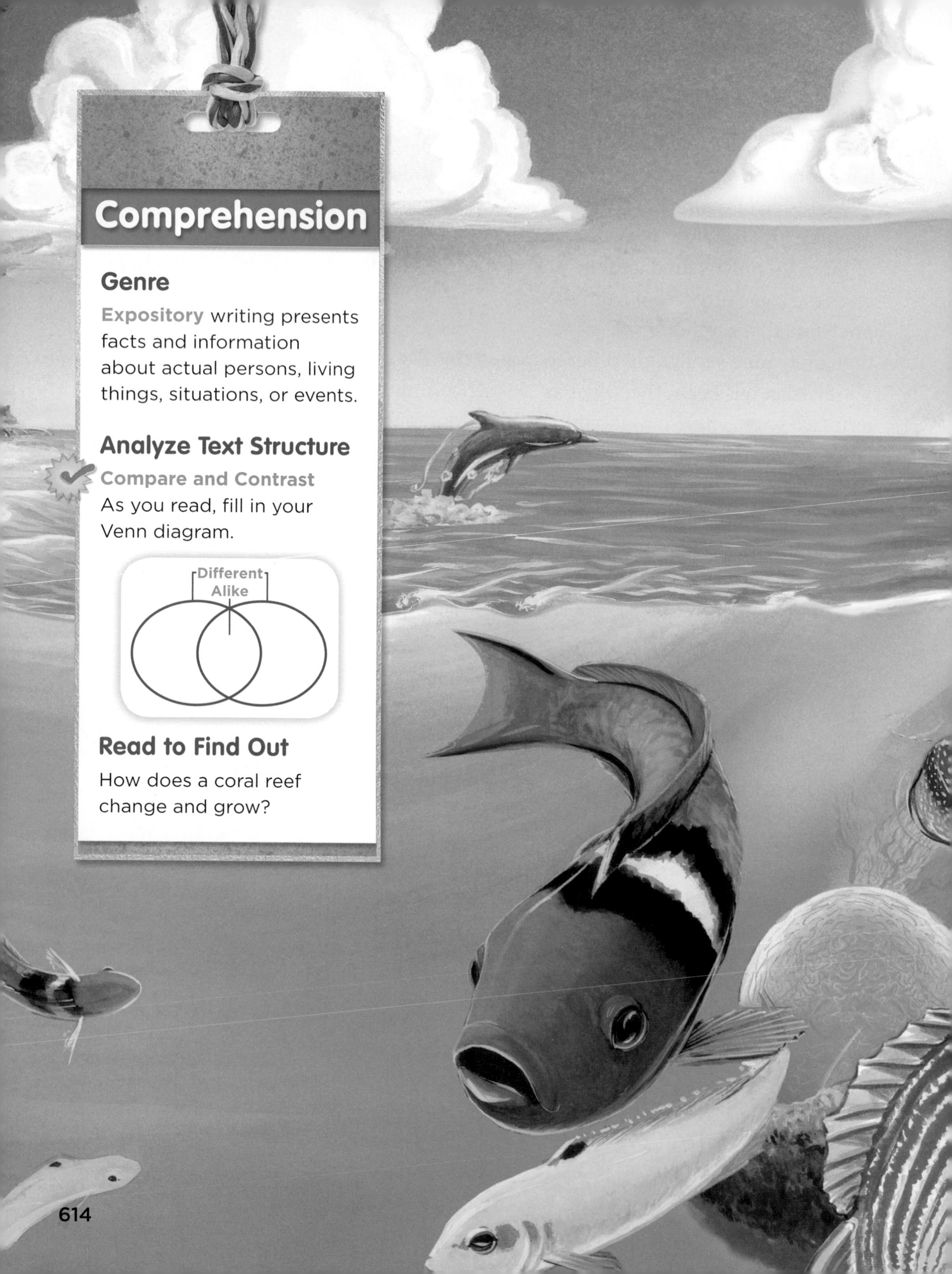

Comprehension

Genre

Expository writing presents facts and information about actual persons, living things, situations, or events.

Analyze Text Structure

Compare and Contrast

As you read, fill in your Venn diagram.

Read to Find Out

How does a coral reef change and grow?

AT HOME IN THE Coral Reef

by Katy Muzik • illustrated by Katherine Brown-Wing

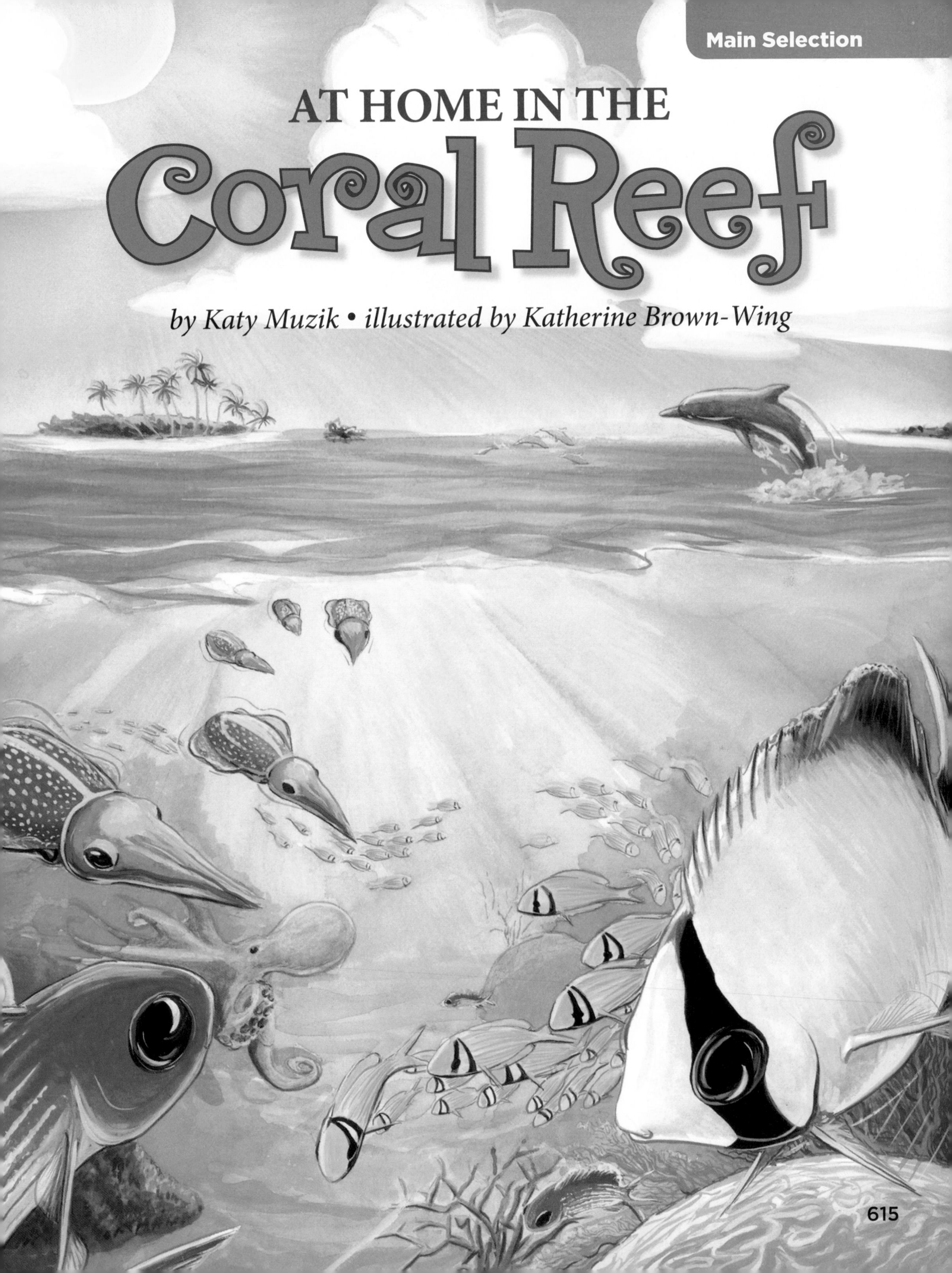

Down, down, down in the tropical clear blue sea lives a beautiful coral **reef**. The coral reef is a wonderful home for hundreds of kinds of fish and thousands of other kinds of creatures. The reef itself is made of zillions of tiny animals called coral polyps.

Each tiny coral polyp catches food with its little arms, called tentacles. The polyps share their food and live so close together that their skeletons are connected.

Some kinds of coral polyps make soft skeletons that sway gently back and forth in the water. These polyps have 8 tentacles. Other coral polyps make skeletons that are as hard as rock. Their hard skeletons form the coral reef. A hard coral polyp has 12, or 24, or 48, or more tentacles! Together, over 50 kinds of hard coral form this reef in the Caribbean Sea.

What are these pink things? Coral eggs! Once a year, coral polyps have babies. Eggs and sperm pop out of the polyps and float up and up to the top of the blue sea. There each fertilized egg becomes a baby coral called a planula. Now it is ready to search for a new home.

The planula is completely covered with little hairs. It swims by waving them through the water, but it cannot swim very fast. Watch out for those hungry wrasses!

Just in time, a big wave carries the planula away to the crest, or top, of the coral reef. Here the water is very shallow. Because it is so shallow, the waves break and crash into the reef.

Splash! Crash! The breaking waves make the water very rough. It's so rough that only a few animals can live here. A fireworm holds on tight. A school of blue tangs darts in and out, hunting for food.

Crash! Splash! Will this be home for the planula? No, it's too rough. The planula is swept along, riding a wave over the crest to the lagoon.

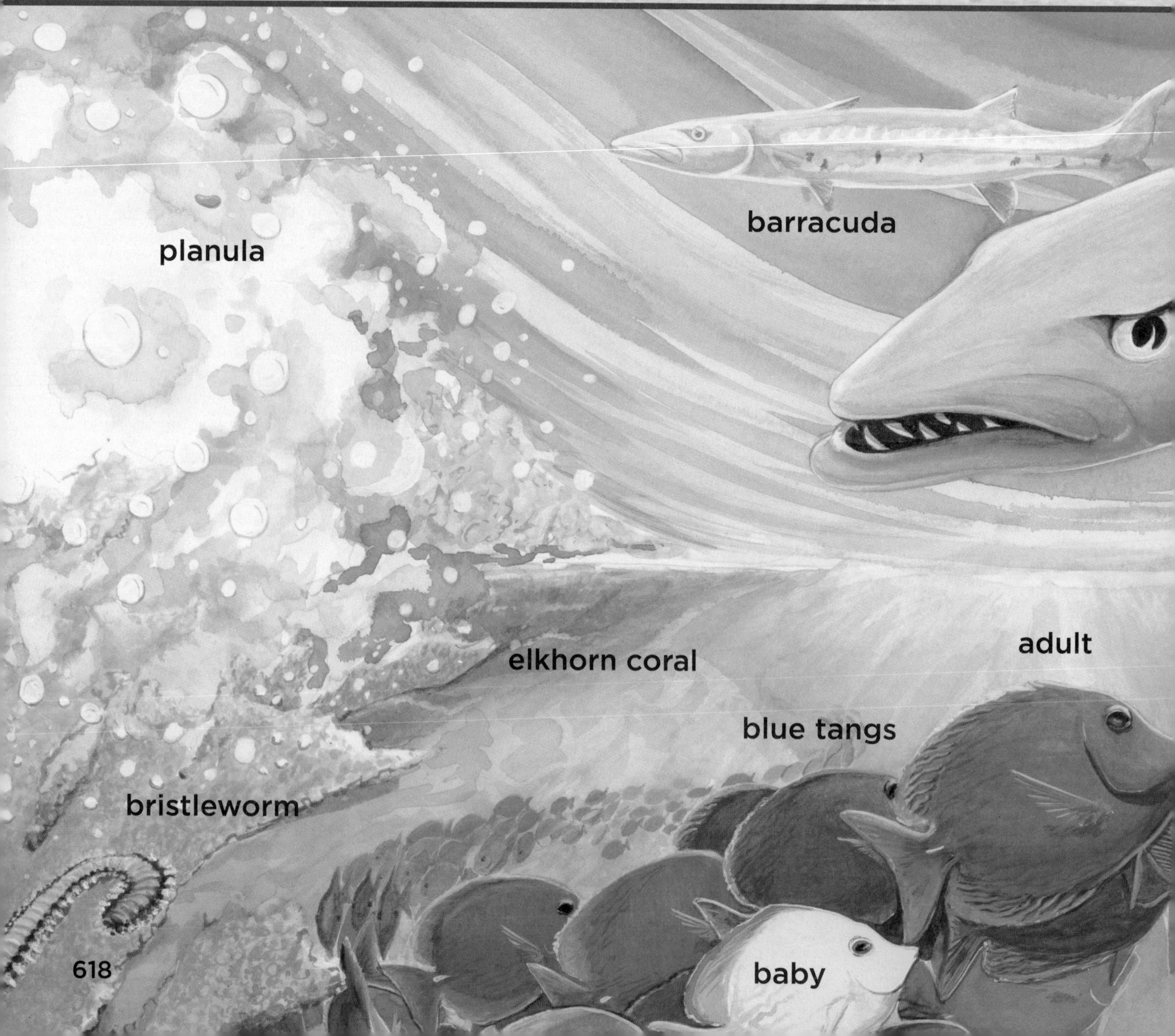

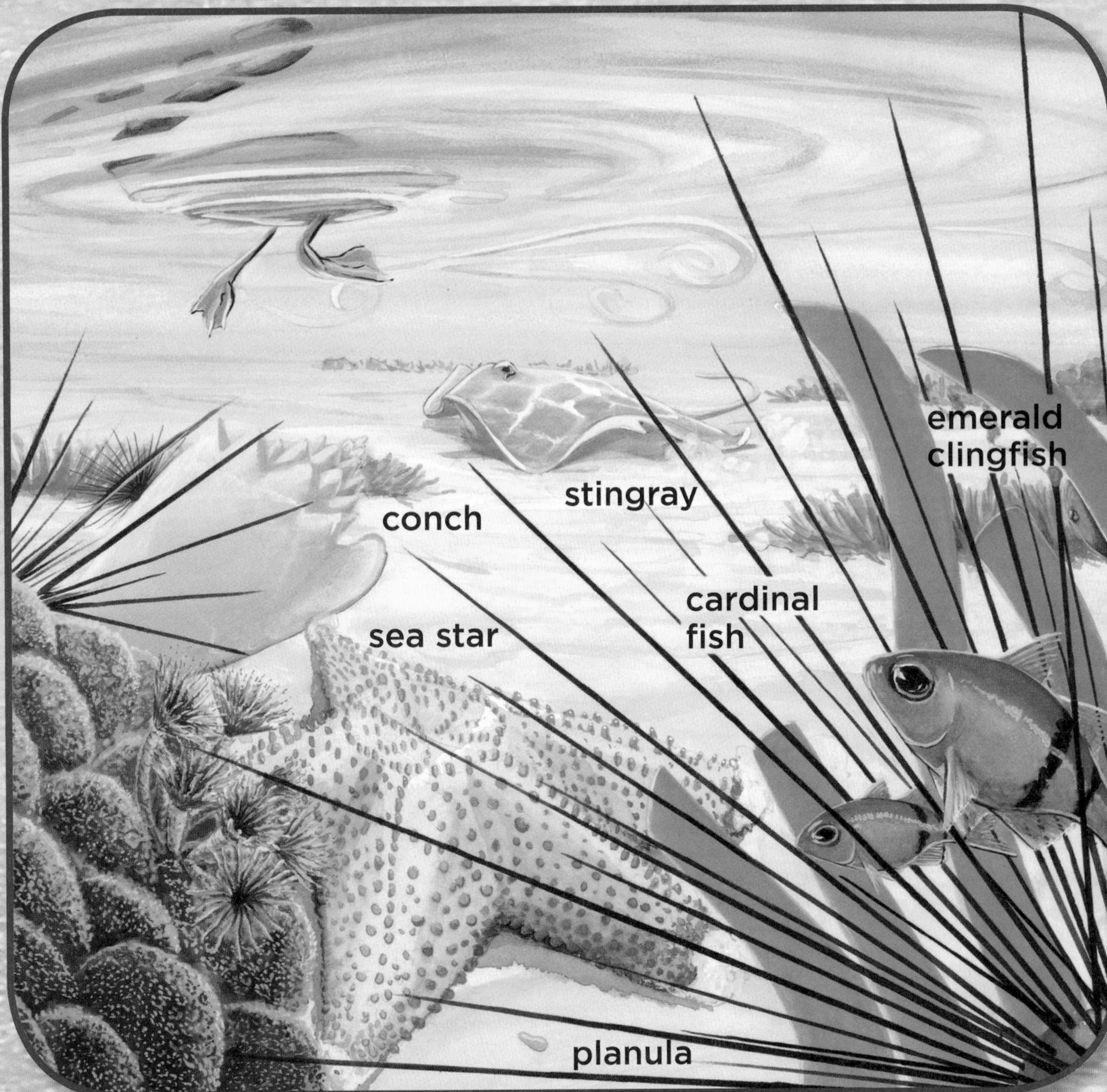

The water in the lagoon is calm. Although the lagoon seems peaceful, it is really a busy place, from top to bottom. At the top, a pelican gulps a pouchful of fish. At the bottom, a stingray slurps up shrimp.

Many animals looking for food in the lagoon are hard to see. An emerald clingfish hides on a blade of turtle grass. Clams and crabs hide in the sand.

Compare and Contrast
Compare the features of the crest of the coral reef and the lagoon.

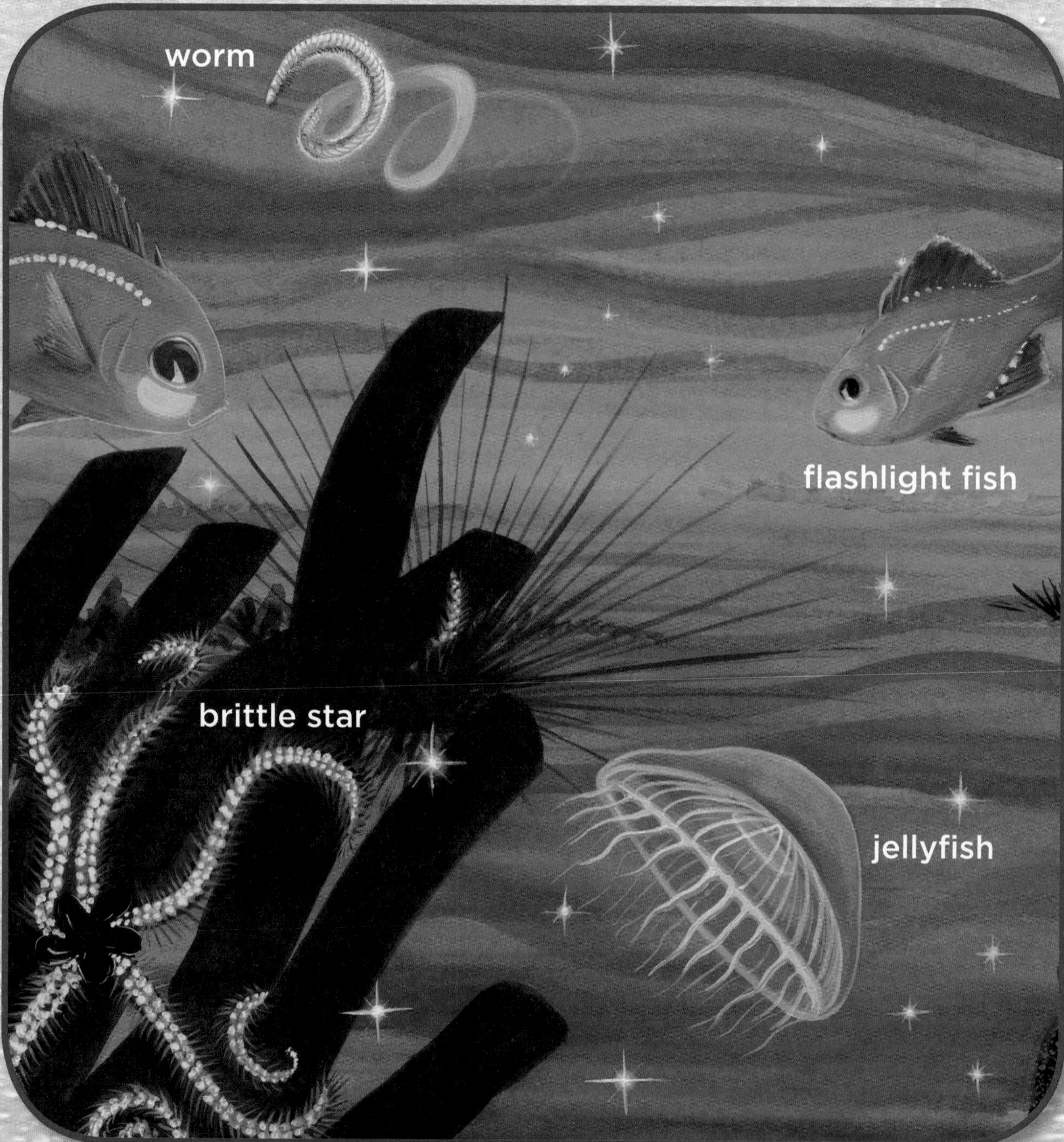

Such a busy place, day and night in the lagoon.

Flash! Glow! Blink! What could these lights be? They twinkle like stars in the sky, but they are all under water.

These lights are made by animals. Animals almost too small to see are twinkling. **Brittle** stars flash to scare away lobsters and crabs. Worms glow to show other worms where they are. Flashlight fish attract their food by blinking.

Can the planula live here? No, it is too sandy.

The planula needs a rocky place. It floats along to the red mangrove trees near the shore of the lagoon. Red mangroves can grow in salty water. Their roots grow out and hang down right into the ocean. Sponges and seaweeds grow on the roots.

Millions of baby fish and baby shrimp start life in the water around mangrove roots. There's lots of food for them there. Will this be a home for the planula, too?

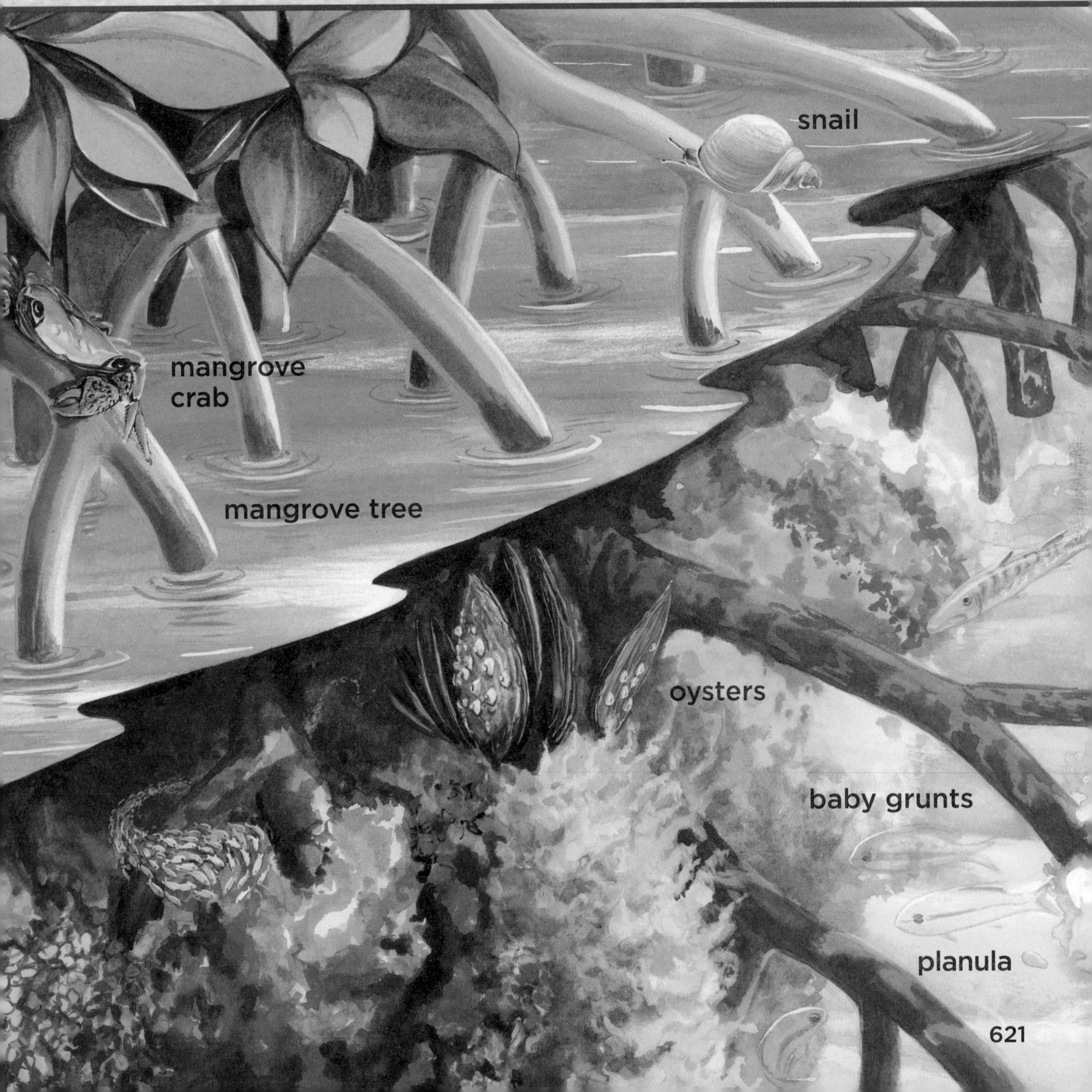

No, the water here is too shady for the planula. It turns away and swims to the shallow water near the beach of the lagoon.

The sunshine heats the sandy beach. The sand was made by the ocean waves. Over thousands of years, the waves have pounded the skeletons of reef animals and plants into smaller and smaller bits. **Eventually**, the bits formed so many grains of sand that they covered the bottom of the lagoon and washed up on shore to make a beach.

Will this be home for the planula? No, it is too shallow and too hot here.

The planula catches a **current** to deeper water. Oh, no, the water is dirty! The water is so dirty, the coral is dying. The dirt smothers the coral polyps and blocks the sunlight they need.

Chemicals washed down the rivers from factories and farms poison the coral. In the dirty water harmful bacteria grow over the coral and kill it. Careless divers hurt the coral too. They step on it and break it with their boat anchors.

Without living coral, the fish and other animals will leave. The planula cannot live here either.

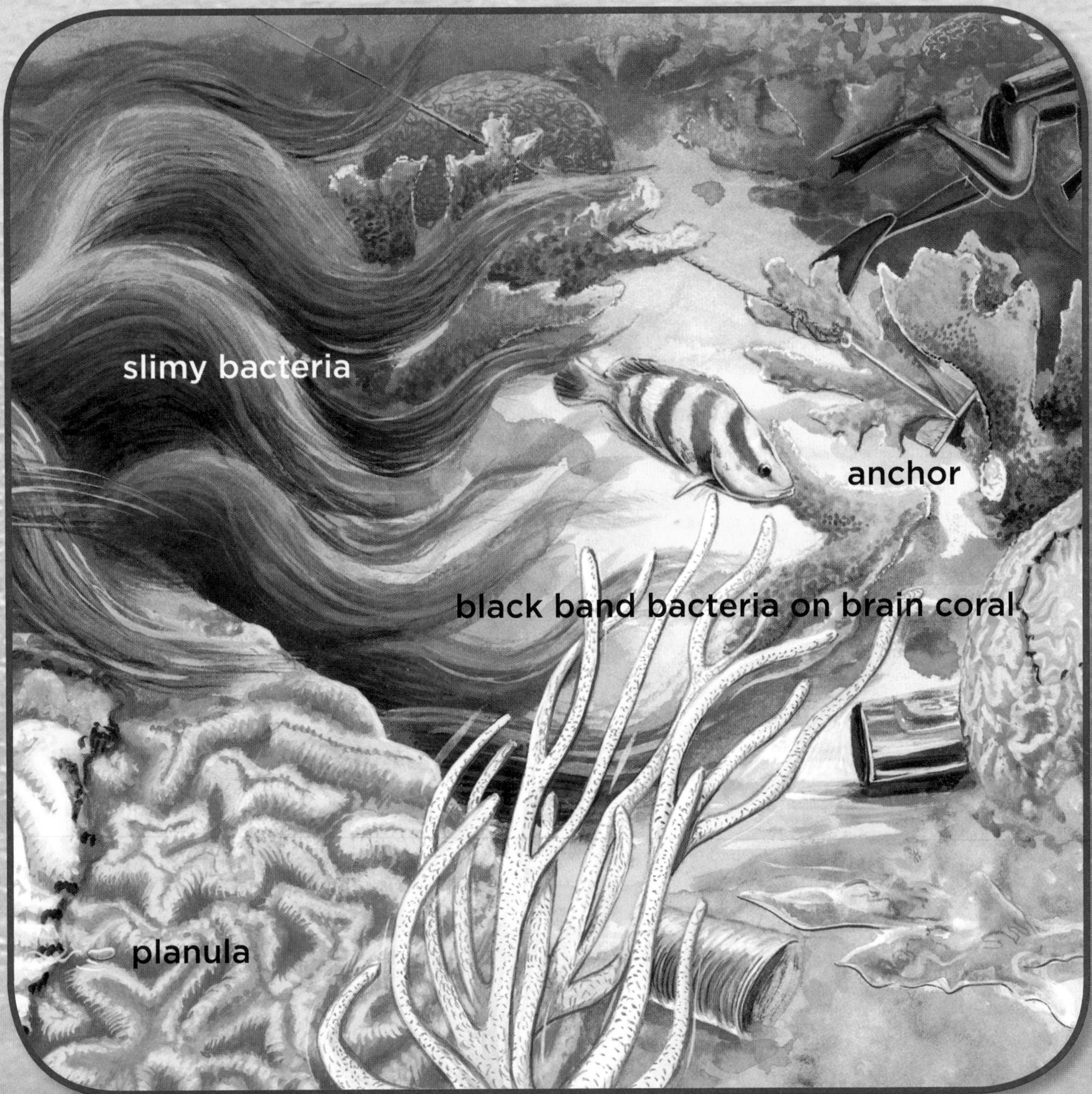

Luckily, a current carries it out of the lagoon, over the top of the reef, and down the other side of the reef deeper and deeper and deeper to a healthy part of the reef.

At last! A safe spot for the planula to settle down. The spot is hard and rocky. It is sunny but not too hot. Gentle currents bring clean water, and plenty of food. It will be a perfect home.

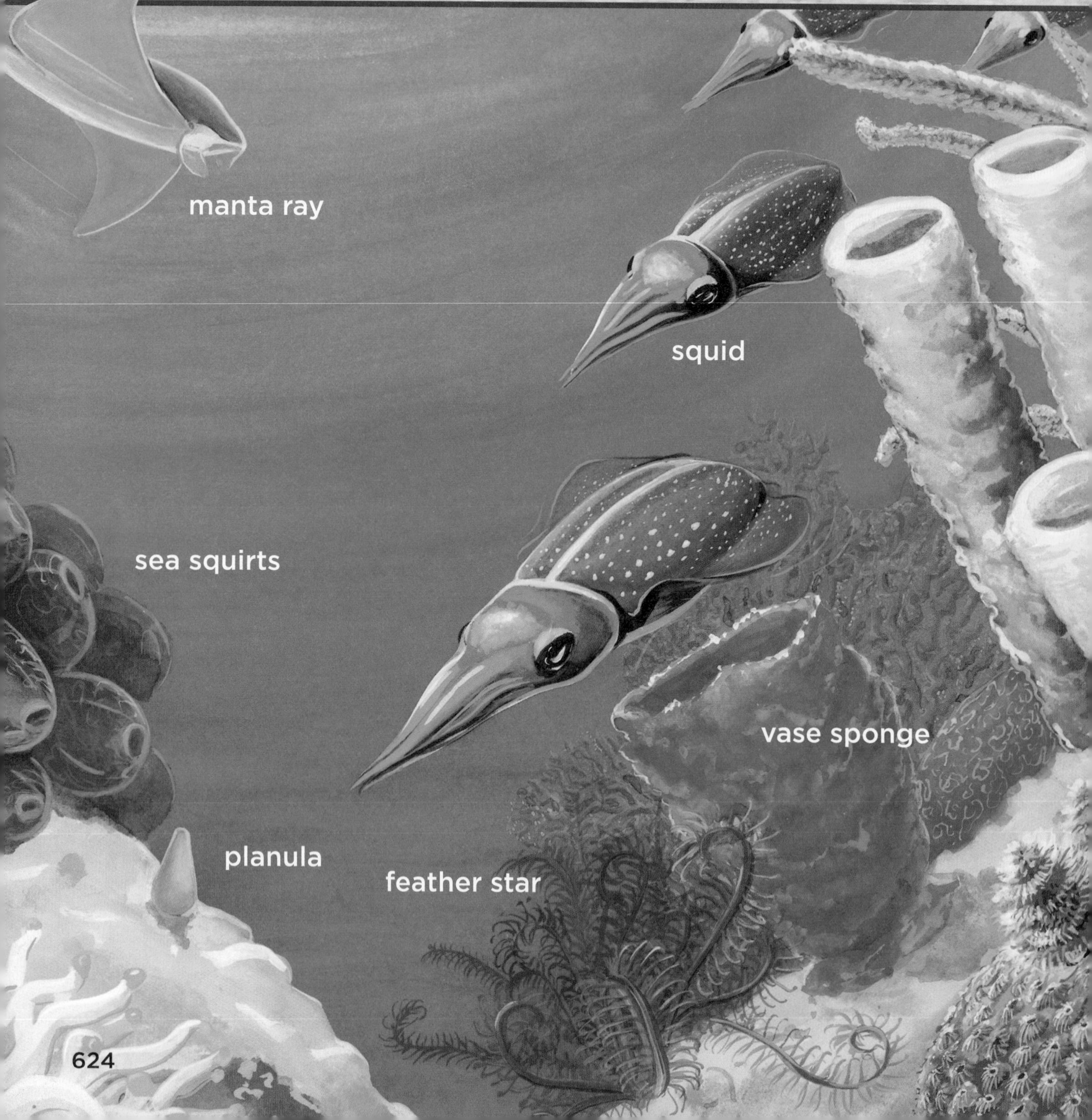

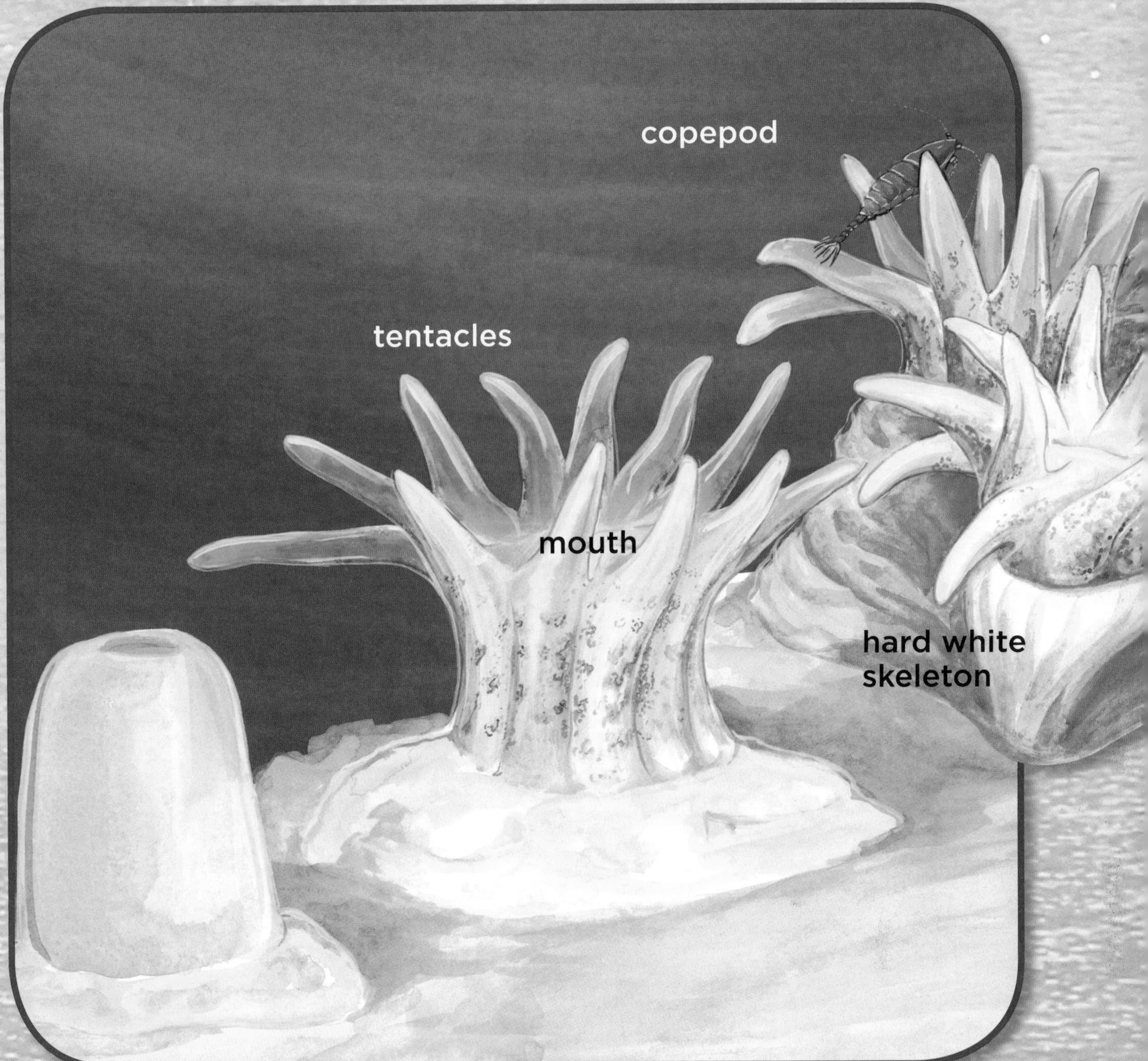

The planula begins to change. First, it sticks itself to a safe spot. Then, around its mouth it grows twelve little tentacles. Now it is a polyp. It looks like a flower, but it really is an animal.

Under its soft body, the polyp starts to grow a hard white skeleton. In a few weeks it makes another tiny polyp exactly like itself. The polyps are connected to each other. Together, the two polyps have twenty-four tentacles for catching food.

The planula is growing up to be a staghorn coral. More polyps grow, and more and more.

Here comes a reef butterfly fish. It eats coral. The coral polyps warn each other of danger. Quick as a wink, they hug their tentacles in. They hide their soft bodies down inside their hard white skeleton. When the danger is past, the coral polyps slowly come out and open up their tentacles again.

Many creatures in the reef are partners that help each other hide or find food. A crab hides in the coral to escape from a hungry octopus. A shrimp lives safely inside a vase sponge.

At a cleaning station, gobies eat what they clean from the teeth of a big grouper. The grouper holds its mouth wide open for the gobies. Away from the station, the grouper would eat gobies!

Even the tiny polyps have partners. The polyps get special food from little golden plants living just inside their skin. In return, the plants get a home. This **partnership** helps the coral grow big enough to form reefs.

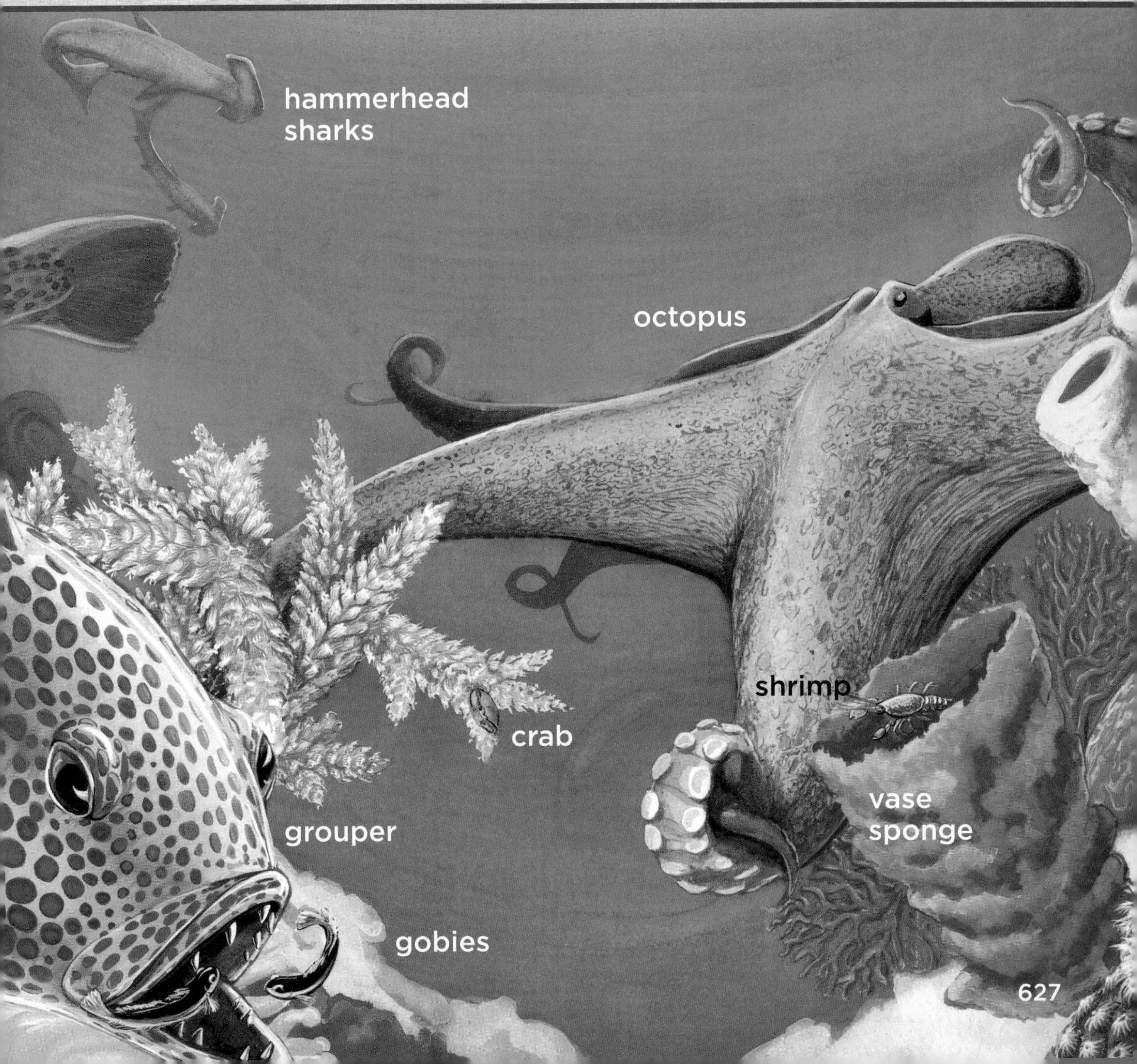

Down, down, down in the tropical clear blue sea, this coral reef is alive and well. The place where it lives is clean. Zillions of coral animals have been adding their skeletons to the reef for over 8,000 years.

It takes thousands of years for a reef to grow but only a few years for one to be destroyed! This reef and other coral reefs all around the world are in danger because the oceans are becoming dirty. Coral reefs need our help.

Compare and Contrast
The planula eventually chooses a safe spot to live. How is this spot different from the other places described in the selection? How is it similar?

What can we do to help a little baby planula grow up to become part of a big coral reef? The first step is to discover how what we do on land affects life in the sea.

All living creatures—including corals and people—need clean water. We all use water on our farms, in our **suburbs**, and in our cities. We throw many things into it that make it dirty. This dirty water flows into rivers, lakes, and underground streams, and eventually ends up in the sea. There it hurts the coral reef and all the creatures that make it their home.

But we can make a difference. We can make our rivers and lakes and oceans clean again. We can learn about life on the coral reef and share what we learn. We can help people everywhere to care about the amazing reefs and the tiny coral animals that build them.

AT HOME WITH Katy & Katherine

Katy Muzik is a marine biologist who specializes in octocorals—commonly known as sea fans. She has dived on coral reefs all over the world, including Fiji, Japan, Australia, and throughout the Caribbean.

Katy wrote *At Home in the Coral Reef* to share both her love of the sea and her concern for its rapidly declining health. She hopes that once people realize how beautiful, fragile, and important corals are, they will change their behavior to help preserve coral reefs. Katy lives near the ocean in Isabela, Puerto Rico.

Katherine Brown-Wing studied at the Art Institute of Boston. She works as a biological illustrator, and her pictures have been published in numerous scientific journals. Katherine lives in North Kingstown, Rhode Island, with her husband.

LOG ON FIND OUT

Author Katy Muzik
Illustrator Katherine Brown-Wing
www.macmillanmh.com

Author's Purpose

What was the author's purpose for writing *At Home in the Coral Reef*? Explain if her purpose was stated or implied.

LOG ON LEARN IT Comprehension www.macmillanmh.com

Comprehension Check

Summarize

To summarize *At Home in the Coral Reef* use the most important details from the selection. Information from your Venn diagram may help you with your summary.

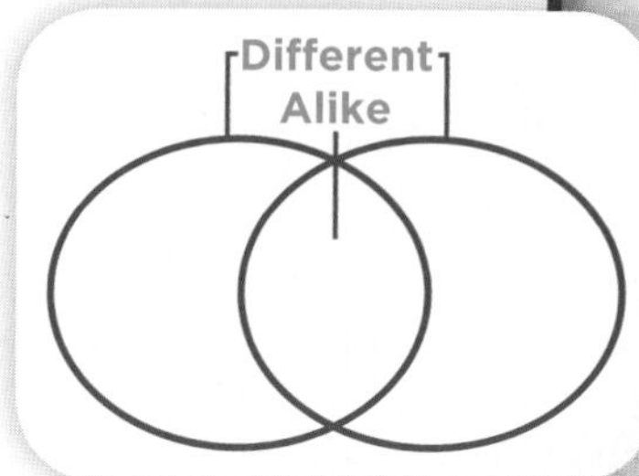

Think and Compare

1. How do coral polyps catch food? Details

2. How is the coral **reef** that lives in dirty water different from the coral reef that lives in clean water? Explain using selection details. Analyze Text Structure: Compare and Contrast

3. Reread page 625. What is the page mainly about? Summarize the main idea and details. Include evidence from the text. Main Idea and Details

4. Reread pages 628–629. Explain how the author uses persuasive language to convince the reader to help save the coral reefs. Author's Purpose

5. Read "Coral Reefs" on pages 612–613 and page 616 of *At Home in the Coral Reef*. What information did each selection provide about hard and soft coral? Reading/Writing Across Texts

Language Arts

Genre

A **Myth** is a made-up story that explains a natural occurrence, with stories about gods and goddesses.

Literary Elements

The **Point of View** is the perspective from which a story is told. In first-person point of view, the narrator is a character in the story. In third-person point of view, the author tells the story.

Hyperbole is the use of exaggeration to create emphasis or drama.

Poseidon and the Kingdom of Atlantis

retold by Gillian Reed

At the beginning of time, the immortal Greek gods of Mount Olympus divided the world among themselves. Zeus, the king of the gods, ruled over the sky and the thunderbolt. Poseidon, his brother, was the god of the sea, the lake, and the earthquake. Poseidon's power and bad temper earned him the name "Earth Shaker." He could stir up the oceans with his trident, a three-pronged fishing spear. He could also calm the sea, riding over the waves in his golden chariot.

In this paragraph, we see that the author is telling the story using third-person **point of view**.

Along with the seas, Poseidon ruled over an island in the middle of the Atlantic Ocean called Atlantis. The people of the island grew wheat, fruit, and vegetables in its fertile soil. Gold and other metals lay beneath the soil. Herds of magnificent elephants and other animals lived in the forests. Poseidon created hot and cold springs, so the people always had fresh water to drink, and warm water in which to bathe.

On the island of Atlantis lived a beautiful woman named Cleito. Poseidon was so taken by Cleito's beauty that he married this mortal woman. He built a palace for Cleito on a graceful hill in the middle of the island. To protect Cleito, Poseidon surrounded the hill with circular belts of water and land. A canal from the ocean to the hill cut across these belts. Cleito and Poseidon became the parents of five sets of twins, all of them boys. The boys grew up to rule over their father's territory, with the oldest, Atlas, ruling as king.

Atlantis was the greatest island kingdom ever known. The power of its rulers extended beyond the island to Europe and Africa. For many generations, Atlantis was a rich and happy land. The walls of the city were lined with brass and tin. Gold covered the temple of Poseidon. The people of Atlantis were noble and virtuous and lived by a set of laws that Poseidon had created. But, over time, the kings and the people became petty and greedy. They ignored Poseidon's laws and began to war against other nations.

Zeus saw what was happening to this great race of people and was angry. He called the gods to Mount Olympus. Pointing his finger at Poseidon, he blamed him for allowing Atlantis to become spoiled.

Using his powers, Poseidon took his trident and furiously whipped up the seas. A gigantic wave washed over the kingdom of Atlantis and flooded the island. Atlantis instantly sank into the sea.

Saying that Atlantis "instantly" sank into the sea is an exaggeration and an example of **hyperbole**.

There are some who believe that the great island kingdom of Atlantis really existed. The Greek philosopher Plato described such a place in his writings. Many people have searched for the sunken island, but no one has ever found it.

Connect and Compare

1. How would this myth have been different if the author had made Poseidon the narrator? **Point of View**
2. How did the people of Atlantis change over time? **Apply**
3. If Atlantis did exist, it might now be covered by coral reefs. Think about what you learned from *At Home in the Coral Reef*. In what kind of waters would Atlantis have to lie to be home to coral reefs? **Reading/Writing Across Texts**
4. On your own, find two myths. Use a Venn diagram to compare and contrast the characters and events in the myths. **Apply**

LOG ON FIND OUT **Language Arts** Myths
www.macmillanmh.com

Writing

Trait: Ideas

Writers use **supporting details** to give readers more information about the main idea.

Reading and Writing Connection

Read the passage below. Notice how the author Katy Muzik uses details to show the distinct things that affect coral.

An excerpt from
At Home in the Coral Reef

The author gives clear details to show the impact of pollution on the coral (called planula) that cannot survive in dirty water.

The planula catches a current to deeper water. Oh, no, the water is dirty! The water is so dirty, the coral is dying. The dirt smothers the coral polyps and blocks the sunlight they need.

Chemicals washed down the rivers from factories and farms poison the coral. In the dirty water harmful bacteria grow over the coral and kill it. Careless divers hurt the coral too. They step on it and break it with their boat anchors.

Without living coral, the fish and other animals will leave. The planula cannot live here either.

Read and Find

Read Raesia's writing below. How did she use details to support her ideas about recycling at her school? Use the checklist below to help you.

Making a Difference

by Raesia S.

Everyone knows that recycling helps the environment. At our school we have a Recycle Club. We help our teachers keep our school clean. My teacher has a recycle box in our classroom. I decorated the box so everyone knows it's for paper and cardboard. Natalie made a sign to show where to find the box. Big bins for plastic are in the hallways. We help carry those big bins so they are ready when the recycle truck comes to collect the recycling from our school.

Read about a recycling club.

Writer's Checklist

- ☑ Does the author give **details** about the recycling process at school?
- ☑ Does the author include details that are relevant and balanced?
- ☐ Does the author persuade you to help by recycling?

Ocean Animals

Talk About It

What do you think of when you see an ocean animal, such as a whale?

LOG ON VIEW IT

Oral Language Activities
Ocean Animals
www.macmillanmh.com

Vocabulary

rumbling **unique** **encounter** **dove** **massive** **tangles**

Dictionary

Homographs are words that are spelled the same but have different meanings and origins. They also may have different pronunciations. You can check the meanings, origins, and pronunciations of homographs in a dictionary.

dove = past tense of *dive*
dove = a type of bird

A Whale of a Trip!

by Kristin Gold

"Ladies and gentlemen," shouted Matty, our guide. He had to yell over the **rumbling** sounds of the boat's engines. "You're in for a special, **unique**, and exciting trip."

Matty continued, "Before your first **encounter** with whales I want to give you a little information about them." First he explained that whales are mammals, not fish. Next he informed us that a group of whales is called a pod.

The first thing we saw were birds flying alongside our boat. One **dove** sharply toward the water, and then flew up again! "That's a dovekie," explained Matty. "Whales may be nearby."

"There are two major groups of whales," Matty continued, "baleen whales and toothed whales. Instead of teeth, baleen whales have plates that act like a big sieve and collect food. These birds hang around to eat the tiny fish that slip out of the whales' mouths!"

Then a whale suddenly surfaced. I couldn't believe how huge it was. It was **massive**!

Soon we saw another whale slap its tail on the water.

"Is it angry?" I asked Matty.

"Probably not," said Matty. "That's called lobtailing. Some scientists think it's a warning to other whales. Others think they're just playing or cleaning their tails."

Matty explained that it's against the law to hunt humpback whales, but whales get killed anyway. The huge nets fishermen use to catch tuna often trap whales, too. Matty said these **tangles** can be prevented by using other kinds of nets. Some concerned people want politicians to help by passing more laws to protect whales.

When we finally reached the dock, we realized that Matty was right. The whale-watching trip had been exciting and one-of-a-kind.

Reread for **Comprehension**

Analyze Text Structure

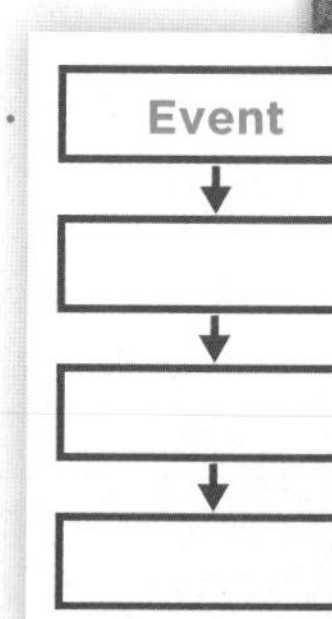

Sequence The way an author organizes information in a selection is called text structure. Sequence is a type of text structure. Authors who use sequence as a text structure present information in time order. Sequence is often an explicit text structure, because the author uses signal words such as *first*, *next*, and *finally* to show the order of events. If there are no signal words, then the author is using sequence as an implicit text structure. Fill in your Sequence Chart as you reread to help you put the events in time order.

LOG ON LEARN IT **Comprehension** www.macmillanmh.com

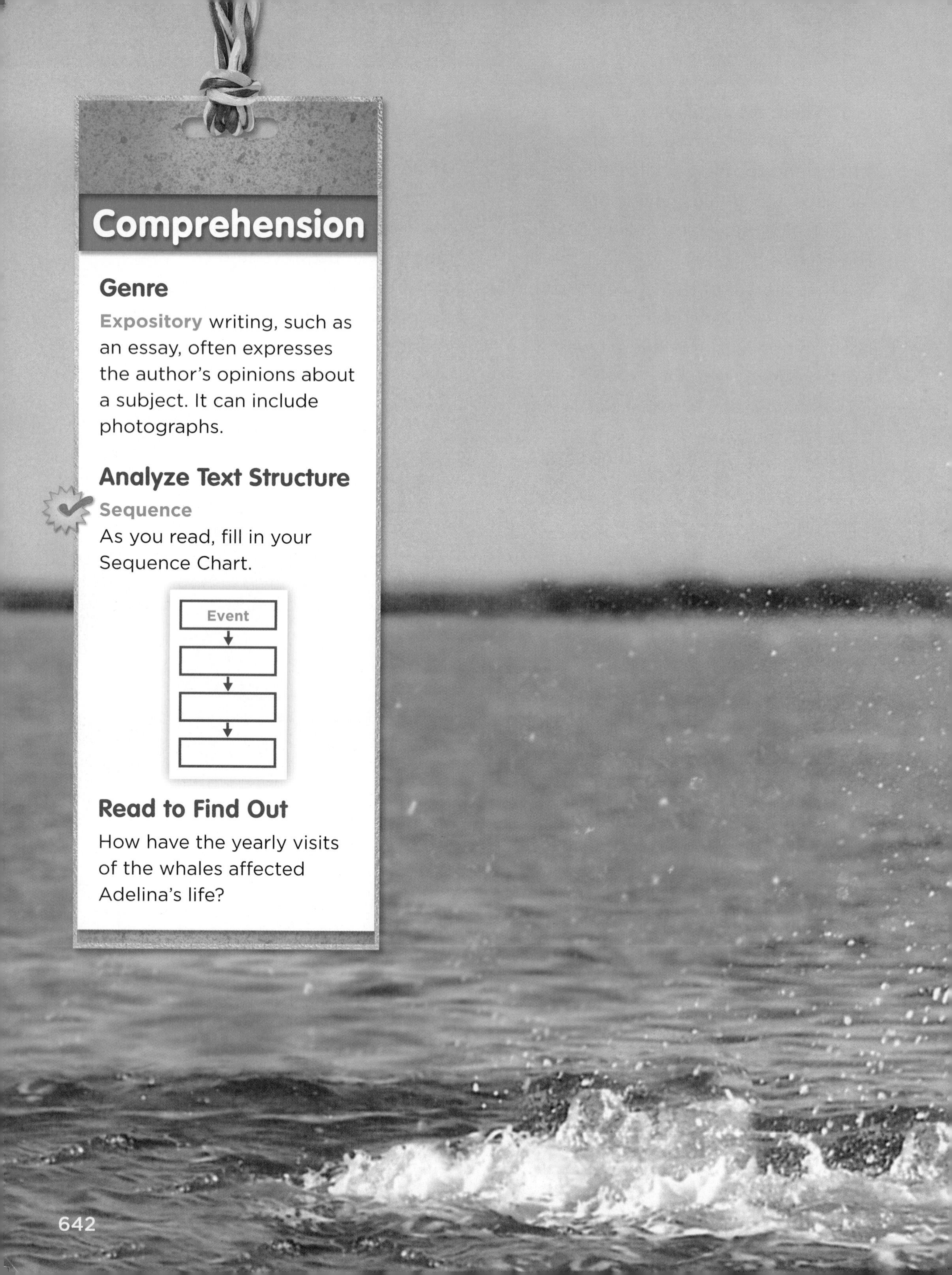

Comprehension

Genre

Expository writing, such as an essay, often expresses the author's opinions about a subject. It can include photographs.

Analyze Text Structure

Sequence

As you read, fill in your Sequence Chart.

Event

Read to Find Out

How have the yearly visits of the whales affected Adelina's life?

ADELINA'S WHALES

Text and photographs by
RICHARD SOBOL

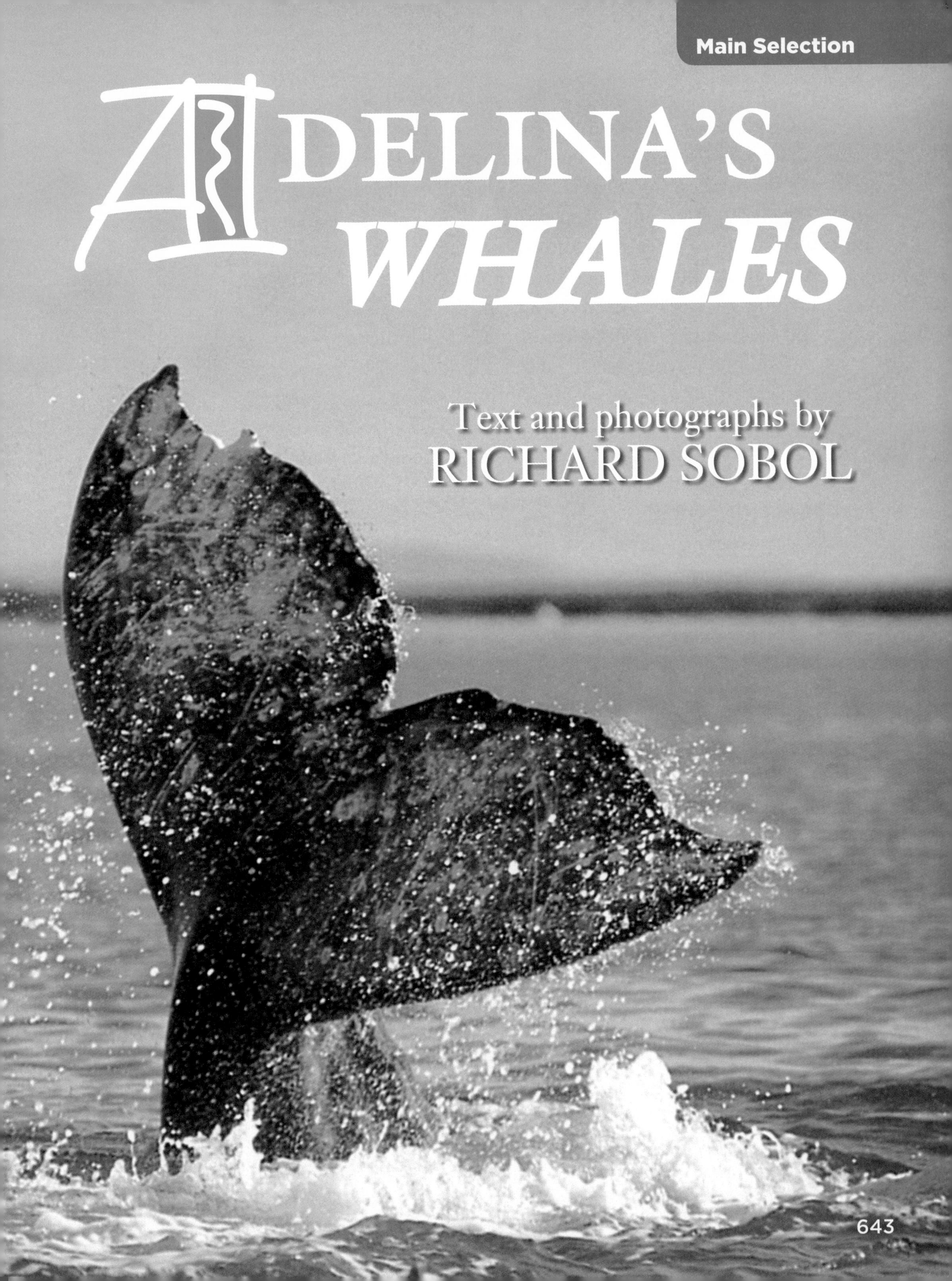

La Laguna is the name of a quiet, dusty fishing village on the sandy shore of Laguna San Ignacio, in Baja California, Mexico. A few dozen homesites are scattered along the water's edge. These little houses are simple one- or two-room boxes patched together with plywood and sheet metal. Drinking water is stored outside in fifty-gallon plastic barrels, and electricity is turned on for only a few hours each day.

Adelina Mayoral has lived her whole life in La Laguna. She is a bright ten-year-old girl. She loves the ocean and the feeling of the ever-present wind that blows her long, dark hair into wild **tangles**. She knows what time of day it is by looking at the way the light reflects off the water. Adelina can tell what month it is by watching the kind of birds that nest in the mangroves behind her home. She can even recognize when it is low tide. Simply by taking a deep breath through her nose, she can smell the clams and seaweed that bake in the hot sun on the shoreline as the water level goes down.

In late January, every afternoon after school, Adelina walks to the beach to see if her friends—the gray whales—have returned. At this same time every year the whales come, traveling from as far away as Alaska and Russia. They slowly and steadily swim south, covering more than five thousand miles along the Pacific Coast during November, December, and January.

One night Adelina is awakened by a loud, low, **rumbling** noise. It is the sound of a forty-ton gray whale exhaling a room-size blast of hot wet air. As she has always known they would, the gray whales have come again to visit. Adelina smiles and returns to her sleep, comforted by the sounds of whales breathing and snoring outside her window. At daybreak she runs to the lagoon and sees two clouds of mist out over the water, the milky trails of breath left by a mother gray whale and her newborn calf.

The waters of the protected lagoon are warm and shallow. The scientists who have come to visit and study the whales have explained that Laguna San Ignacio is the perfect place for the mother whales to have their babies and then teach them how to swim. But Adelina knows why they really come—to visit her!

Adelina's family lives far away from big cities with highways and shopping malls. Her little village does not have any movie theaters or traffic lights, but she knows that her hometown is a special place. This is the only place on earth where these giant gray whales—totally wild animals—choose to seek out the touch of a human hand. Only here in Laguna San Ignacio do whales ever stop swimming and say hello to their human neighbors. Raising their **massive** heads up out of the water, they come face-to-face with people. Some mother whales even lift their newborns up on their backs to help them get a better view of those who have come to see them. Or maybe they are just showing off, sharing their new baby the way any proud parent would.

The whales have been coming to this lagoon for hundreds of years, and Adelina is proud that her grandfather, Pachico, was the first person to tell of a "friendly" visit with one. She loves to hear him tell the story of that whale and that day. She listens closely as he talks about being frightened, since he didn't know then that the whale was only being friendly. He thought he was in big trouble.

Adelina looks first at the tight, leathery skin of her grandfather, browned from his many years of fishing in the bright tropical sun. From his face she glances down to the small plastic model of a gray whale that he keeps close by. As he begins to tell the story of his first friendly whale **encounter**, there is a twinkle in his eye and a large smile on his face. Adelina and her father, Runolfo, smile too, listening again to the story that they have heard so many times before.

In a whisper, her grandfather begins to draw them in. Adelina closes her eyes to imagine the calm and quiet on that first afternoon when his small boat was gently nudged by a huge gray whale. As the boat rocked, her grandfather and his fishing partner's hearts pounded. They held tight and waited, preparing themselves to be thrown into the water by the giant animal. The whale **dove** below them and surfaced again on the opposite side of their boat, scraping her head along the smooth sides. Instead of being tossed from the boat, they were surprised to find themselves still upright and floating.

For the next hour the whale glided alongside them, bumping and bobbing gently—as gently as possible for an animal that is as long as a school bus and as wide as a soccer goal. As the sun started to set behind them, the whale gave out a great blast of wet, snotty saltwater that soaked their clothes and stuck to their skin. The whale then rose up inches away from their boat and dove into the sea. Her first visit was over.

As her grandfather finishes the story, he looks to Adelina, who joins him in speaking the last line of the story: "Well, my friend, no fish today!" they say before breaking into laughter.

Sequence
What happened after the whale gave a great blast of saltwater?

After this first friendly visit with the whales, word quickly spread of the **unique** encounter between a wild fifty-foot whale and a tiny fishing boat. Scientists and whale watchers started to come to Laguna San Ignacio to see the whales themselves. Perhaps word spread among the whales, too, because now dozens of whales began to approach the small boats. With brains as large as a car's engine, gray whales might even have their own language. They "talk" in low rumbles and loud clicks, making noises that sound like the tappings of a steel drum or the ticking that a playing card makes as it slaps against the spokes of a turning bicycle wheel. Maybe they told each other that it was safe to visit here.

Adelina's favorite time of the day is the late afternoon, when her father and grandfather return from their trips on the water, guiding visitors to see the whales. They sit together as the sun goes down behind them, and she listens to stories of the whales. She asks them lots and lots of questions.

Adelina has learned a lot about the gray whales. She knows that when a whale leaps out of the water and makes a giant splash falling back in, it's called breaching. When a whale pops its head straight up out of the water, as if it is looking around to see what is going on, it is called spyhopping. Adelina also learned how the whale's wide, flat tail is called a fluke, and when it raises its tail up in the air as it goes into a deep dive, that is called fluking.

Although her home is a simple one on a sandy bluff hugging the edge of the Pacific Ocean, Adelina has many new friends who come to share her world. She has met people who come from beyond the end of the winding, bumpy road that rings the lagoon. Some are famous actors. Some are politicians. Some speak Spanish. Some speak English. Those that weigh forty tons speak to her in their own magical style. The whales have taught her that the world is a big place.

Adelina knows that she has many choices in her future. Sometimes she giggles with delight at the idea of being the first girl to captain a *panga* (a small open fishing boat) and teach people about the whales in the lagoon. Or sometimes she thinks she may become a biologist who studies the ocean and can one day help to unlock some of the mysteries of the whales in her own backyard. Or maybe she will take pictures like the photographer whom she watches juggling his three cameras as he stumbles aboard the whale-watching boat. But no matter what she chooses, the whales will always be a part of her life.

For these three months Adelina knows how lucky she is to live in Laguna San Ignacio, the little corner of Mexico that the gray whales choose for their winter home. This is the place where two worlds join together. She wouldn't trade it for anything.

Sequence
What events brought whale watchers to Laguna San Ignacio? List the events in correct order.

In the early spring the lagoon grows quiet. One by one the whales swim off, heading north for a summer of feeding. On their heads and backs they carry the fingerprints of those they met, the memories of their encounters in Mexico. Maybe, as the whales sleep, they dream of the colorful sunsets of Laguna San Ignacio.

Every afternoon Adelina continues to gaze across the water. Sometimes now, when she closes her eyes, she can still see the whales swimming by. And if she listens *really* closely, she can even hear their breathing.

A Snapshot of Richard Sobol

Richard Sobol is a photographer who has snapped many different subjects in his long career. For the past few years, Richard has spent a lot of time photographing wildlife, including the whales. He is especially interested in capturing images of endangered species.

Other books by Richard Sobol

LOG ON FIND OUT

Author Richard Sobol
www.macmillanmh.com

Author's Purpose

How does Richard Sobol want the reader to feel about Adelina and the gray whales? Explain your answer using details from the text.

Comprehension Check

Summarize

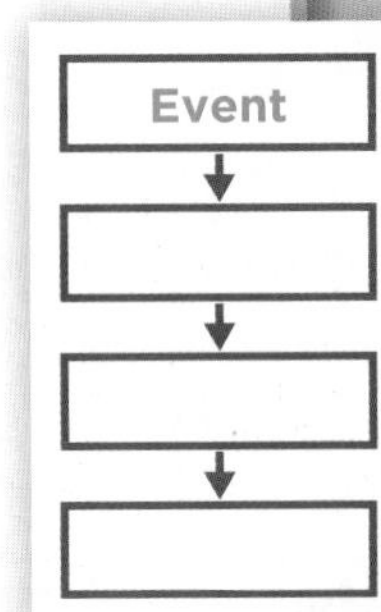

To summarize *Adelina's Whales* use the most important details from the selection. Information from your Sequence Chart may help you.

Think and Compare

1. How many miles do the gray whales cover when they swim south along the Pacific Coast? Details
2. What happens after Adelina is awakened by a loud **rumbling** noise? Explain using details from the selection. Analyze Text Structure: Sequence
3. How does Adelina feel about the gray whales that come every year to Laguna San Ignacio? Use evidence from the text to support your answer. Make Inferences
4. Reread page 647. What language does the author use to persuade the reader that Laguna San Ignacio is a special place? Use examples from the text. Author's Craft
5. Read "A Whale of a Trip!" on pages 640–641. What information about whales was in this article that was not in *Adelina's Whales*? Reading/Writing Across Texts

Limericks

Poetry

Genre

A **Limerick** is a funny poem with a specific pattern of rhyme and meter. All limericks have five lines.

Literary Elements

Meter is the rhythm of the syllables in a line of poetry.

Rhyme Scheme is the pattern of rhymes within a poem.

A Whale of a Meal

There once was a whale named Alene
Who strained all her meals through baleen.
But she dreamed of a lunch
With a food that goes "crunch"
Like a truckload of just-picked string beans.

— *Doreen Beauregard*

Whale Watch

The **meter** in these three lines is created by emphasizing the third, sixth, and ninth syllables.

Near our bóat is a mámmal named Lúke
Who's exceédingly proúd of his flúke.
Just don't call it a tail
Or this dignified whale
Will respónd with a spláshy rebúke.

— *Doreen Beauregard*

The Podless Whale

There once was a whale near Cape Cod
Who just could not locate his pod.
So he joined with a mass
Of bewildered sea bass
Who found this behavior quite odd.

— Doreen Beauregard

The last line of a limerick always **rhymes** with the first two lines. The third and fourth lines have a different rhyme.

Connect and Compare

1. What is the rhyme scheme of "Whale Watch"? If the last line rhymed with the third and fourth lines how would the rhyme scheme change? **Rhyme Scheme**
2. Identify an example of sensory language in "A Whale of a Meal." **Apply**
3. Compare and contrast the whales in these poems to the ones in *Adelina's Whales*. **Reading/Writing Across Texts**

LOG ON FIND OUT **Poetry** Limerick
www.macmillanmh.com

Writing

Trait: Voice

Writers choose special details and language for their particular **purpose and audience**.

Reading and Writing Connection

Read the passage below. Notice how the author Richard Sobol chooses special details to highlight this moment in the mind of the reader.

An excerpt from *Adelina's Whales*

In a whisper, her grandfather begins to draw them in. Adelina closes her eyes to imagine the calm and quiet on that first afternoon when his small boat was gently nudged by a huge gray whale. As the boat rocked, her grandfather and his fishing partner's hearts pounded. They held tight and waited, preparing themselves to be thrown into the water by the giant animal. The whale dove below them and surfaced again on the opposite side of their boat, scraping her head along the smooth sides.

The author uses words and details that show the quiet of the moment and the growing suspense.

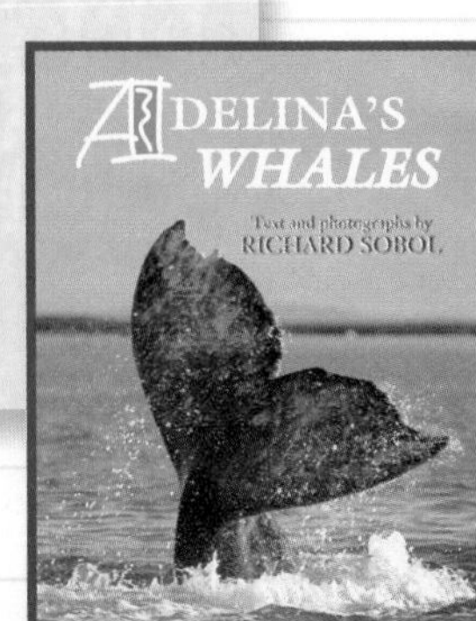

Read and Find

Read Tahrae's writing below. What details does he use to show his audience how he felt? Use the checklist below to help you.

June 12, 2012

Dear Juan,

Remember how I told you I was scared to go down in the basement? I went down there yesterday! My mom needed an extension cord from the basement. I told her I was scared, but she told me I'd be fine. It was dark and dusty, just like I thought it would be. Luckily, there weren't any spiders. I thought for sure I'd see at least one! I jumped when I heard footsteps and a creaking noise, but it was just Mom checking on me.

Your Friend,

Tahrae

Read about a scary basement.

Writer's Checklist

- [x] Does the author use words and details that would help Juan picture what is being described?
- [x] Is the language Tahrae used appropriate for writing a friend?
- [ ] Did Tahrae follow the conventions of a letter?

Review

Compare and Contrast
Problem and Solution
Sequence
Multiple-Meaning Words
Point of View

Tiger's Teacher

A Han Tale from China

Tiger lived in the tip top of a mountain. Although Tiger was strong and brave, he was also clumsy and had a hard time catching animals.

One day he left his cave to look for food. Suddenly, he saw Cat racing by. Tiger was jealous of Cat's quick and easy movements. He thought to himself, "I would be perfect if I could move as easily as Cat!"

Tiger went to Cat and said, "Oh wonderful and honored Cat, could you please teach me your ways, so that I can move as well as you?"

Cat did not trust Tiger, and she worried about teaching him all she knew. She shook her head. "How do I know you won't use this against me?"

Tiger looked shocked. Then he began to charm Cat. "Honored Cat, greatest teacher," he began, "I promise that if you will teach me, I will never forget your goodness. And I will never harm you."

Tiger's words and face were so sweet that Cat began to feel sorry for him. She agreed.

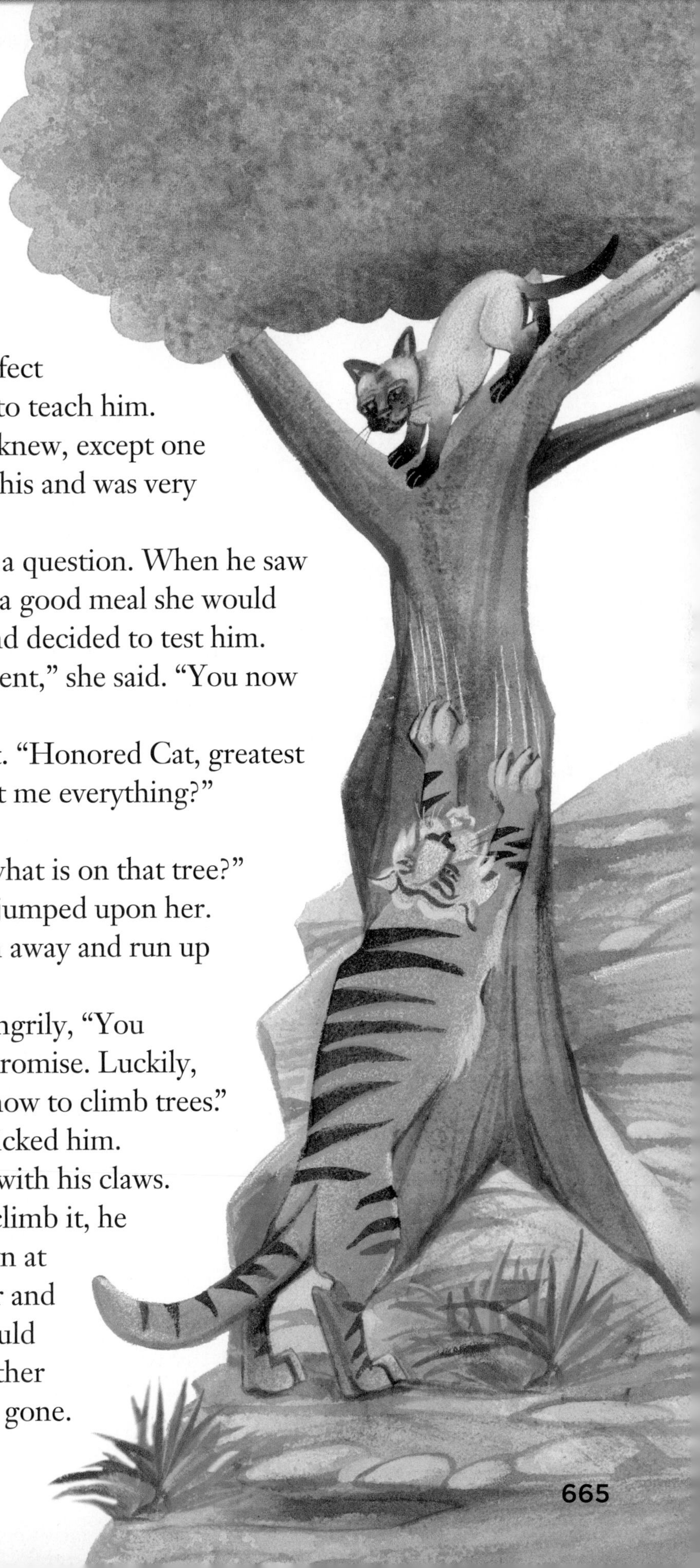

Tiger was overjoyed! He bowed before Cat, saying, "When I have learned to move as beautifully as you, I will never forget you. May I fall into a valley if I am ever ungrateful."

For some time, Tiger was the perfect student. Every day, Cat did her best to teach him. She soon taught him everything she knew, except one skill. However, Tiger did not know this and was very pleased with himself and his teacher.

One day, Tiger came to Cat with a question. When he saw Cat's fleshy body, he imagined what a good meal she would make. Cat saw the look in his eyes and decided to test him.

"Well, you are no longer my student," she said. "You now know everything I know."

Tiger saw his chance to catch Cat. "Honored Cat, greatest teacher, are you sure you have taught me everything?"

"Everything!" said wise Cat.

"Greatest teacher," said Tiger, "what is on that tree?"

When Cat turned to look, Tiger jumped upon her. He batted at her. But Cat had gotten away and run up the tree.

From the tree, Cat called down angrily, "You ungrateful animal! You broke your promise. Luckily, I was wise enough not to teach you how to climb trees."

Tiger couldn't believe Cat had tricked him. He dove at the tree and scratched it with his claws. But because he didn't know how to climb it, he could not reach her. Cat looked down at him with a smile. Tiger grew angrier and angrier, but there was nothing he could do. Finally Cat jumped easily to another tree, and then another, until she was gone.

Turtle Tricks the Trickster

A Native American Tale from the United States

One morning, Rabbit and Turtle met near the brook. They lay in the sunshine on the bank of the brook. Rabbit told tales about how smart and wonderful he was. He bragged that he was the fastest runner in all the land. Turtle wasn't so sure.

"I bet if we race," Turtle said to Rabbit, "I can beat you."

Rabbit stared at Turtle and then burst into laughter. Rabbit kicked his paws against the ground and held his belly. "You are too slow," Rabbit said. "You crawl. You will never beat me!"

Turtle was mad. He didn't like Rabbit's insults or his arrogance. "You meet me here tomorrow," said Turtle. "We will race. I'll wear a white feather so you can see me during the race. We will run over four hills, and the first one to reach that large oak tree at the top of the last hill will be the winner."

"I will be the winner! And I will see you tomorrow at the race!" Rabbit said, and then he skipped off, still laughing to himself.

Turtle was a bit worried, as he knew he could not run faster than Rabbit. But he had an idea. He gathered his family and told them about Rabbit and his bragging. Then, he told them about the race. They quickly agreed to help him. Turtle gave each of the other turtles a white feather. Then together they mapped out the race and decided where each turtle should wait. One turtle waited at the brook, another on the top of the first hill, another in the valley, another at the top of the second hill, and so forth. Turtle himself went to the top of the fourth hill and waited under the large oak tree.

Early the next morning, Rabbit hopped to the brook and found Turtle with his white feather at the starting line.

Rabbit couldn't stop himself from laughing. "Are you ready?" Rabbit smirked. "Okay go," he yelled as he ran off and up the first hill. Turtle with the white feather on his head started crawling. As soon as Rabbit was out of sight, he left the path and disappeared into the bushes.

When Rabbit got to the top of the first hill, he saw Turtle with his white feather crawling ahead of him as fast as he could down into the valley. Rabbit was shocked. He dug his paws into the dirt and passed Turtle with the white feather. As soon as Rabbit's back was to Turtle, the turtle took off the white feather and crawled into the bushes.

When Rabbit reached the bottom of the valley, Turtle with his white feather was ahead of him, yet again. Rabbit hopped harder and faster, leaving Turtle far behind him. Yet every time he reached a hilltop or a valley, there was Turtle again with his white feather, crawling along as fast as he could.

By the time he reached the third valley, Rabbit was so tired he could hardly breathe. He thought he passed Turtle at the top of the third hill, but here Turtle was again moving up to the top of the fourth hill.

Rabbit couldn't stand to lose the race. He gathered his last bit of energy and sprinted up the hill, passing Turtle. When he saw the oak tree, he knew he was almost there. But when Rabbit reached the last stretch of grass, he couldn't believe his eyes. Sitting in the grass under the oak tree, waving his white feather proudly, was Turtle. Turtle had won the race!

Show What You Know

Comprehension

Organizing Information

- In nonfiction, a text structure is an organizational pattern that authors use to present information. Sequence, cause/effect, compare/contrast, and description are all examples of text structures. Text structures can be implicit or explicit. A biography often has an explicit text structure. The events of a person's life are told in sequence using signal words.
- In order to identify an explicit sequence in a text, look for words that signal time, such as *before, after, first, then, next, finally*. Other clues are dates, or steps in a process.
- Reread "Long Journey Home" on page 603. What kind of text structure did the author use? Was it explicit? Explain, using details from the selection including signal words.

Word Study

Multiple-Meaning Words

- Many words have more than one meaning. One way to figure out what a multiple-meaning word means in a sentence is to look for context clues. Look at these two examples for the word *bat*.
- Example: *I bought a new bat for the game.* In this example, a bat is something that you hit a ball with.
- Example: *The bat flew out of the cave.* Here, a bat is an animal.
- Each of the following words has more than one meaning: *drop, fine, well*. Write one sentence for each meaning of the word. Include context clues within your sentences.

Genre

Comparing Tales

- Folktales are stories that are based on the traditions of a people or region. They are handed down from one generation to the next. Folktales often have one character who is very clever and able to fool the other characters in the story.
- With a partner choose two folktales. Discuss the characters and events in each story.
- Then create a Venn diagram and use it to compare the characters and their adventures in the two stories.

Research

What's the Source?

- A bibliography is a list of all the sources you used to write a report. An entry for a book in a bibliography includes the author, title, place of publication, publisher, and date.

Smith, Robert. *Desert Habitats*. New York: Compass, 1996.

- An entry for an online source gives the author, the title of the article, the date you visited, and the URL of the Web site.

Lin, Lucy. "Sahara." March, 2006. http://www.desert.exc

- Choose a book and write a bibliography entry for it. Remember to include the author, title, place of publication, publisher, and year of publication.

Unit 6
Problem Solving

The Big Question

How do we solve problems?

Theme Video
Problem Solving
www.macmillanmh.com

LOG ON VIEW IT

How do we solve problems?

People solve problems in many different ways. The solution depends on the type of problem. To solve a math problem, you may have to apply what you know about numbers or measurement. To solve a health problem, you may have to visit a doctor. To solve a problem with a friend, you may need to sit down with him or her, or know about people and their emotions. Problem solving can be as complex and varied as the problems themselves. Learning about problem solving can help you better understand the problems you face and their possible solutions.

Research Activities

Throughout the unit, you will be gathering information about various types of problems and their solutions. Choose one problem and solution to focus your research on. Use graphic aids to create a booklet explaining the problem and solution.

Keep Track of Ideas

As you read, keep track of all you are learning about problem solving. Use the **Layered Book Foldable**. On the front sheet, write the Unit Theme: *Problem Solving*. On each next sheet, write the facts you learn each week that will help you in your research and in your understanding of the Unit Theme.

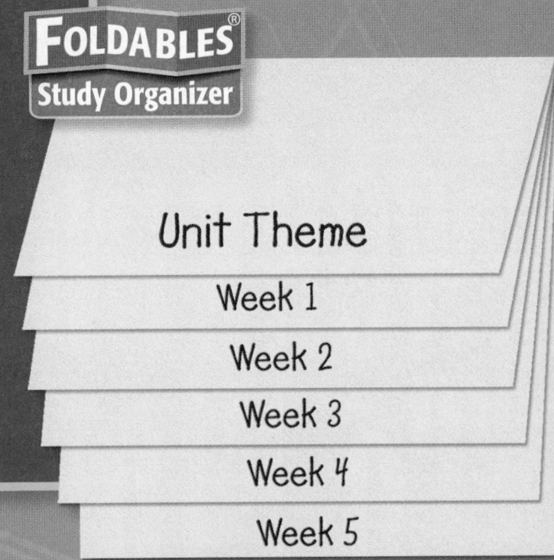

Digital Learning

LOG ON FIND OUT www.macmillanmh.com

StudentWorks Plus

Interactive Student Book

- **Research Roadmap**
  Follow a step-by-step guide to complete your research project.

Online Resources

- Topic Finder and Other Research Tools
- Videos and Virtual Field Trips
- Photos and Drawings for Presentations
- Related Articles and Web Resources
- Web Site Links

People and Places

Lillian Gilbreth 1878–1972

Known as "The First Lady of Engineering," Lillian Gilbreth studied how people could use their time more efficiently. She was also the mother of 12 children. Her children wrote a book, *Cheaper by the Dozen*, about their large, famous family.

WORKING TOGETHER
To Find Solutions

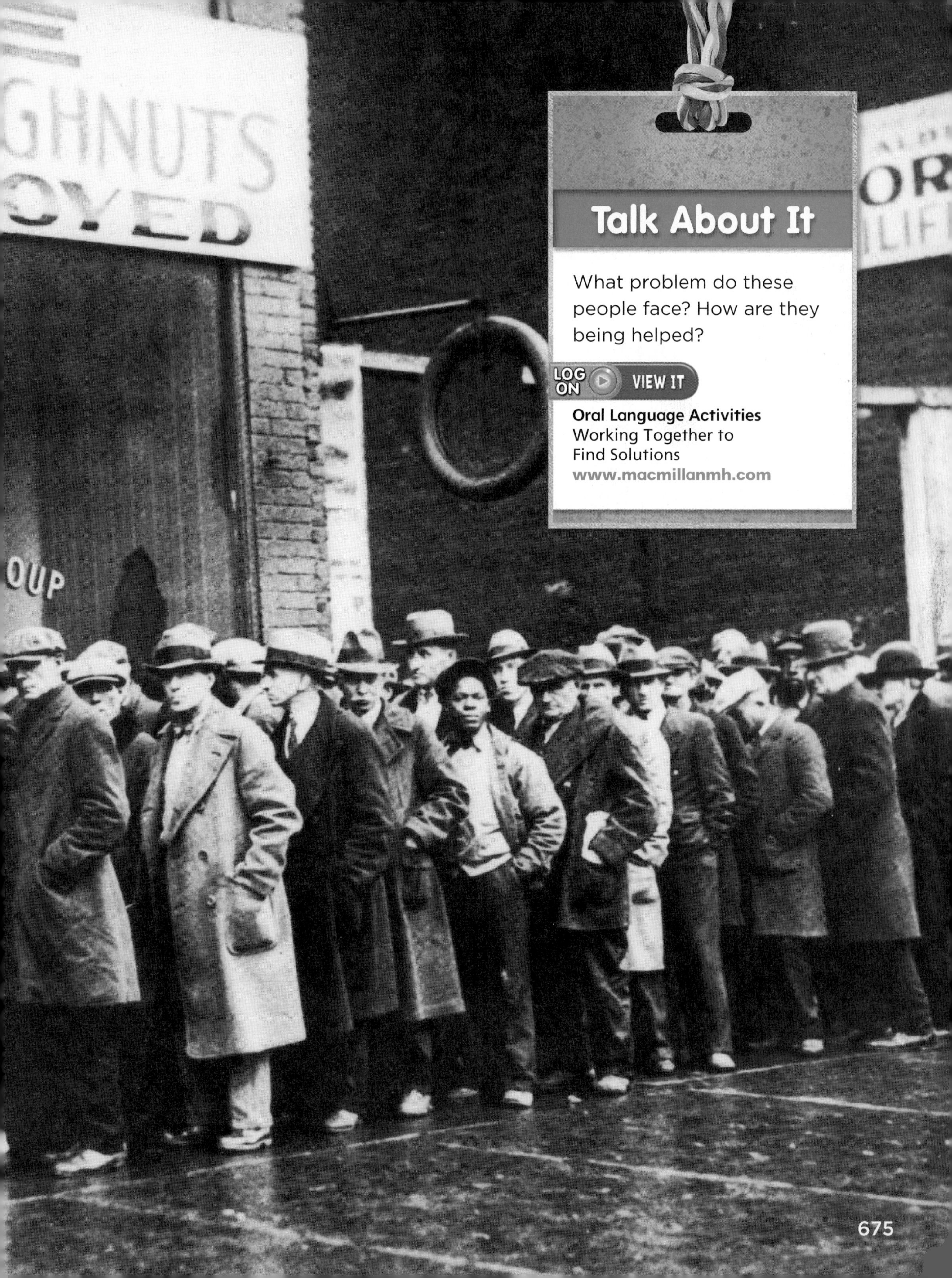

Talk About It

What problem do these people face? How are they being helped?

LOG ON VIEW IT

Oral Language Activities
Working Together to Find Solutions
www.macmillanmh.com

Vocabulary

sturdy **bidding**
items **overflowing**
clustered **glistened**

Dictionary

Unfamiliar Words are words you do not know. You can find the meaning, syllabication, and pronunciation of unfamiliar words in a dictionary. Look up the meaning of the word *clustered*.

Grandma's Story

by Marcus Kharana

My grandmother had been in a wheelchair for a long time. "Why is that, Grandma?" I asked her one day.

"When I was 12," she said, "I had polio." Grandma told me that polio harmed the lungs and muscles. Some people died of it. Many people who lived lost the use of their legs or arms. "President Roosevelt even had it," Grandma said. "Now, thank goodness, there is a vaccine for it." Grandma lived, but she would not be able to walk. Her family felt lucky.

To get around, Grandma told me, she needed a **sturdy**, strong wheelchair. Her family was poor, and this was a hard time for everyone. But the neighborhood decided to help them raise money for a wheelchair by having a sale. Everyone looked around their homes and found **items** that they would be glad to part with.

These things were **clustered** together in the community center basement and given price tags. The nicer pieces, such as furniture and paintings, were placed in an auction. All the money that came from the auction **bidding** and the sale would help pay for the wheelchair.

"The crowd was **overflowing**," Grandma said. "People with little money tried to buy at least one small thing. Wealthy people in the community bid on the expensive things." Grandma's face **glistened** with tears when she told about how her community came together to help her. "I felt that at that moment I would truly be all right."

Reread for Comprehension

Analyze Story Structure

Problem and Solution

Identifying a character's problem in a story can help you understand how an author has organized the story's events. The steps the main character takes to solve the problem make up the story events. A Problem and Solution Chart can help you place the events in sequence and identify how the plot's main events influence future events. Reread the selection to find the problem, the actions taken by the characters, and the solution.

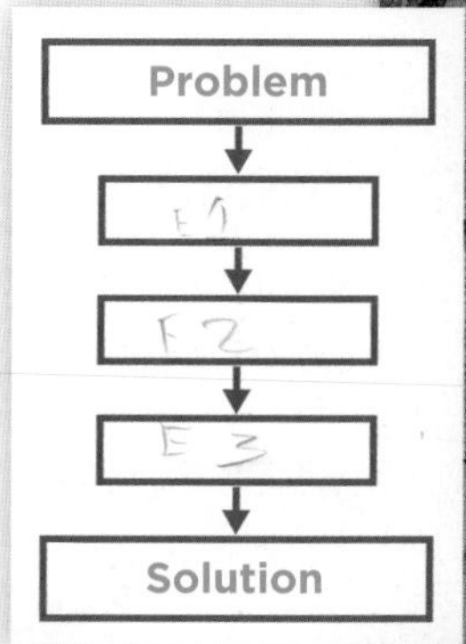

LOG ON LEARN IT **Comprehension** www.macmillanmh.com

Comprehension

Genre

Historical Fiction is set in a real time and place in the past. It may include real people and events that actually happened, along with fictional characters and events.

Analyze Story Structure

Problem and Solution

As you read, fill in your Problem and Solution Chart.

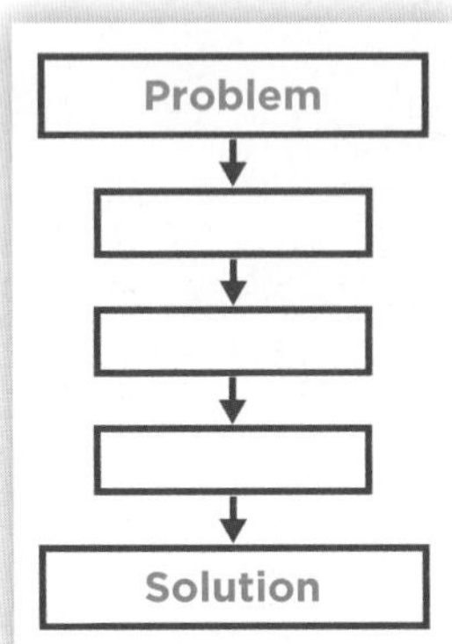

Read to Find Out

What will happen to Leah's pony?

Leah's Pony

Written by Elizabeth Friedrich
Illustrated by Michael Garland

The year the corn grew tall and straight, Leah's papa bought her a pony. The pony was strong and swift and **sturdy**, with just a snip of white at the end of his soft black nose. Papa taught Leah to place her new saddle right in the middle of his back and tighten the girth around his belly, just so.

That whole summer, Leah and her pony crossed through cloud-capped cornfields and chased cattle through the pasture.

Leah scratched that special spot under her pony's mane and brushed him till his coat **glistened** like satin.

Each day Leah loved to ride her pony into town just to hear Mr. B. shout from the door of his grocery store, "That's the finest pony in the whole county."

The year the corn grew no taller than a man's thumb, Leah's house became very quiet. Sometimes on those hot, dry nights, Leah heard Papa and Mama's hushed voices whispering in the kitchen. She couldn't understand the words but knew their sad sound.

Some days the wind blew so hard it turned the sky black with dust. It was hard for Leah to keep her pony's coat shining. It was hard for Mama to keep the house clean. It was hard for Papa to carry buckets of water for the sow and her piglets.

Soon Papa sold the pigs and even some of the cattle. "These are hard times," he told Leah with a puzzled look. "That's what these days are, all right, hard times."

Mama used flour sacks to make underwear for Leah. Mama threw dishwater on her drooping petunias to keep them growing. And, no matter what else happened, Mama always woke Leah on Saturday with the smell of fresh, hot coffee cake baking.

One hot, dry, dusty day grasshoppers turned the day to night. They ate the trees bare and left only twigs behind.

The next day the neighbors filled their truck with all they owned and stopped to say good-bye. “We’re off to Oregon,” they said. “It must be better there.” Papa, Mama, and Leah waved as their neighbors wobbled down the road in an old truck **overflowing** with chairs and bedsprings and wire.

The hot, dry, dusty days kept coming. On a day you could almost taste the earth in the air, Papa said, "I have something to tell you, Leah, and I want you to be brave. I borrowed money from the bank. I bought seeds, but the seeds dried up and blew away. Nothing grew. I don't have any corn to sell. Now I can't pay back the bank," Papa paused. "They're going to have an auction, Leah. They're going to sell the cattle and the chickens and the pickup truck."

Leah stared at Papa. His voice grew husky and soft. "Worst of all, they're going to sell my tractor. I'll never be able to plant corn when she's gone. Without my tractor, we might even have to leave the farm. I told you, Leah, these are hard times."

Problem and Solution
Summarize the problem that Leah's family faces.

Leah knew what an auction meant. She knew eager faces with strange voices would come to their farm. They would stand outside and offer money for her Papa's best bull and Mama's prize rooster and Leah's favorite calf.

All week Leah worried and waited and wondered what to do. One morning she watched as a man in a big hat hammered a sign into the ground in front of her house.

Leah wanted to run away. She raced her pony past empty fields lined with dry gullies. She galloped past a house with rags stuffed in broken windowpanes. She sped right past Mr. B. sweeping the steps outside his store.

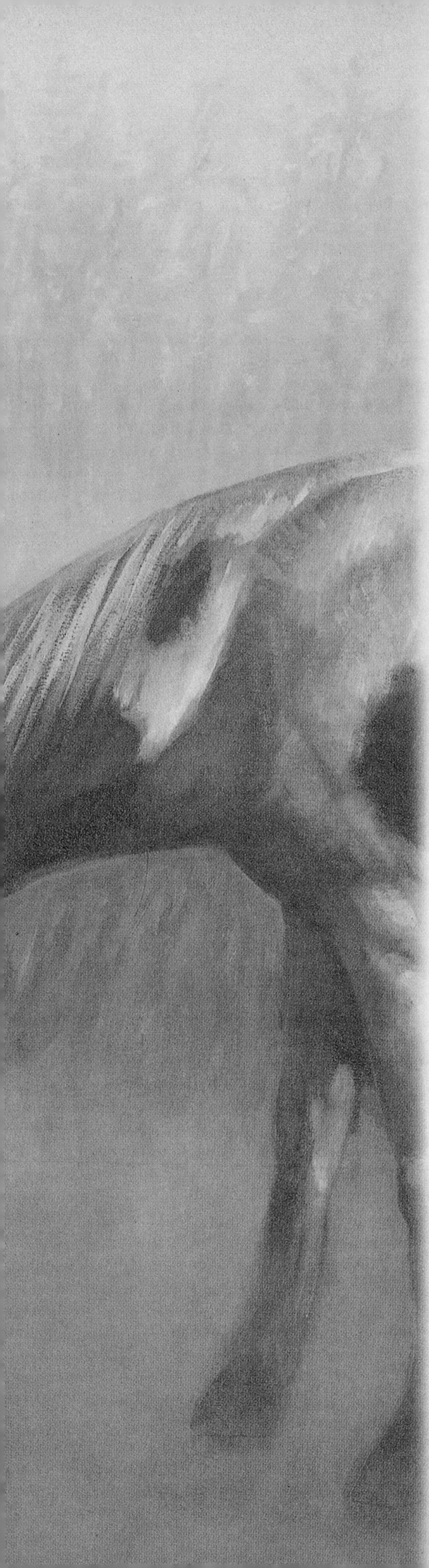

At last Leah knew what she had to do. She turned her pony around and rode back into town. She stopped in front of Mr. B.'s store. "You can buy my pony," she said.

Mr. B. stopped sweeping and stared at her. "Why would you want to sell him?" he asked. "That's the finest pony in the county."

Leah swallowed hard. "I've grown a lot this summer," she said. "I'm getting too big for him."

Sunburned soil crunched under Leah's feet as she walked home alone. The auction had begun. Neighbors, friends, strangers—everyone **clustered** around the man in the big hat. "How much for this wagon?" boomed the man. "Five dollars. Ten dollars. Sold for fifteen dollars to the man in the green shirt."

Papa's best bull.

Sold.

Mama's prize rooster.

Sold.

Leah's favorite calf.

Sold.

Leah clutched her money in her hand. "It has to be enough," she whispered to herself. "It just has to be."

"Here's one of the best **items** in this entire auction," yelled the man in the big hat. "Who'll start the **bidding** at five hundred dollars for this practically new, all-purpose Farmall tractor? It'll plow, plant, fertilize, and even cultivate for you."

It was time. Leah's voice shook. "One dollar."

The man in the big hat laughed. "That's a low starting bid if I ever heard one," he said. "Now let's hear some serious bids."

No one moved. No one said a word. No one even seemed to breathe.

"Ladies and gentlemen, this tractor is a beauty! I have a bid of only one dollar for it. One dollar for this practically new Farmall tractor! Do I hear any other bids?"

Again no one moved. No one said a word. No one even seemed to breathe.

"This is ridiculous!" the man's voice boomed out from under his hat into the silence. "Sold to the young lady for one dollar."

The crowd cheered. Papa's mouth hung open. Mama cried. Leah proudly walked up and handed one dollar to the auctioneer in the big hat.

"That young lady bought one fine tractor for one very low price," the man continued. "Now how much am I bid for this flock of healthy young chickens?"

"I'll give you ten cents," offered a farmer who lived down the road.

"Ten cents! Ten cents is mighty cheap for a whole flock of chickens," the man said. His face looked angry.

Again no one moved. No one said a word. No one even seemed to breathe.

"Sold for ten cents!"

The farmer picked up the cage filled with chickens and walked over to Mama. "These chickens are yours," he said.

The man pushed his big hat back on his head. "How much for this good Ford pickup truck?" he asked.

"Twenty-five cents," yelled a neighbor from town.

Again no one moved. No one said a word. No one even seemed to breathe.

"Sold for twenty-five cents!" The man in the big hat shook his head. "This isn't supposed to be a penny auction!" he shouted.

The neighbor paid his twenty-five cents and took the keys to the pickup truck. "I think these will start your truck," he whispered as he dropped the keys into Papa's shirt pocket.

Leah watched as friends and neighbors bid a penny for a chicken or a nickel for a cow or a quarter for a plow. One by one, they gave everything back to Mama and Papa.

The crowds left. The sign disappeared. Chickens scratched in their coop, and cattle called for their corn. The farm was quiet. Too quiet. No familiar whinny greeted Leah when she entered the barn. Leah swallowed hard and straightened her back.

That night in Leah's hushed house, no sad voices whispered in the kitchen. Only Leah lay awake, listening to the clock chime nine and even ten times. Leah's heart seemed to copy its slow, sad beat.

Leah

The next morning Leah forced open the heavy barn doors to start her chores. A loud whinny greeted her. Leah ran and hugged the familiar furry neck and kissed the white snip of a nose. "You're back!" she cried. "How did you get here?"

Then Leah saw the note with her name written in big letters:

Dear Leah,

This is the finest pony in the county. But he's a little bit small for me and a little bit big for my grandson.

He fits you much better.

Your friend,

Mr. B.

P.S. I heard how you saved your family's farm. These hard times won't last forever.

And they didn't.

Problem and Solution
What did Leah do to help solve her family's troubles?

TRAVEL BACK IN TIME WITH

ELIZABETH FRIEDRICH AND MICHAEL GARLAND

Elizabeth Friedrich was born in San Francisco, California. As a child, she loved to visit her aunt and uncle's farm in Missouri. *Leah's Pony* is based in part on what she learned there.

Today, Friedrich and her family live on a 150-year-old farm in New Hampshire, where she has a horse and six sheep. When she is not writing or working on her farm, she enjoys collecting antiques, reading, and traveling.

Michael Garland was born and raised in New York City. No stranger to children's books, Garland has both written and illustrated many books for young people. His books include *Dinner at Magritte's*, *Circus Girl*, and *My Cousin Katie*. He lives with his wife and three children in Patterson, New York.

LOG ON FIND OUT

Author Elizabeth Friedrich
Illustrator Michael Garland
www.macmillanmh.com

Another book by Michael Garland

Author's Purpose

Explain the message or theme of *Leah's Pony*. Use details from the story.

LOG ON LEARN IT **Comprehension**
www.macmillanmh.com

Comprehension Check

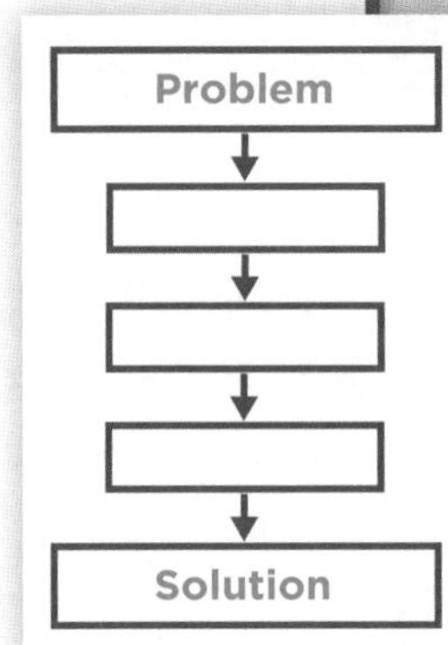

Summarize

To summarize *Leah's Pony* use the most important details in the selection. Your Problem and Solution Chart may help you.

Think and Compare

1. Why do Leah's neighbors go to Oregon? **Details**
2. What happened right before the man in the big hat started the **bidding** for the flock of young chickens? **Sequence**
3. Summarize the problem that Leah's family faced and the events that led to the solution of the problem. **Analyze Story Structure: Problem and Solution**
4. Identify if the narrator of the story is first or third person. How would the story be different if the author had made Leah the narrator? **Author's Purpose**
5. Read "Grandma's Story" on pages 676–677. How are Leah's and Grandma's experiences similar? Use details from both selections in your answer. **Reading/Writing Across Texts**

Social Studies

Genre

Expository selections, such as **textbook excerpts**, present facts and ideas about a topic. They often include text features, such as photographs, primary sources, and maps.

Text Feature

Maps are drawings that show the surface features of an area such as a state or country.

Content Vocabulary

drought
Dust Bowl
Great Depression

SOIL TURNED TO DUST

by Miriam Ramirez

DURING THE 1930s, many states were affected by a **drought**. A drought occurs when little or no rain falls. This drought lasted for so many years that the soil turned to dust.

The map on page 701 shows which states were affected by the drought. This area of the United States became known as the **Dust Bowl**.

Farmers in this area once had plentiful crops. Many had planted larger fields in order to meet the demand for wheat around the world.

Then, during the late 1920s, the rains came less and less often. The soil began to dry up and the wheat died. Strong winds blew the soil away in huge dust storms.

Some farmers borrowed money from banks to help them survive. They had hoped to pay back the banks with money from selling wheat. When there was no wheat to sell, the banks forced the farmers to sell their homes and land. Soon, some of the banks began to have problems and had to close as well.

Many families left the Dust Bowl to find work to support their families and faced great hardships. People all over the country had a hard time finding jobs. This is one reason why those years became known as the **Great Depression**.

The government hired a photographer, Dorothea Lange, to take pictures during this period. One of her photographs is called "Migrant Mother." Lange said that this photo showed a "hungry and desperate mother . . . who had just sold the tires from her car to buy food."

Eventually the rains came back and crops began to grow again. Even so, it took many years for life to return to normal. Most people who lived during those hard times would never forget them.

Dorothea Lange took this photo of a migrant mother in the Dust Bowl.

In April 1935, when he was living in Pampa, Texas, Woody Guthrie wrote this song about a dust storm he saw.

Woody Guthrie

SO LONG, It's Been Good to Know Yuh (Dusty Old Dust)

So long, it's been good to know ye,
So long, it's been good to know ye,
So long, it's been good to know ye,
This dusty old dust is a-getting my home,
And I've got to be drifting along.

A dust storm hit, and it hit like thunder;
It dustedus over and it covered us under;
Blocked out the traffic and blocked out the sun,
Straight for home all the people did run.

Families in the Dust Bowl were often displaced and forced to live in their cars.

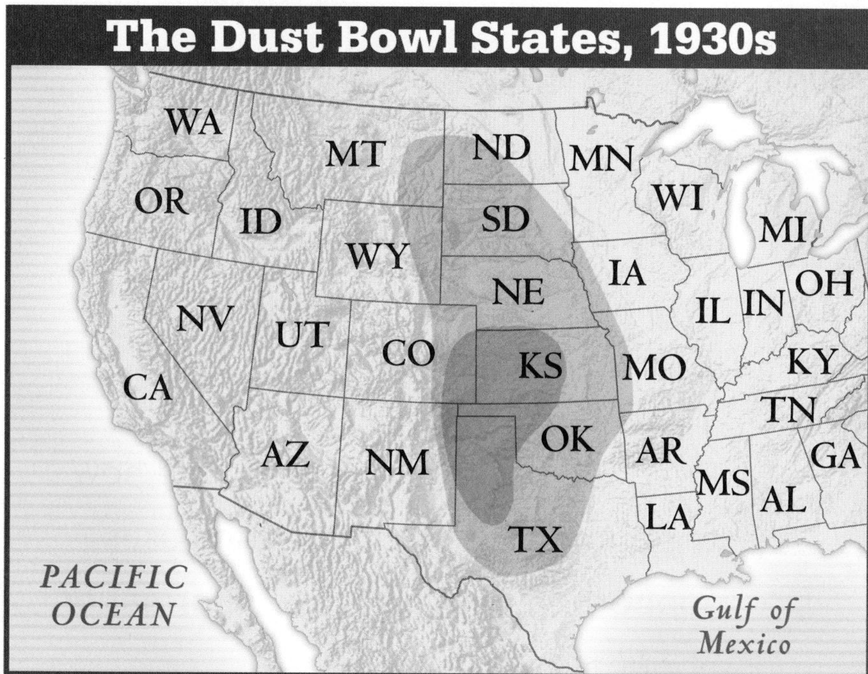

A **Map Key** explains the symbols and color coding used on the map.

▮	Dust Bowl
▯	Other areas damaged by dust storms

Connect and Compare

1. Look at the map on page 701. What states are part of the Dust Bowl? **Reading a Map**
2. How do the photographs, song, and map add to the information presented in the textbook excerpt? **Apply**
3. How does "Soil Turned to Dust" give you a better understanding of the events in *Leah's Pony*? Use details from both texts to explain your answer. **Reading/Writing Across Texts**

Social Studies Activity

Use maps and online references to research the effects of the Dust Bowl in Texas or Kansas. Write a summary of your research and present it to the class.

LOG ON FIND OUT **Social Studies** Dust Bowl **www.macmillanmh.com**

Reading and Writing Connection

Writing

Trait: Ideas

Good writers use **supporting details** to give more information about a topic.

Read the passage below. Notice how the author Elizabeth Friedrich uses supporting details to give information about a topic.

An excerpt from *Leah's Pony*

All week Leah worried and waited and wondered what to do. One morning she watched as a man in a big hat hammered a sign into the ground in front of her house.

Leah wanted to run away. She raced her pony past empty fields lined with dry gullies. She galloped past a house with rags stuffed in broken windowpanes. She sped right past Mr. B. sweeping the steps outside his store.

At last Leah knew what she had to do. She turned her pony around and rode back into town. She stopped in front of Mr. B.'s store. "You can buy my pony," she said.

The author uses supporting details to show what Leah does when she wants to run away. She also uses supporting details to show what Leah decides to do.

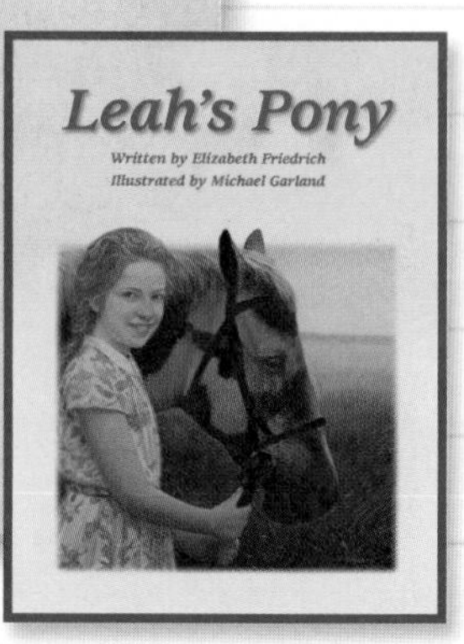

Read and Find

Read Kyle's writing below. How does he use supporting details to show the difference between a pony and a horse? Use the checklist below to help you.

My Pony

by Kyle Y.

Some people think my pony is a horse, but ponies are different from horses. First of all, my pony is smaller than a horse. It has a thicker mane and a thicker tail. My pony has shorter legs than a horse does, too. It also has a smaller head.

If you already know a lot about ponies, you would know right away that my pony is not a horse. If you did not know a lot about ponies, now you do and will be able to tell the difference between a pony and a horse!

Read about Kyle's pony.

Writer's Checklist

- ☑ Does the writing have a topic?
- ☑ Does the author write **supporting details** that tell about the topic?
- ☐ Do all the details support the topic?

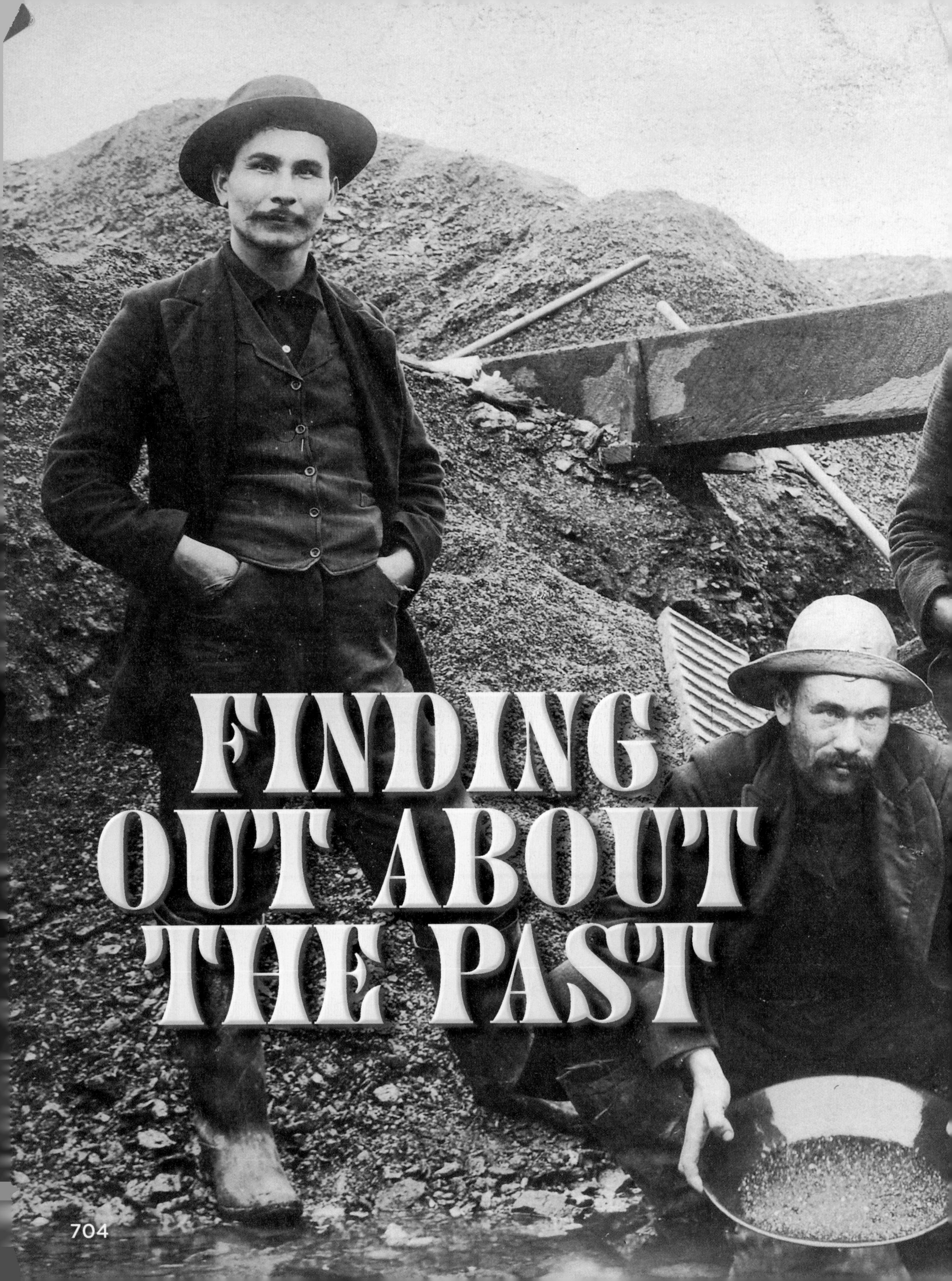

FINDING OUT ABOUT THE PAST

Talk About It

What do you think it would have been like to take part in a gold rush?

LOG ON VIEW IT

Oral Language Activities
Finding Out About the Past
www.macmillanmh.com

Vocabulary

reference **conducted**
disappointment **annoyed**
circular **outstretched**

Suffixes

Suffixes are word parts added to the ends of words to change their meaning. The Latin suffix *-ar* = resembling
circular = resembling a circle

In Search of Gold

by Al Ortiz

Mr. Rodriguez's fourth-grade class was on a field trip at the Sutter Gold Mine. Larry couldn't wait to load up on gold. He even brought along some photos of gold nuggets to use as a **reference**. He didn't want to pick up "fool's gold" by mistake.

Larry's class boarded the Boss Buggy Shuttle that would take them down into the mine. Everyone had to wear a hard hat for safety. On the ride down, their guide, Ron, gave them some information about the Gold Rush.

"Many prospectors came to this area beginning in 1848," explained Ron. "A prospector is someone who searches for valuable metals like gold."

Margaret commented, "Everyone must have gotten rich!"

"Actually," said Ron, "not everyone was successful. Many left the mines filled with regret and **disappointment**. People often turned to farming or ranching to make a living instead."

The underground tour lasted about an hour. Then it was time to go to the mining flumes and pan for gold. Ron handed out pans and demonstrated how to swirl them around in a **circular** motion.

"It's okay to let some of the water splash out," said Ron. "If there's any gold in your pan, it will sink to the bottom."

Larry found an open place at one of the flumes. With his arm **outstretched**, he dipped his pan below the surface of the water. Then he swished around the water. "Nothing," he said with a sigh.

Larry **conducted** the same search several times. He was beginning to get **annoyed**. Then, he noticed something at the bottom of his pan. Larry angled the pan so he could get a better look. Whatever it was, it glinted in the sunlight. Larry pulled out the photos and compared them with what was in his pan. Then he went to show Ron.

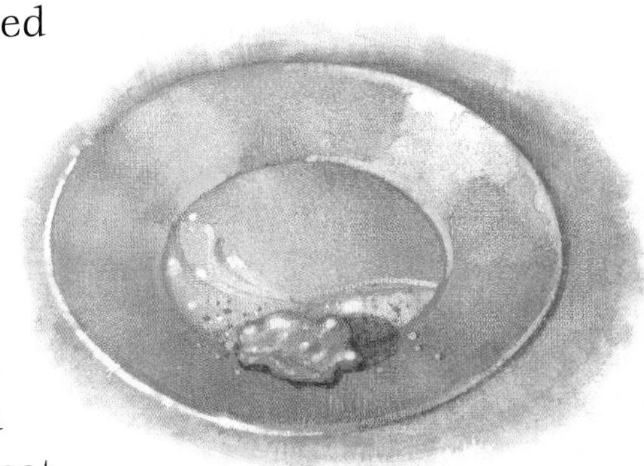

"You've found gold!" Ron exclaimed in surprise.

Everyone gathered around to see. It was just a small piece, but Larry felt like he had hit the jackpot.

Reread for Comprehension

Analyze Story Structure

Cause and Effect A cause is an event or action that causes or makes something happen. An effect is what happens because of an event or action. Identifying them can help you understand how an author has organized these events. A Cause and Effect Chart can help you to sequence cause and effect relationships, and identify how these events influence future events in the plot. Reread the selection and fill in your Cause and Effect Chart to figure out what happens and why.

Cause → Effect
→
→
→
→

LOG ON LEARN IT Comprehension www.macmillanmh.com

Comprehension

Genre

Science Fiction is a story that includes fictional events based on actual or invented scientific or technological discoveries.

Analyze Story Structure

Cause and Effect

As you read, fill in your Cause and Effect Chart.

Cause → Effect
→
→
→
→

Read to Find Out

How did Eric and Matt affect the future by going back into the past?

The Gold Rush Game

by William F. Wu

illustrated by Cornelius Van Wright and Ying-Hwa Hu

Eric Wong looked at his new game on the computer screen. "Let's play." He clicked the button to start.

"The Gold Rush," his friend Matt O'Brien read out loud, as he rolled his chair closer. "What's that mean? I want to see it! Come on, I'm going first."

"I'm older," said Eric. "Besides, it's my game."

"Be nice." Eric's mom came up behind them. "We bought the game so Eric could learn more about the Gold Rush," she said to Matt. "His dad and I are tracing our family tree. Eric's great-great-great grandfather on his dad's side came to California from China during the Gold Rush, but we don't know much about him."

"Hey, look at the game," said Eric. On the screen, he saw steep, mountain slopes covered with tall, green trees. Some men wearing broad-brimmed hats rode horses along a muddy path, leading mules with bundles on their backs. Picks and shovels were tied to the bundles. Chinese men, with long, braided queues down their backs, squatted by a rushing river.

"Who are those guys?" Matt asked. "Are they looking for gold?"

"They might be," said Eric's dad as he came into the room. He held out a small piece of paper with two Chinese characters written on it. "This is the name of our ancestor who first came to California. I don't know Chinese, but my grandfather wrote it down for me when I was growing up."

Eric turned and looked. "What was his name?"

"Daido," his dad said. "I'll say it slower, 'Dye-doe.' It means 'Great Path.' That's a good name for a man who took a great adventure traveling across the Pacific Ocean to a new land. In Chinese, his family name would be given first. And so, he was called Wong Daido."

"Wong Daido," Eric repeated. "Yeah."

"Do you know how to write that?" Matt asked, looking at the name.

"No." Eric shrugged.

"We'll let you play your game," said Eric's mom. "Come on, dear." She and Eric's dad walked away.

"Look." Eric pointed to the screen. A miner wearing a broad-brimmed gray hat lifted a rock showing a button that said, "Press if you dare."

"I dare you," Matt said loudly.

"I'm doing it." **Annoyed**, Eric pressed the button.

Suddenly Eric and Matt found themselves standing in a narrow space between two large, tall rocks by the muddy road in the mountains, with trees towering over their heads. Miners and prospectors walked and rode past. Eric's heart beat faster with excitement, but he was also a little scared.

"What happened?" Matt asked. "This is creepy. Where are we?"

Eric smelled the scent of pine trees and kicked at the mud. "I think we're really in the Gold Rush. We went back in time!"

"Did you say, back in time?" Matt stared around them in shock.

"Come on." Eric walked up to the mysterious miner who had lifted the rock. "Do you know a man named Wong Daido?" Eric carefully pronounced his ancestor's name, remembering to put his family name first.

The miner laughed. Then he looked closely at Eric and Matt. "You're not from around here are you?"

"No, we're not," said Eric hoping the man wouldn't ask any more questions.

"Do you know how many people are in this area? We're on the Feather River upstream from Marysville, in the western foothills of the Sierra Nevada in California. Men came to find gold. We're called the Forty-niners because so many of us have come this year."

"What year?" Matt asked, his eyes wide.

"1849, of course," said the miner. He frowned. "Don't you boys know what year it is? Gold was discovered in this area last year. Now, Forty-niners are coming from all over America and lots of other places."

Cause and Effect
Why did Eric and Matt find themselves back in 1849?

"How do they get here?" Eric asked.

"I came overland from the eastern United States by wagon train. A good friend of mine took a ship from the east coast south around Cape Horn at the tip of South America. From China, other men come on ships across the Pacific Ocean."

"But where do they live?" Eric asked. "I don't see any houses here."

"Marysville is a new town," said the miner. "It was started by miners and prospectors. But men also live in camps, sometimes together and sometimes on their own, while they look for gold." He pointed to the river. "But the best way to find a Chinese miner is to ask other Chinese miners."

Matt ran down to the edge of the river, where a Chinese miner squatted by the rushing water, swirling sand in a metal pan.

Eric hurried after him. "Hey, mister, is your name Wong Daido?"

"No." The man shook his head. Then he gave Eric a little smile and pointed downstream. "You see that man? His name is Wong."

Matt ran down the bank, but this time Eric ran, too. They stopped next to Mr. Wong together, near a big tree growing right beside the river.

"Are you named Wong Daido?" Eric asked.

Mr. Wong was a little younger than the other Chinese miner. His long, braided queue swung behind him as he looked up. "I am," he said, giving both boys a big smile. "Why do you ask?"

Eric was afraid to explain he and Matt had traveled through time from the future. He was sure Mr. Wong wouldn't believe him and might chase them away, so he changed the subject. "My name's Eric, and this is my friend Matt. Have you found any gold?"

"Not today. Some days I find enough gold to buy food that will last until the next time I find gold. I filed this claim so I have the right to pan gold here. The river washes gold dust downstream, so I catch river water, mud, and sand in this pan and try to find it." He moved the pan in a **circular** motion, so that water sloshed out with some of the sand. "Gold is heavy, so it stays in the pan."

"Wow," said Matt. "And the river's so fast."

"Don't you have to get sand from the bottom of the river?" Eric asked. "It looks really deep right here!"

"It's very deep here," said Mr. Wong. "The riverbank drops steeply from the edge of the water and the current's very fast. But I can take the sand and mud right here at the edge and pan it. And the water itself carries sand, even when it looks clear. On a good day, the water brings gold to me."

Suddenly the ground shook. Eric and Matt thumped backward into a sitting position in the mud. Mr. Wong fell into the river with a splash.

"It's an earthquake!" Eric jumped up again. He had felt small earthquakes before, and this one was so quick it had ended already. When he looked up, he saw Mr. Wong in the river, desperately holding onto a tree root with both hands. The power of the river current pulled his legs downstream and he struggled to hold his head above the water. "Help me!"

Eric and Matt grabbed his arms and pulled, but the river current was too strong and Mr. Wong was too heavy for them to help.

"We have to save him," Eric called desperately to Matt. "If we don't, my family won't ever be born. And I won't be here!"

Eric saw a tree branch hanging low. "Come on! Help me pull the branch down!" He took the branch in both hands and bent his knees so his weight pulled it down. When Matt grabbed it, too, the branch lowered to Mr. Wong.

With an **outstretched** hand Mr. Wong grasped the branch.

"Matt, let go!" Eric and Matt released the branch and the branch slowly moved upward again, pulling Mr. Wong out of the water. He got his feet back on the river bank and let go of the branch. Mr. Wong took several moments to catch his breath. His clothes were so wet they stuck to him. "Aiee! You two saved my life. Thank you."

Cause and Effect
What effect did saving Mr. Wong's life have on the future?

"Mine too," said Eric. "You're welcome."

"I thought I was going to drown. Everything I have dreamed about would have come to an end." He paused and looked down at the ground. "I came from a poor peasant village in southern China," Mr. Wong went on. "I hope to find some gold and send for a woman I love. We'll marry here and raise a family in America—at least, I hope so."

"Hey, that's good," said Matt. "Because—"

Eric jabbed Matt with his elbow and interrupted, ". . . because it's a good idea." He smiled, knowing that Mr. Wong's dream was going to come true.

"I don't have much to offer in return for my life," said Mr. Wong. He reached into his pocket and pulled something out. "This is my chop."

Eric and Matt looked. It was a small piece of ivory, with unfamiliar shapes carved on the bottom. "What's it for?" Eric asked.

"I'll show you." Mr. Wong pushed the bottom into a smooth spot of mud next to the river. When he lifted it, three marks were in the mud. "That's my name, Wong Daido. I don't have any gold today. But I would like you to accept this as my gift. I will always remember you."

Eric took the chop. "That's very nice of you. Thanks."

"I should return to my camp and dry off," said Mr. Wong.

"I think we better go home, too," said Eric. "We enjoyed meeting you!" He carefully put the chop in his pants pocket.

"Thank you again for your help," said Mr. Wong. "Goodbye." He picked up his pan and walked away from the river toward the muddy road.

"How do we get back to our time?" asked Matt. "Maybe we should try to find those big rocks. But where are they?"

"Come on," Eric said to Matt. "I remember where they are. Maybe we'll find some kind of clue there that will help us get back." He led Matt back into the space between the two big rocks where they had walked out. Suddenly they were back in Eric's living room in front of the computer.

"Wow! It worked. Those rocks must be some kind of doorway into the past." Matt looked at the computer screen. "That's a great game!"

"Who's winning?" Eric's mom asked, as she and his dad came in.

"Mom! Dad!" Eric called out. "We went into the game and back in time!"

"Yeah," said Matt. "We met Eric's great-great-great grandfather!"

Eric's mom and dad laughed.

"I love the way these games build imagination while they teach history," said Eric's mom. "Isn't that nice?"

"Dad! He told us he filed a claim for his mine along the Feather River!"

"Well, I know from what I read in my grandfather's journal that Daido did file a claim. Let's see if we can find out if it was along the Feather River." Eric's dad moved to the computer and **conducted** an Internet search. After a while he looked up in surprise. "Wong Daido did file a claim in that area in 1849. I found a **reference** to it."

"Do you believe me now?" Eric asked.

"C'mon, Eric. Do you expect me to believe you actually went back in time?"

"No, I guess not." Eric felt a wave of **disappointment**, then suddenly reached into his pocket. "Maybe this will convince you!" He pulled out the chop. "Dad! Look at the name: Wong Daido." Smiling, Eric held it up.

On the chop, a little bit of gold dust from the river glinted in the light.

File a Claim with William, Cornelius, and Ying-Hwa

William F. Wu has liked history since he was a boy. During recess at school, he and his friend acted out famous historical events. William also enjoyed writing stories and poems. He first thought about becoming a writer when he was eight years old.

Cornelius Van Wright and **Ying-Hwa Hu** are a husband and wife team who have been illustrating books for over 15 years. Cornelius studied art in New York City, while Ying developed her art skills in Taiwan and Minnesota. With such different backgrounds, the two try to combine their different cultures into each illustration for this story.

LOG ON FIND OUT

Author William F. Wu
Illustrators Cornelius Van Wright and Ying-Hwa Hu
www.macmillanmh.com

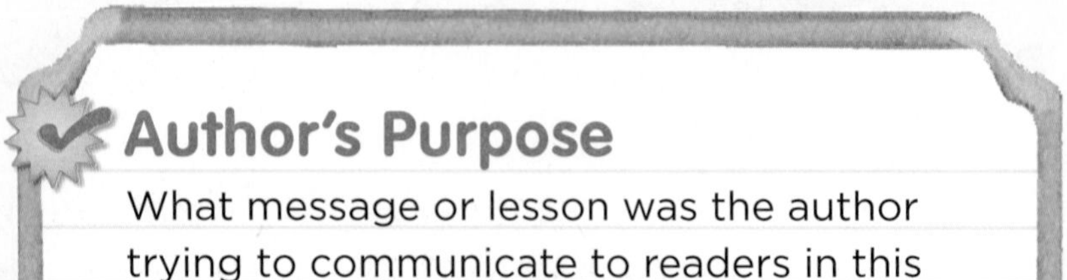

Author's Purpose

What message or lesson was the author trying to communicate to readers in this story? Use evidence and details from the story to support your answer.

LOG ON LEARN IT **Comprehension**
www.macmillanmh.com

Comprehension Check

Summarize

To summarize *The Gold Rush Game* use the most important details from the story. Information from your Cause and Effect Chart may help you.

Cause → Effect
→
→
→
→

Think and Compare

1. What gift did Mr. Wong give to Eric and Matt? **Details**
2. Why did Eric press the button in the computer game? **Analyze Story Structure: Cause and Effect**
3. Summarize the main events in the plot that happen after Mr. Wong fell into the river. **Summarize**
4. Why did the author have Mr. Wong give Eric and Matt his chop? How did this action influence the events at the end of the story? **Author's Purpose**
5. Read "In Search of Gold" on pages 706–707. How is Larry's experience similar to that of the prospectors in *The Gold Rush Game*? How is it different? Use details from both selections to explain. **Reading/Writing Across Texts**

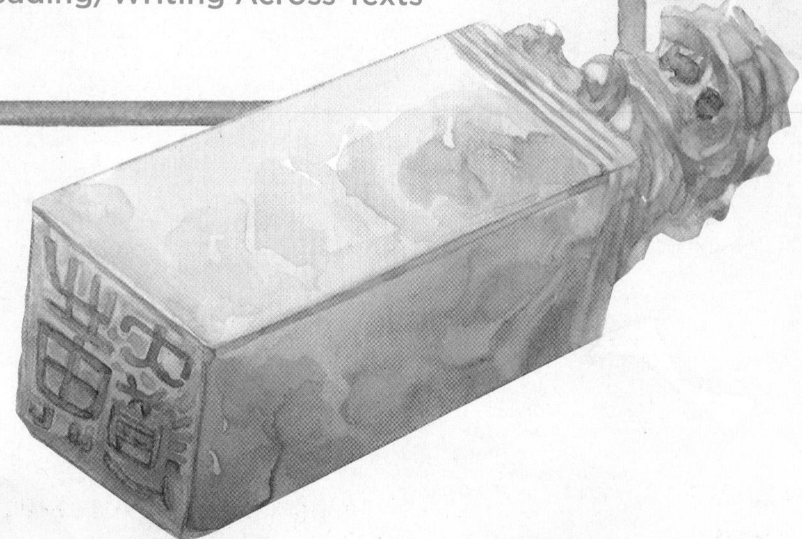

Science

Genre

Expository selections, such as magazine articles, present information, facts, photos, and graphic aids to explain a topic.

Text Feature

Time Lines show historical events in the order in which they occurred.

Content Vocabulary

properties **carat**
alloy

GOLD

by Jan Jensen

People have almost always put a high price on gold. Gold is a valuable mineral that is thinly spread throughout the Earth. People have searched for gold for thousands of years. Even in myths and fairy tales, people are obsessed with gold. Just ask King Midas or Rumpelstiltskin!

Important Properties

The physical **properties**, or qualities, of gold make it a fairly useful metal. Gold is soft and malleable, which means that it can be bent or flattened and worked into different shapes. It also conducts heat and electrical current, making it useful in modern technology. Gold is a very dense mineral. This means that gold is heavy for its size. You can usually tell an object is made of pure gold because of how heavy it is.

"Panning" for gold involves dipping a pan in a river, collecting water, and swishing it around to see if there are any gold pieces.

Gold can be measured using different types of instruments. This gold is being measured using a scale.

A Rare Metal

Perhaps gold's most important property is its rarity. There just isn't much of it around, which is why it is so valuable. Kings and other leaders would often keep most of the gold for themselves. Some of them also believed that gold had magical properties. When they wore crowns and necklaces made of gold, they certainly drew attention wherever they went!

Using Gold

Today, gold is most commonly used as part of an alloy. This means that it is mixed with other metals to make a little bit go a long way. This process can also change the properties of the gold. When mixed with silver or copper, the gold becomes harder. This makes it less likely to get scratched or dented.

GOLDEN FACTS

- If you filled a two-liter bottle with gold, it would weigh over 85 pounds!
- One ounce of gold can be stretched into a thin wire that from end to end would cover 50 miles.

The word *gold* comes from an Old English word, *gelo*, which means *yellow*.

This gold bracelet is 24 carats. It was made in the 1800s in India.

How Many Carats

A carat is a unit of measurement that tells how much actual gold is in an alloy. Pure gold is 24 carats. If you buy a ring that is 12 carat gold, half of it might be another metal, such as nickel or platinum. If something is described as gold-plated, there is only a thin layer of gold on the outside. The rest of the item might be made of a heavy metal such as lead to give it the weight and heft of gold.

Golden Moments in History

Reading a Time Line

This time line shows some important events in the history of gold.

4000 B.C. Gold is first used in parts of Central and Eastern Europe.

3000 B.C. The Egyptians begin mixing gold with metals.

1492 Christopher Columbus comes to the Americas searching for gold.

1849 People rush from all parts of the world to California to search for gold.

1091 B.C. Squares of gold become the legal form of money in China.

Around 250 B.C. Ancient Greek scientist Archimedes creates displacement of water method to measure volume of gold.

1900 The United States adopts the gold standard for its currency.

Rich Prospects

Even today, some people hope to "strike it rich" by finding gold. Though it exists as a hot fluid deep inside the Earth, it most often appears on the surface as flakes or small nuggets in streams and rivers. Because of its weight, gold can be separated from other rocks and minerals using a simple pan. Water washes away the lighter elements, leaving gold behind.

It may take a long time to find a little bit of gold, but with the price of gold still high around the world, it can be well worth the effort!

Gold bars back up the world's currency.

Connect and Compare

1. Look at the time line. What is the next event after the Egyptians began mixing gold with metals? **Using a Time Line**
2. What properties does gold have that makes it useful? **Apply**
3. Think about the setting of *The Gold Rush Game*. From what you have read in this article, why did the boys find Wong Daido near a river? **Reading/Writing Across Texts**

RESEARCH INQUIRY

Science Activity

Choose another metal, such as silver or copper, and use reference sources to research its history. Write a brief report about the metal and include a time line.

LOG ON FIND OUT **Science** Gold
www.macmillanmh.com

Writing

Trait: Ideas

Good writers choose details that support their **main idea**.

Reading and Writing Connection

Read the passage below. Notice how the author Jan Jensen uses details that support a main idea.

An excerpt from *Gold*

The author writes a paragraph about the qualities of gold. The supporting details give information about the main idea.

The physical properties, or qualities, of gold make it a fairly useful metal. Gold is soft and malleable, which means that it can be bent or flattened and worked into different shapes. It also conducts heat and electrical current, making it useful in modern technology. Gold is a very dense mineral. This means that gold is heavy for its size. You can usually tell an object is made of pure gold because of how heavy it is.

Read and Find

Read Eva's writing below. How does she use a main idea and supporting details? Use the checklist below to help you.

Rivers

by Eva C.

Throughout history, people have used rivers in many ways. People get water and food from rivers. They use rivers to travel from one place to another. Loggers float logs down rivers. Many people use rivers for recreation. They kayak, canoe, and fish in rivers. In the 1800s, people looked for gold in rivers like the Feather River in California.

Read about how people use rivers.

Writer's Checklist

- ☑ Does the writing have a main idea?
- ☑ Does the author include details that give information about the main idea?
- ☐ Do all the details support the **main idea**?

Talk About It

How can solving problems in your community improve the lives of others?

LOG ON VIEW IT

Oral Language Activities
Improving Lives
www.macmillanmh.com

Improving Lives

Real World Reading

Vocabulary

decades
transform
active
violated
volunteer

A Fight Against Injustice

Like other immigrant groups, Mexican Americans have faced difficulties in the United States. They have fought hard to overcome prejudice.

From the 1800s through the middle of the 1900s, Mexican Americans were not allowed to vote if they did not understand English. Latinos who knew English had to pay to vote. Finding work was tough because few people would hire Latinos. Like African Americans, they also faced segregation. Latinos weren't allowed in "white-only" public places. Latino children had to go to "Mexican schools."

In 1929, Latino leaders and workers joined together to solve these problems. They formed a group called League of United Latin American Citizens (LULAC). In its first year, LULAC helped desegregate public places in Texas. In 1947, LULAC ended school segregation in California. The organization also worked to make schools better. In the **decades** that followed, LULAC fought for equal rights for Latinos.

Today, the group continues its work. The creation of a LULAC National Youth Group shows that young Latinos are also **active** in this fight for equality.

A Place to Heal

How do you help kids who have lived through wars? One solution is to send them to camp!

The camp is run by the Global Children's Organization (GCO). GCO was started by Judith Jenya in 1993. She wanted to give hope to young war victims. She created camps in Northern Ireland and the Balkans. Jenya says that kids need "air, water, and hope."

"It's impossible to comprehend the horrors these children have lived through," says **volunteer** Carol Tanenbaum. "But it's so amazing to see how quickly some of them **transform**. They're kids again."

Volunteers Carol and Fred Tanenbaum are surrounded by happy campers. ▼

Summer Camp Solution

Camp counselors at Global Children's Organization (GCO) have a tough job. They help child victims of war do typical camp activities, such as swimming, dancing, and singing. Teaching kids to swim is easy. Trying to fix their personal problems is hard.

Jesse Bernstein is a volunteer. She saw that war had **violated** the kids' feelings of trust and security. A few campers even had trouble sleeping. "We'd have to stay with them until they had fallen asleep," she says.

Volunteers like Jesse help campers with their fears. They also show kids that problems can be solved peacefully, as a team.

Kids enjoy swimming at a Global Children's Organization camp. It is located on an island in Croatia.

Comprehension

Genre

Expository text, such as a magazine article, presents facts and information.

Generate Questions

Fact and Opinion

A fact is something that can be proven true using reference sources. An opinion is a belief that does not have to be supported by facts.

Taking the Lead

How did Dolores Huerta help solve the problems faced by farmworkers?

Dolores Huerta is an important leader in the Latino community. She has spent the last few **decades** helping farmworkers. After college, Huerta became a teacher. Many of her students' parents worked on farms. Their children often came to school hungry. Huerta realized that these families needed help.

"I couldn't stand seeing farmworker children come to class hungry and in need of shoes," Huerta has said. "I thought I could do more by organizing their parents than by trying to teach their hungry children."

▼ Dolores Huerta and supporters celebrate the birthday of César Chávez in Los Angeles in 2006.

▲Dolores Huerta during a grape pickers' strike

Law and Order

Huerta believed she could be of great service to her community. She became **active** in 1955, when she helped to form the Community Service Organization (CSO). The CSO helped Latinos and farmworkers in California. Huerta listened to the problems farmworkers faced and fought hard to fix them.

While working with the CSO, Huerta tried to make laws fair for farm laborers. One problem she faced was that many farmworkers couldn't read or understand English. Huerta pushed for a law to allow people to vote in Spanish. She also supported a law to let Californians take their driver's license exam in their native language. Without these laws, Huerta argued, people's rights would be **violated**.

Doing More

At the CSO, Huerta worked with another powerful organizer, César Chávez. He also fought for the rights of farmworkers. In 1962, the two began another labor group called the National Farm Workers Association. The group's goal was to organize farmworkers.

Over the years, Huerta and Chávez have helped **transform** the lives of farmworkers. Together, they worked to get higher wages for farm laborers. Huerta organized meetings between large farming companies and workers. She helped save the farmworkers' jobs when they were about to lose them. She stood up for their rights and quickly became a leader and hero to many.

Dolores Huerta and César Chávez meet during a strike by grape pickers.▼

Huerta and Chávez saw a need to do more for others, so they formed the National Farm Workers Service Center. They found that many workers did not have houses. To help solve this problem, the Center built 4,200 homes and apartments for working families. The dwellings are priced so that farmworkers and Latino families can afford to live there. People in Texas, Arizona, New Mexico, and California are helped by these lower-cost homes.

Family First

Families are important to Dolores Huerta. She is the mother of 11 children, and she has 20 grandchildren and five great-grandchildren. She has won many awards for her **volunteer** efforts. Her work isn't easy, but even in her 70s, she continues to fight for equal rights for poor and working families. She shows no signs of slowing down.

Today, she is the president of the Dolores Huerta Foundation. She often travels around the country to give speeches and to teach future leaders. Crowds of people gather to hear Huerta talk about issues that affect immigrants, families, and workers.

"No matter how poor you are," Huerta has said, "no matter if you lack a formal education, we can do things, we can change things. The secret is taking responsibility."

▲ Dolores Huerta still draws crowds. Here she speaks at a rally in Los Angeles.

TIME FOR KIDS

Think and Compare

1. Who formed the National Farm Workers Service Center?
2. Identify a fact from the article. How would you verify, or check the fact?
3. Summarize the main idea and supporting details in this article.
4. How is the organization LULAC in "A Fight Against Injustice" similar to the Community Service Organization?

Famous Women

Dolores Huerta joined the National Women's Hall of Fame in 1993. Read about some of the other women who have also made a big difference in the world.

Hermine Dalkowitz Tobolowski worked hard for equal rights. She was given the nickname "Mother of the Texas Equal Rights Amendment" after she helped pass an equal rights amendment to the Texas constitution.

Virginia Apgar developed a test called the Apgar Score in 1952. This test lets doctors know whether a newborn baby needs special help to stay alive. The Apgar Score has saved the lives of countless infants.

Patricia Locke worked to preserve the languages and spiritual traditions of Native Americans. She helped start Native American-run colleges and helped guarantee Native Americans the right to practice their traditions.

Building a Better GADGET

Test Practice

Answering Questions

Right There answers are found in one place in the text.
Think and Search answers are found in more than one place.
Author and Me answers ask the reader to look for clues.

Keagan Bolibol won $25,000 for her invention. ▶

1 For every problem, there is a solution. That could be why more and more invention contests keep popping up. The contests offer big prizes to people who can invent clever gadgets that make life easier.

2 Many contests give inventors a specific problem to solve. One contest challenges people to create a new office product. Another contest asks entrants to come up with an invention for pets. Even the U.S. government holds invention contests. A Department of Defense competition is looking for inventions that will lighten the equipment load soldiers carry.

There are even invention contests 3
for kids. One contest asks students to invent something to make school life easier. Keagan Bolibol, 10, from Woodinville, Washington, saw her homework was getting sloppy, so she invented the Problem Pad. This dry-erase page lets kids work out homework problems without messing up a notebook. She won $25,000 for her solution!

Students at Adobe Bluffs 4
Elementary School in San Diego came up with a new way to put out fires. Their solution uses chemicals, so it doesn't cause water damage. Thomas Edison would have been proud of all these young inventors!

Use "Building a Better Gadget" to answer questions 1–4.

1 Keagan Bolibol invented —

- **A** a new office product
- **B** the Problem Pad
- **C** a chemical solution
- **D** a pet gadget

2 Which of the following is a fact?

- **F** The U.S. government should not have invention contests.
- **G** Thomas Edison would have been proud.
- **H** One student won $25,000 for her invention.
- **J** Students at Adobe Bluffs Elementary School are creative.

3 Paragraph 2 is mainly about —

- **A** invention contests that ask inventors to solve a specific problem
- **B** inventors who want to make more money from their inventions
- **C** the U.S. government wanting to find jobs for inventors
- **D** students who want to find ways to make school life easier

4 Which is the best summary of the selection?

- **F** There are invention contests for kids. Keagan Bolibol won a large prize for her invention. Kids at an elementary school in San Diego invented something that puts out fires. Thomas Edison would have been proud of these kids.
- **G** The U.S. government wants people to make inventions that help soldiers. They have an invention contest. They don't want soldiers to have to carry so much heavy equipment. Another contest helps pets.
- **H** Keagan Bolibol won $25,000 for her invention. There are lots of different kinds of invention contests. Some people win big prizes like Keagan. One contest wants people to invent office products.
- **J** There are many different invention contests. Some contests ask people to solve a specific problem, such as creating an invention for pets. There are also contests for kids. One girl won $25,000 for her invention.

Write to a Prompt

Write a composition about a person that you think is interesting.

Think about the purpose of your composition.

As you write, think about what makes an effective sentence.

Below, see how one student begins a response to the prompt above.

The writer used specific details to support her opinion.

Dolores Huerta has worked hard to get equal rights for all people. Without her, life would be very different for many people today, especially children.

As the author says in "Taking the Lead," Huerta worried about farmworker children who came to school hungry and without shoes. Instead of trying to teach them, she worked for the rights of their parents. She knew that if their parents earned equal pay in the fields and could vote on important issues, their children would have better lives and more opportunities.

Writing Prompt

Respond in writing to the prompt below. Review the hints below before and after you write.

Write a composition about a person who made a difference to your family or your community.

Writing Hints

- ☑ Remember to write about a person who made a difference. Think about genre.
- ☑ Plan your writing by organizing your ideas.
- ☑ Include important details to support your ideas.
- ☑ Check that each sentence you write helps the reader to understand your ideas.
- ☑ Review and edit your writing.
- ☑ Use correct spelling, grammar, and punctuation.

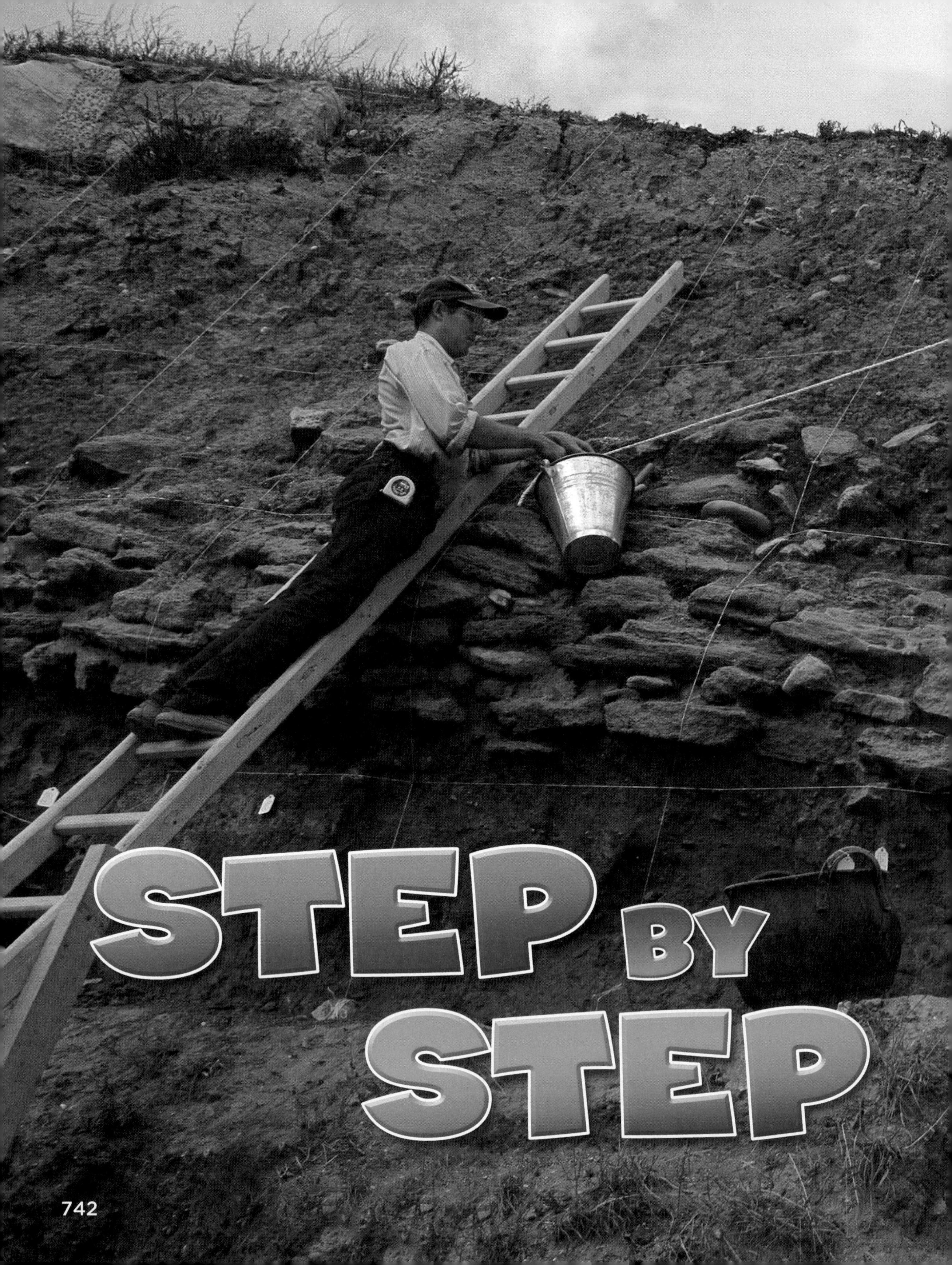

STEP BY STEP

Talk About It

What steps are these scientists taking to find a solution?

LOG ON VIEW IT

Oral Language Activities
Step by Step
www.macmillanmh.com

Vocabulary

technique **inspire**
foolishness **evaporate**
annual **magnify**

Dictionary

Multiple-Meaning Words are words that have more than one meaning. Use context clues to figure out the meaning of *annual*. Then use a dictionary to find its other meanings.

Let It Snow

by Cynthia Robey

Do you have a method or **technique** for catching snowflakes? Some people run in circles trying to catch them. Others stand perfectly still with their tongue sticking out. It might look like **foolishness**, but it's a fun, **annual** activity!

Crystals to Flakes

A snowflake's shape is formed long before it lands on Earth. First an ice crystal forms around a tiny piece of dirt in a cloud. Now it's a snow crystal. The crystal's shape depends on the temperature of the cloud.

Finally, as the crystals fall from the clouds, they stick together to form snowflakes. Each snowflake is made up of 2 to 200 separate snow crystals.

Studying Snowflakes

Snow crystals form into one of seven shapes. You probably know the stellar crystal best. These star-shape crystals are not the most common, but they're the kind that **inspire** the work of most artists.

How can you study snowflakes before they **evaporate** and disappear? First, go outside when it's not windy and about 25°F. Second, bring a piece of dark cloth with you. This will make it easier to see the crystals. Finally, you will need to use a microscope that will **magnify** and enlarge the crystal so that you can get a good look at it.

Wilson "Snowflake" Bentley learned how to make the crystals show up in photographs. He cut away the dark parts of the negatives to make them visible.

Dangerous Snowflakes

If conditions are just right, beautiful snowflakes can turn into a dangerous storm called a blizzard. In blizzards, strong winds can blow the snow around. This causes "whiteout" conditions, making it very difficult to see where you are going.

Always pay attention to the weather. That way you can safely catch and study all the snowflakes you want.

Reread for Comprehension

Generate Questions

Draw Conclusions When you draw conclusions, you think about two or more facts or details an author presents. You add to this your own experience that is connected to this information to arrive at a new understanding about a text or story. Generating questions as you read can help you to draw conclusions, and identify the devices authors use to present information. Reread the selection and use your Conclusions Chart to help you understand how snowflakes are formed.

Text Clues	Conclusion

LOG ON LEARN IT **Comprehension** www.macmillanmh.com

Comprehension

Genre

A **Biography** is a story about the life of a real person written by someone else.

Generate Questions

Draw Conclusions

As you read, fill in your Conclusions Chart.

Text Clues	Conclusion

Read to Find Out

What did Snowflake Bentley give to the world?

SNOWFLAKE BENTLEY

By Jacqueline Briggs Martin
Illustrated by Mary Azarian

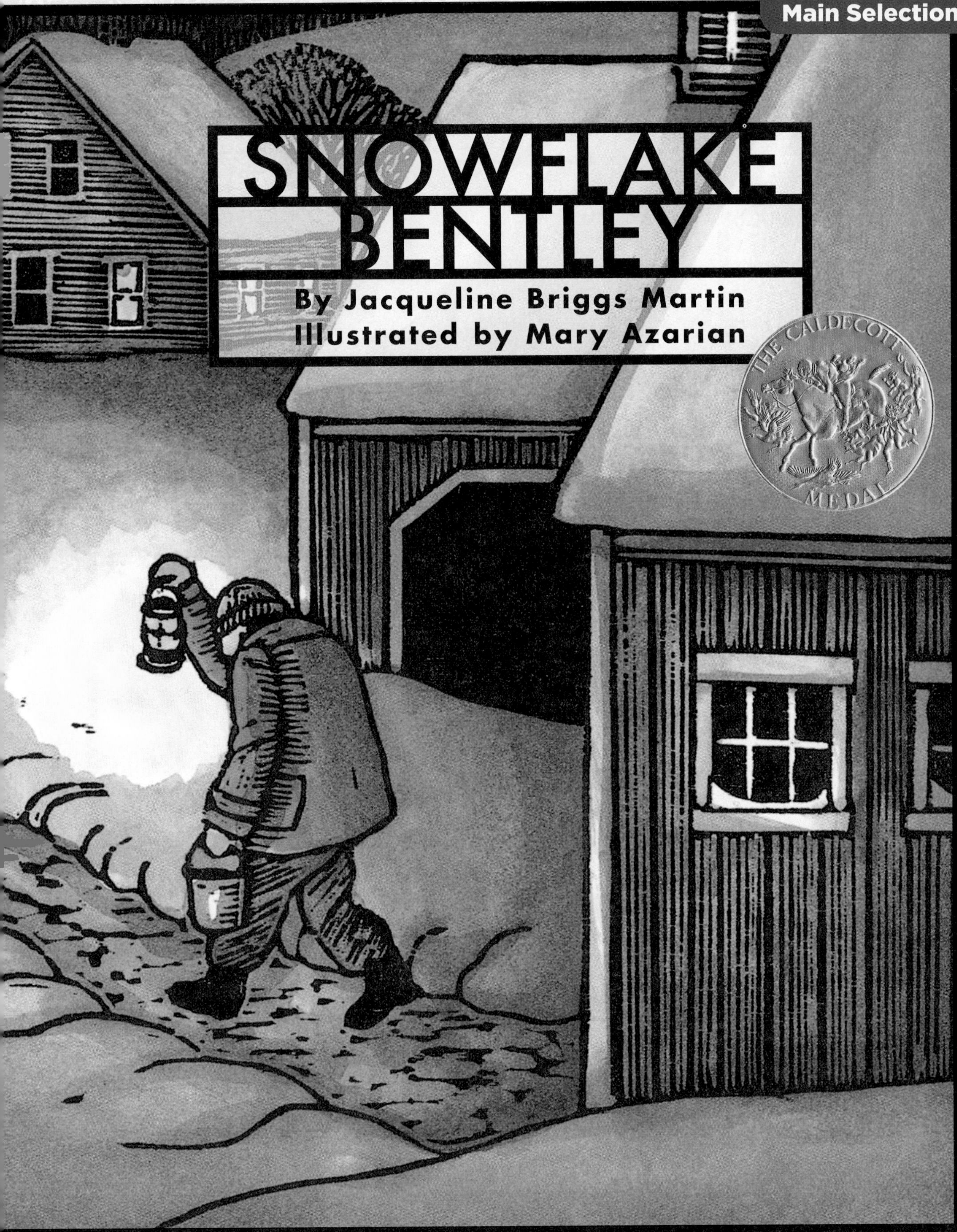

Wilson Bentley was born February 9, 1865, on a farm in Jericho, Vermont, between Lake Champlain and Mount Mansfield, in the heart of the "snowbelt," where the **annual** snowfall is about 120 inches.

In the days when farmers worked with ox and sled and cut the dark with lantern light, there lived a boy who loved snow more than anything else in the world.

Willie Bentley's happiest days were snowstorm days. He watched snowflakes fall on his mittens, on the dried grass of Vermont farm fields, on the dark metal handle of the barn door. He said snow was as beautiful as butterflies, or apple blossoms.

Willie's mother was his teacher until he was fourteen years old. He attended school for only a few years. "She had a set of encyclopedias," Willie said. "I read them all."

He could net butterflies and show them to his older brother, Charlie. He could pick apple blossoms and take them to his mother. But he could not share snowflakes because he could not save them.

From his boyhood on he studied all forms of moisture. He kept a record of the weather and did many experiments with raindrops.

When his mother gave him an old microscope, he used it to look at flowers, raindrops, and blades of grass. Best of all, he used it to look at snow.

While other children built forts and pelted snowballs at roosting crows, Willie was catching single snowflakes. Day after stormy day he studied the icy crystals.

He learned that most crystals had six branches (though a few had three). For each snowflake the six branches were alike. "I found that snowflakes were masterpieces of design," he said. "No one design was ever repeated. When a snowflake melted . . . just that much beauty was gone, without leaving any record behind."

Starting at age fifteen he drew a hundred snow crystals each winter for three winters.

Their intricate patterns were even more beautiful than he had imagined. He expected to find whole flakes that were the same, that were copies of each other. But he never did.

Willie decided he must find a way to save snowflakes so others could see their wonderful designs. For three winters he tried drawing snow crystals. They always melted before he could finish.

The camera made images on large glass negatives. Its microscope could **magnify** a tiny crystal from sixty-four to 3,600 times its actual size.

When he was sixteen, Willie read of a camera with its own microscope. "If I had that camera I could photograph snowflakes," he told his mother.

Willie's mother knew he would not be happy until he could share what he had seen.

"Fussing with snow is just **foolishness**," his father said. Still, he loved his son.

When Willie was seventeen his parents spent their savings and bought the camera.

It was taller than a newborn calf, and cost as much as his father's herd of ten cows. Willie was sure it was the best of all cameras.

Even so his first pictures were failures—no better than shadows. Yet he would not quit. Mistake by mistake, snowflake by snowflake, Willie worked through every storm.

Winter ended, the snow melted, and he had no good pictures.

Willie's experiment: He used a very small lens opening, which let only a little light reach the negative, but he kept the lens open for several seconds—up to a minute and a half.

He learned, too, that he could make the snow crystals show up more clearly by using a sharp knife to cut away all the dark parts of the negative around the crystals. This etching meant extra hours of work for each photograph, but Willie didn't mind.

He waited for another season of snow. One day, in the second winter, he tried a new experiment. And it worked!

Willie had figured out how to photograph snowflakes! "Now everyone can see the great beauty in a tiny crystal," he said.

The best snowstorm of his life occurred on Valentine's Day in 1928. He made over a hundred photographs during the two-day storm. He called the storm a gift from King Winter.

But in those days no one cared. Neighbors laughed at the idea of photographing snow.

"Snow in Vermont is as common as dirt," they said. "We don't need pictures."

Willie said the photographs would be his gift to the world.

While other farmers sat by the fire or rode to town with horse and sleigh, Willie studied snowstorms. He stood at the shed door and held out a black tray to catch the flakes.

When he found only jumbled, broken crystals, he brushed the tray clean with a turkey feather and held it out again.

He waited hours for just the right crystal and didn't notice the cold.

If the shed were warm the snow would melt. If he breathed on the black tray the snow would melt. If he twitched a muscle as he held the snow crystal on the long wooden pick the snowflake would break. He had to work fast or the snowflake would **evaporate** before he could slide it into place and take its picture. Some winters he was able to make only a few dozen good pictures.

Some winters he made hundreds.

He learned that each snowflake begins as a speck, much too tiny to be seen. Little bits—molecules—of water attach to the speck to form its branches. As the crystal grows, the branches come together and trap small quantities of air.

Draw Conclusions
Think about what you have read so far. What conclusions can you draw about Willie?

Many things affect the way these crystal branches grow. A little more cold, a bit less wind, or a bit more moisture will mean different-shaped branches. Willie said that was why, in all his pictures, he never found two snowflakes alike.

Willie's nieces and nephews lived on one side of the farmhouse that Willie shared with his brother Charlie. Willie often played the piano as they sang and shared stories and games with them.

Willie so loved the beauty of nature he took pictures in all seasons.

In the summer his nieces and nephews rubbed coat hangers with sticky pitch from spruce trees. Then Willie could use them to pick up spider webs jeweled with water drops and take their pictures.

On fall nights he would gently tie a grasshopper to a flower so he could find it in the morning and photograph the dew-covered insect.

But his snow crystal pictures were always his favorites. He gave copies away or sold them for a few cents. He made special pictures as gifts for birthdays.

Many colleges and universities bought lantern slide copies of his photographs and added to their collections each year. Artists and designers used the photographs to **inspire** their own work.

He held evening slide shows on the lawns of his friends. Children and adults sat on the grass and watched while Willie projected his slides onto a sheet hung over a clothesline.

Even today, those who want to learn about snow crystals begin with Wilson Bentley's book, *Snow Crystals*.

By 1926 he had spent $15,000 on his work and received $4,000 from the sale of photographs and slides.

He wrote about snow and published his pictures in magazines. He gave speeches about snow to faraway scholars and neighborhood skywatchers. "You are doing great work," said a professor from Wisconsin.

The little farmer came to be known as the world's expert on snow, "the Snowflake Man." But he never grew rich. He spent every penny on his pictures.

Willie said there were treasures in snow. "I can't afford to miss a single snowstorm," he told a friend. "I never know when I will find some wonderful prize."

Other scientists raised money so Willie could gather his best photographs in a book. When he was sixty-six years old Willie's book—his gift to the world—was published. Still, he was not ready to quit.

Less than a month after turning the first page on his book, Willie walked six miles home in a blizzard to make more pictures. He became ill with pneumonia after that walk and died two weeks later.

The plaque on the monument says

"SNOWFLAKE"
BENTLEY

Jericho's world famous snowflake authority

For fifty years Wilson A. Bentley, a simple farmer, developed his **technique** of micro-photography to reveal to the world the grandeur and mystery of the snowflake—its universal hexagonal shape and its infinite number of lovely designs.

A monument was built for Willie in the center of town. The girls and boys who had been his neighbors grew up and told their sons and daughters the story of the man who loved snow. Forty years after Wilson Bentley's death, children in his village worked to set up a museum in honor of the farmer-scientist.

And his book has taken the delicate snow crystals that once blew across Vermont, past mountains, over the earth. Neighbors and strangers have come to know of the icy wonders that land on their own mittens—thanks to Snowflake Bentley.

Draw Conclusions
What happened to Willie and his work over time?

"SNOWFLAKE"
BENTLEY

SNAPSHOTS OF JACQUELINE AND MARY

Jacqueline Briggs Martin began to write this story after she saw a snowflake and thought about an article she had read about a man who loved snow. Jacqueline saw lots of snow when she was growing up. She lived on a farm in Maine where she enjoyed nature, stories, and history.

Other books illustrated by Mary Azarian

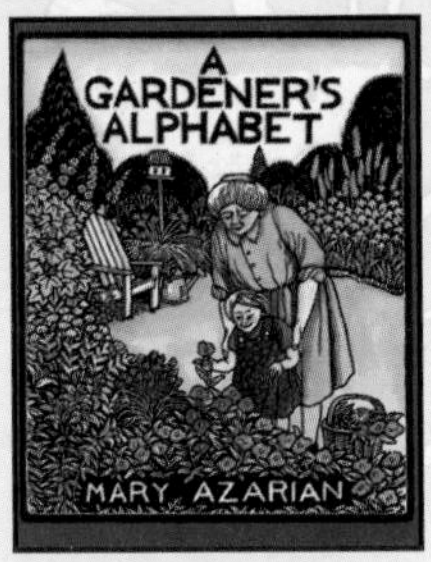

Mary Azarian has also seen a lot of snow. Just like Wilson Bentley, she lives on a farm in Vermont. Mary used her experiences on the farm to create her woodcut illustrations.

LOG ON ▶ FIND OUT

Author Jacqueline Briggs Martin
Illustrator Mary Azarian
www.macmillanmh.com

✔ Author's Purpose

Why did Jacqueline Briggs Martin write *Snowflake Bentley*? Was her purpose for writing this biography stated or implied? Explain using details from the selection.

LOG ON LEARN IT **Comprehension** www.macmillanmh.com

Comprehension Check

Text Clues	Conclusion

Summarize

To summarize *Snowflake Bentley* use the most important details from the selection. Information from your Conclusions Chart may help you.

Think and Compare

1. What did Willie want when he was sixteen that would **magnify** tiny crystals? Details
2. Why was it that some years Willie was able to make only a few dozen good snowflake pictures? Cause and Effect
3. What can you conclude about Wilson Bentley's decision to make photographing snowflakes his life's work? Explain using details from the story. Generate Questions: Draw Conclusions
4. Reread pages 752–753. How does the author show the reader how Willie's parents feel about him? Use details from the selection to explain your answer. Author's Purpose
5. Read "Let It Snow" on pages 744–745. How is the information about snow in that selection the same as in *Snowflake Bentley*? How is it different? Explain using details from both selections. Reading/Writing Across Texts

HAIKU

Poetry

Haiku is poetry that uses three short lines to describe a scene or just one moment. The first and third lines often have five syllables each, and the second line may have seven syllables.

Literary Elements

Imagery is the use of sensory language to create a picture in the reader's mind.

Metaphor is the comparison of two different things without the use of *like* or *as*.

Winter solitude—
in a world of one color
the sound of wind.

— *Matsuo Basho*

The words "a world of one color" create an **image** of a snow-covered scene.

Mountains and plains,
all are captured by the snow—
nothing remains.

— *Joso*

The snow is melting
and the village is flooded
with children.

— *Kobayashi Issa*

Children do not really flood the village. This **metaphor** compares children running through the streets to an overflow of water.

No sky at all;
no earth at all—and still
the snowflakes fall....

— *Hashin*

Connect and Compare

1. In the haiku by Joso, what phrase tells the reader that the poet thinks of the snow as an invader? **Metaphor**

2. Compare the three haiku by Joso, Basho, and Hashin. How do these poets feel about snow? Use details from the haiku in your answer. **Analyze**

3. Compare the poets' feelings about snow to Willie's feelings about snow in *Snowflake Bentley*. How are they alike and different? **Reading/Writing Across Texts**

4. Think of a metaphor that compares two different things. Now use the metaphor to write a haiku. Include sensory language in your haiku. **Apply**

Writing

Trait: Sentence Fluency

Good writers use **transition words and phrases** to connect their ideas and to make their writing flow smoothly.

Reading and Writing Connection

Read the passage below from *Snowflake Bentley*. Notice how the author uses transition words to connect ideas.

An excerpt from *Snowflake Bentley*

The author uses transition words to connect supporting details within paragraphs and ideas between paragraphs.

When Willie was seventeen his parents spent their savings and bought the camera.... Willie was sure it was the best of all cameras.

Even so his first pictures were failures.... Mistake by mistake, snowflake by snowflake, Willie worked through every storm.

Winter ended, the snow melted, and he had no good pictures.... One day, in the second winter, he tried a new experiment. And it worked!

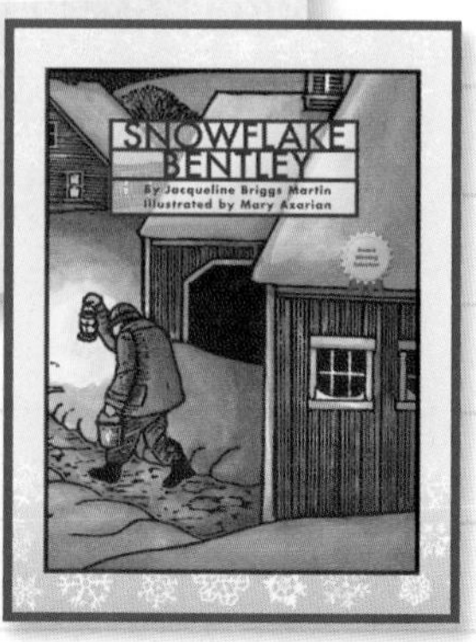

Read and Find

Read Caitlin's writing below. What transition words does she use to connect ideas? Use the checklist below to help you.

Polar Bears

by Caitlin K.

Polar bears are big. In fact, they are the biggest predators on land. Even though their fur is white, they have black noses and black skin. Polar bears have two kinds of fur. Guard hairs keep them dry, and thick fur next to their skin keeps them warm. In addition to their fur, they have a thick layer of fat.

Although polar bears are land animals, they spend a lot of time in the water. That's because these strong swimmers hunt for seals.

Read about polar bears.

Writer's Checklist

- [x] Does the author use transition words?
- [x] Do the transition words connect information and ideas?
- [ ] Do the **transition words** make the writing flow more smoothly?

Invent It

Talk About It

How does this invention make this worker's job a little easier?

LOG ON VIEW IT

Oral Language Activities
Invent It
www.macmillanmh.com

Vocabulary

hilarious **dizzy**
mischief **came in handy**
independence **nowadays**

Dictionary

Idioms are phrases that have a meaning different from the meaning of each word in them. Use a dictionary to find out what "came in handy" means.

He Made the World Brighter

by Susan Dickson

As a teen, Edison printed his own newspaper called *The Weekly Herald*.

Thomas Edison was a poor student. **Hilarious**? It is funny when you know what he grew up to become. Even if his grades didn't show it, the mother of this future inventor was convinced he was smart. After a few disappointing months in school, she decided to teach Thomas herself at home.

Thomas's Childhood

Thomas Alva Edison was born in 1847 in Ohio. Although curious and prone to **mischief**, Thomas read whenever he could.

Thomas's first job, at thirteen, was selling newspapers. Back then that's when most boys started working. At sixteen he became a telegrapher. This gave Thomas **independence** and an opportunity to travel. Shortly after this, Edison decided to be an inventor.

The Young Inventor

Not everything Thomas invented was a success. In fact his first invention, an electric vote recorder, failed. Edison thought it would help count votes. No one else found it useful, but that didn't stop Edison.

Edison's Greatest Challenge

Back then gas was the best lighting source, but burning it was dirty and unhealthful. Gas could also be very dangerous. The idea of using electricity for lighting had been around for more than 50 years. But nobody had developed anything practical or safe.

Edison set out to solve this problem. He improved upon what others had learned about electricity. He tested thousands of ideas in a whirlwind of activity. Several men helped Edison with his experiments. By 1880 they had burned a light bulb for more than 1,500 hours. They must have felt **dizzy** with excitement!

This was just the beginning. Edison's success led to the invention of an entire electric lighting system. That invention certainly **came in handy**! Many appliances and lights run on electricity **nowadays**. It is hard to imagine life without it. Next time you turn on your computer, think of Thomas Edison—and say "Thanks."

Edison with lamps he created

Reread for Comprehension

Generate Questions

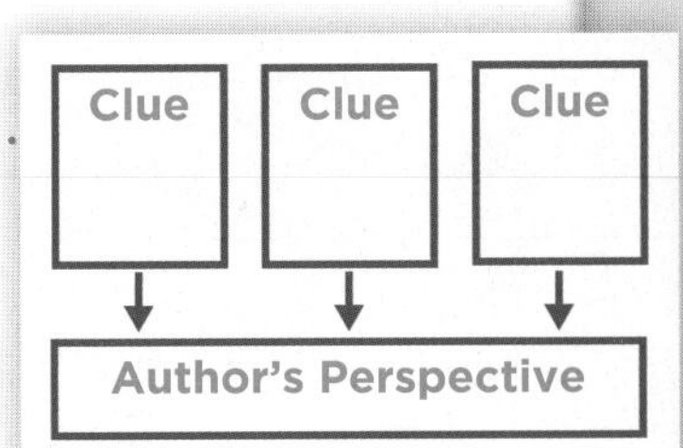

Author's Perspective Authors have attitudes and opinions about the subjects they choose to write about. Asking questions about the way an author presents information about a subject can help you identify the author's perspective, or how the author feels about a subject. Use your Author's Perspective Map to find clues about the author's perspective.

LOG ON LEARN IT Comprehension www.macmillanmh.com

Comprehension

Genre

A **Biography** is a story about the life of a real person written by someone else.

Generate Questions

Author's Perspective

As you read, fill in your Author's Perspective Map.

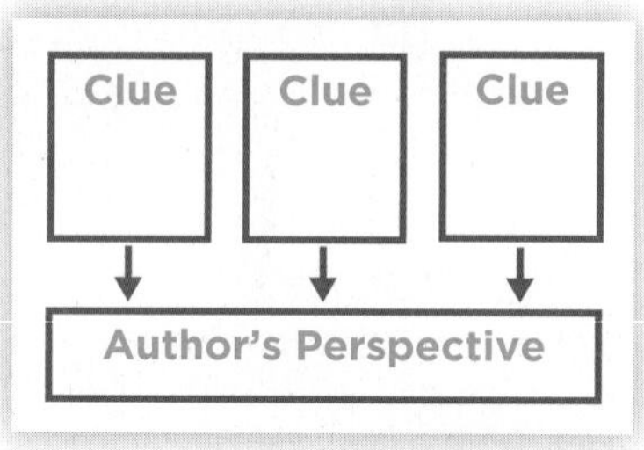

Read to Find Out

What does the author think Ben Franklin's greatest achievement is?

Award Winning Author and Illustrator
How
BEN FRANKLIN
STOLE THE
LIGHTNING
ROSALYN SCHANZER

Early to bed and early to rise makes a man healthy, wealthy and wise.
Silence Dogood
BENJ. FRANKLIN
SOAP
OINTMENT for the ITCH
Set

It's true!

The great Benjamin Franklin really did steal lightning right out of the sky! And then he set out to tame the beast. It goes to figure, though, because he was a man who could do just about anything.

Why, Ben Franklin could swim faster, argue better, and write funnier stories than practically anyone in colonial America. He was a musician, a printer, a cartoonist, and a world traveler! What's more, he was a newspaper owner, a shopkeeper, a soldier, and a politician. He even helped to write the Declaration of **Independence** and the Constitution of the United States!

Ben was always coming up with newfangled ways to help folks out, too. He was the guy who started the first lending library in America. His post office was the first to deliver mail straight to people's houses.

He also wrote almanacs that gave **hilarious** advice about life and told people when to plant crops, whether there might be an eclipse, and when the tides would be high or low.

And he helped to start a hospital!

A free academy!

A fire department!

In colonial days, fire could break out at any time. And it was lightning that caused some of the worst fires. Whenever thunderstorms were brewing, they would ring the church bells for all they were worth, but it didn't do anybody a lick of good.

Of course, after Ben stole the lightning, there weren't nearly as many fires for firefighters to put out. "Now, why was that?" I hear you ask. "And how did he steal any lightning in the first place?" Well, it's a long story, but before we get to the answer, here's a hint. One of the things Benjamin Franklin liked to do best was to make inventions.

Author's Perspective
What clues reveal how the author feels about Ben so far?

Why, Ben was a born inventor. He loved to swim fast, but he wanted to go even faster. So one day when he was a mere lad of eleven, he got some wood and invented swim paddles for his hands and swim fins for his feet. Ben could go faster, all right, but the wood was pretty heavy, and his wrists got plumb worn out.

That's why his second invention was a better way to go fast. He lay on his back, held on to a kite string, and let his kite pull him lickety-split across a big pond. (You might want to remember later on that Ben always did like kites.)

Ben kept right on inventing better ways to do things for the rest of his life.

Take books, for example. Ben read so many books that some of them sat on shelves way up high near the ceiling. So he invented the library chair. If he pulled up the seat, out popped some stairs to help him reach any books on high shelves. And in case climbing stairs made him **dizzy**, he invented a long wooden arm that could grab his books, too.

He also invented an odometer that told how far he had ridden to deliver the mail. And the first clock with a second hand. And he even thought up daylight saving time. Then he invented bifocals so older folks could see up close and far away without changing glasses.

Everybody and his brother and sister just had to find better ways to heat their houses in wintertime. So Ben came up with a Franklin stove that could warm up cold rooms faster and use a lot less wood than old-fashioned stoves and fireplaces.

People all over Europe and America loved Ben's glass armonica. This instrument could spin wet glass bowls to make music that sounded like it came straight from heaven. Mozart and Beethoven wrote music for it, and it was even played at a royal Italian wedding.

But as popular as warmer stoves and glass armonicas were, they aren't anywhere near as celebrated **nowadays** as the invention Ben made after he stole the lightning.

Another hint about Ben's most famous invention is that it helped make life easier for everyone. His scientific ideas were helpful, too, and were often way ahead of their time. For example, he had a lot of ideas about health. He said that exercise and weight lifting help keep folks fit, but they have to work hard enough to sweat if they want to do any good.

He wrote that breathing fresh air and drinking lots of water are good for you. He was the guy who said "an apple a day keeps the doctor away."

And before anyone ever heard of vitamin C, he wrote that oranges, limes, and grapefruit give people healthy gums and skin. Sailors soon got wind of this idea. They began eating so many limes to stop getting sick from scurvy at sea that they became known as limeys.

Didn't the man ever stop to rest? Even when he was outside, Ben kept right on experimenting.

For instance, he often sailed to England and France to do business for America. As he crossed the Atlantic Ocean, he charted the Gulf Stream by taking its temperature. Once sailors knew the route of this fast, warm "river" in the cold ocean, they could travel between America and Europe in a shorter time than ever before.

He was probably the first person to write weather forecasts, too. Once he chased a roaring whirlwind by riding over the hills and forests of Maryland just to find out how it worked.

Ben had an old scientific trick that he liked to show people every chance he got. He used to store some oil inside a bamboo walking stick, and whenever he poured a few drops onto angry waves in a pond or lake, the water became smooth as glass!

Meanwhile, over in Europe, people called "electricians" had started doing some tricks of their own. One trick was to raise a boy up near the ceiling with a bunch of silk cords, rub his feet with a glass "electric tube," and make sparks shoot out of his hands and face.

Another mean trick made the king of France laugh so hard he could hardly stop. His court electrician had run an electric charge through 180 soldiers of the guard, and they jerked to attention faster than they ever had in their entire lives.

But although people were doing lots of tricks with electricity, nobody had a clue about why or how it worked. So Benjamin Franklin decided to find out. He asked a British friend to send him an electric tube so that he could do some experiments.

In one experiment, he made a cork "electric spider" with thread for legs. It kept leaping back and forth between a wire and an electric tube just like it was alive.

Another time he asked a lady and gentleman to stand on some wax. One held an electric tube, the other held a wire, and when they tried to kiss, they got shocked by all the sparks shooting between their lips.

Ben even figured out how to light up a picture of a king in a golden frame. Anyone trying to remove the king's gold paper crown was in for a shock!

Doing all these tricks gave Ben his idea for stealing lightning out of the sky. He believed that lightning was nothing more nor less than pure electricity. Now he set out to prove it.

First he made a silk kite with a wire on top to attract some lightning. Next he added a kite string, tied a key to the bottom, and knotted a silk ribbon below the key. Ben and his son William stood out of the rain inside the doorway of a shed on the side of a field. To keep from getting shocked, Ben held on to the dry silk ribbon. Then he flew his kite straight up toward a big rain cloud.

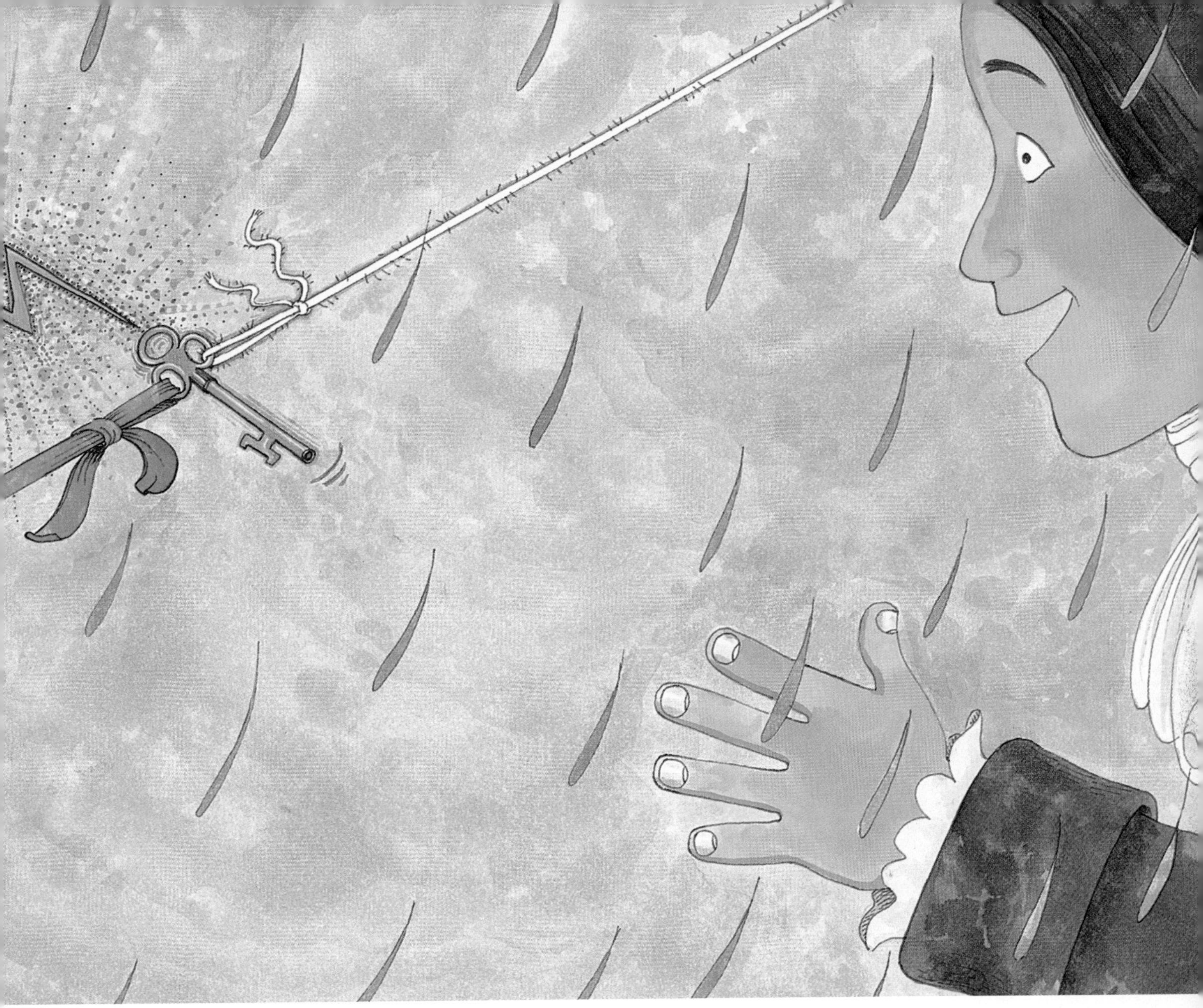

For the longest time, nothing happened.

Just as Ben and William were about to give up, the hair on that wet kite string began to rise up and stand at attention. Ben put his knuckle near the key, and YIKES!!!! Out jumped a bright spark of genuine electricity!

Real lightning had traveled all the way down that kite string! Ben had stolen electric fire out of the heavens and proven that he was right.

(Of course, now we know that if the storm had been any stronger, the great inventor would have been toast.)

Finally! Here's the part of the story where Ben's practice from thinking up all those inventions **came in** so **handy**. Way back then, you remember, lightning was always setting fire to ships, houses, and church spires. Even the best fire departments couldn't keep entire towns from going up in smoke. So Ben decided to make his most famous invention of all—the lightning rod!

The whole idea was to pull lightning safely out of the sky before it could do any **mischief**. Ben showed people how to put a pointed iron rod on the tip-top of a roof or ship's mast and connect it to a wire leading all the way down under the ground or into water. Now the lightning could follow a safe path without burning up a thing.

Author's Perspective
Explain how the author feels about Ben's invention of the lightning rod.

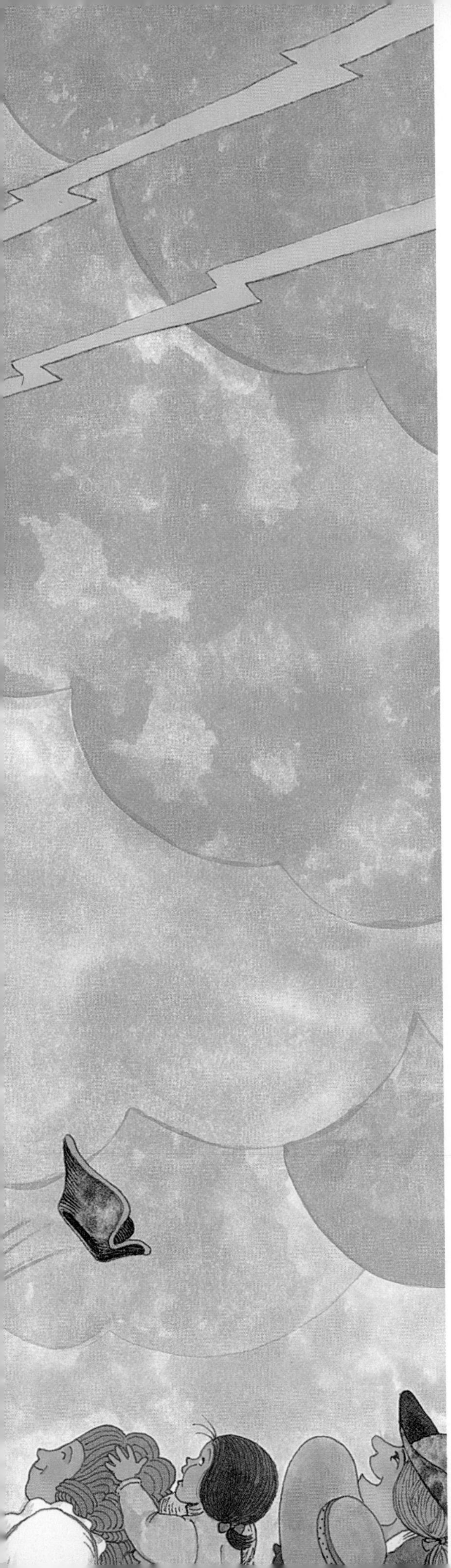

This simple but brilliant invention worked beautifully. It saved more lives than anyone can count and made Ben Franklin a great hero.

Scientists from around the world lined up to give Ben medals and awards. But during his long life, he became much more than the master of lightning. Why, when America fought against Great Britain for the right to become a free nation, Ben convinced France to come help win the war, and when it was over, he helped convince Great Britain to sign the peace. He had helped in so many ways that the people of France honored him with a beautiful medallion. It says "He snatched the lightning from heaven and the scepter from tyrants."

And he did.

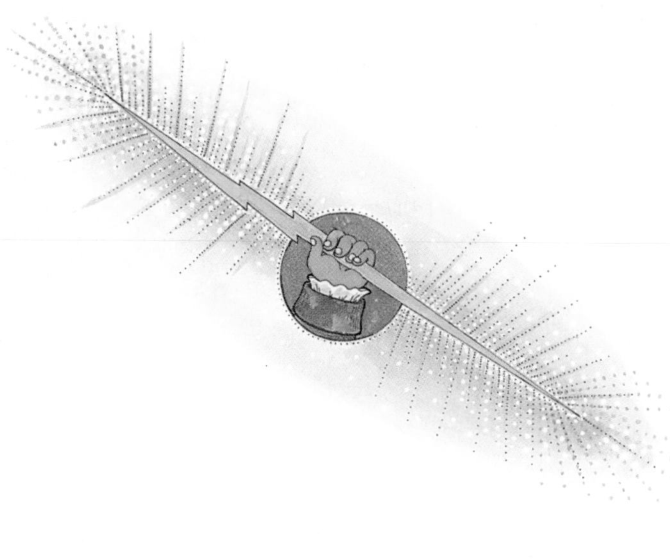

MEET THE INVENTOR

*R*OSALYN *S*CHANZER spent a lot of time in Philadelphia to write this piece. She visited the places where Ben Franklin lived and worked to make sure that her words and pictures would be accurate. Rosalyn probably would have gotten along really well with Ben. She is a great swimmer, just like he was. Once she even swam past sharks on a trip to Belize! Rosalyn also shares Ben's curiosity about the world. She's explored a jungle, visited an ancient city, and sailed a boat more than 800 miles.

Other books by Rosalyn Schanzer

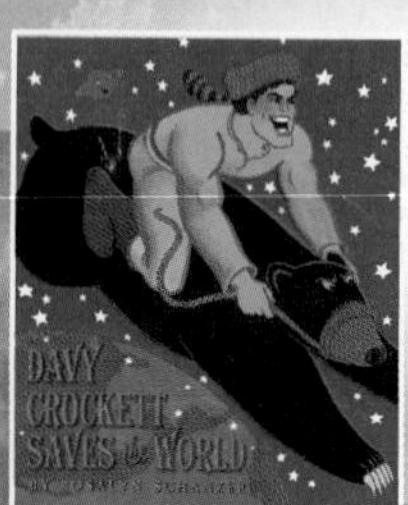

LOG ON FIND OUT

Author Rosalyn Schanzer
www.macmillanmh.com

Author's Purpose

Why did the author choose to focus on Benjamin Franklin's inventions? Use evidence from the text to support your answer.

LOG ON LEARN IT **Comprehension** www.macmillanmh.com

Comprehension Check

Summarize

To summarize *How Ben Franklin Stole the Lightning* use the most important details from the selection. Information from your Author's Perspective Map may help you.

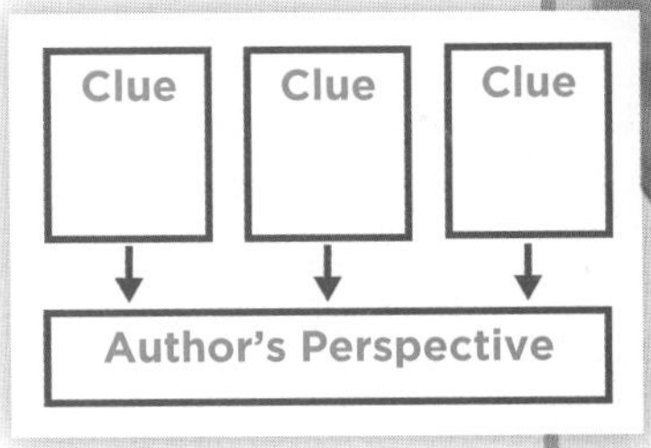

Think and Compare

1. What did Ben Franklin invent when he was eleven? **Details**
2. The text structure the author uses to present information on pages 790–791 is sequence. Is this text structure stated or implied? Explain using details from the selection to support your answer. **Sequence**
3. What do Ben Franklin's inventions tell about him? Use evidence from the text to explain your answer. **Make Inferences**
4. Why does the author believe that Ben Franklin was much more than an inventor, or "master of lightning"? Explain using details from the selection. **Generate Questions: Author's Perspective**
5. Read "He Made the World Brighter" on pages 776–777. How was Thomas Alva Edison like Ben Franklin? Use evidence from both selections to explain your answer. **Reading/Writing Across Texts**

Poetry

A **Concrete Poem** has words and lines arranged in the shape of the thing it describes.

Literary Elements

Figurative Language uses words to create mental images.

Alliteration is the repetition of the same consonant sound in a series of words.

Light Bulb

Thomas
Edison didn't
hesitate to let
ideas incubate, and
try again, if they
weren't right. One
day to his intense
delight, he **squeezed**
his thoughts
into a bulb
and then
turned
on the
light
light
light
!!!

— *Joan Bransfield Graham*

Edison didn't really squeeze his thoughts into a bulb. This example of **figurative language** helps the reader picture how hard Edison was thinking.

Lightning Bolt

NEWS FLASH !
BEN
FRANKLIN
USES
KITE & KEY
TO UNLOCK
ELECTRICITY!

This use of "kite" and "key" is an example of **alliteration**.

— *Joan Bransfield Graham*

Connect and Compare

1. Identify an example of figurative language in the poem "Lightning Bolt." **Figurative Language**
2. What do the shapes of these poems have to do with their topics? Explain. **Apply**
3. Compare the information presented in "Lightning Bolt" to the information in *How Ben Franklin Stole the Lightning*. In what ways is it similar? **Reading/Writing Across Texts**

LOG ON FIND OUT **Poetry** Concrete Poem
www.macmillanmh.com

Reading and Writing Connection

Writing

Trait: Organization

An expository paragraph often ends with a **concluding sentence** that sums up the author's ideas.

Read the passage below. Notice how the author Rosalyn Schanzer uses a concluding sentence.

An excerpt from
How Ben Franklin Stole the Lightning

The whole idea was to pull lightning safely out of the sky before it could do any mischief. Ben showed people how to put a pointed iron rod on the tip-top of a roof or ship's mast and connect it to a wire leading all the way down under the ground or into water. Now the lightning could follow a safe path without burning up a thing.

The author uses the last sentence as a concluding sentence to sum up ideas in the paragraph.

Read and Find

Read Reema's writing below. How did she conclude the paragraph? Use the checklist below to help you.

Painting

by Reema A.

Drawing sounded fine, but painting seemed weird to Shaheed. At first, he wouldn't paint at all. He didn't think he could do it. Then, for no good reason, he started. He looked around, saw a green tree, and painted a little blob of color. Then, he decided it looked like more than a blob. A few more strokes and Shaheed's picture was coming together. He could express himself without words–using shapes and colors to do it.

Read about the art of painting.

Writer's Checklist

- [x] Does the paragraph have a main idea? What is it?
- [x] What supporting details give information about the main idea?
- [ ] Does the paragraph have a **concluding sentence**? What is it?

Review

Problem and Solution
Cause and Effect
Fact and Opinion
Idioms
Primary Source

Pitch for Fish

"ORDER! THIS MEETING WILL NOW COME TO order!" barked Alison as she slammed her fist down on the desk. Rosa and Javier rolled their eyes at one another as Alison kept talking. "We have to decide what to do for the school fair. I think we should do a game of some sort. Like the game where people throw a ball in a jar from three feet away. And if they get it in, they win a prize."

"They'll win a prize? What?" asked Javier.

"A goldfish!" said Alison excitedly. "Don't you just love the idea of seeing all those little goldfish bowls lined up together? We can call our booth *Pitch for Fish*!"

Javier bit his lip. He nodded, knowing his opinion was insignificant. It didn't matter what he thought. Alison wanted a goldfish game and Alison always got what she wanted.

"Great," Alison said. "Rosa? What about you? Don't you think this is the best idea ever?"

Rosa looked down, her face burning. She didn't want to say anything to upset Alison, but she didn't like the idea.

Alison frowned. "Okay, you agree then. Now, I hate painting so you two have to lend a hand. You should construct the booth and paint it pink. The letters should be—"

"Alison," Rosa interrupted.

Alison paused at the timid interruption. She looked angry. "Did you just interrupt me, Rosa?"

When she heard the anger in Alison's voice, Rosa felt more intimidated than ever. But she thought of those poor fish, trapped in tiny bowls, and gained enough courage to say, "I think goldfish make terrible prizes."

"Well, I think it's a great idea. And Javier agrees."

"He didn't hear my side yet." Rosa took a deep breath. "It's not fair to the fish. Getting a pet is an important decision. You have to really want one and be willing to take care of it. You should never give someone a pet as a prize or present. Most people who win a fish won't take care of it. Most of those fish will be dead in a few weeks and it will be our fault. I don't want to be responsible for that."

Alison looked stunned. She was not used to people disagreeing with her.

"Actually, I agree with Rosa," Javier said in a firm voice. "We can still have the pitching game, but let's think of another prize. We shouldn't give away something live."

Alison looked really upset. Rosa knew they were right, but she didn't want to rub it in.

"Let's give away stuffed fish instead," Rosa suggested. "Then we can still use your name, Alison. Pitch for Fish is a great name."

Alison smiled again. "It is, isn't it?"

CAVES

MYSTERIOUS UNDERGROUND WORLDS

ARE YOU LOOKING for something new to explore? Check out a cave! Caves are natural spaces, like rooms, that have openings you can reach from the inside. They are often so deep below the ground that natural light does not reach inside. There are about 40,000 caves in the United States. This means there is a very good chance you can find one somewhere near you. There are caves in every state except Louisiana and Rhode Island.

There are four basic types of caves: **solution caves**, **sea caves**, **lava caves**, and **glacier caves**. Solution and sea caves are both formed by water. The constant flow of water dissolves and wears away the rock. Over time, the path deepens and creates a cave. Lava caves are formed from volcanic eruptions. The outer layer of lava cools and hardens while the center stays hot and keeps flowing. When the lava in the center drains, it creates a cave. Glacier caves form when melting water runs through a glacier.

Many caves are protected by state law. This ensures cavers respect the caves while exploring them!

Caves can be exciting places to explore, but they can also be dangerous. The number one rule to remember is never to go in a cave alone. It is best to go with an expert who knows the cave well. You also need to be prepared. Remember, there is no natural light in a cave, so you need to bring your own light with you. Most cave explorers wear a helmet that has a light on the front. The light allows you to see and to inspect the wonders of the cave. It also helps you in tricky areas that might need more of your attention because you do not have to hold a light in your hands. This is important because then your hands are free to help you keep your balance.

Choose your clothing carefully before you go caving. Wear comfortable shoes that help you keep your balance on steep or slippery paths. Temperatures are often colder in caves, so wear layers of clothing that you can add or remove as necessary. Wearing cotton as the inside layer and wool as the outside layer will help you keep dry and trap in heat.

Finally, you also need to be sure not to cause any damage. Do not go off alone or remove any objects. Be sure to leave the cave exactly the way you found it. That way, other people can enjoy the same mysterious underground world!

TRAVEL JOURNAL

June 20-21
This weekend, my family and I visited Mammoth Cave National Park. Did you know Mammoth is the longest cave in the United States? It is about 169 miles long and right here in our home state of Kentucky. My brother and I took a tour and got to crawl and slide through really narrow parts of the cave. After that, we decided to call it a day and go back to the campsite for a dinner of hotdogs and hot chocolate!

June 27-29
My family and I traveled to Cumberland Caverns in Kentucky. All I can say is WOW! Even though Cumberland is shorter than Mammoth, I think I liked it better. The cave is 23 miles long but very tricky. We brought sleeping bags and did an overnight tour. It was scary but a lot of fun!

Show What You Know

Comprehension

Using Text Features

- Text features in expository text, such as a magazine article, give an overview of the article. As you look at an article think about what information you can learn from the title, the headings, and the photographs.
- Graphic aids such as maps, graphs, and diagrams will also give an overview of the information that is being presented.
- Look at the article "Taking the Lead" on pages 734–737. On a separate sheet of paper, answer the following questions: *What can you tell about the topic of the article by reading the title, the question under the title, and the other headings? What kind of information do the photographs and captions provide?*

Word Study

Suffixes

- A suffix is a word part added to the end of a base word or root that changes the meaning of the word. Many suffixes used in English come from Greek, Latin, and other languages. Some suffixes change a word from a noun to an adjective. For example: *joy* + *-ful* = "joyful."
- Some suffixes change a verb into a noun. For example: *teach* + *-er* = the noun "teacher."
- Create at least eight words using the following suffixes: *-or*, *-er*, *-less*, *-ful*. Then sort the words by putting the nouns in one column and the adjectives in another column.

Genre

Expository Text

- Expository text, such as a magazine article, presents facts and information about an event, person, place, or thing.
- The introduction tells what the article is about and usually includes a topic sentence. The main text of the article gives information, facts, and details about the topic. Text features provide details and facts in easy-to-read formats.
- The conclusion gives the author's ideas about what is the most important information in the article.
- With a partner read a magazine article. Together write a summary of the article.

Research

In Your Own Words

- When you paraphrase information, you use your own words to restate what you have read. Paraphrasing information can help you better understand what you are reading.
- When you take notes, paraphrase the information unless you plan to use an exact quote. If you don't paraphrase, you run the risk of copying another person's written words. Copying somebody else's words and ideas without giving him or her credit is called *plagiarism*. In order to avoid plagiarizing, you must give credit whenever you use another person's written words, facts, statistics, charts, or diagrams.
- Choose a reference book. Paraphrase part of a chapter and write the source of your information. When you write the source include the author, title, place published, publisher, and year of publication.

LOG ON FIND OUT

Glossary

What Is a Glossary?

A glossary can help you find the **meanings** of words in this book that you may not know. The words in the glossary are listed in **alphabetical order**. **Guide words** at the top of each page tell you the first and last words on the page.

Each word is divided into syllables. The way to pronounce the word is given next. You can understand the pronunciation respelling by using the **pronunciation key**. A shorter key appears at the bottom of every other page. When a word has more than one syllable, a dark accent mark (′) shows which syllable is stressed. In some words, a light accent mark (') shows which syllable has a less heavy stress. Sometimes an entry includes a second meaning for the word.

prehistoric

reptiles

script/splendid

Guide Words

First word on the page — Last word on the page

Sample Entry

Pronunciation — Part of speech

Main entry & Syllable division: **sketch•es** (skech'əz) *plural noun.*

Definition: Simple drawings that are done quickly.

Example sentence: *I made several **sketches** before finally painting the tree.*

Pronunciation Key

Phonetic Spelling	Examples
a	at, bad, plaid, laugh
ā	ape, pain, day, break
ä	father, calm
âr	care, pair, bear, their, where
e	end, pet, said, heaven, friend
ē	equal, me, feet, team, piece, key
i	it, big, give, hymn
ī	ice, fine, lie, my
îr	ear, deer, here, pierce
o	odd, hot, watch
ō	old, oat, toe, low
ô	coffee, all, taught, law, fought
ôr	order, fork, horse, story, pour
oi	oil, toy
ou	out, now, bough
u	up, mud, love, double
ū	use, mule, cue, feud, few
ü	rule, true, food, fruit
u̇	put, wood, should, look
ûr	burn, hurry, term, bird, word, courage
ə	about, taken, pencil, lemon, circus
b	bat, above, job
ch	chin, such, match

Phonetic Spelling	Examples
d	dear, soda, bad
f	five, defend, leaf, off, cough, elephant
g	game, ago, fog, egg
h	hat, ahead
hw	white, whether, which
j	joke, enjoy, gem, page, edge
k	kite, bakery, seek, tack, cat
l	lid, sailor, feel, ball, allow
m	man, family, dream
n	not, final, pan, knife, gnaw
ng	long, singer
p	pail, repair, soap, happy
r	ride, parent, wear, more, marry
s	sit, aside, pets, cent, pass
sh	shoe, washer, fish, mission, nation
t	tag, pretend, fat, dressed
th	thin, panther, both
<u>th</u>	these, mother, smooth
v	very, favor, wave
w	wet, weather, reward
y	yes, onion
z	zoo, lazy, jazz, rose, dogs, houses
zh	vision, treasure, seizure

Aa

ab•sorbed (ab zôrbd′) *verb.* Soaked up something such as a liquid or the sun's rays. *It was a hot day, so the plant **absorbed** the water immediately.*

a•chieved (ə chēvd′) *verb.* To have done or carried out successfully. *She studied hard and **achieved** the grade she wanted.*

ac•quaint•ance (ə kwān′təns) *noun.* A person one knows, but who is not a close friend. *Carole is an **acquaintance** from camp.*

ac•tive (ak′tiv) *adjective.* Lively, busy. *Carlos is always **active**; he hardly ever sits still.*

ad•vanced (ad vanst′) *adjective.* Beyond the beginning level; not elementary. *As a singer, Sheila was really **advanced** for her age.*

ag•ile (aj′əl) *adjective.* Able to move and react quickly and easily. *Bonita is an **agile** softball player.*

al•loy (al′oi) *noun.* A metal formed by fusing two or more metals. *Brass is an **alloy** of copper and zinc.*

a•maze•ment (ə māz′mənt) *noun.* Great surprise or wonder. *To the **amazement** of the audience, the children played some difficult music perfectly.*

am•bu•lance (am′byə ləns) *noun.* A special vehicle that is used to carry sick or injured people to a hospital. *My neighbor once had to call an **ambulance** to take him to the hospital.*

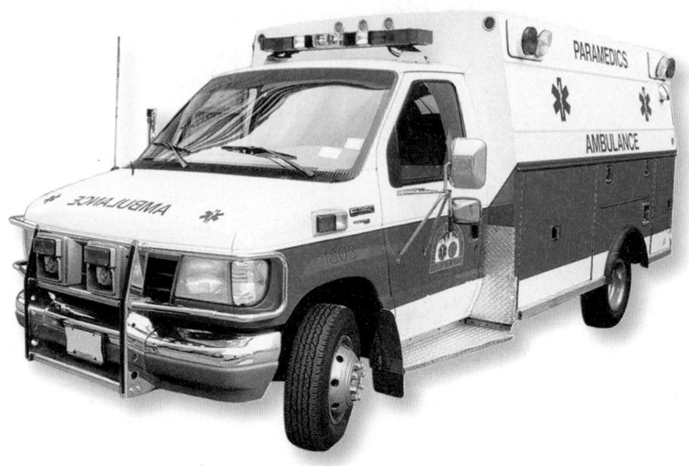

an•ces•tors (an′ses tərz) *plural noun.* People in the past from whom one comes. *Your great-grandparents are some of your **ancestors**.*

an•noyed (ə noid′) *adjective.* Bothered or disturbed. *Kevin looked **annoyed** when his little sister came out to join the game.*

an•nu•al (an′yū əl) *adjective.* Measured by the year. *The **annual** rainfall in our hometown is close to 20 inches.*

an•tic•i•pa•tion (an tis′ə pā′shən) *noun.* A feeling of excited expectation. *Tim was full of eager **anticipation** as he got on the roller coaster.*

a•pol•o•gize (ə pol′ə jīz′) *verb*. To say one is sorry or embarrassed; make an apology. *Aaron said, "I'd like to **apologize** for being late."*

ap•plaud•ed (ə plôd′əd) *verb*. Showed approval for or enjoyment of something by the clapping of hands. *The crowd **applauded** the soldiers as they came off the ship.*

ap•pre•ci•at•ed (ə prē′shē āt′əd) *verb*. Understood the value of; was grateful for something. *The boss **appreciated** how much his workers did for the company.*

as•sem•bled (ə sem′bəld) *verb*. To have put or fit together. *Anita and Grace **assembled** their wagon in just three hours.*

as•sured (ə shůrd′) *verb*. Made certain or sure. *Our hard work **assured** the success of the festival.*

a•void•ed (ə void′əd) *verb*. Stayed away from. *Butch **avoided** doing hard work.*

a•ware (ə wâr′) *adjective*. Knowing or realizing. *I don't wear headphones when I run, so I am **aware** of what is around me.*

awk•ward (ôk′wərd) *adjective*. Lacking grace in movement or behavior; clumsy or uncomfortable. *Until Julio learned the steps, his dancing was **awkward**.*

Bb

bar•be•cue (bär′bi kū′) *noun*. A meal, usually meat, cooked outdoors over an open fire. *We had a great **barbecue** in the park.*

at; āpe; fär; câre; end; mē; it; īce; pîerce; hot; ōld; sông; fôrk; oil; out; up; ūse; rüle; půll; tûrn; chin; sing; shop; thin; <u>th</u>is; hw in white; zh in treasure.

The symbol ə stands for the unstressed vowel sound in about, taken, pencil, lemon, and circus.

bar•gained (bär′gind) *verb.* To have talked over the terms of an agreement or sale. *My dad **bargained** with the salesperson to get a deal on our new car.*

bid•ding (bid′ing) *noun.* A period in which bids, offers of payments, are made or received. *The auction house started the **bidding** for the antiques.*

bor•der (bôr′dər) *noun.* A line between one country, state, county, or town and another. *A river runs along the **border** between the two states.*

boy•cotts (boi′kots) *plural noun.* Protests in which people refuse to buy from or work for a person, nation, or business. *The **boycotts** against the unfair company were very successful.*

Word History

Boycotts comes from Charles Boycott, who was shunned by Irish farmers for his harsh actions against them.

brit•tle (brit′əl) *adjective.* Likely to break or snap. *Susan's fingernails became **brittle** and started to break.*

Cc

cam•ou•flage (kam′ə fläzh′) *verb.* To hide or conceal by using shapes or colors that blend with the surroundings. *The chameleon is able to **camouflage** itself by changing the color of its skin.*

car•at (kar′ət) *noun.* A unit of weight equal to 1/5 of a gram, usually used to measure gems. *The ring had a three **carat** diamond in the center.*

chal•leng•es (chal′ənj ez) *plural noun.* Those things that call for work, effort, and the use of one's talents. *Ted's greatest **challenges** are in Art and Spanish.*

char•i•ty (char′i tē) *noun.* The giving of help to the poor or needy. *After the flood, some of the families refused to accept any **charity**.*

cir•cu•lar (sûr′kyə lər) *adjective.* Having or making the shape of a circle. *The referee's arm made a **circular** motion as he blew the whistle.*

cit•i•zen (sit′ə zən) *noun.* A person who was born in a country or who chooses to live in and become a member of that country. *Carmine is an Italian **citizen** but often visits the United States.*

civ•il•i•za•tions (siv'əl ə zā'shənz) *plural noun*. Human societies in which agriculture, trade, government, art, and science are highly developed. *Charles studies the ancient **civilizations** of Asia.*

cli•mate (klī'mit) *noun*. The average weather conditions of a place or region through the year. *Most deserts have a hot, dry **climate**.*

clus•tered (klus'tərd) *verb*. To have grown, or grouped together, things of the same kind. *The grapes were **clustered** in a bunch.*

col•lage (kə läzh') *noun.* A picture made by pasting paper, cloth, metal, and other things in an arrangement on a surface. *Once I made a **collage** of my day's activities by using clippings from magazines.*

Word History

Collage comes from the French word *collage*, from *colle*, meaning "glue" or "paste."

col•o•ny (kol'ə nē) *noun*. A group of animals or plants of the same kind that live together. *I found a **colony** of ants in my yard.*

com•mo•tion (kə mō'shən) *noun*. A noisy disturbance; confusion. *We ran into the hall to see what was causing the **commotion**.*

com•mu•ni•ca•tion (kə mū'ni kā'shən) *noun*. An exchange or sharing of feelings, thoughts, or information. *Music is one form of **communication** that does not require speech.*

com•ple•ted (kəm plēt'əd) *verb*. Finished; did. *I had to wait until I **completed** my homework before I could go to the movies.*

con•ceived (kən sēvd') *verb*. To have formed an idea; thought up. *The plan was **conceived** after everyone had gone to bed.*

con•densed (kən densd') *verb*. To have made thicker or more compact; to have reduced the volume of. *The chef **condensed** the sauce by boiling it for 20 minutes.*

con•di•tions (kən dish'ənz) *plural noun*. The state something is in. *Because of the **conditions** at the playground, we weren't allowed to play there.*

at; āpe; fär; câre; end; mē; it; īce; pîerce; hot; ōld; sông; fôrk; oil; out; up; ūse; rüle; pu̇ll; tûrn; chin; sing; shop; thin; <u>th</u>is; hw in white; zh in treasure.

The symbol ə stands for the unstressed vowel sound in about, taken, pencil, lemon, and circus.

con•duc•ted (kən dukt′tid) *verb.* To have directed, led, guided, or transmitted. *When Susie lost her sneaker, she **conducted** a search of the entire locker room.*

con•sis•ted (kən sis′təd) *verb.* Contained; was made up. *The batter **consisted** of a cup of flour, one egg, and a cup of milk.*

con•vinced (kən vinst′) *verb.* To have caused a person to do or believe something. *Raj finally **convinced** his father he was old enough to go on the trip.*

crank•y (krang′kē) *adjective.* To be cross or in a bad temper; grouchy. *Roni is always **cranky** before she's had breakfast.*

cur•i•ous (kyůr′ē əs) *adjective.* Eager to learn new, strange, or interesting things. *We were all **curious** to know who our new teacher might be.*

cur•rent (kûr′ənt) *noun.* A portion of a body of water or of air flowing continuously in a definite direction. *The **current** took the raft far out to sea.*

Dd

dec•ades (dek′ādz) *plural noun.* Periods of ten years. *Our family has lived in the same city for nearly six **decades**.*

Word History

Decades comes from the Greek *deka*, meaning "ten."

de•cayed (dē kād′) *adjective.* Having undergone the process of decomposition; rotted. *We walked in the woods past **decayed** stumps of trees.*

de•fend (di fend′) *verb.* Guard against attack or harm. *The rabbit could not **defend** itself against the snake, so it ran away.*

def•i•ni•tion (def′ə nish′ən) *noun.* An explanation of what a word or phrase means. *Our teacher Mr. Mitchell asked us what the **definition** of "like" is.*

de•mon•stra•ted (de′mən strā′təd) *verb.* Showed by actions or experiment. *The performer **demonstrated** great skill with both the piano and the drums.*

de•scen•dants (di send′ənts) *plural noun.* People who come from a particular ancestor. *My neighbors are **descendants** of a French explorer.*

de•signed (di zīnd′) *verb*. To have made a plan, drawing, or outline of something. *Penelope's sister **designed** the perfect sundress for her.*

des•per•ate (des′pər it) *adjective*. Very bad or hopeless. *I needed money, but the situation was not **desperate**.*

di•ges•ted (di jes′tid) *verb*. To have broken down food in the mouth, stomach, and intestines. *After my dog had **digested** his dinner he was hungry again.*

dis•ap•point•ment (dis′ə point′mənt) *noun*. A feeling of being disappointed or let down. *Losing the match was a **disappointment**, but I still like tennis.*

dis•miss (dis mis′) *verb*. To discard or reject. *John was able to **dismiss** the story he heard as a rumor.*

dis•play (di splā′) *noun*. A show or exhibit. *The children's artwork is the main **display** on the family refrigerator.*

dis•rupt (dis rupt′) *verb*. To throw into disorder or confusion. *An argument might **disrupt** the meeting.*

diz•zy (diz′ē) *adjective*. Having the feeling of spinning and being about to fall. *I was **dizzy** when I got off the Ferris wheel.*

dove (dōv) *verb*. Plunged head first into water. *We watched as the woman **dove** perfectly off the board and into the deep pool.*

dove (duv) *noun*. A medium-size bird of the pigeon family. *The **dove** cooed quietly on the window ledge.*

draw•backs (drô′bāks) *plural noun*. Things that make something more difficult or unpleasant. *One of the **drawbacks** of his job is the long hours.*

drought (drout) *noun*. A period of time in which there is little or no rainfall. *The terrible August **drought** affected the wheat crop.*

at; āpe; fär; câre; end; mē; it; īce; pîerce; hot; ōld; sông; fôrk; oil; out; up; ūse; rüle; pu̇ll; tûrn; chin; sing; shop; thin; <u>th</u>is; hw in white; zh in treasure.

The symbol ə stands for the unstressed vowel sound in about, taken, pencil, lemon, and circus.

Dust Bowl (dust bōl) *noun*. The region in the central United States that suffered from the great dust storms of the 1930s. *Oklahoma was part of the **Dust Bowl**.*

Ee

eaves•drop•ping (ēvz'drop'ing) *noun*. Listening to other people talking without letting them know you are listening. *He was **eavesdropping** on her neighbors.*

ech•o•lo•ca•tion (ek'ō lō kā'shən) *noun*. A way to find out where objects are by making sounds and interpreting the echo that returns. *Bats rely on **echolocation** when they hunt for insects.*

ee•rie (îr'ē) *adjective*. Strange in a scary way. *We heard an owl's **eerie** hooting as we walked home in the dark.*

e•lec•tri•cal (i lek'tri kəl) *adjective*. Relating to the form of energy carried in wires for use to drive motors or as light or heat. *Dad carefully connected the **electrical** cables to the new DVD player in the den.*

e•merge (i mûrj') *verb*. To come into view or become known. *After months in hibernation, the bears **emerge**.*

en•coun•ter (en koun'tər) *verb*. To meet or face, usually unexpectedly. *Katie listens to the traffic report so she does not **encounter** any delays.*

en•cour•aged (en kûr'ijd) *verb*. To have inspired with courage, hope, or confidence. *The bright sunlight **encouraged** us to continue our hike.*

end•less (end'lis) *adjective*. Having no limit or end. *The line of people for the show seemed **endless**.*

en•dured (en dùrd' *or* en dyùrd') *verb*. Survived or put up with. *The workers **endured** the hot sun all day.*

e•nor•mous (i nôr'məs) *adjective*. Much greater than the usual size, amount, or degree; extremely large. *The **enormous** pumpkin weighed over 300 pounds.*

en•ter•pri•sing (en'tər prī'zing) *adjective*. Showing energy and initiative; willing or inclined to take risks. *Brian, an **enterprising** young man, ran for class president and won.*

e•sta•blished (i stab'lishd) *verb*. To have begun, created, or set up. *We **established** a scholarship in memory of my mother.*

e•va•po•rate (i vap'ə rāt') *verb*. To change from a liquid or solid into a gas. *Heat makes water **evaporate**.*

Word History

Evaporate comes from the Latin *evaporatus*, "dispersed in vapor," from *ex*, "out," and *vapor*, "exhalation."

e•ven•tu•al•ly (i ven'chü ə lē) *adverb*. In the end; finally. *We **eventually** got a DVD player because the good movies were not being shown on television.*

ex•as•per•at•ed (eg zas'pər āt'əd) *verb*. Annoyed greatly; made angry. *Helping me with my math so **exasperated** my dad that my mom took over.*

ex•po•sure (ek spō'zhər) *noun*. The condition of being presented to view. *After each **exposure** to the new toy, the dog began to recognize it and would pick it up without being asked.*

Ff

fam•ished (fam'isht) *adjective*. Very hungry; starving. *After a long day of running and swimming, the children were **famished** and wanted to eat as soon as possible.*

flinched (flincht) *verb*. Drew back or away, as from something painful or unpleasant; winced. *When the door suddenly slammed, Myra **flinched**.*

fool•ish•ness (fü'lish nəs) *noun*. The act of not showing good sense. *I wanted to race across the street, but my mom will not allow that **foolishness**.*

frag•ile (fraj'əl) *adjective*. Easily broken; delicate. *My toothpick ship is too **fragile** to take to show-and-tell.*

freeze-dried (frēz'drī'd) *verb*. To dry while frozen under high vacuum for preservation. *On the camping trip, John mixed a cup of boiling water with a teaspoon of **freeze-dried** coffee.*

fre•quent•ly (frē'kwənt lē) *adverb*. Happening often. *I **frequently** eat cereal for breakfast.*

fron•tier (frun tîr') *noun*. The far edge of a country, where people are just beginning to settle. *Many Americans moved to the **frontier** in covered wagons.*

fu•els (fū'əlz) *plural noun*. Substances burned as a source of heat and power, such as coal, wood, or oil. *When the world runs out of fossil **fuels**, we will be forced to use alternate energy sources.*

at; āpe; fär; câre; end; mē; it; īce; pîerce; hot; ōld; sông; fôrk; oil; out; up; ūse; rüle; pùll; tûrn; chin; sing; shop; thin; this; hw in white; zh in treasure.

The symbol ə stands for the unstressed vowel sound in about, taken, pencil, lemon, and circus.

Gg

gaped (gāpt) *verb*. Stared with the mouth open, as in wonder or surprise. *The audience **gaped** at the acrobats.*

gen•u•ine (jen'ū in) *adjective*. Sincere; honest. *My friends and I made a **genuine** effort to help all the kids that were new to the school.*

glanced (glansd) *verb*. To take a brief or hurried look. *He **glanced** at the magazines on the table.*

glist•ened (glis'ənd) *verb*. To shine with reflected light. *The snow on the fir trees **glistened** in the sun.*

globe (glōb) *noun*. Earth (as a shape). *Our **globe** is the home of billions of people.*

glo•ri•ous (glor'ē əs) *adjective*. Having or deserving praise or honor; magnificent. *The colors of the maple leaves in autumn are **glorious**.*

Great De•pres•sion (grāt dē presh'ən) *noun*. A worldwide economic downturn that began in 1928. *My grandparents tell stories about how difficult it was to find a job during the **Great Depression**.*

guard•i•an (gär'dē ən) *noun.* A person or thing that guards or watches over. *My older brother sometimes acts like he is my **guardian**.*

Hh

hab•i•tat (hab'i tat') *noun*. The place where an animal or plant naturally lives and grows. *A swamp is a common **habitat** for many creatures.*

han•dy (han'dē) *adjective*. Within reach, nearby; easy to use. To **come in handy** is to be useful. *It's amazing how many times a dictionary can **come in handy**.*

harm•less (härm'les) *adjective*. Not able to do damage or hurt. *My dog looks mean, but really she is **harmless**.*

head•lines (hed'līnz) *plural noun*. Words printed at the top of a newspaper or magazine article. *The most important news has the biggest **headlines**.*

hi•ber•nate (hī′bər nāt′) *verb*. To sleep or stay inactive during the winter. *Bears eat a lot to get ready to **hibernate**.*

hi•lar•i•ous (hi lâr′ē əs) *adjective*. Very funny. *Keisha tells **hilarious** jokes that make everyone laugh.*

hoist•ing (hoist′ing) *verb*. Lifting or pulling up. ***Hoisting** logs out of the water, the men soon grew tired.*

Ii

i•den•ti•fied (ī den′tə fīd′) *verb*. Proved that someone or something is a particular person or thing. *The fingerprints on the gold watch **identified** the butler as the thief.*

im•pres•sive (im pres′iv) *adjective*. Deserving admiration; making a strong impression. *The track team won five races, which was its most **impressive** result all year.*

in•ci•dent (in′si dənt) *noun*. An event or act. *After the pep rally, there was a funny **incident** involving bales of hay and the school mascot.*

in•de•pen•dence (in′di pen′dəns) *noun*. Freedom from the control of another or others. *America gained its **independence** from Great Britain.*

in•jus•tice (in jus′tis) *noun*. Lack of justice; unfairness. *The workers felt it was an **injustice** that they could not vote on the issue.*

in•sec•ti•cides (in sek′ti sīdz′) *plural noun*. Chemicals for killing insects. *Our family room was sprayed with **insecticides**.*

at; **ā**pe; f**ä**r; c**â**re; **e**nd; m**ē**; **i**t; **ī**ce; p**î**erce; h**o**t; **ō**ld; s**ô**ng; f**ô**rk; **oi**l; **ou**t; **u**p; **ū**se; r**ü**le; p**ů**ll; t**û**rn; **ch**in; si**ng**; **sh**op; **th**in; **th**is; **hw** in **wh**ite; **zh** in trea**s**ure.

The symbol **ə** stands for the unstressed vowel sound in **a**bout, tak**e**n, penc**i**l, lem**o**n, and circ**u**s.

in•spire (in spīr′) *verb.* To stir the mind, feelings, or imagination. *Nature can **inspire** some people to write poetry.*

in•sult (in′sult) *noun.* A remark or action that hurts someone's feelings or pride. *It would be an **insult** not to invite Marta to the party.*

in•tel•li•gent (in tel′i jənt) *adjective.* Able to understand and to think especially well. *An **intelligent** person was needed to solve the difficult puzzle.*

in•ter•act (in′tər akt′) *verb.* To act together, toward, or with others. *My teacher and our class **interact** on a daily basis.*

in•ter•fere (in′tər fîr′) *verb.* To take part in the affairs of others when not asked; to meddle. *My mom hates to **interfere** with my business, but she often gives me good advice.*

in•ter•vals (in′tər vəlz) *plural noun.* The spaces or time between two things. *There are **intervals** of 50 miles between each rest stop on the highway.*

in•ves•ti•gates (in ves′ti gāts′) *verb.* Looks at something carefully in order to gather information. *Every morning, our dog Lulu **investigates** our yard for cats.*

Word History

Investigates comes from the Latin *investigare*, meaning "to track."

is•sues (ish′üz) *plural noun.* 1. Subject matters under discussion. *2.* Individual copies of a magazine. *1. My brother and I disagree on certain **issues**. 2. All the **issues** of my favorite comic book were stacked on the shelf.*

i•tems (ī′təmz) *noun.* Things in a group or list. *Christine always makes a list of the **items** she needs from the grocery store.*

Jj

jour•ney (jûr′nē) *noun.* A trip, especially one over a considerable distance or taking considerable time. *Ping made a **journey** to China to meet his grandparents and uncles.*

jum•ble (jum′bəl) *noun.* A confused mixture or condition; mess. *My messy room is a **jumble** of toys and books.*

Ll

la•bor (lā′bər) *noun*. 1. Hard work. 2. People who work at jobs that require physical strength. *1. We all needed naps after a day of **labor** in the yard. 2. The mayor's new construction plan was good news for **labor**.*

leg•a•cy (leg′ə sē) *noun*. Something handed down from the past; heritage. *The medical research foundation she founded will be her **legacy**.*

leg•en•dary (lej′ən der′ē) *adjective*. Relating to a legend, or a story that has been handed down for many years and has some basis in fact. *Johnny Appleseed's efforts to spread the apple tree have become **legendary**.*

log•i•cal (loj′i kəl) *adjective*. Sensible; being the action or result one expects. *When it rains, I do the **logical** thing and put my bicycle in the garage.*

loos•ened (lü′sənd) *verb*. Made looser; set free or released. *Brad **loosened** his necktie when the ceremony was over.*

lum•ber•ing (lum′bər ing) *adjective*. Moving in a slow, clumsy way. *Put a **lumbering** hippo in the water, and it becomes a graceful swimmer.*

lurk (lûrk) *verb*. To lie hidden. *Many animals **lurk** in their dens so they can surprise their prey when it walks by.*

Mm

mag•ni•fy (mag′nə fī′) *verb*. To make something look bigger than it really is. *Devices such as microscopes help to **magnify** small things.*

mas•sive (mas′iv) *adjective*. Of great size or extent; large and solid. *The sumo wrestler had a **massive** chest.*

at; **ā**pe; f**ä**r; c**â**re; **e**nd; m**ē**; **i**t; **ī**ce; p**î**erce; h**o**t; **ō**ld; s**ô**ng; f**ô**rk; **oi**l; **ou**t; **u**p; **ū**se; r**ü**le; p**u̇**ll; t**û**rn; **ch**in; si**ng**; **sh**op; **th**in; **th**is; **hw** in **wh**ite; **zh** in trea**s**ure.

The symbol **ə** stands for the unstressed vowel sound in **a**bout, tak**e**n, penc**i**l, lem**o**n, and circ**u**s.

midst (midst) *noun.* A position in the middle of a group of people or things. *"There is a poet in our **midst**," said the principal, "and we need to clap for her."*

mi•grant work•ers (mī′grənt wûr′kərz) *plural noun.* Persons who move from place to place for work. *The **migrant workers** traveled from farm to farm.*

mis•chief (mis′chif) *noun.* Conduct that may seem playful but causes harm or trouble. *The kittens were always getting into **mischief** when we weren't home.*

mis•un•der•stood (mis′un dər stůd′) *verb.* Understood someone incorrectly; got the wrong idea. *I **misunderstood** the directions my teacher gave and did the wrong page for homework.*

mo•ti•vate (mō′tə vāt′) *verb.* To provide with a move to action. *The thought of a college scholarship will always **motivate** me to study hard.*

mut•tered (mut′ərd) *verb.* Spoke in a low, unclear way with the mouth closed. *I could tell he was mad by the way he **muttered** to himself.*

mys•te•ri•ous (mi stîr′ē əs) *adjective.* Very hard or impossible to understand; full of mystery. *The fact that the cookies were missing was **mysterious**.*

Nn

nat•u•ral (nach′ər əl) *adjective.* 1. Unchanged by people. 2. Expected or normal. *1. We hiked through **natural** surroundings of woods, streams, and meadows. 2. The **natural** home of the dolphin is the open ocean.*

ne•glec•ted (ni glekt′əd) *verb.* Failed to give proper attention or care to; failed to do. *I **neglected** to finish my science project and could not present it at the fair.*

now•a•days (nou′ə dāz′) *adverb.* In the present time. *People hardly ever write with typewriters **nowadays**.*

nu•mer•ous (nü′mər əs *or* nū′mər əs) *adjective*. Forming a large number; many. *The mountain climbers faced **numerous** problems, but they still had fun.*

nu•tri•ents (nü′trē ənts *or* nū′trē ənts) *plural noun*. Substances needed by the bodies of people, animals, or plants to live and grow. *Sometimes we get ill because we are not getting the proper **nutrients**.*

Oo

o•be•di•ence (ō bē′dē əns) *noun.* The willingness to obey, or to carry out orders, wishes, or instructions. *It is important to show **obedience** to safety rules.*

Word History

Obedience comes from the Latin word *obedire*, meaning "to hearken, yield, or serve."

o•pin•ions (ə pin′yənz) *plural noun*. Beliefs or conclusions based on a person's judgment rather than on what is proven or known to be true. *I want to find out what my classmates' **opinions** are about recycling.*

op•por•tu•ni•ties (op′ər tü′ni tēz) *plural noun*. Good chances or favorable times. *School offers students many **opportunities** to join clubs and organizations.*

or•a•to•ry (ôr′ə tôr′ē) *noun*. Eloquence and skill in public speaking. *The President was a master of campaign **oratory**.*

out•stretched (out′strechtd′) *adjective*. Stretched out; extended. *His **outstretched** palm held the quarter I had dropped.*

o•ver•flow•ing (ō′vər flō′ing) *verb*. To be so full that the contents flow over. *The trunk was **overflowing** with old toys.*

at; āpe; fär; câre; end; mē; it; īce; pîerce; hot; ōld; sông; fôrk; oil; out; up; ūse; rüle; pu̇ll; tûrn; chin; sing; shop; thin; this; hw in white; zh in treasure.

The symbol ə stands for the unstressed vowel sound in about, taken, pencil, lemon, and circus.

Pp

par•a•lyzed (par′ə līzd′) *adjective.* 1. Having lost movement or sensation in a part of the body. 2. Powerless or helpless. *Sue was **paralyzed** by stage fright.*

part•ner•ship (pärt′nər ship′) *noun.* A kind of business in which two or more people share the work and profits. *Janell, Pat, and Erik formed a gardening **partnership**.*

pe•cul•iar (pi kūl′yər) *adjective.* Strange; not usual. *I had the **peculiar** feeling that I was being watched.*

per•sis•tence (pər sis′təns) *noun.* The ability to keep trying in spite of difficulties or obstacles. *In order to run a business, a person must have a lot of **persistence**.*

phras•es (frāz′iz) *plural noun.* Groups of words expressing a single thought but not containing both a subject and predicate. *When I proofread my report, I made **phrases** into complete sentences.*

pol•i•cy (pol′i sē) *noun.* A guiding plan that people use to help make decisions. *The school has a strict "no t-shirt" **policy**.*

pos•i•tive (poz′i tiv) *adjective.* Certain; sure. *I am **positive** I left my backpack right here on the counter.*

pre•his•tor•ic (prē′his tôr′ik) *adjective.* Belonging to a time before people started recording history. *Explorers found **prehistoric** drawings along the cave walls.*

pro•claimed (prə klāmd′ *or* prō klāmd′) *verb*. Announced publicly. *The principal* ***proclaimed*** *May 20 as the day for our class trips.*

prop•er•ties (prop′ər tēz) *plural noun*. Characteristics of matter that can be observed. *Scientists measured the* ***properties*** *of gold in their lab.*

pro•tes•ted (prō test′əd) *verb*. Complained against something. *When the workers lost their jobs in the factory, they* ***protested****.*

pur•chased (pûr′chəsd) *verb.* Got by paying money; got by sacrifice or hardship. *Sally* ***purchased*** *the chess board using what she saved from her monthly allowance.*

Rr

ranged (rānjd) *verb*. To go between certain limits. *The prices for a music player* ***ranged*** *from fifty to two hundred dollars.*

re•al•is•tic (rē′əlis′tik) *adjective*. Seeing things as they are; practical. *I dream of being a famous rock star, but I should also be* ***realistic*** *and stay in school.*

reef (rēf) *noun*. A ridge of sand, rock, or coral at or near the surface of the ocean. *Boaters have to be careful not to scrape against the* ***reef*** *below.*

ref•er•ence (ref′ər əns *or* ref′rens) *noun*. A statement that calls or directs attention to something. *The speech makes a* ***reference*** *to a play written by William Shakespeare.*

re•form (ri fôrm′) *noun*. A change for the better. *She worked for a* ***reform*** *of the political system.*

reg•i•ster (rej′i stər) *noun*. 1. A formal record or list. 2. The range of a voice or instrument. *verb.* To enroll. *Every college student must* ***register*** *before attending class.*

re•lays (rē′lāz) *plural noun*. Fresh sets, teams, or supplies that replace or relieve another. *Post office workers work in* ***relays*** *in order to get your letters from one place to another quickly.*

at; **ā**pe; f**ä**r; c**â**re; **e**nd; m**ē**; **i**t; **ī**ce; p**î**erce; h**o**t; **ō**ld; s**ô**ng; f**ô**rk; **oi**l; **ou**t; **u**p; **ū**se; r**ü**le; p**u**ll; t**û**rn; **ch**in; si**ng**; **sh**op; **th**in; **th**is; **hw** in **wh**ite; **zh** in trea**s**ure.

The symbol **ə** stands for the unstressed vowel sound in **a**bout, tak**e**n, penc**i**l, lem**o**n, and circ**u**s.

re•leased (ri lēsd′) *verb*. To have set free or loose. *The girl opened the gate to the pen and **released** the pigs.*

re•lo•cat•ed (rē lō′kā tid) *verb*. To have moved to a different location. *The store **relocated** down the block from the park.*

rep•tiles (rep′tīlz) *plural noun*. Cold-blooded vertebrates of the group Reptilia, which includes lizards, snakes, alligators, crocodiles, and turtles. *Most **reptiles** lay eggs, although some give birth to live young.*

res•i•dent (rez′i dənt) *noun*. A person who lives in a particular place. *The new **resident** shocked neighbors by planting the entire front yard with sunflowers.*

re•spon•si•bil•i•ty (ri spon′sə bil′i tē) *noun*. The quality or condition of having a job, duty, or concern. *Taking care of the dog was my **responsibility**.*

roamed (rōmd) *verb*. Moved around in a large area. *The grizzly bear **roamed** over the valley and the nearby mountains.*

route (rüt *or* rout) *noun*. A road or course used for traveling. *Trucks must follow a special **route**.*

rum•bling (rum′bling) *noun*. A heavy, deep, rolling sound. *The **rumbling** of thunder woke me up.*

Ss

sanc•tu•ar•y (sangk′chü er′ē) *noun*. A protected place for wildlife where predators are controlled and hunting is not allowed. *My friend runs a **sanctuary** for injured hawks and owls.*

scorn•ful•ly (skôrn'fəl ē) *adverb*. In a way that shows that something or someone is looked down upon and considered bad or worthless. *The critic was unhappy with the new artist's paintings so he spoke **scornfully** about them.*

seg•re•ga•tion (seg'ri gā'shən) *noun*. The practice of setting one racial group apart from another. *The Civil Rights movement fought against **segregation**.*

se•lec•ting (si lek'ting) *verb*. Picking out among many; choosing. *I spent a long time **selecting** the right gift.*

self•ish (sel'fish) *adjective*. Thinking only of oneself; putting one's own interests and desires before those of others. *A second piece of cake sounded good, but I didn't want to be **selfish**.*

sen•si•ble (sen'sə bəl) *adjective*. Having or showing sound judgment; wise. *If you make a mistake, the **sensible** thing to do is apologize.*

sev•e•ral (sev'ə rəl *or* sev'rəl) *adjective*. More than two, but not many. *Louisa slept for **several** hours.*

shim•mer (shim'ər) *verb*. To shine with a faint, wavering light; glimmer. *The lake began to **shimmer** in the rays of the setting sun.*

silk•en (sil'kən) *adjective*. 1. Made of silk. 2. Like silk in appearance. *1. The queen's **silken** robe was exquisite. 2. Antonio wrote a poem about the girl's long **silken** hair.*

Silk Road (silk rōd) *noun*. A trade route that connected China with the Roman Empire. *The **Silk Road** was about 4,000 miles long.*

sim•il•ar (sim'əl ər) *adjective*. Having many but not all qualities alike. *Zack and Nick have **similar** haircuts.*

sky•scrap•ers (skī'skrā'pərz) *plural noun*. Very tall buildings. *The city has many **skyscrapers**, and some of them are 50 stories tall!*

slen•der (slen'dər) *adjective*. Thin, especially in an attractive or graceful way. *The swan stretched its long **slender** neck and flapped its wings.*

slith•ered (slith'ərd) *verb*. Slid or glided like a snake. *When the snakes **slithered** across the ground, they moved quickly and hardly made a sound.*

snick•er•ing (snik'ər ing) *verb*. Laughing in a mean or disrespectful manner. *The children stopped **snickering** when their mother told them to be kinder.*

at; **ā**pe; f**ä**r; c**â**re; **e**nd; m**ē**; **i**t; **ī**ce; p**î**erce; h**o**t; **ō**ld; s**ô**ng; f**ô**rk; **oi**l; **ou**t; **u**p; **ū**se; r**ü**le; p**ů**ll; t**û**rn; **ch**in; si**ng**; **sh**op; **th**in; **th**is; **hw** in **wh**ite; **zh** in trea**s**ure.

The symbol **ə** stands for the unstressed vowel sound in **a**bout, tak**e**n, penc**i**l, lem**o**n, and circ**u**s.

soft•ware (sôft'wâr') *noun*. Written or printed programs of information that are used on a computer. *The artist used a new design* ***software*** *to help plan her latest sculpture.*

sol•i•tar•y (sol'i ter'ē) *adjective.* Living, being, or going alone. *After everyone else quit, Jim was the* ***solitary*** *player left in the game.*

Word History

Solitary comes from the Latin *solitarius*, meaning "alone, lonely."

sores (sôrz) *plural noun*. Places where the skin has been broken and hurts. *My hands had* ***sores*** *after raking leaves all morning with no gloves on.*

spe•cial•ized (spesh'ə līzd') *verb*. To have concentrated on a particular product, activity, branch of a profession, or field of study. *When she went to cooking school, she* ***specialized*** *in bread baking.*

spe•cial•ty (spesh'əl tē) *noun*. A special thing that a person knows a great deal about or can make very well. *Making quilts is my aunt Lisa's* ***specialty***.

spin•off (spin'ôf') *noun*. A product derived from another field. *This new plastic used in eyeglass frames is a* ***spinoff*** *from the aerospace industry.*

strikes (strīks) *plural noun*. 1. The stopping of work to protest something. 2. Pitched balls in the strike zone or that a batter swings at and misses.
1. The workers threatened ***strikes*** *if conditions did not improve.*
2. One rule of baseball is three ***strikes*** *and you're out.*

strut•ting (strut'ing) *verb*. Walking in a self-important way. *When Marilyn returned from her trip to Europe, she came* ***strutting*** *in showing off her new Italian boots.*

stur•dy (stûr'dē) *adjective*. Having strength; hardy. *The bookshelf we built was* ***sturdy*** *enough to hold our entire collection of books.*

sub•urbs (sub'ûrbz) *plural noun*. The areas around a city where people live. *Many people commute from the* ***suburbs*** *to the city using public transportation.*

Word History

Suburbs comes from the Latin *suburbium*—from *sub-* "under" and *urbs*, meaning "city."

sul•tan (sul'tən) *noun.* The king or ruler in certain Muslim countries. *Modern-day Turkey was ruled by a **sultan** at one time.*

swarms (swôrmz) *plural noun.* Large groups of insects flying or moving together. *When the hive fell, **swarms** of angry bees flew out.*

Tt

tan•gles (tang'gəlz) *plural noun.* Knotted, twisted, confused masses. *The garden hose had not been rolled back up and was full of **tangles**.*

tech•nique (tek nēk') *noun.* A method or way of bringing about a desired result in a science, an art, a sport, or a profession. *Part of Orli's **technique**, when she is running, is to breathe in and out through her mouth.*

Word History

Technique comes from the Greek word *teknikos*, meaning "relating to an art or a craft."

tech•nol•o•gy (tek nol'ə jē) *noun.* Electronic products and systems that have various uses. ***Technology** has changed the ways that artists create their work.*

tel•e•graph (tel'i graf') *noun.* A system or equipment used to send messages by wire over a long distance. *Before the telephone, a **telegraph** may have been used to relay a message.*

tem•po•rar•y (tem'pə rer'ē) *adjective.* Lasting or used for a short time only. *We recorded a **temporary** message for the answering machine.*

at; **ā**pe; f**ä**r; c**â**re; **e**nd; m**ē**; **i**t; **ī**ce; p**î**erce; h**o**t; **ō**ld; s**ô**ng; f**ô**rk; **oi**l; **ou**t; **u**p; **ū**se; r**ü**le; p**u̇**ll; t**û**rn; **ch**in; si**ng**; **sh**op; **th**in; **th**is; **hw** in **wh**ite; **zh** in trea**s**ure.

The symbol **ə** stands for the unstressed vowel sound in **a**bout, tak**e**n, penc**i**l, lem**o**n, and circ**u**s.

ter•ri•to•ry (ter′i tôr′ē) *noun.* Any large area of land; region. *My brother's **territory** for selling medical office supplies is North Carolina.*

threat•ened (thret′ənd) *adjective.* Having a sense of harm or danger. ***Threatened** by the hawk circling above, the mouse escaped under a log.*

trans•form (trans fôrm′) *verb.* To change in form, appearance, or structure. *To **transform** a barn into a modern home, you need to invest a lot of time and expense.*

Word History

Transform comes from the Latin *transformare*, meaning "to change in shape."

trans•la•tion (trans lā′shən) *noun.* A changing of a speech or piece of writing into another language. *Maria's grandmother spoke only Spanish, so Maria needed a **translation** of the letter from her.*

Uu

un•fair (un fâr′) *adjective.* Not fair or just. *Punishing all of us for the actions of my little sister seemed **unfair**.*

un•ions (ūn′yənz) *plural noun.* Groups of workers joined together to protect their jobs and improve working conditions. *Some labor **unions** stage strikes to get workers the safety equipment they need.*

u•nique (ū nēk′) *adjective.* Having no equal; the only one of its kind. *The Everglades is **unique** in that there is no other place on Earth like it.*

un•sta•ble (un stā′bəl) *adjective.* Not settled or steady; easily moved or put off balance. *Although the raft looked **unstable**, it floated very well.*

Vv

var•ied (vâr'ēd) *adjective.* Consisting of many different kinds. *The organisms in this coral reef are **varied**.*

ven•ture (ven'chər) *noun.* A business or some other undertaking that involves risk. *Rea's new **venture** was a carpet-cleaning service.*

vi•o•lat•ed (vī'ə lā'tid) *verb.* To have failed to obey; to have broken. *Mel was yelled at because she **violated** the "no talking during a test" rule.*

vis•i•bly (viz'ə blē) *adverb.* Plainly seen. *The firemen were **visibly** fatigued.*

vol•un•teer (vol'ən tîr') *noun.* A person who offers to help or does something by choice and usually without pay. *I am a **volunteer** at the nursing home.*

W

week•days (wēk'dāz') *plural noun.* The days of the week except Saturday and Sunday. *We go to school only on **weekdays**.*

at; **ā**pe; f**ä**r; c**â**re; **e**nd; m**ē**; **i**t; **ī**ce; p**î**erce; h**o**t; **ō**ld; s**ô**ng; f**ô**rk; **oi**l; **ou**t; **u**p; **ū**se; r**ü**le; p**u̇**ll; t**û**rn; **ch**in; si**ng**; **sh**op; **th**in; **th**is; **hw** in **wh**ite; **zh** in trea**s**ure.

The symbol **ə** stands for the unstressed vowel sound in **a**bout, tak**e**n, penc**i**l, lem**o**n, and circ**u**s.

Acknowledgments

The publisher gratefully acknowledges permission to reprint the following copyrighted material:

"Adelina's Whales" text and photographs by Richard Sobol. Text and photographs copyright © 2003 by Richard Sobol. Reprinted by permission of Dutton Children's Books, a division of Penguin Books USA Inc.

"The Adventures of Ali Baba Bernstein" by Johanna Hurwitz. Copyright © 1985 by Johanna Hurwitz. Reprinted by permission of William Morrow and Company.

"The Ant and the Grasshopper" retold and illustrated by Amy Lowry Poole. Copyright © 2000 by Amy Lowry Poole. Reprinted by permission of Holiday House.

"The Astronaut and the Onion" by Ann Cameron from GLORIA RISING. Text copyright © 2002 by Ann Cameron. Reprinted by permission of Frances Foster Books, an imprint of Farrar, Straus and Giroux.

"At Home in the Coral Reef" by Katy Muzik, illustrated by Katherine Brown-Wing. Text and illustrations copyright © 1992 by Charlesbridge Publishing. Reprinted by permission.

"Because of Winn-Dixie" by Kate DiCamillo from BECAUSE OF WINN-DIXIE. Copyright © 2000 by Kate DiCamillo. Reprinted by permission of Candlewick Press.

"Brave New Heights" by Monica Kulling from MORE SPICE THAN SUGAR: POEMS ABOUT FEISTY FEMALES compiled by Lillian Morrison. Compilation copyright © 2001 by Lillian Morrison. Reprinted by permission of Marian Reiner from the author.

"The Cricket in Times Square" by George Selden, illustrated by Garth Williams from THE CRICKET IN TIMES SQUARE. Copyright © 1960 by George Selden Thompson and Garth Williams. Reprinted by permission of Farrar, Straus and Giroux. [McGraw-Hill acknowledges the use of a trademark due to illustrator restrictions.]

"Dear Mrs. LaRue" written and illustrated by Mark Teague. Copyright © 2002 by Mark Teague. Reprinted by permission of Scholastic Press, a division of Scholastic, Inc.

"How Ben Franklin Stole the Lightning" by Rosalyn Schanzer. Copyright © 2003 by Rosalyn Schanzer. Reprinted by permission of HarperCollins Publishers.

"I Love the Look of Words" by Maya Angelou from SOUL LOOKS BACK IN WONDER. Copyright © 1993 by Tom Feelings. Reprinted by permission of Dial Books, a division of Penguin Books USA Inc.

"Ima and The Great Texas Ostrich Race" by Margaret Olivia McManis, illustrated by Bruce Dupree. Text copyright © 2002 by Margaret McManis. Illustrations copyright © 2002 by Bruce Dupree. Reprinted by permission of Eakin Press/A Division of Sunbelt Media, Inc.

"Leah's Pony" by Elizabeth Friedrich, illustrated by Michael Garland. Text copyright © 1996 by Elizabeth Friedrich. Illustrations © 1996 by Michael Garland. Reprinted by permission of Boyds Mills Press.

"The Life and Times of the Ant" by Charles Micucci from THE LIFE AND TIMES OF THE ANT. Copyright © 2003 by Charles Micucci. Reprinted by permission of Houghton Mifflin Company.

"Light Bulb" and "Lightning Bolt" by Joan Bransfield Graham from FLICKER FLASH. Text copyright © 1999 by Joan Bransfield Graham. Reprinted by permission of Houghton Mifflin Company.

"Me and Uncle Romie" by Claire Hartfield, paintings by Jerome Lagarrigue. Text copyright © 2002 by Claire Hartfield, paintings copyright © 2002 by Jerome Lagarrigue. Reprinted by permission of Dial Books, a division of Penguin Books USA Inc.

"Mighty Jackie: The Strike-Out Queen" by Marissa Moss, illustrated by C. F. Payne. Text copyright © 2004 by Marissa Moss, illustrations copyright © 2004 by C. F. Payne. Reprinted by permission of Simon & Schuster Books for Young Readers.

"Mountains and plains" and "No sky at all" from AN INTRODUCTION TO HAIKU: AN ANTHOLOGY OF POEMS AND POETS FROM BASHŌ TO SHIKI. Copyright © 1958 by Harold G. Henderson. Reprinted by permission of Doubleday Anchor Books, a Division of Doubleday & Company, Inc.

"My Brother Martin: A Sister Remembers, Growing Up with the Rev. Dr. Martin Luther King, Jr." by Christine King Farris, illustrated by Chris Soentpiet. Text copyright © 2003 by Christine King Farris, illustrations copyright © 2003 by Chris Soentpiet. Reprinted by permission of Simon & Schuster Books for Young Readers.

"My Brothers' Flying Machine" by Jane Yolen, paintings by Jim Burke. Text copyright © 2003 by Jane Yolen, illustrations copyright © 2003 by Jim Burke. Reprinted by permission of Little, Brown and Company.

"My Diary from Here to There" story by Amada Irma Pérez, illustrations by Maya Christina Gonzalez from MY DIARY FROM HERE TO THERE. Story copyright © 2002 by Amada Irma Pérez, illustrations copyright © 2002 by Maya Christina Gonzalez. Reprinted by permission of Children's Book Press.

"Mystic Horse" by Paul Goble. Copyright © 2003 by Paul Goble. Reprinted by permission of HarperCollins Publishers.

"The New Kid" from AT THE CRACK OF THE BAT: Baseball Poems compiled by Lillian Morrison, illustrated by Steve Cieslawski. Text copyright © 1992 by Lillian Morrison. Illustrations copyright © 1992 by Steve Cieslawski. Reprinted by permission of Hyperion Books for Children.

"Roadrunner's Dance" by Rudolfo Anaya, pictures by David Diaz. Text copyright © 2000 by Rudolfo Anaya, illustrations copyright © 2000 by David Diaz. Reprinted by permission of Hyperion Books for Children.

"Snowflake Bentley" by Jacqueline Briggs Martin, illustrated by Mary Azarian. Text copyright © 1998 by Jacqueline Briggs Martin, illustrations copyright © 1998 by Mary Azarian. Reprinted by permission of Houghton Mifflin Company.

"The snow is melting" and " Winter solitude" from THE ESSENTIAL HAIKU: VERSIONS OF BASHŌ, BUSON, AND ISSA. Introduction and selection copyright © 1994 by Robert Hass. Unless otherwise noted, all translations copyright © 1994 by Robert Hass. Reprinted by permission of The Ecco Press.

Excerpt from "So Long, It's Been Good to Know Yuh." Words and music by Woody Guthrie. www.woodyguthrie.org Copyright © 1940 (Renewed), 1950 (Renewed), 1951 (Renewed) by TRO-Folk. Reprinted by permission of The Richmond Organization (TRO).

"A Walk in the Desert" by Rebecca L. Johnson with illustrations by Phyllis V. Saroff from A WALK IN THE DESERT. Text copyright © 2001 by Rebecca L. Johnson, illustrations copyright © 2001 by Phyllis V. Saroff. Reprinted by permission of Carolrhoda Books, Inc.

"When I Went to the Library" by Ken Roberts from WHEN I WENT TO THE LIBRARY edited by Debora Pearson. Copyright © 2001 by Ken Roberts. Reprinted by permission of Groundwood Books/Douglas & McIntyre.

"Wild Horses: Black Hills Sanctuary" by Cris Peterson, photographs by Alvis Upitis. Text copyright © 2003 by Cris Peterson, photographs copyright © 2003 by Alvis Upitis. Reprinted by permission of Boyds Mills Press, Inc.

ILLUSTRATIONS

Cover Illustration: Gloria Domingo Manuel.

10–31: Maya Christina Gonzalez. 40–41: Ginger Nielson. 42–59: Brian Biggs. 60–63: Olwyn Whelan. 65: Ken Bowser. 80: Kim Johnson. 82–97: Anna Rich. 120–121: Robert Casilla. 125: Viviana Diaz. 140–155: Chris Soentpiet. 166–183: C.F. Payne. 184-185: Steve Cieslawski. 220–223: Ande Cook. 230–251: Paul Goble. 258–259: Darryl Ligasan. 270: Ann Boyajian. 272–285: Nicole Wong. 296–319: Mark Teague. 330: Dean Macadam. 340–341: David LaFleur. 342–361: Renato Alarcão. 362: Wendy Born Hollander. 363: (tr)(ml) Renato Alarcão; (bl)(cr) Wendy Born Hollander. 364: (t) Renato Alarcão; (tr)(bl) Wendy Born Hollander. 365: (bkgd) Renato Alarcão; (insets) Wendy Born Hollander. 372–391: Jerome Lagarrigue. 396–397: Susan Swan. 408–409: Loretta Krupinski. 410–429: Garth Williams. 433: Argosy. 440–455: Charles Micucci. 456–459: Amy Lowry Poole. 465: Bridget Starr Taylor. 476–477: James Bentley. 478-497: Bruce Dupree. 508–525: Jim Burke. 527: Jim Burke. 528–529: Bandelin-Dacey Studios. 532–533: Bill Cigliano. 534–535: Argosy. 548: Laura Westlund. 550–559: Phyllis V. Saroff. 574–595: David Diaz. 614–631: Katherine Brown-Wing. 632–635: David Groff. 658: Richard Sobol. 660–661: Jesse Reisch. 664–665: Fabricio Vandenbroeck. 666–667: Marion Eldrige. 676–677: Stacey Schuett. 678–697: Michael Garland. 706–707: Greg Shed. 708–723: Ying-Hwa Hu & Cornelius Van

Acknowledgments

Wright. 746–769: Mary Azarian. 770–771: Tina Fong. 778–797: Rosalyn Schanzer. 802–803: Stacey Schuett. 804: Paul Mirocha.

PHOTOGRAPHY

iv: Purestock/SuperStock. v: (t) Jeff Greenberg/PhotoEdit; (b) © 2005 Twentieth Century Fox. All rights reserved. vi: Kayte M. Deioma/PhotoEdit. vii: (t) Brian Bahr/Getty Images. viii: Masterfile. ix: Masterfile. x: Bob Daemmrich/PhotoEdit. xi: Bill Heinsohn/Alamy. xii: (tl) Lon Lauber/OSF/Animal Animals/Earth Scenes; (cl) Martin J. Miller/Visuals Unlimited; (cl-bkgd) Tom Bean. xiii: William Smithey Jr/Getty Images. xiv: Comstock/SuperStock. xv: AP Images/Neil Eliot. 2-3: Purestock/SuperStock. 4: Veronique Krieger/Getty Images. 4-5: Ryan McVay/Getty Images. 5: Bettmann/Corbis. 6-7: Jose Luis Pelaez/Corbis. 8: Rusty Hill/FoodPix/Jupiter Images. 9: David Hiser/Getty Images. 30: (tl, c) Children's Book Press. 32: (bl) Ted Streshinsky/Corbis. 33: (c) Morton Beebe/Corbis; (br) Najlah Feanny/Corbis. 34: (bl) Arthur Schatz/Time Life Pictures/Getty Images; (tr) PunchStock. 35: Walter P. Reuther Library/Wayne State University. 37: Myrleen Ferguson Cate/PhotoEdit. 38-39: Tom & Dee Ann McCarthy/Corbis. 58: (bl) Brian Biggs; (tr) Ben Hurwitz. 65: Photodisc/Getty Images. 66–67: Jeff Greenberg/PhotoEdit. 68: (t) Getty Images; (cr) Russel Illig/Photodisc/PunchStock; (br) C Squared Studios/Getty. 70-71: (all) Mi Won Kim /Time For Kids. 72: (t) Esta Shapiro/Time For Kids; (bl) Courtesy David Hsu. 73: Courtesy David Hsu. 74: Lewis Wickes Hines/Corbis. 77: (tcr) Brand X Pictures/PunchStock; (cr) PhotoLink/Getty Images. 78-79: Mitch Tobias/Masterfile. 81: Stock Trek/Getty. 96: (tl) Das Anuda/Courtesy Farrar, Straus and Giroux; (cr) Courtesy Anna Rich. 98: NASA Johnson Space Center Collection. 98-99: (bkgd) NASA/CORBIS. 99: (br) PatitucciPhoto/Aurora Photos; (t) NASA Johnson Space Center Collection. 100: (tr) GustoImages/Artemi Kyriacou/Jupiter Images. 100-101: (bkgd) BigStockPhoto. 101: (tr) NASA/Roger Ressmeyer/Corbis; (br) NASA/Corbis. 103: Dan Bigelow/Getty Images. 104-105: Don Mason/Blend Images/Jupiter Images. 106:Steven Weinrebe/Index Stock Imagery. 107: Don Smetzer/Stone/Getty Images. 108-114: © 2005 Twentieth Century Fox. All rights reserved. 116-117: (bkgd) Wetzel & Company. 117: © 2005 Twentieth Century Fox. All rights reserved. 120: (tr) Courtesy Candlewick Press; (bl) © 2005 Twentieth Century Fox. All rights reserved. 121: © 2005 Twentieth Century Fox. All rights reserved. 124: © 2005 Twentieth Century Fox. All rights reserved. 125: Ryan McVay/Getty Images. 126: Brand X Pictures/PunchStock. 128: Michael Okoniewski/AP-Wide World Photos. 129: (br) Michael Okoniewski/AP-Wide World Photos; (bl) Hemera Technologies/Alamy. 131: (cr) Nic Hamilton/Alamy; (tr) Ryan McVay/Getty Images; (br) Pixtal/PunchStock. 132-133: Kayte M. Deioma/PhotoEdit. 134: Digital Vision Photography/Veer. 134-135: Ingram Publishing/AGEfotostock. 135: Owen Franken/Corbis. 136-137: Corbis. 138: Bettmann/Corbis. 139: (cl,cr) Bettmann/Corbis. 154: (c) Courtesy Chris Soentpiet/www.soentpiet.com. 156: Bettmann/Corbis. 156-159: Macmillan/McGraw-Hill. 157: AP Photo. 158: Jack Balletti/Bettmann/Corbis. 161: Michael Newman/PhotoEdit. 162-163: Lori Adamski Peek/Getty Images. 164: Bettmann/Corbis. 165: Bernard Hoffman/Getty. 182: (cr) Courtesy C.F. Payne. 187: Royalty-Free/Corbis. 188-189: Brian Bahr/Getty Images. 190: (t) Brian Nicholson/AP Photo; (b) Bryn Lennon/Getty Images. 191: (tr) Al Grillo/AP Photo; (bl) Phil Cole/Getty Images. 192: Brian Bahr/Getty Images. 193: (tr) Todd Warshaw/Pool/Getty Images; (bl) Petros Giannakouris/AP Photos. 194: Nadia Borowski Scott/Zuma Press/Newscom. 195: (tr) STR/AFP/Getty Images; (bl) Petros Giannakouris/AP Photo. 196:Tamara Reynolds. 199: (bl) Photodisc/PunchStock; (bc) Ana de Sousa/Shutterstock; (r) Stockdisc/PunchStock. 200-201: Steve Bloom Images/Alamy. 202: Scott Neville/AP Photos. 204-217: (all) Alvis Upitis. 218: (tl) Boydsmills Press; (cr) Alvis Upitis. 218-219: Alvis Upitis. 225: Kevin Peterson/Getty Images. 226-227: Carson Ganci/Design Pics Inc./Alamy. 228: TiConUno s.r.l./Alamy. 228-229: (bkgd) Photographers Choice RF/SuperStock. 229: Macmillan/McGraw-Hill. 250: Courtesy Paul Goble. 252: (bl) Getty Images: (bkgd) Wetzel & Company. 253: Getty Images. 253-255: (bkgd) Wetzel & Company. 257: Robert Llewellyn/Alamy. 260: (br) Michael St. Maur Sheil/Corbis; (t) Jerry Driendl/Getty Images. 260-261: Jerry Driendl/Getty Images. 263: (tr) Stockbyte/PunchStock; (cr) Royalty-Free/Corbis; (bl) McVay/Getty Images. 264-265: Masterfile. 266: Dennis MacDonald/AGEfotostock America. 266-267: Gary He/Macmillan/McGraw-Hill. 267: Charles Krupa/AP Images. 268-269: Whit Preston/Stone/Getty Images. 271: (tl) Daryl Balfour/Getty Images; (cr) Stephen Cooper/Getty Images. 284: (tl) Courtesy Groundwood Books; (cr) Courtesy Nicole Wong. 286: John Cancalosi/DRK. 287: Michael & Patricia Fogden/Minden. 288: (tl) Michael Fogden/Animal Animals; (bl) Bruce Coleman, Inc/Alamy. 291: Tipp Howell/Getty Images. 292-293: Masterfile Royalty-Free. 294: (bl) Ulrike Schanz/Animal Animals; (b) Royalty-Free/Corbis. 295: Mary Grace Long/Asia Images/Getty Images. 318: Courtesy Scholastic. 320: Okapia/Hund/Kramer/Photo Researchers. 321-323: Manuela Hartling/Reuters/Corbis. 325: Royalty-Free/Corbis. 326-327: Masterfile. 328: Time & Life Pictures/Getty Images. 329: (tl) Time & Life Pictures/Getty Images; (tr) Corbis. 331: Marc Longwood. 332: Eric L. Stewart/Lyon College. 333: Warner Brothers/Everett Collection. 337: (tcr, br) Brand X Pictures/PunchStock; (cr) Siede Preis/Getty Images; (bl) PhotoLink/Getty Images; (bc) Ana de Sousa/Shutterstock; (b) Michael Scott/Macmillan/McGraw-Hill. 338: Group 4/Image Source Black/Alamy. 360: (tl) Courtesy Peachtree Publishers; (br) Courtesy Renato Alarcão. 367: Amos Morgan/Getty Images. 368-369: Jeff Greenberg/Alamy. 370: (bl) Chris Steele-Perkins/Magnum; (bc) Getty Images; (br) Comstock Images/Getty Images. 371: Photodisc/Getty Images. 390: (cl) Courtesy of Penguin Group; (tr) Photo by Jessica Tampas. Courtesy Claire Hartfield. 392: Frank Chmura/Alamy. 395: Alan Levenson/AGEfotostock America. 398: Time & Life Pictures/Getty Images. 399: Danita Delimonte/Alamy. 401: (bl) Pixtal/PunchStock; (cr) Stockdisc/PunchStock. 402-403: Bob Daemmrich/Photo Edit. 404: Marta Lavandier/AP Images. 404-405: (bkgd wooden blocks) Dynamic Graphics/Jupiter Images; (bkgd wood texture) Dynamic Graphics/PunchStock; (bkgd close-up of wood grain) Ryan McVay/Getty Images. 405: The Granger Collection, New York. 406-407: Gabe Palmer/Corbis. 428: (tl) Marcia Johnston. Courtesy Farrar, Straus & Giroux; (cr) Courtesy Estate of Garth Williams c/o Frost National Bank. 430: (tr) B. G. Thomson/Photo Researchers; (cr) Karen Marks/Bat Conservation International/Photo Researchers. 430-431: Steve Kaufman/Corbis. 431: Pat Little/AP Images. 432: Jeff Lepore/Photo Researchers. 432-433: Tim Flach/Stone/Getty Images. 435: Dan Bigelow/Getty Images. 436-437: Michael & Patricia Fogden/Corbis. 438: Masterfile. 439: Steve Hopkin/Ardea. 454: Anita Lambrinos/Courtesy Charles Micucci. 461: Amos Morgan/Getty Images. 462-463: Bill Heinsohn/Alamy. 464: Bob Stefko/Getty Images. 465: (tr) Bettmann/Corbis; (tl) Christopher and Sally Gable/Getty Images. 466: Stephen Pingry/AP Photo. 467: AGEfotostock/SuperStock. 468: Doug Mazell/Jupiter Images. 469: Mary Altaffer/AP Photo. 470: OJPhotos/Alamy. 473: (cr) Ryan McVay/Getty Images; (bl) PhotoLink/Getty Images; (bc) Ana de Sousa/Shutterstock; (br) Photodisc/PunchStock. 474-475: Troy Wayrynen. 496: (tl) Justin A. Woods; (br) Donna Freeman courtesy of Pelican Publishing Company. 498: Richard Hutchings. 499: North Wind Picture Archives/Alamy. 500: (tl) The Ima Hogg Papers/The Center for American History/The University of Texas at Austin; (b) Travelwide/Alamy. 501: Thais Llorca/epa/Corbis. 503: Rubberball Productions/Getty Images. 504-505: Library of Congress/Getty Images. 506-507: Bettmann/Corbis. 507: Science Museum, London/Topham-HIP/Image Works. 526: (tr) Jason Stemple/Curtis Brown Limited; (bcl) Courtesy Jim Burke. 531: Frank Siteman/AGEfotostock America, Inc. 537: (l) Brand X Pictures/PunchStock; (cr) Ken Cavanagh/Macmillan/McGraw-Hill; (br) Stockbyte/PunchStock. 538-539: Lon Lauber/OSF/Animal Animals/Earth Scenes. 540: George H. H. Huey/Corbis. 540-541: Brand X Pictures/PunchStock. 541: Jeff Foott/Getty Images. 542-543: Stephen Krasemann/NHPA. 544: Jack Barrie/Bruce Coleman. 545: Dave Tipling/Alamy. 546-547: Bruce Clendenning/Visuals Unlimited. 547: Martin J Miller/Visuals Unlimited. 549: (tr) Steve Warble; (b) Brian Vikander. 550: Barbara Gerlach/Visuals Unlimited. 551: (t) Richard Day/Daybreak Imagery; (b) Tom Bean. 552: (tr) Bayard A. Brattstrom/Visuals Unlimited; (br) Rob Simpson/Visuals Unlimited. 553: John Cunningham/Visuals Unlimited. 554: (t) LINK/Visuals Unlimited; (b) John and Barbara Gerlach/Visuals Unlimited. 555: Hal Beral/Visuals Unlimited. 556: Malowski/Visuals Unlimited. 557: John Gerlach/Visuals Unlimited. 558: (tr) Barbara Gerlach/Visuals Unlimited; (b) Joe McDonald/Visuals Unlimited. 559: Tom J. Ulrich/Visuals Unlimited. 560-561: Bruce Clendenning/Visuals Unlimited. 562: (tr) Courtesy Lerner Publishing Group; (b) Martin J Miller/Visuals Unlimited. 562-563: Bruce Clendenning/Visuals Unlimited. 563: (bl) Barbara Gerlach/Visuals Unlimited; (bc) Rob Simpson/Visuals Unlimited; (br) Steve Warble. 564: Mitsuaki Iwago/Minden Pictures. 565: (tl) Steve Kazlowski/Danita Delimont.com; (br) Robert W. Ginn/Alamy. 566: (tl) Inside OutPix/PunchStock; (cl) Renee Morris/Alamy; (bc) blickwinkel/Alamy; (br) Andrew Harrington/Alamy. 567: Royalty-Free/Corbis. 569: Jim Jordan/Getty Images. 570-571: Joel Sartore/National Geographic Image Collection. 572-573: John Cancalosi/Ardea. 573: ZSSD/SuperStock. 590: (tl) Photo by Mimi. Courtesy Rudolfo Anaya; (cr) Courtesy of David Diaz. 597: BananaStock/Alamy. 598-599: William Smithey Jr/Getty Images. 600: Frank Staub/Index Stock Imagery. 601: Corey Rich/Aurora Photos. 602-603: Ken Wilson/Wildfaces. 605: William Campbell/Corbis Sygma. 606: Galen Rowell/Corbis. 609: (cr) PhotoLink/Getty Images; (bc) Ana de Sousa/Shutterstock; (br) Stockbyte/PunchStock. 610-611: Jupiter Images/Comstock/Alamy. 612: (t) Boden/Ledingham/Masterfile; (bl) Brandon Cole Marine Photography/Alamy. 612-613: Boden/Ledingham/Masterfile. 613: Brandon Cole/Visuals Unlimited. 616-629: (bkgd) Wetzel & Company/Janice McDonald. 630: Yuusuke Itagaki, Courtesy Charlesbridge Publishers. 630-631: (bkgd) Wetzel & Company/

Janice McDonald. 637: BananaStock/AGEfotostock. 638-639: (bkgd) James Watt/Animal Animals/Earth Scenes. 640: (tr) Amos Nachoum/ Corbis; (br) Roger Tidman/Corbis. 640-641: (bkgd) Stephen Frink Collection/Alamy. 642-657: Richard Sobol. 658: (author) Courtesy Robert Sobol. 658-659: Richard Sobol. 663: (cr) Rubberball Productions/Getty Images. 669: (cr) Stockdisc/PunchStock; (br) Tracy Montana/PhotoLink/Getty Images. 670-671: Comstock/SuperStock. 672: Comstock/SuperStock. 673: Underwood & Underwood/Corbis. 672-673: Digital Vision/Getty Images. 674-675: Corbis. 696: Alice Garland. 698-699: Corbis. 699: Dorothea Lange/Stringer/2005 Getty Images. 700: (t) John Springer Collection/Corbis; (c) Bettmann/Corbis. 703: Comstock Images/Alamy. 704-705: The Granger Collection, New York. 722: (tr) Rob Layman; (cl) Courtesy Cornelius Van Wright and Ying-Hwa Hu. 724: James L. Amos/Corbis. 724-725: Joe Ginsberg/Getty Images. 725: (t) Pat Roque/Associated Press; (b) Joe Ginsberg/Getty Images. 726: (t) Victoria & Albert Museum, London/Art Resource, NY. 726-727: Joe Ginsberg/Getty Images. 727: ImageDJ/Jupiter Images. 729: Tipp Howell/Getty Images. 730-731: Damian Dovarganes/AP Photo. 732: Brian Harkin/Getty Images. 733: (all) Taro Yamasaki. 734: Ric Francis/ AP Photo. 735 (all) Arthur Schatz/Time Life Pictures/Getty Images. 736-737: Aurelia Ventura/La Opinion Photos/Newscom. 738: Staples, Inc. 741: (br) Royalty-Free/Corbis; (bc) Ana de Sousa/Shutterstock. 742-743: Randy Olson/National Geographic/Getty Images. 744: Gary Buss/Getty Images. 745: Richard Hutchings/Corbis. 768: (tl) Sharron L. McElmeel/ McBookwords LLC; (cr) Courtesy Mary Azarian. 773: ImageState/ Alamy. 774-775: Justin Sullivan/Getty Images. 776: (tr) Schenectady Museum; Hall of Electrical History Foundation/Corbis; (bl) W. Dickson/ Corbis. 777: Bettmann/Corbis. 796: Courtesy Roz Schanzer. 801: Michael Newman/PhotoEdit. 804-805: Chris Howes/Wild Places Photography/ Alamy. 807: (tr) Stockdisc/PunchStock; (br) Photodisc/PunchStock. 808: (l) Digital Vision Ltd./Getty Images; (r) Ingram Publishing/Alamy. 810: Comstock/Alamy. 811: Photodisc Collection/Getty Images. 814: Creatas/ SuperStock. 815: Adam Jones/Visuals Unlimited. 818: Jeremy Woodhouse/Getty Images. 819: Charles George/Visuals Unlimited. 821: Mel Curtis/Getty Images. 822: Jeff Foott/Discovery Images/Getty Images. 825: Digital Vision Ltd./Getty Images. 826: (r) S. Solum/ PhotoLink/Getty Images; (l) Ingram Publishing/Alamy. 829: Digital Vision Ltd. 830: Peter Yates/Corbis. 831: Robert Harding World Imagery/ Getty Images.